Trotskyism and the Second World War
Ted Grant Writings: Volume 1 (1938-1942)

Wellred Books
London

Trotskyism and the Second World War

Ted Grant Writings
Volume 1 (1938-1942)

Ted Grant at Speakers' Corner in Hyde Park,
Mid 1942 [Ted Grant Archive]

Trotskyism and the Second World War
Ted Grant Writings
Volume One 1938-1942

First published by Wellred 2010
2023 printing

Copyright © Estate of Ted Grant
Introduction © Wellred

UK distribution: Wellred Books, wellred-books.com
152-160 Kemp House, City Road
London
EC1V 2NX
books@wellred-books.com

USA distribution: Marxist Books, marxistbooks.com
WR Books
250 44th Street #208
Brooklyn
New York
NY 11232
sales@marxistbooks.com

DK distribution: Forlaget Marx, forlagetmarx.dk
Degnestavnen 19, st. tv.
2400 København NV
forlag@forlagetmarx.dk

Ted Grant Internet Archive: www.tedgrant.org

Cover design by Manuel Reichetseder

Layout by Espe Espigares

ISBN: 978 1 900007 35 1

Contents

3—The internal debate of WIL on the revolutionary military policy
[February – March 1941]

4—A turning point: the attack on the USSR
[July 1941 – December 1942]

5—WIL's pre-conference documents and updates
[August 1942]

Appendices

Acknowledgements

We would like to thank all those who helped to uncover the material produced in this book. Extensive research was carried out by Paolo Brini, Francesco Giliani, Alun Morgan, Rob Sewell and Harry Whittaker in different archives and universities. We would like to specially thank Carol McCullam and Philip Wallace from the Glasgow Caledonian Archive of the Trotskyist Tradition; the universities of Hull and Warwick where the archives of Jock Haston and Jimmy Deane are hosted; the Senate House archives of Al Richardson in London; the Trotsky archive in Harvard.

The bulk of the research was based on the archives of Sam Bornstein and Ted Grant which were reorganised and put into order by Francesco Merli. We also thank Alan Woods for providing us with WIL and RCP internal documents from his personal archives that would have otherwise been impossible to trace.

Many comrades have helped in transcribing and proofreading the material for this project. Special thanks to Miriam Díaz Crespo, Lynne Faulkes, Julianna Grant, Ana Muñoz, Harry Nielsen, Rob Sewell, Maarten Vanheuverswyn and Harry Whittaker. We would like to express our special gratitude to Francesco Merli for the systematic research and editing work and for taking up the task of coordinating the project. Thanks to Emil Vaughn for his proofreading and pioneering work on the Ted Grant archive website and to Maarten Vanheuverswyn, Niklas Albin Svensson and Manuel Reichetseder for guaranteeing its regular update. A special thanks to Fred Weston and Harry Nielsen for the final proofreading of all the texts published here, to Espe Espigares and Harry Nielsen for the layout of the book, Steve Jones and Mick Brooks for the index and to Manuel Reichetseder for the cover design.

Preface

It is with great pleasure that we introduce this first volume of the writings of Ted Grant. It represents the first step of a very long project that aims at publishing all his writings. Our aim is to make available to a broader public Ted's contribution to the history of the revolutionary movement. We believe this project will contribute to the education of the next generation of Marxist cadres in the traditions that Ted kept alive throughout his long-standing activity in the labour movement.

The history of the Workers' International League is so closely linked with the work of Ted Grant that it is impossible to separate them. Especially after Ralph Lee's departure in 1940, Ted emerged as the WIL's most prominent theoretician. From that time on he drafted the majority of the main political documents of the movement.

In a number of cases we have been able to trace Political Bureau or Central Committee minutes where we find Ted being put in charge of drafting a certain document. Some other documents carry the fingerprint of Ted's style so evidently that there can be no doubt about their authorship. Clearly, the documents, although drafted by Ted, would have had input from other members and can be considered the fruit of collective effort. Ted, however, was the main driving force. These documents reflect the views of the collective leadership of the WIL, which Ted played a significant role in formulating.

For these reasons we have decided to include in this volume all the main political documents of the WIL that we could trace. We also decided to include all materials relating to the important debate of February-March 1941 on the proletarian military policy, in which Ted Grant, Gerry Healy and Andrew Scott defended a Majority EC position and Jock Haston, Sam Levy and Millie Kahn put forward a Minority view. This debate was instrumental in forging a genuine principled unity amongst the WIL leadership and in orientating the activities of the WIL during the war.

The authorship of all texts is indicated when different from Ted Grant and where there is known authorship.

Ted would have drafted or written many lead articles in *Youth For Socialism*, *Socialist Appeal* and *Workers' International News* that were published unsigned because they represented an official statement of the WIL. We decided not to include this material in the present volume and hope to publish it separately at a later date. The same decision was taken in relation to Ted's complete correspondence, because of the amount of research work needed to collect and edit that material. Again, it is our intention to publish this at a later date .

All texts have been checked against the original documents and are published here in their original form, except for evident typing errors that have been corrected and formatting characters that have been standardised throughout. Where editorial insertions were necessary for clarification, they have been introduced in square brackets [].

Footnotes in the original texts have been marked with (*). Other numbered footnotes have been introduced in the present volume.

Ted Grant's mother and father c.1910

Introduction

During the early years of the Second World War, Ted Grant (1913-2006), as editor of the *Socialist Appeal* and political secretary of the Workers' International League (WIL), emerged as the principal theoretician of British Trotskyism. Basing himself on a profound understanding of the writings of Marx, Engels, Lenin and Trotsky, Ted drafted the main documents and resolutions of the movement for a period of over 60 years. His participation in the revolutionary movement was to span a period of more than 70 years from 1928, when he was introduced to Marxism, through to his death. Throughout this long period, Ted never lost either his faith in Marxism, his sense of humour or his (slight) South African accent.

These decades of Ted Grant's political activity embraced the titanic events of the Wall Street crash, the great depression, the victory of fascism in Germany, the Spanish Civil War, the Moscow trials, the Second World War, the abolition of capitalism in China and Eastern Europe, the post-war upswing, the revolutionary 1970s, and the eventual collapse of Stalinism. Throughout these years of revolution, counter-revolution, capitalist stability and the re-emergence of capitalist crisis, Ted remained firmly committed to the ideas of world revolution and the absolute correctness of Marxism. However, he was no mere commentator on events, but a man who actively dedicated his whole life to the cause of revolutionary socialism. For all those who knew him, he was a truly remarkable and inspiring figure.

The articles and documents contained in this first volume of Ted Grant's *Writings* coincided with the emergence of the Workers' International League as one of the most successful Trotskyist groups in the world. This present volume covers a period of some five years, dealing with the immediate pre-war period and the first three years of the Second World War, a decisive time in world history. It was the most testing time for British and World Trotskyism. As Hitler occupied Europe, the WIL was alone on the continent in applying the proletarian military policy that had been outlined by Trotsky. This it managed to do in the most successful fashion, allowing the WIL to establish an important proletarian base. Pierre Broué, the celebrated Marxist historian, believed that the

British Trotskyists conducted the most successful work during the war of any Trotskyist group in the world. These writings of Ted Grant therefore constitute an essential and rich part of the theoretical heritage of our tendency. Above all, they will serve to educate the new generation of workers and youth who are entering into political activity at this time of deep capitalist crisis, in the ideas, methods, and outlook of the Marxist tendency.

It must be said that there was a problem in the selection of this material. We publish here only the articles that were either signed by Ted or that he drafted in his role as the WIL's political secretary. He would have certainly written the vast bulk of the editorials of *Socialist Appeal*, but these have not been included. This is somewhat of a disservice to Ted's colossal contribution, but it is hoped that we will publish them later in a separate volume as a supplement to his wartime writings. Of course, other leading comrades of the WIL, such as Ralph Lee, Jock Haston, and Andrew Scott, would have also contributed to the drafting of important unsigned documents or material. This should certainly be recognised. Ted was certainly appreciative of their collaboration. Nevertheless, Ted emerged during these years as the organisation's undisputed theoretician, as demonstrated by his political and theoretical output. He was a cadre of over ten years' experience. This role was further underlined with the subsequent return of Ralph Lee to South Africa for personal and health reasons in the middle of 1940.

In South Africa

Ted Grant was born in Germiston, near Johannesburg, in South Africa in July 1913, a year before the outbreak of the First World War and four years before the Bolshevik Revolution of 1917, an event that was going to have a profound effect on his later life. His family upbringing had little effect on his future political evolution except for a family lodger, Ralph Lee, who had been a member of the South African Communist Party since 1922. Ralph, who was about five years older than Ted, had been expelled from the party for opposition views. As a teenager, Ted had been systematically introduced by Ralph to the writings of Bernard Shaw, HG Wells, Maxim Gorky and Jack London. After these authors he progressed to the writings of Marx, Engels and Lenin. By the age of 15, Ted had become a convinced and committed Marxist and remained so for the rest of his life. "It changed my life completely", stated Ted later, "and I started on a political road that now spans more than seventy years."

Ted made regular visits to a left-wing bookshop in Johannesburg which was receiving copies of the newly-established paper called *The Militant*. These were produced by the American Trotskyists headed by James P. Cannon, who had recently been expelled from the American Communist Party. These papers introduced Ralph and Ted to the ideas of Leon Trotsky and the Left Opposition on a whole series of burning questions, beginning with his *Critique of the draft programme of the Communist International.* This had a massive and lasting impact upon them. "We read them avidly from cover to cover, especially the writings of Trotsky himself," explained Ted. "These contributions made an enormous difference to our understanding."

The Left Opposition had been established by Trotsky in 1923 as part of the struggle against the Stalinist degeneration taking place within the Soviet Union. With the defeat of the German Revolution, followed by the death of Lenin, Stalin came forward with the anti-Marxist theory of Socialism in One Country. This theory reflected the outlook of the bureaucracy which turned its back on world revolution and sought to consolidate its privileged position. With each defeat and blow against world revolution, the Russian masses were worn down after years of deprivation and isolation. In November 1927, the Stalin clique succeeded in consolidating itself further by expelling Trotsky and the Left Opposition from the party. Early in 1928, Trotsky was exiled firstly to Alma Ata and later to Turkey. From there he organised the international Left Opposition as an expelled faction of the Communist International in a fight to restore the genuine programme and methods of Leninism and reform the Soviet state.

In solidarity with Trotsky, Ralph and Ted organised the beginnings of a Left Opposition group in Johannesburg and soon recruited Ted's younger sister Zena and her boyfriend Raymond Lake. Others soon joined, including Millie Kahn, who was to later play an important role in the British Trotskyist movement. Her sister Hilda had joined the Stalinists, which, according to Millie, provoked a "war" between them. Shortly she was to marry Ralph and change her name to Millie Lee. Her steady income from a job in her mother's hat business served to maintain Ralph as a "professional revolutionary" for the group.

Some years ago, just before she died, I took Ted to meet Millie for the last time. Millie had played an extremely active role in the Trotskyist movement in the period covered by this book, assisting Ted and others to build the Workers' International League in Britain. She subsequently moved away from Trotskyism, as did many others, after 1950 with the break-up of the Revolutionary Communist Party. She had not met Ted since that time until this meeting at her home in September 2001. It was quite a remarkable meeting as Ted and Millie began to recall events and experiences of the past. She remembered with great pride the time she was arrested and sent to Holloway prison in August 1940 after trespassing on private property during a protest outside the Russian embassy against Trotsky's assassination in Mexico. The WIL protesters carried placards, "Stalin murdered Trotsky". After nine days she was finally released and fined £30, which was a considerable sum of money in those days. Despite her advanced years, Millie seemed to come to life as she described the building of the Trotskyist movement during the Second World War. She marvelled at the work they had done at that time in preparing for the British Revolution. "We were optimistic throughout, weren't we?" as she nodded in

Ted's direction. "Considering everything, we had a fantastic time." (*Interview with Millie Haston and Ted Grant*, September 8 2001). Millie supplied us with a host of photographs of the period, many of which appear in this volume.

In the early 1930s, the small group of South African Trotskyists struggled bravely to make their mark, even leading the Johannesburg laundry workers' strike of 1934. However, the situation was very difficult. The comrades realised that the real centre of future revolution would take place thousands of miles away in Europe. Hitler had come to power in Germany and preparations were being made for world war. In Spain the workers had launched the heroic Asturian Commune, providing a new impetus to the Spanish Revolution. As a result, the South African comrades decided over a period to uproot their small forces and place them where they could better serve the world revolution. Ted and another member of the group, Max Bosch, left South Africa for England in late 1934 for "broader horizons", to use Ted's words. Both decided to change their names at this point. Max Bosch became Sid Frost, and a certain Isaac Blank became Ted Grant. Most of the other comrades, including Ralph and Millie, followed in the middle of 1937. "We decided there was no real future for us in South Africa, so we came to England", stated Millie.

In search for "broader horizons"

On his voyage to London, Ted and Sid stopped off in Paris and discussed with Leon Trotsky's son, Leon Sedov, who was the main organiser of the international Trotskyist movement. From this conversation it was clear that Sedov had many reservations about the British Trotskyists who were working at this time within the Independent Labour Party (ILP), a centrist party that had split from the Labour Party in 1932. Trotsky had advised the newly formed British Left Oppositionists to join the ILP as a means of winning over the leftward-moving workers to Marxism.

This had constituted a sharp change in the tactics of the Left Opposition and resulted from the fact that the road to the Communist workers had been effectively blocked at this stage. The consolidation of the Stalinist regime with the successes of the Five Year Plans served to strengthen the grip of Stalinism. By the mid-1930s, the purges had produced a river of blood which separated Stalinism and Trotskyism. At the same time, the world capitalist crisis had created colossal ferment in the ranks of the social-democratic organisations. Trotsky explained the urgent need for the Trotskyists in this period to break out of their isolation and turn towards the opportunities within the reformist organisations. With correct work, this could result in the rapid crystallisation of a revolutionary tendency with deep roots in the working class. This tactic became known as the "French turn", although it was first carried out in Britain.

Ralph Lee

Trotsky's proposal led, however, to great controversy and resulted in a split in the British group. The main leaders of the group strenuously upheld the independence of the party as a principle, which simply served to reinforce their sectarian isolation. A dozen of the younger less experienced comrades took Trotsky's advice and entered the ILP. The Trotskyists—known as the Marxist Group—nevertheless (mainly due to their inexperience) struggled to take advantage of the opportunities within the ILP.

The Marxist Group

On his arrival, Ted joined the Marxist Group in Paddington and began to give regular talks on the lessons of the South African workers' movement. Ever since he was introduced to the ideas of Marxism, Ted had developed a keen interest in theory. He devoured the classics of Marxism and especially the new articles of Trotsky. Ted also absorbed the perspectives of a new imperialist world war and the development of world revolution in the coming period. Both Ted and Sid Frost, who worked closely together at this time, repeated the perspectives at every opportunity within the ILP. "Here comes 'War' and 'Revolution'," sneered the hardened centrists wherever the South Africans turned up. Such slurs were water off a duck's back and in any event the two young South Africans were

The WIL Centre, 61 Northdown Street, Kings Cross, London

proved right.

The Marxist Group was clearly in bad shape by this time. There had been an opportunist adaptation amongst some of the group's leaders to the centrist milieu, causing dissatisfaction amongst the membership. Ted, with other members, wrote to Leon Sedov expressing their deep concerns with the functioning of the group and the lack of prospects (See appendix). At this time, the ILP was haemorrhaging members and losing influence. Most of those who remained were die-hard centrists. There were far better prospects for Trotskyism developing within the Labour Party, especially in the Labour League of Youth.

Trotsky, who would have seen the report, was quick to realise that the ILP episode was clearly coming to an end. The shift to the left in the Labour Party was producing much greater opportunities. "The British section will recruit its first cadres from the thirty thousand young workers in the Labour League of Youth", wrote Trotsky, as he urged the comrades to leave the ILP and enter the Labour Party. This, yet again, produced another row, with the leaders of the group yet again opposing this turn. Nevertheless, many of the young comrades followed Trotsky's advice and individually joined the Labour Party, especially its youth section. This new group soon began to produce a paper called *Youth*

Militant mainly aimed at work in the Labour League of Youth (LLY). Ted followed Trotsky's advice and joined the LLY. Here the comrades battled with the Stalinists who had taken control of the youth. With the growing threat from Mosley's blackshirts, the comrades, and Ted in particular, also took an active part in the anti-fascist street battles in East London.

The following year, a small number of South African Trotskyists, including Ralph and Millie Lee, arrived in Britain. After discussions with Ted and Jock Haston, a former member of the Communist Party, they decided to join the Militant Group. Along with Ted and Jock, they became members of the group's Paddington branch. They were extremely energetic in building the branch and were making a considerable impact on the group. Amazingly they were soon regarded with suspicion by the group's leadership, fearing that these "new-comers" would challenge their positions. These leaders were involved in clique politics and consumed with their own personal prestige. As a result, rumours were deliberately spread by the leadership about Ralph Lee which claimed he had stolen money from the Laundry Workers' Union. This was a slander spread by the Stalinists in Johannesburg. In fact Ralph had spent everything he had on the strike personally and was held in high esteem by the workers. This poisonous atmosphere in the group led to an almighty row at a London aggregate meeting and a walk-out by several members led by Jock Haston, including, amongst others, Ralph Lee, Millie Lee, and Ted Grant. They were then informed by the group's leaders that they had been expelled.

The formation of the WIL

After lengthy discussions over a number of days and nights, the comrades decided to turn their back on the "Militant Group" and their clique politics. The old group could not be considered a serious revolutionary organisation. It was a petty-bourgeois clique incapable of doing serious work. In any case, relations were completely poisoned. The comrades decided to launch themselves as a new organisation with a clean banner. With eight comrades, they set themselves up as the Workers' International League in late December 1937 as the only genuine Trotskyist group in Britain.

They continued with their work within the Labour Party. Their first task, however, was to quickly produce a magazine called the *Workers' International News*. The first issue came off the press in January 1938, with an article by Trotsky. The comrades also produced *Youth For Socialism* from September until the middle of 1941 when it became *Socialist Appeal*, aimed at the members of the Labour League of Youth. Ralph Lee, as the most experienced comrade, played the leading role in the group, assisted by Ted, Millie and Jock, which acted as the leadership of the organisation. Of course, much of the material of the group concentrated upon Trotsky's material and the rapidly approaching war. Within about six months they had managed to grow to thirty members, mostly young workers. They were very energetic, selling their papers at Hyde Park, Tottenham Court Road and other central locations. They were very keen to build up their membership and establish themselves on a national basis. Ted wrote several leading articles, all re-produced in this volume, concerning the nature of the war, the developing international situation and the tasks posed before the working class.

1938 "unity" conference

A year before the war, in September 1938, a "unity conference" had been convened in an attempt to unify the four Trotskyist groups in Britain. It was an initiative of the International Secretariat of the International Communist League, the forerunner of the Fourth International, and was hosted by James Cannon who had come over from the United States. This conference was held in order to present a British unified group to the founding conference of the Fourth International which was soon to take place in Paris. However, the problem was that these four groups had different methods and tactics. While the WIL attended the "unity conference" in London, it opposed the unification as unprincipled and unworkable. They argued that it was not possible to fuse different groups with different traditions, methods and tactics into a single organisation. The fusion conference was chaotic with faction meetings taking place, people coming and going, and doors opening and closing. Ralph branded it as more like a French bedroom farce. While the WIL refused to join the fusion, the group did not want to sever all its links with the international movement and asked to be recognised as a sympathetic section of the Fourth International. At the founding conference of the Fourth, Cannon scandalously opposed the WIL's sympathetic affiliation and secured a vote against the proposal. Unfortunately, the WIL could not afford to send a delegate to Paris as most of the comrades were unemployed. "We became the bastard child of the International", explained Ted later.

James P. Cannon, who was a prestige politician, never forgave the WIL for its principled stand against the 1938 fusion and its future successes. His reputation had been dented. This was to colour his role in the international movement after Trotsky's death and his negative relations with the British Trotskyists, as will become clear in future volumes. In the years covered in this volume, however, Cannon's standing in the Fourth International was very high, as was that of the American Socialist Workers' Party. On October 27 1941, the trial of 28 members of the SWP and Teamsters' Union, Local 544 had begun. Eighteen were found guilty of "advocating the desirability of overthrowing the government by force and violence", which resulted in the imprisonment of Cannon and other SWP leaders. The sections of the "Fourth" tended to look up to the Americans for guidance and inspiration. The WIL was no different and, despite being officially outside the International, it regularly reproduced material and news from the American SWP. For a more comprehensive appraisal of Cannon's contribution throughout this period, readers should refer to Ted Grant's book on the *History of British Trotskyism.*

Following the "fusion" conference, the new "unified" group in Britain took the name of the Revolutionary Socialist League (RSL). As predicted, the "unified" group started to break up as soon as the conference was over. "The adoption of different tactics", explained Ted, "was a recipe for uniting four groups into ten!" And that is what happened. The WIL however continued to make steady progress, even taking chunks out of the RSL. They won over the entire RSL Liverpool and Leeds groups, bringing over the entire Deane family in Liverpool in the process.

It is worth noting that Trotsky never attacked the WIL or its decision to remain outside of the International as an unofficial sympathising group. He basically adopted a wait-and-see approach, which was justified by subsequent events. Within six weeks of establishing the WIL, Ralph Lee wrote a letter to Trotsky on behalf of the group dated February 12 1938, explaining that they had established a printing press. "Up to now we have published two issues of *Workers' International News* and the pamphlet *Summary of the final report of the commission of enquiry into the charges made against Leon Trotsky in the Moscow trials.* Copies of these have been sent to you under separate cover", stated the letter. The original of this letter is in the Trotsky archives at Harvard. As was usual, Trotsky marked the more interesting passages of any correspondence in a blue and red pencil. This he did with the sentences already quoted. He also wrote a question mark in the margin, probably indicating the need to find out more about this English group. Ralph's letter ended:

> "Hitherto we have been dependent on the initiative and energy of the American comrades but this has meant, among other things, prohibitive prices for our publications that have prevented their wide distribution. In seeking to end this dependence on an external section of Fourth Internationalists we hope that we will have your blessing."

The last eight words were also underlined in pencil by Trotsky.

In his discussions with members of the American SWP a month or so later, Trotsky praised the WIL for obtaining a printing press, and urged the American comrades to follow this excellent example (Trotsky's *Writings 1937-38*, p.394). He also wrote to the WIL thanking them for re-publishing his pamphlet *Lessons of Spain*, which contained an introduction by Ralph and Ted that is also reprinted in this volume.

War preparations

The whole period was overshadowed by the rush to war by the European powers. The war was a continuation of the First World War, precipitated by the attempts of German imperialism to force a re-division of the world in its own interests. Hitler's mission was world domination through the displacement of France and Britain, and eventually the United States. While Germany acted as a bulwark against Bolshevism, Britain assisted her re-armament programme. This was fully exposed in the *Socialist Appeal* of June 1941 when it published extracts from the diary of William E. Dodd, the US ambassador to Germany between June 1933 and December 1937. Dodd revealed that Britain and France had been preparing for war long before Hitler had come to power. In an entry for March 17 1935, he explains, "I think the Goering air programme is truly belligerent but France, Italy and England have armed in violation of the Versailles Treaty too." He also reveals the policy of French and British diplomacy was to aid Hitler's rearmament in preparation for war against the Soviet Union. In a conversation with Lord Lothian in May 1935 he shows the clear attitude of British imperialism.

> "Lord Lothian, who as Philip Kerr was secretary to Lloyd George during the world war, wrote me…a letter which I received today…he indicated clearly that he favours a coalition of the democracies to block any German move in their direction and to turn Germany's course eastwards. That this might lead to a war between Russia and Germany does not seem to disturb him seriously. In fact he seems to feel this would be a good solution of the difficulties imposed on Germany by the Versailles Treaty. The problem of the democracies, as he sees it, is to find for Japan and Germany a stronger place in world affairs to which, in his opinion, they are entitled because of their power and tradition. He hopes this can be accomplished without any sacrifice to the British Empire and with as little destruction to human liberty as possible."

On January 11 1937, six months after Franco's uprising, Dodd writes of the leading British diplomats:

> "Sir Eric Phipps was as discreet as ever, but he revealed more sympathy for the Fascist crowd in Spain than I had noted before. I believe now that he is almost a Fascist, as I think are Baldwin and Eden."

In relation to German rearmament, his diary reveals Britain's role.

> "I visited Sir Eric Phipps and repeated in all confidence a report that Armstrong-Vickers, the great British armament concern, had negotiated a sale of war material here (Berlin) last week, just before a British government commission arrived to negotiate some plan with Schacht for payment of short-term debts…due on current deliveries of British cotton yarn from Lancashire. It is impossible, Schacht said to me yesterday, to pay British debts. Yet, last Friday, I reported to Sir Eric, the British arms people were selling for cash enormous quantities of war supplies. And I was frank enough—or indiscreet enough—to add that I understood that representatives of Curtiss-Wright from the United States were here this

week to negotiate similar sales. The British Ambassador pretended to be surprised..."

He gives much more material to show what the real attitude of the "democracies" was towards Hitler prior to the war. It demonstrates without any doubt that the Second World War was not a war between "democracy" and "fascism" as the "democratic" imperialists wanted us to believe. Dodd was forced to conclude:

"In the United States, capitalists are pressing in their same Fascist direction, supported by capitalists in England. Nearly all our diplomatic service people here have indicated their drift in the same direction."

Again Churchill, reflecting the attitude of the British ruling class, was a great admirer of both Mussolini and Hitler. "One may dislike Hitler's system and yet admire his patriotic achievement", wrote Churchill. "If our country were defeated, I hope that we should find a champion as indomitable to restore our courage and lead us back to our place among the nations." (*Strand* magazine, November 1935). The British imperialists supported Hitler at Munich after he seized Czechoslovakia in the hope that he would be satisfied with central Europe. But to their cost, they finally realised that German imperialism was striving towards world domination, which collided with Britain's interests. This could not be tolerated. The "war against fascism" provided a convenient cover to rally the masses behind their real war aims.

Stalin-Hitler pact

The isolation and degeneration of the Russian revolution had resulted in the usurping of power by the Stalinist bureaucracy. Stalin carried through the Purge Trials to exterminate all those who had any connection with the October Revolution. Zinoviev, Kamenev, Bukharin and other "Old Bolsheviks" were framed as counter-revolutionary "Trotsky-fascists" and murdered. Stalin decapitated the Red Army and systematically strangled the Spanish Revolution to prove to the western powers how reliable he was as a potential ally. He feared Hitler and therefore sought an alliance with the imperialist "democracies". This, however, proved fruitless, despite Stalin's continuous efforts, as the "democracies" were rearming Germany (and Italy) for war with the Soviet Union.

Hitler had decided to move west. A "non-aggression" pact with Stalin suited his interests and in August 1939 the Stalin-Hitler Pact was signed. "We have always held that a strong Germany is an indispensable condition for a durable peace in Europe", stated Molotov. This pact allowed Hitler access to Russia's important raw materials as well as guaranteeing the Soviet Union's "neutrality" in the approaching war. "Stalin acts as his (Hitler's) quartermaster", noted Trotsky. The "non-aggression" Pact also allowed Stalin to take Eastern Poland and occupy strategic positions in the Baltic, as well as invading Finland. Above all, for a temporary period, it allowed Hitler to concentrate on conquering Western Europe before turning his attentions towards the USSR.

"The Communist Party leaders represent nothing but the narrow interests of the Kremlin"—stated a leaflet issued by the WIL—"Yesterday they supported the war. Today they are calling for an imperialist 'peace' and are quite prepared to sacrifice the German, Czech and Polish workers to rule of German fascism. Tomorrow, if Stalin makes a pact with Chamberlain they will again support the war. The working class can have nothing but contempt for such scoundrels." (No date, Ted Grant's archives)

Two days after the signing of the Stalin-Hitler Pact, Germany invaded Poland, and France and Britain declared war against Germany. By April 1940, Germany invaded Norway and Denmark. A month later, she invaded the Low Countries and France. Within six weeks British forces evacuated Dunkirk and France fell. On July 10 1940 the Germans began the bombing of London. This was the international background in which the Workers' International League was established and conducted its work.

The WIL and the fascist threat

In the 18 months up to the outbreak of war, the Workers' International League had been engaged in feverish work to build up its forces.

"We published *Workers' International News*, a very large part of our activity was making contacts through the *Workers' International News*, apart from our entrist work in the Labour Party", stated Jock Haston much later. "In the main, it was a conflict with the Communist Party. We used the documents also for contact with militants in the ILP. We participated actively in the anti-fascist movement which was fairly strong at that time and some of our publications were devoted to the anti-fascist, anti-Mosley struggle. Ted in particular—I have a picture somewhere of Ted at the barricades in the East End of London, in Cable Street."

"It was mostly selling *Workers' International News* outside meetings and Hyde Park"—interjected Millie—"And attending Communist Party meetings dealing with the Moscow Trials"—continued Jock—"We never allowed any Communist Party meetings to take place on the Moscow Trials in which we didn't intervene and attack the Stalinists on their line on the Moscow Trials. I think probably one might say that our principal source of contacts was the YCL and the Paddington Young Communist League on at least two occasions, almost to a man, came over to the WIL group, and Johnny Gollan was actually sent up to Paddington when he was leader of the YCL with the object of re-establishing the YCL and we challenged him. Every time they had a public meeting we challenged them."

Jock Haston, who was the group's national organiser, also reveals some of the basic problems facing the WIL, particularly the paucity of resources.

> "Well, the problems were that first of all, we were an organisation that almost entirely consisted of workers. We didn't have any money, so money was the pre-occupying activity for us, for our publications, the theoretical bag and baggage that we had wasn't very great, we were mainly followers, rather than initiators, you know of the broad Trotskyist point of view. The problem was getting up and down the country to make contacts with the people we had heard about in different parts of the country, and it was very difficult due to the lack of cash. The problem was getting our publications out on time with what limited resources we had, so here was a question of really working all the hours god sent. We were almost all of us professionals, practically all of us were on the dole, and we had tons of time, but no money, in which to conduct the work we were carrying out." (*Interview given to Al Richardson by Jock Haston on April 30 1978, with Millie (Lee) Haston participating*, Bornstein archives)

The pace of work of this small group of comrades was immense. On top of their other activities, from October 1939 to May 1940, the WIL, mainly due to the work of Ralph Lee, produced a duplicated sheet on practically a daily basis, entitled *Workers' Diary*.

The proletarian military policy

In the period before the war, the WIL conducted an anti-war policy explaining that any new world war was dictated by imperialism's desire to re-divide the world in its search for new markets and profits. The only solution to imperialist war was to fight our real enemies at home as part of the struggle for socialism. This line was reflected in the party press until the adoption by the WIL of the proletarian military policy in the autumn of 1940, which saw a new military emphasis to the articles in the League's publications. The political thrust was still to call upon Labour to break the war-time coalition and carry through a socialist programme, but additional demands were added for a revolutionary military policy to fight against fascism, and in particular the need to arm the working class in the struggle against Nazism.

Ted Grant explained in a speech he had made towards the end of 1940 of how the policy evolved.

> "The policy remains essentially the same, but the emphasis has changed," he said. "The policy remains irreconcilable opposition to the war-making imperialists. However, with the outbreak of war and the vic-

tory of the Nazis, the policy is given a new emphasis. Popular agitation could not be conducted on the basis of revolutionary defeatism, which could never win the masses." (Notes of a speech on the proletarian military policy in the Ted Grant archives)

He went on to explain that the defeat of Hitler remained the aim, however only the workers could defeat fascism. The ruling class was not waging a war against fascism, but only to defend its own material interests. Without giving any support whatsoever to British imperialism's war aims, the revolutionary tendency needed to take into account the mood of the working class and its hatred of fascism. In such a struggle, the hopeless inadequacies of pacifism were clearly exposed. What was needed was an independent workers' policy to serve the needs of the workers. Such a policy needed to emphasise the capitalist character of the army and the need to dissolve the standing army into an armed people. This raised the question of the election of officers, the government to finance schools under the control of the trade unions for training worker-officers, instead of the sons of the ruling class. Such a programme would also make workers conscious of the role of the army, the state and the capitalists. It would pose the need for the working class to take power and wage a revolutionary internationalist war.

This proletarian military policy was first put forward by Trotsky shortly before his death in 1940 and adopted wholeheartedly by the WIL.

"If one proceeds only on the basis of the overall characterisation of the epoch, and nothing more, ignoring its concrete stages, one can easily lapse into schematism, sectarianism, or quixotic fantasy"—wrote Trotsky—"With every serious turn of events we adjust our basic tasks to the changed concrete conditions of the given stage. Herein lies the art of tactics." (Trotsky *Writings*, 1939-40, p. 103)

He went on to outline the Marxist approach to the war:

"Without in any way wavering from our programme we must speak to the masses in a language they understand. 'We Bolsheviks also want to defend democracy, but not the kind that is run by sixty uncrowned kings. First let's sweep our democracy clean of capitalist magnates, then we will defend it to the last drop of blood. Are you, who are not Bolsheviks, really ready to defend *this* democracy? But you must, at least, be able to the best of your ability to defend it so as not to be a blind instrument in the hands of the Sixty Families and the bourgeois officers devoted to them. The working class must learn military affairs in order to advance the largest possible number of officers from its own ranks.'

" 'We must demand that the state, which tomorrow will ask for the workers' blood, today give the workers the opportunity to master military technique in the best possible way in order to achieve the military objectives with the minimum expenditure of human lives.'

" 'To accomplish that, a regular army and barracks by themselves are not enough. Workers must have the opportunity to get military training at their factories, plants, and mines at specified times, while being paid by the capitalists. If the workers are destined to give their lives, the bourgeois patriots can at least make a small material sacrifice.'

" 'The state must issue a rifle to every worker capable of bearing arms and set up rifle and artillery ranges for military training purposes in places accessible to the workers.'

"Our agitation in connection with the war and all our politics connected with the war must be as uncompromising in relation to the pacifists as to the imperialists.

" 'This war is not our war. The responsibility for it lies squarely on the capitalists. But so long as we are still not strong enough to overthrow them and must fight in the ranks of their army, we are obliged to learn to use arms as well as possible!'

"Women workers must also have the right to bear arms. The largest possible number of women workers must have the opportunity, at the capitalists' expense, to receive nurses' training.

"Just as every worker, exploited by the capitalists, seeks to learn as well as possible the production techniques, so every proletarian soldier in the imperialist army must learn as well as possible, when the conditions change, to apply it in the interests of the working class.

"We are not pacifists. No. We are revolutionaries. And we know what lies ahead for us." (Ibid, pp. 104-5)

When Trotsky raised the proletarian military policy, it provoked widespread opposition within the ranks of the Fourth International. Many leaders, such as those of the Belgian and British (the RSL) sections, deliberately purged any references to this policy. The Belgian group, for example, struck out several paragraphs on this question from the clandestine version of the May 1940 *Manifesto*. There were also "reservations" held by the French section and even the European Secretariat of the Fourth International. As a consequence, their whole approach, rooted in a false appraisal of the real situation, completely failed to connect with the working class faced with the onslaught of Hitler fascism. Their tactics were stuck in the past and tainted with pacifism. As a result, they were confined to the fringes. Even the American SWP, which had adopted the military policy under Trotsky's pressure, interpreted the policy in a passive fashion, reducing it to mere propaganda divorced from any perspective for workers' power.

In an article about this question, written by Pierre Broué in 1985, he explained that apart from Jean Van Heijenoort, who had worked very closely with Trotsky, "nobody in or on the fringe of the Fourth International had understood the question of militarisation." This represented a damning indictment of the whole of the Fourth International which was not able to grasp this change of direction, so essential for an understanding of the entire epoch. However, Broué was not aware of the WIL's position when he wrote this article. Subsequently, through his collaboration with the International Marxist Tendency and his contact with Ted Grant, he came to the conclusion that the WIL had conducted the most successful work during the war of any Trotskyist group in the world.

Leaflet for Trotsky memorial meeting, London
August 21 1941

The success of the Workers' International League during the war was based on its application of the military policy. While Cannon and the SWP were emphasising their propaganda approach, the WIL was posing the question of power before the working class. It is no accident that the group's 1942 perspectives document was entitled *Preparing for power*, a position ridiculed by the RSL from the comfort of their sofas. The WIL's perspective was however the same as Trotsky's.

In an article he dictated just before he died, Trotsky addresses not only the SWP but also the world Trotskyist movement.

"No occupation is more completely unworthy than that of speculating whether or not we shall succeed in creating a powerful revolutionary leader-party. Ahead lies a favourable perspective, providing all the justification for revolutionary activism. It is necessary to utilise the opportunities which are opening up and to build the revolutionary party...

"Reaction wields today such power as perhaps never before in the modern history of mankind. But it would be an inexcusable blunder to see only reaction. The historical process is a contradictory one. Under the cover of official reaction profound processes are taking place among the masses who are accumulating experience and are becoming receptive to new political perspectives. The old conservative tradition of the democratic state which was so powerful even during the era of the last imperialist war exists today only as an extremely unstable survival. On the eve of the last war the European workers had numerically powerful parties. But on the order of the day were put reforms, partial conquests, and not at all the conquest of power.

"The American working class is still without a mass labour party even today. But the objective situation and the experience accumulated by the American workers can pose within a very brief period of time on the order of the day the question of the conquest of power. This perspective must be made the basis of our agitation. It is not merely a question of a position on capitalist militarism and of renouncing the defence of the bourgeois state, but of directly preparing for the conquest of power and the defence of the proletarian fatherland." (Trotsky, *Writings 1939-40*, pp. 413-414)

WIL Trotsky memorial meeting, London
(standing Ajit Roy, seated Ted Grant, Sid Bidwell and Gerry Healy)

It must be said, however, that the adoption of the military policy did not take place without some political frictions within the WIL leadership. While they all agreed with the general thrust of the policy, there were some criticisms by Jock, Millie and Sam Levy about the slant given to articles in the paper and particularly the nature of the Home Guard and how it could be transformed into a workers' militia. The Minority believed the group had made concessions to defencism. Ted Grant, supported by Andrew Scott and Gerry Healy, defended the Majority line taken in the paper, which had correctly embraced the policy of proletarian militarism. It can be said that Ted, as opposed to the other leading comrades, grasped the real significance of the military policy as argued by Trotsky. This dispute led to exchanges within the internal bulletin between February and March 1941. The issue was resolved at a conference of the group based on a resolution drafted by Ted on behalf of the Political Bureau, which together with the articles in the internal bulletin are reprinted in their entirety for the first time in this volume.

True to form, the sectarian RSL, which was the official British section of the Fourth International, *officially* rejected the entire proletarian military policy in September 1941, describing it as a capitulation to chauvinism, and calling instead for the war to be turned into a civil war. They even made rejection of the policy a condition of membership! This politically hopeless sectarian group turned in on itself, keeping its r-r-revolutionary whispering for the dressing room. It was a sterile approach. They were simply repeating parrot-fashion what Lenin had written at the time of the First World War, without understanding that Lenin was not addressing the masses, but the cadres. But Lenin changed his approach during 1917 as the Bolshevik party sought not to educate the cadres, but to win over the Russian masses.

Anti-militarism and defeatism could never win the masses. This was especially the case in Britain when, following the fall of France, the masses were alarmed at the prospect of a Nazi occupation and all the horrors that would mean. The Trotskyists also wanted to defeat Hitler, but pointed out that the British workers could not rely on the British ruling class, who supported the fascists when it suited them, to carry out this task. The WIL agitated for a genuine war against Hitler on the basis of the British workers taking power, and an internationalist appeal to the German workers to overthrow Hitler.

As Trotsky explained:

> "The present war, as we have stated more than once, is a continuation of the last war. But a continuation does not imply a repetition. As a general rule, a continuation implies a development, a deepening, a sharpening. Our policy, the policy of the revolutionary proletariat towards the second imperialist world war, is a continuation of the policy elaborated during the last imperialist war, primarily under the leadership of Lenin. But a continuation does not imply a repetition. In this case, too, a contin-

uation means a development, a deepening and a sharpening." (Trotsky, *Writings 1939-40*, p.411)

Work in the Labour League of Youth

As a result of their sectarian approach, the RSL suffered a steep decline in its membership. At the same time, the WIL made significant progress in the recruitment of industrial workers and built important points of support in the factories. By the time of its first national conference it was 300-strong, 90 percent of which were industrial workers.

Before the outbreak of war, the WIL conducted consistent work within the Labour League of Youth against the Stalinists, however, its independent work began to take on greater and greater importance. This was especially the case with the declaration of war in September 1939 and the conscription of the youth into the army. The political truce reduced the local Labour Party branches to mere shells with little internal life. In the middle of 1940, the Labour Party entered a coalition government under Winston Churchill. Under these circumstances, any potential gains in the Labour Party completely dried up. The WIL adopted a flexible approach and made a turn towards the ILP, which had started to grow on the basis of its anti-war stance. Moreover, with the upturn in the number of strikes, the WIL turned increasingly to the industrial front, changing the name of its paper from *Youth For Socialism* to *Socialist Appeal* in June 1941. This gave it a much broader appeal. In the lead article in the first issue of the *Appeal* it argued for Labour to power on the following programme:

> "(1) Arming and organising of the workers under their own control to resist any danger from invasion or any Pétainism at home. (2) Election of officers by soldiers. (3) The establishment of special officers' training camps, financed by the government and controlled by the trade unions, to train workers to become officers. (4) Expropriation of the arms industries, mines, banks, land and heavy industry. (5) Workers' control of production. (6) Freedom for India and the Colonies. (6) A Socialist appeal to the workers of Germany and Europe for the Socialist struggle against Hitler." (*Socialist Appeal*, June 1941)

Impact of the Nazi attack on the USSR

This transformation of the WIL's newspaper was not only due to the growing influence of the organisation, but it also coincided with Hitler's attack on the Soviet Union and her entry into the world conflagration. The need to unconditionally defend the Soviet Union from imperialist attack was a long-standing position of the Trotskyist movement. This did not change the general imperialist character of the war, but the defence of the USSR featured more prominently in the WIL's programme. The banner heading of the July 1941 issue read

Defend the Soviet Union and explained

"The war has now taken a new turn with the attack by German imperialism on the Soviet Union. A terrible danger now threatens the first workers' state with destruction. The greatest clash in the history of the world on a 1,800-mile front has thrown the whole international situation into a state of flux. The assault of world imperialism on the first workers' state is no longer a Marxist perspective, but a grim reality."

Prior to this, the Stalin-Hitler Pact, the Soviet invasion of Poland and Finland, and the war itself, had produced a wave of anti-Soviet propaganda throughout the capitalist "democracies". This shook a section of the American SWP to the core, resulting in a substantial minority led by Max Shachtman and James Burnham buckling under pressure. This led them to challenge the class nature of the Soviet Union as a deformed workers' state resting on nationalised property rights. They stated that the USSR had become a new bureaucratic collectivist state with its own imperialist ambitions. They regarded it as some kind of new class society which could not be defended. This clearly reflected the pressures of bourgeois public opinion. While the Trotskyists opposed the Stalin dictatorship, their revolutionary duty was to defend the remaining gains of the October Revolution, the nationalisation of the means of production and the monopoly of foreign trade. This position was linked with the need for political revolution to remove the bureaucracy and re-introduce workers' democracy. The Shachtman-Burnham group finally split from the SWP and abandoned any pretence at defending the Soviet Union.

Despite Hitler's attack on the Soviet Union in June 1941, the WIL did not change its characterisation of the war as an imperialist war, despite the fact that the USSR had allied itself with the "democratic" imperialist powers. For the Stalinists, however, this changed everything. Ever since the signing of the Stalin-Hitler Pact, the Communist Party characterised the war as imperialist and campaigned for, in essence, peace on Hitler's terms. They branded Britain and France as the real enemies. This showed that the Stalinist parties were simply the mouthpieces of the Russian bureaucracy, twisting and turning with every change of policy emanating from Moscow.

For the Stalinists, as soon as the Soviet Union was drawn into the war, the war suddenly changed to become a "just war" against fascism, which should be given unqualified support. In the space of 24 hours, the Communist Party became the greatest supporter of the war and opposed all strikes which served to undermine the war effort. They became the greatest cheerleaders of the Churchill government. The Stalinists had turned into strike breakers and chauvinists of the worst kind. As a result, the WIL launched an immediate struggle against the pro-war line of the Stalinists in the trade unions and in the factories, exposing their weaknesses and posing a revolutionary alternative.

The work of the WIL during this period began to have an effect on the best workers in the ranks of the CP and a number of its best militants joined the Trotskyists. A growing part of the work of the WIL was directed towards the best CP workers in an attempt to win them away from its Stalinist leadership. The Trotskyists gave whole-hearted support to the increasing number of strikes, to the profound displeasure of the bosses, trade union bureaucracy and the Stalinists.

Stalinist attacks

In November 1941, the WIL held a successful 200-strong public meeting in London on the anniversary of the Bolshevik Revolution. It was described by the *Socialist Appeal* as "one of the most enthusiastic left-wing gatherings held in Britain since the outbreak of the war." The speakers were Haston, Healy and Ted Grant. In the report it explains:

> "The last speaker was comrade Ted Grant who exposed the real meaning of Churchill's aid for the USSR. Amidst loud applause he dealt a slashing attack upon [the] treacherous role of the Communist Party. 'If Hitler was confronted with a Russian victory,' said comrade Grant, 'then in 24 hours Churchill would make peace with German Nazism and inaugurate a universal imperialist line up against the first workers' state.' In reply to discussion our comrade satisfactorily dealt with a number of issues raised by CP members of the audience." (*Socialist Appeal*, December 1941)

The meeting had coincided with a public attack on the WIL by the *Sunday Dispatch*, accusing the comrades of acting in the interests of the Nazis. *Socialist Appeal* replied to this attack by a front-page article exposing the role of the *Dispatch* and its sister paper, the *Daily Mail*, for its lies, adding that these gutter newspapers had been ardent supporters of Hitler and Mussolini before the war. The *Dispatch* reprinted all the Stalinist lies contained in a manifesto that the Trotskyists were disrupters and agents of Hitler, Mussolini and Franco! They repeated these slanders and ended with the Stalinist phrase: "Treat the Trotskyists as you would a Nazi." In the December issue of *Labour Monthly*, R.J. Campbell described the Trotskyists as the "agents of the Gestapo in the Labour movement."

Throughout these months, the success of the WIL brought a witch-hunt down on the heads of the Trotskyists, instigated by Will Lawther, national president of the Miners' Federation, Joe Hall, the president of the Yorkshire miners, the capitalist press and, of course, the Stalinists. All accused the Trotskyists of sabotaging the war-effort and helping Hitler. There was a massive uproar against the WIL in the capitalist press and the Stalinists issued a pamphlet in August 1942 called *Clear out Hitler's agents*, by William Wainwright, urging their members to physically attack the Trotskyists. They even raised the matter in the House of Commons through their MP Willie Gallacher, urging that Home Secretary Herbert Morrison ban the WIL and close down its newspaper. Morrison was not convinced, although he stated inquiries would be made. He turned to Gallacher, reminding him of his past saying:

> "I ask Mr. Gallacher not to be too keen to suppress this organisation; they are only pursuing much the same political policy which he and his own political friends pursued some time ago." (Quoted in *War and the International* by Bornstein and Richardson, p. 64)

The Communist Party's hooligan tactics were to encourage physical assaults upon *Socialist Appeal* sellers, who were invariably attempting to sell outside CP meetings and engage the rank and file in discussions. In late 1941, a circular was sent by YCL leaders to its branches:

> "We are too tolerant of these people. They are allowed to sell their paper *Socialist Appeal* outside meetings. They have even become members of the Communist Party and YCL. We must be utterly ruthless with these people. They spread confusion amongst the working class and do serious harm to our party." (Quoted in *Socialist Appeal*, December 1941)

Dozens of reports were made to the WIL headquarters of Stalinist attacks and paper-snatching, from Liverpool, Birmingham, Wimbledon, Wood Green, Ilford, Stoll and Chiswick, to name a few. An article outlining these incidents appeared in the January 1942 issue of the *Appeal*. The report from Liverpool explained, "Replying in the only way such near-fascist methods deserve, the Stalinist was soon on the floor, not much hurt, but certainly disinclined to try any more funny business." This issue of increasing Stalinist violence, which was akin to the methods of fascist reaction, was also discussed at the Political Bureau of the WIL in January 1942. The minutes record the advice to be given to comrades:

> "Discussion on how to counter Stalinist hooligan tactics. Task was not to over-reach. Be friendly, even joke—stop things coming to a clash. Of course, if assaulted the comrades to protect themselves." It concluded with the instruction, "Don't call the police." (*Political Bureau minutes*, January 3 1942)

In general, the WIL comrades responded magnificently, turning the political attacks to their advantage. They turned the tables on their attackers. For instance, *Socialist Appeal* counter-attacked with a leaflet entitled, *Clear out the bosses' agents*, exposing the strike-breaking policies of the Communist Party. In its issue of September 1942, the paper offered a £10 reward to "any member of the CP who can show any page of this pamphlet [*Clear out Hitler's agents*] which does not contain a minimum of five lies." Needless to say, the reward remains unclaimed to this very day.

Growth of the WIL

From eight or so members in January 1938, the WIL had grown to around 300 members by their first national conference in August 1942. It was held in the Holborn Hall in London, attended by some 120 delegates and visitors. It was here that the document *Preparing for power* was debated and enthusiastically endorsed. In preparation for this important conference a Central Committee meeting was held on June 27 for which Ted was asked by the Political Bureau to draft a resolution on military policy. The RSL, the official section of the Fourth International, plagued by factionalism, had, by this time, to all intents and purposes collapsed.

The WIL had been proved absolutely correct in breaking with the old "Militant Group" and launching out on its own. It was proved correct in practice for the comrades to turn their back on the Trotskyist sects and their "fusion conference". The WIL was built on the rock solid foundations of Marxist theory, flexible tactics and confidence in the future. The group was now conducting the most successful work in the war of any Trotskyist group in the world. This was due to a correct political line and the assembling of a core of leading comrades that were self-sacrificing and dedicated to the cause of world socialism. Key amongst them was Ted Grant who above all else grasped the ideas and methods of genuine Trotskyism. Today these ideas and traditions are being advanced by the International Marxist Tendency—a real testament to the work and heritage of comrade Ted Grant.

"Our untrained and untested organisation will, within a few years at most, be hurled into the turmoil of the revolution. The problem of the organisation, the problem of building the party, goes hand in hand with the mobilisation of the masses..."—explained Ted—"Every member must raise himself or herself to the understanding that the key to world history lies in our hands. The conquest of power is on the order of the day in Britain—but only if we find the road to the masses." (*Preparing for power*, June 1942)

Rob Sewell, July 2010

1 – Pre-war period

Introduction

The Workers' International League was founded at the end of 1937 in the middle of the preparations for the Second World War. Through the publications of the WIL we can see how this group of young comrades were preparing for the imminent war without making any concessions to pacifist or ambiguous positions. Their characterisation of the war as an imperialist war gave them the theoretical basis to resist the pressure of petty-bourgeois pacifism which was dominant in the ILP at that time. It also put them firmly against the CP's "peace on Hitler's terms", then the complete somersault of a war of "democracy against fascism".

The WIL, from its inception, stood out for its active agitation and propaganda, and for the efficient organisation that allowed them to produce two monthly publications, *The Searchlight*, then *Youth For Socialism*, the theoretical magazine *Workers' International News*, and also many pamphlets. The WIL became the main voice of British Trotskyism and it is thanks to this small organisation that the most advanced British workers had the possibility of reading and debating the ideas put forward by Trotsky—a task that the then bigger Revolutionary Socialist League was never able to accomplish.

The documents of this section give a reduced sample of the ideological battle for the political rearmament of the movement that was taking place in such difficult conditions. We have decided to include the document produced by the WIL political bureau for the June 1938 "unification" conference of Trotskyist groups. Suffice to say that the principled position of the WIL was soon vindicated by the continuous crises of the RSL provoked by the hasty fusion of groups without a real political agreement. On these grounds, although standing as an independent organisation outside of the official section, the WIL appealed for membership to the founding congress of the Fourth International.

Ted Grant's lead articles for *Youth For Socialism* provide the theoretical grounds for the future evolution of the WIL and the adoption of Trotsky's military policy.

Cover of the 1938 WIL pamphlet *The lesson of Spain—The last warning!* [Ted Grant Archive]

Lessons of Spain

By Ted Grant and Ralph Lee

Introduction to Leon Trotsky's pamphlet,
The lesson of Spain—the last warning! May or June 1938

Under the transparent disguise of the "peace alliance" agitation, the popular front[1] of Britain now makes its first steps towards entering the political arena. The Liberals cock their ears attentively, the Labour Party heads strenuously oppose the project and the Communist Party, the initiator of the agitation, is utilising every resource it possesses to bring the popular front into being. It now becomes urgently necessary for British workers to draw conclusions from the events in Spain, to examine the experience of popular frontism as it appears in practice in the civil war in order to face up to the problems of tomorrow.

Leon Trotsky, in a series of articles and pamphlets on the Spanish situation has consistently pointed the road which the Spanish masses must travel if fascism is to be conquered, [and] has called insistently for the only guide along that road, the revolutionary workers' party, to take up its position at the head of the awakening Spanish masses. Trotsky concludes his pamphlet *The Revolution in Spain*, written in 1931, with these words: "For a successful solution of all these tasks, three conditions are required: a party; once more a party; again a party."

The conditions for a workers' victory over reaction, thus epigrammatically summed up, are still unfulfilled: this is the lesson that must be brought to the consciousness of the working class in Britain as in Spain.

While the Spanish fascists openly prepared, with aid from abroad, to strike their blow, the popular front government conspicuously failed to make that counter preparation which would have destroyed the enemy swiftly and easily. The army was left undisturbed in the hands of the reactionaries; under the noses of the popular front government they consolidated a powerful basis among the

---

[1] The popular front or people's front was a name given to coalitions between workers' parties and so-called liberal or radical capitalist parties. The Communist International adopted the people's front policy in 1935, after the debacle of Hitler's rise to power.

Moors[2] who, finding the chains of the new government no less galling than those of the monarchy, fell an easy prey to Franco's specious promises. On the other hand, the workers were prevented by their reformist leaders from taking those measures which would have frustrated the fascist plans—the setting up of workers' militia and factory committees. When, in spite of the entreaties of their leaders who begged them not to "provoke" the reaction, not to "antagonise" their republican-capitalist partners in the popular front, the workers struck and the peasants seized land, the government answered by arresting strikers, breaking up workers' meetings, censoring workers' papers, shooting down peasants. Such is the story related by the press dispatches and the official communications in the months of popular front power leading up to the civil war. In this way the popular front in the months preceding Franco's uprising gagged and tied the masses and drove numbers into the opposite camp to join the Moors in opposing a "democratic" government that perpetuated their misery and oppression.

Neither the popular front nor any other capitalist government could solve the basic problems of modern Spain. Five million peasant families with insufficient land, three million of them with no land at all, were squeezed by taxation and were starving. Only the expropriation of the big landowners and the redivision of the land among the poor peasants could relieve their famine. But this solution was impossible under capitalism, because the whole structure of Spanish banking rests on the land mortgages, so that the ruin of the big landowners would mean the ruin of the capitalists and bankers. Only a Spanish "October"[3] could, by dealing a death blow at the capitalist and landowning classes alike, relieve the hunger of the perishing masses of the countryside.

The conditions of the workers in the cities likewise presented a problem insoluble under capitalism. Spanish industry, born too late to compete with the cheap goods which a well-developed foreign industry is able to pour into jealously guarded markets, is unable to find even a home market because of the impoverished peasant population. Marx and Lenin taught that there is no way out for the workers from their prison of meagre wages and growing unemployment except by smashing down the barriers of capitalism and placing the control of industry into the hands of the working class.

In the first months of the civil war the workers of Spain spontaneously sought this way out as an essential part of their struggle against reaction, for it is not by military method alone that Franco can be defeated. Measures necessary to rouse the masses, by giving them something to fight for, were put into operation: factory, village and shop councils, and workers' tribunals were set up;

---

2 The Arab population of North West Africa. They struggled for years in Morocco for autonomy from Spanish rule. Where the popular front government did nothing, Franco promised them independence

3 The Russian revolution took place in October 1917 on the old Russian calendar.

a workers' police force and militia were initiated. The beginnings of a workers' state thus came into being to conduct a revolutionary war against the fascists, and existed side by side with the popular front, challenging its authority and wresting away its functions.

The Communist and Socialist Parties came to the rescue of the capitalist government thus threatened with extinction. They entered the popular front government and Caballero[4], hailed as "the Spanish Lenin", became the prime minister. Step by step the conquests of the workers were filched back in the name of the "defence of democracy". The workers' militia was dissolved into the republican army, workers' courts were eliminated, workers' police corps disbanded.

The same process went on in Catalonia where the POUM entered the coalition government, proclaiming it the workers' government. But the POUM also proclaimed that the civil war was fundamentally a question of socialism versus capitalism, a truth which undermines the very foundations of the popular front. Republicans and Stalinists united in a vile campaign of calumny against the POUM accusing it of being in the pay of Franco, driving it from government, suppressing its propaganda and journals, arresting and imprisoning its leaders.

At the beginning of May 1937, the government launched its provocative attack on the workers to regain possession of the factories and buildings which were under workers' control. The resistance of the workers was overcome and full control was regained by the bourgeoisie in the economic as in the political and military fields.

The alternatives that confront the Spanish masses today are on the one hand the victory of Franco initiating a totalitarian regime or on the other hand the now problematic victory of a "democratic" capitalist regime which in a spent and devastated Spain can only rule by a scarcely veiled dictatorship. In either case the chains will be more securely riveted on the limbs of the workers, peasants and the colonial people, exhausted and cheated.

From its very inception, the popular front disavowed in its programme not only socialist but even semi-socialist measures. It was openly and admittedly the guardian of capitalist property, dangling grandiose plans for future reforms before the eyes of the people to distract their attention from present miseries. The projected popular front in Britain is cut on the same pattern. "Any idea of real socialism would have to be put aside for the present," declares Sir Stafford Cripps[5] in the *Tribune* (April 14 1938) in pleading for a "democratic front" gov-

---

4 Largo Caballero, leader of a left tendency in the Spanish Socialist Party in the 1930s. Prime Minister from September 1936 to May 1937.

5 Stafford Cripps, Labour MP from 1931, expelled from the party for a period in 1939 for campaigning for a popular front. As Chancellor of the Exchequer 1947-50, he introduced an austere economic programme. *Tribune* was the paper of the reformist left in the party which Cripps helped to found in 1937.

ernment. The *Daily Worker* supports the Liberal candidate in a by-election as against the Labour candidate, and sneered at Labour's "astonishing 'discovery' that Liberals are not socialist, as if Liberals ever made this claim." (May 11 1938).

For Britain as for Spain, the struggle against fascism is the struggle for socialism. The arms plans and the food plans, the spy scares and the air raid precautions serve to warn the workers that the "peace" period draws rapidly to a close. The American recession in industry spreads to Britain; in the first three months of 1938 the decline of new capital issues, 33,000,000 as against 49,505,000 for the corresponding period last year, indicates the dimensions of the coming industrial slump. The increased employment in the armaments industry and the increased recruiting for the army serve for the time being to mask the growth of industrial unemployment, and the shifting centre of gravity in national economy is not visible in the general statistics of trade and industry because the artificial stimulus of war preparations helps to conceal the real process of economic breakdown. The disease that grips the vitals of capitalism in decay produces as its symptom a feverish activity in certain branches of industrial activity, accompanied by that false sense of well-being which must be recognised as pre-war "prosperity", the delirium before the crisis.

As long as the pre-war boom continues and the British masses continue in a comparatively passive state, the right wing bureaucrats of the trade unions and the Labour Party oppose the popular front. When the masses start to move, as they did in Spain and France, towards a militant socialist solution of their difficulties, the Labour bureaucracy will not scruple to follow the example of its counterparts in Spain and France, to put a bridle on the mass movement and lead it into the safe bye-paths of popular frontism. If today they resist the popular front, it is not because it is the open, treacherous abandonment of even the pretence of socialism, but because they are quite satisfied with their own status in capitalist society, because they fear the inevitable exposure to which the taking of political power will subject them. Today they attack the Liberals as non-socialists, tomorrow they will justify and defend them, and work hand in hand with them in the "strike-breaking conspiracy" of the popular front, as their brother reformists of the Communist Party are already doing.

The Communist Party of Great Britain pleads for the popular front and supports the Liberals on a programme of "arms for Spain", "defence of democratic liberties," "economic and social advancement of the people." The French popular front[6] in power supplied no arms for Spain; the French colonial slaves of

---

6 The alliance of the French Communist Party (PCF), the Socialist SFIO and the Radical and Socialist Party won the May 1936 legislative elections, leading to the formation of a government headed by SFIO leader Léon Blum. Léon Blum's government lasted from June 1936 to June 1937 but eventually collapsed from the pressure of the bourgeois right wing within the front.

North Africa and Indo-China received as their share of "democratic liberties"—bullets and prison sentences; the French popular front government nibbled at the concessions wrested from the ruling class by the direct strike action of the French workers and frustrated their wage gains by currency manipulation. The Liberals and "progressive" capitalists offer, in place of reforms, grandiloquent *plans* for reforms.

The past writings of the Communist Party leaders prove that they are well aware of the treacherous role of the Liberals. Today they are able to exploit the reputation for militancy which has been won by the work of party members in the trade union struggle, in order to lead militant workers along the political path mapped out by their paymasters in the Kremlin. Stalin and company are prepared to sacrifice the socialist aspirations of the British working class for the sake of a war alliance with the British bourgeoisie and to this end they have ordered a popular front in Britain. The Communist Party heads leap to obey; they flatly and brazenly contradict their arguments of a few months back, they consciously and deliberately manoeuvre the workers into supporting a coalition government with the class enemy, they blindfold the worker while the Liberals prepare the dagger which will be plunged into his back.

The Communist Party carries out its traitorous work with loud cries of "Unity! Unity!" But the British working class constitutes in itself two-thirds of the population, and would draw behind itself the majority of the lower middle class if it pressed forward with a bold programme of socialist demands. The workers have no need for an alliance with any section of the class foe, least of all with the decayed, long ago bankrupt Liberals. They instinctively know that unity is an all-powerful weapon in their struggle—unity *of the working class*. The popular front is a caricature of unity. The genuine united front on a class basis, binding together the workers, their organisations, their parties on a programme of common struggle is the crying need of today, the only means of defending those rights and privileges which the workers have won in generations of struggle and sacrifice. The successful defence of concessions already gained must lead inevitably to the campaign for full workers' rights, to the struggle for workers' power.

The experience of Spain is a warning and a lesson to the workers of the world, above all to the British workers. Yesterday's drama in Spain is being rehearsed today in Britain. Tomorrow it will be enacted if the British workers have failed to realise the nature of the tasks which history has placed before them. And in preparing to tackle those tasks, the working class has need above all, of "a party, once more a party; again a party".

Contribution by WIL
to the discussion on the tasks of
Bolshevik-Leninists in Britain

[*Original document*, June 1938]

The Bolshevik-Leninists of the various groupings in Britain are united in the matter of the adoption of the broad programme of the Fourth International—the characterisation of the present epoch as the eve of new international economic convulsions heralding the death throes of capitalism [and] imperialism, the acceleration of frantic preparations for another universal war of imperialist cannibalism and the encroachment of fascism as the overtures to the coming crisis; the role of reformism and Stalinism as the crutches of moribund imperialism; the vacillating character of centrism; the need for a new Fourth International and for a revolutionary party in Britain, a section of the new international, to lead the struggle of the British workers. It is of course on the question of how to overcome the present exasperating isolation of the revolutionary elements from the broad masses of the working class that differences of opinion have risen that keep British Bolshevik-Leninists disunited. It is therefore only with this question of immediate tactics in facing present tasks that this statement deals.

On October 7 1858, Engels was able to write to Marx:

> "The British working class is actually becoming more and more bourgeois, so that this most bourgeois of all nations is apparently aiming ultimately at the possession of a bourgeois aristocracy and a bourgeois proletariat as well as a bourgeoisie. Of course, this is to [a] certain extent justifiable for a nation which is exploiting the whole world."

This classic characterisation of the British labour movement recurs again and again throughout Marxist writings and is underlined by the growing opportunism of the British labour movement under the leadership of its aristocratic stratum, bribed by a share of the super profits arising from the colonial monopoly of the world market. The Labour Party is the culmination of decades of opportunism and social chauvinism, and today seeks to qualify as the managing board of the British bourgeoisie, to conduct tomorrow wars for it in the same spirit as liberalism conducted its wars of yesterday. Today encroaching rival imperialism by threatening the British bourgeoisie, thereby threatens also the vested interests of the Labour bureaucracy. In its open wholehearted support for

British war preparations, the labour bureaucracy seeks merely to protect its own.

The plunder seized by the victors in the last great war gave a new infusion of blood not only to British capitalism but to its opportunist lackeys in the labour movement. Where in the vanquished and cheated imperialist countries the bourgeoisie was compelled to turn to fascism as the last mean to maintain its domination, in Britain as in France the labour bureaucracy was given a new lease of life! The same crisis that carried the German social democratic leaders into exile or into Hitler's concentration camps carried the Ramsay MacDonalds into Downing Street.

Today the social economic basis for British labour opportunism is disappearing. Rearmed German imperialism, Italian aggression, Japan's war of plunder, sharpening antagonism with the other victors in the last war, colossal armaments expenditures, increasing demands by the national bourgeoisie in the Dominions and India, colonial revolts, the approach of a new world slump—all these factors undermine the privileged position of monopolist British imperialism [and] destroy the basis of British Labour opportunism. Far from winning new concessions, the British proletariat find its old concessions increasingly threatened, its standards of life steadily gnawed away.

If there are British workers today who vote for the Tories, it is on account of the reputation which the Tories won in a past epoch when they led the struggle for the abolition of child labour, for the Factories Act, etc. The rural worker who votes Tory as his grandfather did, does so for the same reason—because it represents for him a progressive force which did after all win reforms, whereas Labour, he will point out, has gained nothing for the workers. The treachery of past Labour governments, far from clearing the road for the revolutionary party, has reconsolidated Toryism in Britain. The experience of two Labour governments does not in itself serve to guide the working class to the correct conclusions; there is needed in addition the presence within the labour movement of a vanguard which successfully drives the lesson into workers' consciousness by means of sustained, serious and systematic criticism of policies. Where such criticism comes from select coteries external to the mass organisations, it is generally ignored, however deserving it may be of a better fate; only when it is uttered by workers within the organisations who have earned the right to criticise by means of steady work side by side with the other active members, only then is there the chance of driving the lesson home.

This piece of ABC wisdom is apparently not part of the equipment of one section of revolutionary socialists. Comrades belonging to our grouping have reported to us that they heard read out at a meeting of their trade union, the AEU[1] a circular letter which had been issued by the executive committee of the

---

[1] Amalgamated Engineering Union

Revolutionary Socialist League to all AEU branches. The letter contained a correct criticism of the arms policy of the AEU leadership, but it aroused no discussion and was ignored. In other branches the letter was not even read.

Criticism from outside is sometimes more damaging to the cause it seeks to serve than no criticism at all. As in this concrete instance, so in its general attitude towards reformist mass organisations, the RSL, which lacks a sufficiently strong voice to make its criticism heard from the outside, fails on the other hand to take the only alternative path and organise an effective internal criticism. The utterly ineffective, and indeed damaging, tactic adopted towards the AEU is in the case of the Labour Party glorified into a Marxist principle, and called "the independence of the revolutionary proletarian party." The Labour bureaucracy is left entirely free to organise yet another betrayal of the British workers who are abandoned by "revolutionaries" to find their own way out of the debacle which means in effect to retrace their footsteps, to return to Toryism or even more extreme reaction.

The Labour Party reached its peak membership of nearly 4.5 million in 1919-1920, the revolutionary post-war years. Today it has less than half that number of members but there can be no doubt that it will again reflect in an increasing membership the struggle of the British workers to smash down the political barriers that baffle their efforts to maintain their standards of life.

In their attempts to cut a way through the legislative measures that hemmed them in, the workers in the British trade unions created the Labour Party as a political adjunct to the trade unions. Every time the efforts of the trade unionists to gain their demands or safeguard their interests through the unions were baffled by judicial decisions the Labour Party gained new access of strength. Future trade union struggles must inevitably come into conflict with the reactionary measures introduced by the national government and so force upon the consciousness of the workers the necessity for political action to implement trade union action. The Labour Party must inevitably experience a new growth after the next offensive or defensive struggle of the trade unions since it functions as a subsidiary political arm of the trade unions which impress upon it their own fundamentally reformist character.

Because it is an outgrowth of the trade unions and functions entirely within the framework of bourgeois democracy, the Labour Party shares one basic characteristic with the trade unions: it dwindles in "peace time" to a mere skeleton.

It is the experience of every active trade unionist that between periods of major struggle—against wage cuts, for wage increases—the trade union is carried on by a small minority of members. The majority of members do not attend meetings, although they continue to pay subscriptions and support the union passively. It is in these periods of ebb that the trade union bureaucracy consolidates itself.

For the Labour Party, functioning as it does within bourgeois democracy, war time is election time, and in the peace time period between elections, it becomes a mere skeleton, passively supported by its individual, trade union and co-operative members. At the present moment, except for the passive ripples of by-elections, its work is carried on by a small minority consisting in the main of the bureaucracy, a sprinkling of ambitious careerists, a few veterans who support the bureaucracy and the factions sent in by external organisations. In such a structure, party activity consists in a series of manoeuvres executed mainly between Stalinists and right wingers. The mass membership for whose benefit the various postures are adopted are notably absent from the auditorium.

This is the party into which a number of revolutionary socialists have entered, and their participation in the life of the party is conditioned by this skeleton structure which gives to the reigning bureaucracy a practically free hand. But far from negativing the activity of the revolutionary socialists within the Labour Party, the peace time structure gives them a political weight out of all proportion to their numerical strength.

There is in the first place the opportunity of coming into contact with politically awakening workers who in the ordinary functioning of the Labour Party would pass through the organisation as through a sieve. By posing before them a militant programme of struggle, the disillusionment that arises from the reformist character of the Labour Party is replaced with the hope of accomplishing working class aims. In this way the left wing within the Labour Party is strengthened and consolidated.

Secondly there arises the possibility of utilising the national machinery of the Labour Party as a sounding board. Where normally there would be merely the factional struggle between right wing reformism and Stalinist reformism, there is now introduced a third point of view, the revolutionary position. For example, in the present struggle between the Stalinist popular front and the right wing "independence of the Labour Party" it is possible to introduce the correct policy of the workers' united front. In the absence of a revolutionary wing, the entire question is distorted.

In the struggle to magnify the weak voice of revolutionary socialism it is necessary to capture positions, delegations, seats on committees and councils, and this brings the socialists into direct conflict with the expert manoeuvrers on the other side. Repeated defeats, when they are examined self critically, are the soil from which spring future successes. The necessity of responding swiftly and correctly to the questions raised day after day brings valuable experience.

Thus even in the skeletonised party of the inter-election period there is to be gained new blood for the left wing movement, a magnification for revolutionary propaganda and political experience.

At the present moment the right wingers search for a stick with which to beat the Stalinists who threaten to tear the machine from out of their hands. They do not hesitate to publish selected articles by Trotsky in *Forward*[2] and to quote from the Trotskyites. Only from within the Labour Party is it possible to exact a price from the bureaucracy, forcing it to acknowledge the revolutionary content of Trotskyism instead of merely utilising the anti-Stalinist aspect of its revolutionary programme.

The revolutionary elements correctly oriented within the mass workers' party grow with the growth of the party. As the crisis forces increasing numbers of workers from passive to active support of the Labour Party, they find within the party a nucleus around which to gather, and party growth means growth of the left wing. To gain the maximum development along lines of revolutionary struggle requires the throwing of the entire available forces of the militants into the work of building the left wing. It is possible to learn from military theoreticians, who have summed up the central principle of military tactics in the formula: "all strength at the point of attack." The adoption of this formula in "the contiguous field of political strategy" means the abandonment of any external "independent" organisation. The experience of our grouping has proved that it is possible to carry out the special work of an independent organisation, publication of pamphlets, propaganda, news, etc. even though its entire forces are immersed in the Labour party, attempting to carry out the functions of building the left wing, voicing the revolutionary policy and training cadres. The actual carrying out of this policy has consolidated the numbers of the Workers' International League in opposition to any concession whatsoever to the sectarianism which seeks to concentrate the efforts of militants on the framing of unread manifestoes and unread criticism.

These arguments apply with even greater force to the task of mobilising working class youth, now being drawn increasingly into economic struggles, under the banner of revolutionary socialism. Within the Labour League of Youth, which is a rallying ground for the younger and fresher elements of the politically awakening proletariat, there are basically the same trends and an even better field of work than in the senior party. It is among the youth that the Stalinists who have entered the Labour Party exert the greatest influence, utilising their virtual control of the organisation for the purpose of lining up the youth for imperialist war. Failure to build a left wing in the Labour League of Youth means the abandonment of working class youth to social patriotism and to wholesale slaughter.

The struggle for the winning of the youth opens up new avenues for reach-

---

2 *Forward* was a Glasgow-based socialist journal established by the Independent Labour Party in 1906.

ing that section of the youth that has already come under Stalinist influence. The increasing disintegration within the Communist Party manifests itself in a growing internal opposition to popular frontism, deepened by the recent defeats for the peace alliance. Side by side with the instinctive rejection by a part of the membership of the Stalinist policies of class collaboration there is the havoc brought by the latest Moscow Trial. The possibility is now created of taking advantage of those self-inflicted breaches in the Stalinist wall both by a direct tackling of the problem of reaching the Stalinist rank and file and through the Labour Party.

Since the dissolution of the Socialist League[3] there has been no left wing organisation within the Labour Party to serve as a rallying point for Labour militants. Both the Socialist Left Federation and the Militant Labour League have been still born; neither has met with any response within the Labour Party. On the other hand if the movement of the ILP towards re-affiliation to the Labour Party culminates as most observers expect, the ILP with its long tradition and its verbally left programme must become the core of the left wing. Events in Spain have driven the ILP away from the Communist Party and towards the Labour Party. On February 3 1938, Fenner Brockway was reported as declaring: "We would be prepared to re-affiliate to the Labour Party if we had the conditions from that Party which would enable us to maintain our revolutionary socialistic views." The Labour Party executive refuses "any special reservations or privileges for ILP members as MPs."

The re-entry of the ILP into the Labour Party will relegate both the Socialist Left Federation and the Militant Labour League into oblivion. Our entire perspective within the Labour Party must be adapted to the new conditions now arising, which necessitate working upon the ILP to hasten the process of differentiation which has already begun in the ILP in the movement of its parliamentary section towards the Labour Party bureaucracy. With our small forces opposed to the overwhelming numbers and resources of the enemy, we are forced to adopt guerrilla tactics, to offset our smallness of numbers with greater mobility, resourcefulness and activity. As our forces grow and spread in their scope, practical problems of co-ordination and unification are raised. The solution to these problems are found as they arise and it is in the actual solving of concrete problems that the organisation is created to serve as the living instrument of workers' militant struggle. Only a brief breathing space is allotted to us for the forging of that instrument. We must utilise the time at our disposal in the most effective manner, and that means—all our forces into the Labour Party—full strength at the point of attack.

---

3 The Socialist League was a left group formed in 1932, led by Stafford Cripps, as a split from the Independent Labour Party in opposition to the ILP's policy of disaffiliating from the Labour party.

Statement of WIL to the international congress of the Fourth International[1]

[*Original document*, September 1938]

The Workers' International League supports the principle that there shall be wherever possible in each country one section and only one section of the Fourth International.

The objective situation in Britain, the extension of capitalist decay and acceleration of war preparations, coupled with the isolation and numerical smallness of the Bolshevik Leninists, dictates the tactic of entering the mass organisations of the working class as a semi-legal fraction. The Workers' International League stands consistently and unequivocally on this basis, refusing to make any concession to sectarianism which will cancel out the effects of this activity.

The new Revolutionary Socialist League is founded on a compromise with sectarianism, and arising out of the political compromise there is naturally a dual organisational structure. The membership is left free to decide, each for himself, the milieu of work; the principle of centralism is thrown overboard, and with it any pretence of democratic discipline. In effect, the new RSL consists of two organisations masquerading under a single name, a state of affairs that cannot be hidden from the outside world, even if internal friction is sufficiently overcome to enable the organisation to begin to function.

The WIL alone subscribes consistently and unequivocally to the programme agreed upon at the first international congress of the Fourth International for Britain in the present period. By laying, not merely the "main emphasis", but the *entire weight* of its forces on work in the Labour Party, it thereby underlines its claim to be the official British section of the Fourth International. If however, the 1938 congress of the Fourth International decides that it is necessary to

---

[1] In 1938 the Workers' International League issued a statement to request affiliation to the Fourth International as the official British section. Although the WIL stood entirely for the programme and methods of the Fourth, the affiliation was thwarted thanks to the manoeuvres of Cannon and other leaders of the Fourth, who retaliated against the WIL's opposition to the unprincipled fusion which led to the formation of the Revolutionary Socialist League.

dilute the decision of the previous congress, and to modify that section of the draft thesis: *The death agony of capitalism*, entitled *Against Sectarianism*, (particularly the final sentence: "The cleansing of the ranks of the Fourth International of sectarianism and incurable sectarians is a primary condition for revolutionary success"); if the congress decides upon these modifications and accepts the new Revolutionary Socialist League as the official British section of the Fourth International, then the Workers' International League has no recourse but to request that it be accepted as a body sympathetically affiliated to the Fourth International. The real bond that unites the national sections in the Fourth International is of course the common programme which determines the activity of each section; the WIL embraces the fundamentals of this common programme and thereby establishes its claim to affiliation as an *entrist* group, i.e., as a body not openly and avowedly affiliated.

By virtue of our sympathetic affiliation to the Fourth International, we will be ipso facto a body fraternally affiliated to the new RSL, to which our attitude becomes one of fraternal collaboration in those fields of work which we both enter: trade unions, Labour parties, youth organisations. Joint work, with the relations between the two groups subject to continual review, will produce the maximum possible benefit for our tendency in Britain, and the basis for such joint work must be the fraternal status of the two groups within the framework of the Fourth International.

Dear Comrade Trotsky,

At the beginning of this year Workers' International Press was founded on the basis of a hand printing press and a group of comrades numbering thirty odd who are all working in the Labour Party for our tendency. We are not associated with any of the British groups calling themselves Trotskyists.

Up to now we have published two issues of Workers' International News and the pamphlet "Summary of the Final Report of the Commission of Enquiry into the Charges made against Leon Trotsky in the Moscow Trials." Copies of these have been sent you under separate cover. We do not regard this activity as anything more than a subsidiary function to our main activity as propagandists within the mass reformist organisations and we are pressing forward towards the publication of a left wing labour paper. This is at present beyond our financial resources.

Workers' International Press, in putting out its paper and pamphlets is initiating a programme of publication which aims at providing for an audience of British workers and their friends among the intelligentsia an exposition of the international viewpoint of our tendency. In this project we have met with response and assistance that encourages us to believe that the press fills a gap in Britain and will prove a permanent institution.

Extract of letter from WIL to Trotsky, 12 February 1938

Against "national defence"

By Ted Grant

[*Youth For Socialism*, Vol. 1, No. 7, March 1939]

In the recent debate in Parliament, Chamberlain[1] announced that the loans for armaments were to be increased to £800,000,000. £1,000 a minute is being spent on arms in Britain at the present time. All the resources of the country are being squandered on building up a colossal war machine.

This war machine is for the defence of the trading interests and the colonial loot of British imperialism, for what is making for war is the intensified and sharpened struggle for markets between the different countries of the world. As the *Daily Telegraph* of February 20 1939 says in discussing the coming trade visit of R. S. Hudson, the Secretary of Overseas Trade, and Sir Oliver Stanley, President of the Board of Trade to Germany and Russia, "...national hostilities aroused in the trading field can be all too easily inflamed till they reach the battlefield..."

The background of these trade talks will be the "export or die" policy of Germany which is leading her inevitably to financial and economic collapse. The *Volkswirt*, Nazi organ of economics, points out:

> "...The only remaining possibility [for Germany] is an increase in exports of 25 percent to 30 percent, thus subjecting the world market to that sharp competition which was one of the most important causes of the world war."

With this perspective on both sides of the North Sea the discussions between Germany and Britain must end in utter failure or at best put off for a short period a renewed trade war of a more intense and bitter character.

That is why one eighth of the national income is being spent for war preparations. At the same time millions are being made by the arms profiteers in prof-

---

[1] Arthur Neville Chamberlain (1869–1940) was a British Conservative politician and Prime Minister of the United Kingdom from 1937 to 1940. Chamberlain is best known for signing the Munich Agreement in 1938 with Hitler, conceding the Sudetenland region of Czechoslovakia to Germany.

its at the expense of the workers. The Bristol Aeroplane Company announces a 75 percent bonus on shares and in addition a bonus on the stock market worth 130 percent. These figures are not exceptional and represent more or less the trend in the armaments industry.

That is the real meaning of "national service". Profits for the capitalists, service by the workers. The opposition among the rank and file of the Labour Party and the trade unions to national service has been increased during the last few weeks. The rank and file realise that they are to be harnessed to the war machine of British imperialism and demand that the Labour and trade union leaders should not ally themselves with the enemy. They demand that an independent stand should be made by the working class.

The whole of the national debt before the last war was only slightly higher than the cost of the rearmament programme: £580,000,000 for next year. All the capitalist governments bleat and bewail the crushing burden of armaments which threatens to lead to the collapse of world economy. But all continue to pile up arms for the continuance of the struggle—which is now waged by tariffs, export subsidies and diplomatic manoeuvres—to its inevitable and only outcome. To decide who is to dominate the markets of the world, the imperialists will resort to the mass slaughter of the peoples.

Chamberlain openly declared that if the armaments race were to be continued for much longer the world was heading for bankruptcy. His only satisfaction was that Britain would go bankrupt last! However, despite the admitted lunacy of the arms race, the thought of any agreement between the different countries to limit arms production was out of the question. To call a disarmament conference would only aggravate the position as it was bound to fail. No country of course had any aggressive intentions. The arms race was due to a misunderstanding! In these utterances by a leading spokesman the capitalists show their complete inability not merely to prevent war but even to prevent the ruinous and catastrophic accumulation of the weapons of destruction in every country of the world, which, since all countries join in the race, mutually cancel each other out.

In the meantime Chamberlain has hinted what the arms programme will mean to the workers: increased taxes on food, harder work, a general attack on the standard of living. As the *Times* quite brutally and cold-bloodedly puts it:

> "...it is clear that such conditions [rearmament] would imply that there must be a restriction of consumption all round in order that the necessary amount of capital goods and armaments could be produced."

Instead of bread we are to make bullets, instead of clothing we are to make machine guns, instead of houses, tanks and battleships are to be built. The already low standard of living of the workers is to be cut down further in order to pay for this monstrous armaments programme, while the capitalists make super profits out of the armaments rackets.

The working class must be prepared to resist all encroachments on their standard of living made in order to pile up arms for their own destruction. The £2,000,000,000 for rearmament must be devoted to a scheme of public works, housing, roads and other schemes which will be of benefit to the workers.

All the lying propaganda that these arms are to be used for the "defence of liberty and democracy" are seen to be hollow shams concocted in order to cover up the real motive: the defence of capitalist trade interests. The hypocrisy and cant of the call to "defend liberty and freedom" by the spokesmen of the "great democracies" is clearly seen in the development of the civil war in Spain. Eagerly and with the greatest gusto Britain and France are making great haste to help Franco destroy the Republican government and the last relics of democracy in Spain by granting him recognition even before he has completely succeeded in conquering Spain, and at the same time are withdrawing recognition from the Madrid government. That is how much they treasure the "sacred trust" of "liberty and freedom".

The position is clearly revealed by the actions of "the greatest democracy of all", the United States. Roosevelt, Ickes and other spokesmen of the government have announced their determination to stand up to the menace of dictatorship and the aggressor states. Key Pittman, chairman of the Senate, has demanded that a stand be made once and for all. He is prepared to face up to war right now: "It is better to die fighting than retreat cravenly before the destroyers of liberty." For the purpose of meeting the menace, arms are to be supplied by America to Britain and France, sister-democracies facing up to the same threat. But the United States is not prepared to send a single gun or plane to "defend democracy" in republican Spain!

The policy of the Communist Party and the Labour leaders in supporting rearmament for "national defence" is a betrayal of the working class. Attlee, Morrison and company in the House of Commons had no criticism to offer to the rearmament programme except that it should be made more efficient.

While the *Daily Telegraph* talks openly about the economic reasons for the coming war, the Labour and communist leaders still continue to deceive and sow illusions in the minds of the workers about "democracy", "freedom", and the "menace of fascist aggression". The *Daily Telegraph* weighs up almost without concealment the chances of the trade war being turned into armed conflict. The communist and Labour leaders demand that the national government should take further action against their rivals in the trade war in defence of "British" (capitalist) trade interests. They demand an increase in the efficiency of arms production. They attempt to outdo the capitalists themselves in their eagerness to defend capitalist interests.

The capitalists make huge profits out of war and war preparations. We demand the confiscation of all armaments profits. Not alone "profiteering" but all profit must be taken away from the arms manufacturers. The traffic in the lives of the people must be stopped.

These preparations for war, and the mass butchery which will follow, can only bring hunger, misery and want to the workers of Britain and the world. A struggle must be waged in the labour movement against all war preparations. We must fight against the real cause of war, and against the people that benefit from it. Our enemy is not the German, Italian or French workers. It is capitalism everywhere. Our strongest blows must be directed against our main enemy, British capitalism at home. The fight for socialism is the fight for peace.

Confiscate all arms profits!
Workers' homes, not battleships!
To abolish war, abolish capitalism!

Vol. 1, No. 7   MARCH, 1939   One Penny

YOUTH
FOR SOCIALISM

AGAINST "NATIONAL DEFENCE"

IN the recent debate in Parliament Chamberlain announced that the loans for armaments were to be increased to £800,000,000. £1,000 a minute is being spent on arms in Britain at the present time. All the resources of the country are being squandered on building up a colossal war machine.

This war machine is for the defence of the trading interests and the colonial loot of British imperialism, for what is making for war is the intensified and sharpened struggle for markets between the different countries of the world. As the *Daily Telegraph* of February 20th, 1939 says in discussing the coming trade visit of R. S. Hudson, the secretary of Overseas Trade, and Sir Oliver Stanley, President of the Board of Trade, to Germany and Russia, " . . . national hostilities aroused in the trading field can be all too easily inflamed till they reach the battlefield . . . "

The background of these trade talks will be the "export or die" policy of Germany which is leading her inevitably to financial and economic collapse. The *Volkswirt*, Nazi organ of economics, points out " . . . The only remaining possibility [for Germany] is an increase in exports of 25% to 30%, thus subjecting the world market to that sharp competition which was one of the most important causes of the World War."

With this perspective on both sides of the North Sea the discussions between Germany and Britain must end in utter failure or at best put off for a short period a renewed trade war of a more intense and bitter character.

That is why one-eighth of the National Income is being spent for war preparations. At the same time millions are being made by the arms profiteers in profits at the expense of the workers. The Bristol Aeroplane Co. announces a 75% bonus on shares and in addition a bonus on the stock market worth 130%. These figures are not exceptional and represent more or less the trend in the armaments industry.

That is the real meaning of "National Service". Profits for the capitalists, service by the workers. The opposition among the rank and file of the Labour Party and the trade unions to National Service has been increased during the last few weeks. The rank and file realise that they are to be harnessed to the war machine of British imperialism and demand that the Labour and Trade Union leaders should not ally themselves with the enemy. They demand that an independent stand should be made by the working class.

The whole of the National Debt before the last war was only slightly higher than the cost of the re-armament programme £580,000,000 for next year. All the capitalist governments bleat and bewail the crushing burden of armaments which threatens to lead to the collapse of world economy. But all continue to pile up arms for the continuance of the struggle which is now waged by tariffs, export subsidies and diplomatic manoeuvres, to its inevitable and only outcome. To decide who is to dominate the markets of the world, the imperialists will resort to the mass slaughter of the peoples.

Chamberlain openly declared that if the armaments race were to be continued for much longer the world was heading for bankruptcy. His only satisfaction was that Britain would go bankrupt last! However, despite the admitted lunacy of the arms race, the thought of any agreement between the different countries to limit arms production was out of the question. To call a disarmament conference would only aggravate the position as it was bound to fail. No country of course had any aggressive intentions. The arms race was due to a misunderstanding! In these utterances by a leading spokesman the capitalists show their complete inability not merely to prevent war but even to prevent the ruinous and catastrophic accumulation of the weapons of destruction in every country of the world, which, since all countries join in the race, mutually cancel each other out.

In the meantime Chamberlain has hinted what the arms programme will mean to the workers. Increased taxes on food, harder work, a general attack on the standard of living. As the *Times* quite brutally and cold-bloodedly puts it. " . . . it is clear that such conditions (rearmament) would imply that there must be a RESTRICTION OF CONSUMPTION ALL ROUND in order that the necessary amount of capital goods and armaments could be produced."

Instead of bread we are to make bullets, instead of clothing we are to make machine guns, instead of houses, tanks and battleships are to be built. The already low standard of living of the workers is to be cut down further in order to pay for this monstrous armaments programme, while the capitalists make super profits out of the armaments rackets.

The working class must be prepared to resist all encroachments on their standard of living made in order to pile up arms for their own destruction. The £2,000,000,000 for rearmament must be devoted to a scheme of public works, housing, roads and other schemes which will be of benefit to the workers.

KARL MARX

KARL MARX, the great founder of revolutionary socialism, died on the fourteenth of March, 1883. The stern fighter and vigorous thinker who inaugurated the First International and threw a bright beam of light to illuminate the future path of the working class of the world has bequeathed to us the task of continuing his life-long fight for the emancipation of humanity from capitalist chains. The best way in which we can honour his memory is in the continuance of that struggle. Our daily fight for the victory of Marxist ideas is the wreath which we lay on the tomb of the grand old revolutionary warrior. It is in that fight that Marx still lives and leads.

Above all he leads the revolutionary youth, born into a world of capitalist decline that brings us not peace but war, not work but stagnation, not life but hunger and death. It is for us to continue the class struggle on the lines of militancy that he laid down, to the ultimate victory of socialism.

All the lying propaganda that these arms are to be used for the "defence of liberty and democracy" are seen to be hollow shams concocted in order to cover up the real motive: the defence of capitalist trade interests. The hypocrisy and cant of the call to "defend liberty and freedom" by the spokesmen of the "great democracies" is clearly seen in the development of the civil war in Spain. Eagerly and with the greatest gusto Britain and France are making great haste to help Franco destroy the Republican Government and the last relics of democracy in Spain by granting him recognition even before he has completely succeeded in conquering Spain, and at the same time are withdrawing recognition from the Madrid Government. That is how much they treasure the "sacred trust" of "liberty and freedom".

The position is clearly revealed by the actions of "the greatest democracy of all" the United States. Roosevelt, Ickes and other spokesmen of the Government have announced their determination to stand up to the menace of dictatorship and the aggressor states. Key Pittman, chairman of the Senate, has demanded that a stand be made once and for all. He is prepared to face up to war right now: "It is better to die fighting than retreat cravenly before the destroyers of liberty." For the purpose of meeting the menace, arms are to be supplied by America to Britain and France, sister-democracies facing up to the same threat. But the United States is not prepared to send a single gun or plane to "defend democracy" in Republican Spain!

The policy of the Communist Party and the Labour leaders in supporting rearmament for "national defence" is a betrayal of the working class. Attlee, Morrison and Co. in the House of Commons had no criticism to offer to the rearmament programme except that it should be made more efficient.

While the *Daily Telegraph* talks openly about the economic reasons for the coming war, the Labour and Communist Leaders still continue to deceive and sow illusions in the minds of the workers about "democracy", "freedom", and the "menace of fascist aggression". The *Daily Telegraph* weighs up almost without concealment the chances of the trade war being turned into armed conflict. The Communist and Labour leaders demand that the National Government should take further action against their rivals in the trade war in defence of "British" (capitalist) trade interests. They demand an increase in the efficiency of arms production. They attempt to outdo the capitalists themselves in their eagerness to defend capitalist interests.

The capitalists make huge profits out of war and war preparations. We demand the confiscation of all armaments profits. Not alone "profiteering" but all profit must be taken away from the arms manufacturers. The traffic in the lives of the people must be stopped.

These preparations for war, and the mass butchery which will follow, can only bring hunger, misery and want to the workers of Britain and the world. A struggle must be waged in the Labour movement against all war preparations. We must fight against the real cause of war, and against the people that benefit from it. Our enemy is not the German, Italian or French workers. It is capitalism everywhere. Our strongest blows must be directed against our main enemy, British capitalism at home. The fight for Socialism is the fight for peace.

CONFISCATE ALL ARMS PROFITS!
WORKERS' HOMES, NOT BATTLESHIPS!
TO ABOLISH WAR, ABOLISH CAPITALISM!

         EG

Youth For Socialism, March 1939, carrying the lead article *Against "national defence"* by Ted Grant (Ted Grant Archive)

The robbers quarrel over Tientsin[1]

By Ted Grant

[*Youth For Socialism*, Vol. 1 No. 11, July 1939]

The war between China and Japan has now been dragging on for more than two and a half years. The quick successes anticipated by the Japanese have failed to materialise. The costs of the war have meant a steady drain on the financial and economic resources of Japan. The Japanese military clique can feel the rumble of the coming revolt which it has suppressed temporarily by diverting the anger aroused in the masses by the social crisis in Japan into the channels of "patriotism" and "nationalism". But the contrast between the misery and privation by the workers and peasants and the enormous super profits being made by the landlords and capitalists is driving the masses on to the road of revolution as the only way out.

These conditions have driven the military clique in control in Japan completely off their balance. In sheer panic they have been compelled to try and make some desperate coup which will save the situation. Now that the war crisis in Europe is about to reach its peak (Churchill has warned of the coming period of crisis during the next three months which can easily lead to war in Europe), the Japanese imperialists have calculated that now is the time to strike a blow against their imperialist rivals in the Far East.

That is the meaning of the crisis over Tientsin and now the treaty pacts of Swatow and Foochow have been drawn into the struggle. The newspapers have been featuring with blazing headlines the "unprecedented treatment of British subjects. The deliberate insults, searching and stripping naked at the barrier, manhandling, the blockade of the British concession itself, indicate the lengths to which the Japanese are prepared to go."

---

[1] On June 14 1939 Japanese forces blockaded the foreign concessions of Tientsin over the refusal of the British authorities to hand over four Chinese who had assassinated a Japanese collaborator (a customs official). The incident unleashed a nationalistic outburst in defence of British prerogatives over China. Labour and Communist Party leaders advocated for a "firm" defence of British interests and of China against Japan.

What the Japanese are aiming at is indicated by their demands. They want to force the British to concede the major part of the Chinese market and to preserve China as an exclusive Japanese colony in fact if not in name, like her puppet state of Manchukuo and North China.

The British imperialists, purely for their own greedy ends, have been helping the struggle of Chiang Kai Shek and the Chinese by supplying them with arms and other necessities imported through the foreign concessions and the treaty ports. The Japanese in return for minor concessions are demanding that all aid to China shall cease and that Britain exert pressure on the Chinese to force them to surrender.

The loathsome hypocrisy of the moral indignation shown by the British capitalist press at the "barbarism", the "inhuman", "uncivilised", etc., conduct of the Japanese is shown by a report which has just come through of what is taking place in the British West African "protectorate" of Sierra Leone. In order to collect the monstrous and burdensome taxes inflicted on the natives, tortures and flogging are officially used on women as well as men in the best traditions of "Anglo-Saxon" gentle methods of government.

The quarrel between Britain and Japan is a quarrel between two sets of thugs and gangsters over the division of the booty from the exploitation of the Chinese people. Because of her difficulties in Europe, Britain has been attempting to make a robber's agreement at the expense of the Chinese masses. The motives which inspire the actions and diplomacy of Britain and other imperialist countries can be clearly seen in the horse deals which they are attempting to arrange behind the scenes in secret discussions at Tokyo.

Under these conditions the shameful role played by the "Labour" and "communist" leaders is transparently demonstrated. Instead of exposing the economic and political motives of the actions of the British government, they attempt to show themselves as better and more zealous defenders of the "interests" of the British capitalists than the capitalists themselves. They are demanding a "firm" stand and no retreat in the face of Japanese "insolence," "protection" of the rights of Britain in China, that is, of the robber treaties forced at the point of the bayonet on the Chinese. As if any action undertaken by the imperialists can be for any purpose except the protection of their profits.

We must demand the cancellation of all privileges enjoyed by the British and other imperialist nations in China, and the handing over to the Chinese of the plunder wrung from them in imperialist wars of conquest. That is the way to strike a blow not only in favour of China, but against British capitalism as well. We cannot trust the British capitalists to carry out any act in the interests of the workers of Britain and the world.

We can help the Chinese people only by independent action. For the workers' boycott of Japan! Transport workers, dockers, all workers must rely only on their own might by refusing to handle goods to and from Japan.

The Far Eastern situation reveals the precarious state of the world. The imperialists are preparing to sacrifice the youth of all nations on the altar of profits. There is only one road for youth to travel, the road of unrelenting opposition to imperialism and capitalism as the only way to abolish the nightmare of the worldwide slaughter which they are preparing for us. No support for imperialist war preparations, diplomacy or horse-deals!

WORKERS' INTERNATIONAL NEWS

Incorporating "WORKERS' FIGHT".

VOL. 4, No. 7.	JULY 1941	TWOPENCE

DEFEND THE SOVIET UNION!

MANIFESTO OF THE FOURTH INTERNATIONAL IN BRITAIN

The last stronghold of the world working class is now being stormed by the armies of the blackest reaction history has known. The workers' state is in mortal danger. The achievments of the immortal October revolution—the social ownership and planned economy are in danger of destruction. Every conscious socialist worker must rally unconditionally to the defence of the Soviet Union. But this is not enough! We have to understand who is responsible for the present situation. The Stalinist bureaucracy and the Communist International! Stalin sought, with the reactionary theory of Socialism in one country, to detach the Soviet Union from the fate of the world working class. When Trotsky warned of the inevitable clash of world imperialism with the isolated Socialist State if revolution in the West did not intervene, he and his partisans were branded as enemies of the working class. But today our warnings have become the ghastly reality.

But all is not yet lost! The crisis of World imperialism, the terrible oppression of the totalitarian vice of the Nazis, the crushing national and social oppression of Europe, raises the possibility of waging a victorious war for a socialist Europe.

The die is cast. There can be no turning back. The fate of the Soviet Union, the fate of Europe, the fate of culture and civilisation itself, is in the balance. Either victory of world imperialism or the extension of the socialist revolution. Those are the two alternatives. In the words of Lenin "There is no middle way."

Workers want peace—
bosses prepare for war!

By Ted Grant

[*Youth For Socialism*, Vol. 1 No. 12, August 1939]

All the elements that are making for an international crisis are maturing at the present time. The capitalist drive towards war is assuming irresistible dimensions. Elaborate preparations, hidden and open are being made for a new show down in August or September which may lead to war. Diplomatic military preparations are going on in every country in Europe.

The British fleet will be at full war strength in these months. A million men will be under arms in England, the biggest peacetime number on record. France is calling up extra reservist and keeping the Maginot line fully manned. The British army is being kept ready for immediate action. British troops have marched side by side with the French in parades in Paris, and British bombers have flown over France in demonstration flights.

In the meantime in Danzig, the key point in the crisis, contrary to threats and in defiance of Poland the Nazis have feverishly fortified, armed and sent thousands of troops in preparation of a coup. In an article in the *Daily Telegraph* it is stated that "Germany's military concentrations in the east and west are tremendous and almost complete." The French premier has declared that this is "Europe's gravest situation for 20 years."

The same article emphasises the international crisis. "Nobody believes," says the *Frankfurter Zeitung*, "that a change of direction in British policy will satisfy Germany's vital claims...The trouble must therefore go on."

In bellicose speeches Poland's rulers have announced that any attempt to annex Danzig to the *Reich* will mean war, and Britain and France have guaranteed support to Poland. "In event of further aggression we are resolved to use at once the whole of strength in fulfilment of our pledges to resist it," declared Lord Halifax for the government on June 30.

Hore Belisha has indicated the seriousness of the position of French and British imperialism in a speech made in France:

"Their peoples [read British and French capitalists—EG] know that the long period during which they have been privileged to enjoy great wealth and great sway on easy terms has been closing."

In order to keep their hands free of European complications, the British capitalists have been compelled to beat a temporary retreat in the Far East. Japan, taking advantage of the troubled situation, has forced British imperialism to grant them indirect support for their war in China. This horse deal in itself is a significant proof of how little the British imperialists are genuinely concerned for peace or in fighting "aggression". Their main concern, as of all imperialists, is with protecting and adding to their pitiless exploitation of the colonial and other peoples in the world.

The armaments expenditure still goes on, mounting to staggering proportions; £730,000,000 is being spent on arms in Britain this year alone. The British and other governments are preparing colossal burdens for the masses of the people in order to further their war preparations.

The negotiations in Moscow for a military pact are still dragging on, with Britain and the Soviet manoeuvring for advantages and haggling over the details of military commitments. Here again can it clearly be seen that the aim of the British imperialists is the protection of their interests and nothing else.

The ideological preparations for the slaughter continue apace. Goebbels' propaganda ministry continues to broadcast attacks on the inhuman treatment of the colonial peoples by the "pluto-democracies", which for their part monotonously retort with denunciations of the atrocities committed in the totalitarian states.

Marshal Smigly-Rydz announces that the Polish people will fight to the last man for Danzig. "Poland does not want war but for us there are things worse than war and one of these is the loss of our liberties." In the house of the hanged one should not speak of the gallows. The Polish capitalists who have murdered, terrorised and oppressed Ukrainians, Galicians, Germans, Jews and other minorities, in addition to the suppression of the workers and peasants, have the astounding impudence solemnly to talk of the "defence of liberty".

The British press has quoted these words approvingly, including the workers' press. Arthur Greenwood for the Labour Party has said that much as he loves peace he loves liberty more and demands that Nazi Germany be stopped. The Labour Party has issued a manifesto to the German people to take action against their rulers in the interests of peace. The BBC have had the major part broadcast to Germany. This has resulted in a fury of indignation among the Nazis in Germany. The *Daily Herald* of July 5 comments:

> "They [German newspapers—EG] do not like it because the Labour appeal treats the German people as human beings, as comrades, as partners in a common heritage. But the German government treats them as pawns, as counters, as gun-fodder."

The laying of the burden for conducting the struggle against war on the shoulders of the German workers has aroused the righteous indignation of the Communist Party of Great Britain. Referring to the Labour appeal they point out that our task is to struggle at home, and then go on to demand a redoubled effort for the overthrow of Chamberlain as the ally of Hitler, Hitler's fifth column, etc.

If anything the hypocrisy of the Communist Party is even more blatant than that of the Labour Party. Both deceive the workers of Germany and of Britain as to the real causes of the conflict which is impending. True enough, Hitler uses the German people as pawns, counters and gun-fodder. But in the cold-blooded calculations of British, French and Polish imperialism, the workers in these countries too are so much cannon fodder to be used to defend their capitalist interest—nothing more.

The new found interest of Britain in "liberty loving" Poland and the integrity of Eastern Europe is by no means motivated by an altruistic love of humanity. It is fear of the successful rivalry of German imperialism.

The *Daily Herald* of July 1 admits the real cause of the conflict to be not different ideologies but the clash of interests of rival imperialisms. The old imperialism must be ended, they appeal, if lasting peace is to be preserved. To urge the imperialists to cease to be imperialists is like asking carnivorous beasts of prey to cease eating meat and live on porridge. So long as imperialism and capitalism exist they must perforce go to war because of the conflict of economic interests.

The British capitalists are no better and a great deal more hypocritical than their German rivals. Our job lies at home. If there is one thing which is preventing the capitalists from going to war up to now, it has been fear of the wrath of the working class.

Desperately the Brawn capitalists are attempting to find some way out of the impasse in which they have landed. The offer of a loan of £1,000,000,000 to Germany by R. S. Hudson, Minister for Overseas Trade, was an impulsive attempt to find some compromise. All the capitalists of the world are afraid of the war which is developing, not because of any concern for human life but for fear of the inevitable revolutions which will arise from it. But even so they find a solution impossible. They may manage to delay the outbreak of war for a short period but that is all.

To the workers, and especially the youth who are now being trained in the use of arms in the militia and the army, we say: your enemy is not the youth in other lands; it is the capitalist class at home. There is only one way to prevent war and if it breaks out to end it, namely, by the overthrow of capitalism, the real root from which war springs.

Down with the war!
"The main enemy is at home"

By Ted Grant

[Youth For Socialism, Vol. 2 No. 1, September 1939]

Today the youth of Britain as of other countries face the gravest threat to their lives and liberties they have ever had to consider. War or peace trembles in the balance. The nations confront one another mobilised and armed to the teeth. "We are ready," boasts Chamberlain, pointing to the navy, army and air force preparedness, to the methodical preparations of ARP[1] and evacuation schemes. Yes, they even have ready 250,000 shrouds for those they expect to be killed in the first weeks and months of air raids, for London alone. Across the Channel, on both sides of the Rhine, the state of preparation is just as, or even more complete.

It requires merely the signal, on either side, and the ghastly tragedy of 1914-1918 will have begun. Millions, tens of millions, will be killed in the insane slaughter, whole cities and countries will be devastated, women and children as well as men will be in the front-lines to be butchered. Famine and disease will sweep over all Europe. The flower of European manhood will be exterminating one another. And for what?

The British capitalist press has been attempting to picture the situation as if it were all due to the "lust for power" on the part of a lunatic who controls Germany. This man, they say, has an insane desire to dominate Europe—and the world. After his conquest of Austria and Czechoslovakia, it is now the turn of Poland. It is time, they say, that British "democracy" made a stand.

It is true that German imperialism desires to dominate the continent of Europe. But the reason for this lies in the insoluble contradictions of German capitalism. In the most highly industrialised country in Europe, with the coming to power of fascism in Germany and the consequent savage lowering of the standard of living of the German people, the German capitalists find themselves in a position where they must find new markets in order to get rid of their surplus goods, which they cannot sell at home. In addition they want sources of raw material and new peoples to exploit, having squeezed almost the last *pfennig*,

---

[1] The Air Raid Precaution committee was set up in May 1924 to plan and overview the evacuation of British cities.

the last ounce of energy out of the German working class. They have openly demanded that Central and South Eastern Europe must become a "German sphere of influence".

But the British and French capitalists, despite the huge resources of their empires, with their millions of colonial slaves, out of whom super profits are wrung, also despite the few crumbs given to the upper layers of the working class, find themselves in a similar position.

Cabinet minister after cabinet minister has openly stated that they are not willing to give up a single one of their markets anywhere in the world. That is the cause of the quarrel between these different gangs of imperialist bandits. Stripped of all the pious phrases about "defence of democracy", "liberty", "the rule of law, not force", on the one hand, and "Germany's sacred rights", "living space", "the wrongs of Versailles" on the other, it can be reduced to the quarrel between the different cliques of monopoly capitalists as to who shall have the dominant right to make profits at the expense of the peoples of the whole world.

The attempt to picture the struggle as one between barbarism and civilisation, fascism versus democracy, tyranny against liberty, is made laughable by the attempt of the British capitalists to win over to their side Franco, the butcher of millions of Spanish workers, bloodiest tyrant in Europe, and Mussolini, not a whit better or worse than his fellow dictator. And there is no need to point out that thousands of workers are languishing in the jails of fascist Poland in whose defence we are to die.

In addition, by means of the Emergency Powers Act the liberties of the workers in England will be swept away soon. In France the move towards dictatorship has gone even further than in England. Freedom of the press, freedom to hold meetings, etc., has already been taken away, and rule by an "inner cabinet" of four dictators resorted to. As soon as the sound of the first shots has died away, behind the smoke of battle the last vestiges of freedom and democracy will disappear. War on the totalitarian scale will begin.

Already the capitalists have exacted "sacrifices" in the "national interests" from the rail workers and engineers. Dearly bought trade union conditions in the engineering industry have gone by the board. "Dilution", leading to a lower standard of living has begun. This is just the start. Other attacks on all sections of the working class are to come. It will be noticed that the railway owners, engineering bosses, and armament profiteers are not being called on to make sacrifices.

War, if it comes, will mean immense profits to the monopoly capitalists on both sides of the frontier. It is the working class and small people generally who will be the sufferers. "But what about the defence of our country?" plead the millionaires and their hired prostitutes of the boss class press. Defence of whose country? Defence of the landlord and the boss!

We defend the country when we have a country to defend. Cut down the profits out of war 100 percent first. Let the mines, factories, railways and workshops come under the control of the working class. The working class on both sides of the frontier has no interest in the struggle of one or another group of vultures fattening on the corpses of the working people. If British capitalists win the war, they are preparing to carve up Germany among their allies and themselves. Already the *Evening News*, formerly an enthusiastic supporter of Hitler, when he was destroying the trade unions and other organisations of the working class, former enthusiastic backer of Mosley and British fascism, has hinted in its leader columns of this intention upon the part of the British ruling class. If Hitler wins he will impose his monstrous tyranny on the whole of Europe and the colonies, as he has upon the Czech people. British workers and German workers have no reason to slaughter one another. Let us turn upon our real enemies, the German and British capitalist class.

If world capitalism has no solution for its problems excepting new and more horrible slaughter of whole nations, it is time this insane system were ended. And meantime, what is the message of the Labour and Communist Party leaders to the workers of the world? They are betraying us into the hands of our worst enemies.

Working youth, capitalism can only continue to exist on your bones. The sole way out for the youth lies in the overthrow of capitalism and workers' power and socialism. Our path lies in building up the revolutionary socialist youth which alone can lead us away from the nightmare of war which hangs over us.

2 – Imperialist slaughter [September 1939 – July 1940]

Introduction

In this series of lead articles for *Youth For Socialism* Ted Grant highlighted the main reason for the war, the conflict between German and Anglo-American imperialism for domination of Europe and the world.

The war was presented as one against Nazi dictatorship, but at the same time the British ruling class had a liking for Franco and were also courting Mussolini, revealing the fact that their opposition to "dictatorship" was pure hypocrisy. After the first few months of war in early 1940, preparations for an even worse scenario of slaughter were being undertaken by all imperialist powers by mobilising the masses of each country against the "enemy". The Labour leaders' bankrupt policies of backing a national unity government led by Churchill left the workers disarmed.

On the other hand, fake anti-war agitation was carried out by the Stalinist leaders of the Communist Party of Great Britain, which in the last analysis amounted to accepting peace on Hitler's terms. These criminal policies were hampering the ability of the working class movement to adopt an independent stance in relation to the war. The betrayal of the Stalinist leaders of the CPGB was the British side of the coin of the Stalin-Hitler pact signed in August 1939.

The propaganda of the WIL focused on the hypocrisy of the British bourgeoisie which was responsible for the rise of Hitler and which had tried until the last moment to reach a gentlemen's understanding with Hitler through the Munich Agreement that allowed Nazi Germany to invade Czechoslovakia. The WIL denounced the real interests behind the calls for national unity, while arguing that the solution would not be that of accepting peace on Hitler's terms, as the Stalinists were proposing, but to wage a class revolt against the imperialist war.

In the early stages of the war, Germany wished to maintain nominal neutrality among the other nations in Europe, especially among those with whom she shared a common frontier. Britain, in order to strike at Germany, tried to spread the war as widely as possible, not being in the least concerned with the "rights of small nations". As Ted Grant wrote, "The people of Europe can look forward to a few months more or less of the present deadlock, then the sanguinary slaughter—there is no other prospect."

By the summer of 1940, the French ruling class had miserably succumbed to Nazi domination, refusing to organise popular resistance for fear that the arming of the working class might threaten their interests, and preferring to reach a deal with the Nazi occupier. The capitulation of the French bourgeoisie was a turning point in the war that was reflected in a change of tone in the propaganda of the WIL. Now Britain faced the threat of invasion. In France the bourgeoisie refused to arm the workers for fear that these arms would eventually be turned against them. As a result of this experience the revolutionary socialists in Britain posed the demand of expropriating the capitalists, freeing the colonies from the imperialist yoke and arming the workers as the only means to stop any Nazi invasion.

Our war is the class war

By Ted Grant

[*Youth For Socialism*, Vol. 2 No. 5, February 1940]

The war drags on without any possibility of a quick and decisive victory for either side. February finds all Europe immobilised in the grip of the severest winter for a generation. It is as if the elements themselves, contemptuous of the stupidity of the human race, had added their quota to the sufferings of men. At the moment, with the western front snowbound, there is no likelihood of any large-scale military action.

It has taken the cold to give the soldiers some respite. But the outlook in the immediate future is as grim as the weather: a respite, not a reprieve, has been given to the people of Europe. Relentlessly and with set purpose the belligerents are preparing for the spring offensive.

Intense diplomatic activity in all the countries of Europe, striving for domination by one group or another, is taking place. The war is waged with economic and political weapons, but in the background remains the certain knowledge that it will be decided only by force of arms.

Meanwhile, what the war is being fought over is being revealed by the deeds and words of both belligerents. First, Germany has threatened the small neutrals: "If they do not comport themselves in a manner calculated to conform to an interpretation of neutrality made in Berlin, the Reich will have to consider taking measures for its own protection." A thinly veiled threat of military action which fits in well with the declared aim of Germany "that the domination of Europe by England must be ended forever."

The British press featured prominently the blustering and bullying of small nations by the Nazi "Prussian" bully, and waxed eloquent on the dire fate awaiting them in the event of a German victory. Comparisons were made between the methods of the allies and the methods of the Nazis. Chamberlain explained that the allies were fighting for the rights of small nations to "live their own lives" without fear of aggression. But Churchill, in a speech which showed his eagerness to have done with any hesitation or vacillation to grapple with the enemy as soon as possible, lifted the mask off the benign face of British imperialism perhaps too clearly for the ideological purposes of the ruling class: "The neutrals must do their duty, for their fate too is at stake," he threatened, emulating the classic Nazi technique; their duty of course being to enter the war on the same side as Britain and France. The small nations, having observed how Britain had "defended" Abyssinia, Albania, Austria, Czechoslovakia (when it suited her interests to compromise with the aggressor), do not appreciate the difference between "living their own lives" for the benefit of Britain or of Germany.

The hapless capitalists in the smaller countries attempt to maintain a precarious balance between the two warring camps. They know that neither side will hesitate to invade their territory when it suits the purpose of their military and strategical staff. They are mere pawns in this game of power politics, and it is to decide who shall dominate them and the colonies that war is being waged.

The role of Britain and France in this war to end "Nazism" and "aggression" is shown by their assiduous courting of Italy. Mussolini is to be the protector of the independence of small nations in the Balkans against the twin evils of Nazi aggression and Bolshevism. The allies are attempting to win Italy over to the side of "democracy and liberty." But Italy was bribed to betray her alliance with Germany in the last war; she was promised a fortune and given a dime. So Mussolini is shyly waiting to see where he can obtain the best advantage before committing himself.

In the conquered territories of Czechoslovakia and Poland, the Nazis organise an exploitation and repression unparalleled in modern Europe. The British press is full of stories of the horror of the regime of national and social barbarism which Hitler has imposed in these areas: a savagery not of the clumsy and ill-organised brutality of medieval times, but operated by modern means and machinery. And it is indeed unnecessary, as in the last war, for the allies to invent tales of German atrocities. The truth is far more appalling than any number of lies.

The Nazis, however, are merely acting in time-honoured imperialist fashion, a little more open, a little cruder. It was with methods such as these that the British Empire was built up and maintained, and the Germans have not been slow to retort to the mock indignation of the imperialists in London. All Empires have been built in this fashion; the difference exists only in geography and time. Hitler has transferred to the continent of Europe the methods of Britain in Asia and Africa. Lacking colonies and resources overseas, German imperialism is compelled to attempt to reduce the Czech and Polish workers and peasants to the level of the coolies and peasants in India. Imperialism does not distinguish between the colour of white and brown in the selection of its slaves. There is nothing to distinguish today between the German and allied diplomacy. The tender admiration now expressed for Franco, who decimated the Spanish people, the courting of Mussolini, the alliance with Turkey and Rumania (two of the most ruthless dictatorships in Europe), all show the concern with which allied imperialism regards Hitler's methods when they can be used to the advantage of their own money-bags.

Already Chamberlain, Churchill and other spokesmen of the government have monotonously reiterated that "the whole German people" is responsible for prolonging the war, thereby proving the assertion of Goebbels that the aim of the allies is to starve Germany, not to destroy Nazism. This gives an insight into what Europe will look like under the domination of Threadneedle Street[1]. The system of Asiatic despotism will pervade Europe whichever side wins the war. It is this fear that drives the German masses to support the Nazi regime—they have good reasons to dread the prospect of becoming the slaves of British and French capital.

Thus, in methodical and business-like fashion, both sides prepare for the spring and the neutrals wait in apprehension; for there is no knowing where the new front will be created. The war must be "opened up" and both sides will attempt to use the terrain which suits them best.

March winds and April showers will bring forth not flowers, but a grim harvest of slaughter, and the ordeal will not be of short duration. "We will fight for eight, for ten years, to gain victory," says Hitler, while Chamberlain comfortingly assures the British people: "We must prepare for a long and grim struggle."

But we, the youth of Britain, have learned the lessons of the past. We will not allow ourselves to be sacrificed as our fathers were, to the Moloch[2] of capitalism.

No, we know our enemies, it's not the youth of Germany, but those who are exploiting us at home! The task of Germany's youth is to settle with its boss class. Our job at home is to overthrow the capitalist system and establish workers' power in Britain.

---

[1] Location of the Bank of England since 1734, often called for this reason "the old lady of Threadneedle Street ".

[2] See footnote, p. 79.

DEFEND THE
SOVIET UNION

Since the foundation of the Soviet Republic the imperialists have been aiming to discredit the idea of socialism in order to overthrow the first Workers State. What could not be achieved by all the slanders and lies of the capitalist press, has been accomplished by the policy of Stalin.

This attack on Finland is not in the interests of the Finnish or the Russian workers

This is the ultimate act of treachery towards the world working class which Stalin's regime has perpetrated since he seized power in 1923.

In a frantic attempt to organise a defence against the inevitable capitalist attack on the Soviet Union, the Stalin Government shamelessly violates the idea of Lenin, that *the socialist revolution cannot be imposed on peoples; they must be won over to it.* The liberation of Finland can only be achieved by the Finnish workers themselves. The Red Army should assist but cannot take the place of workers' action.

By his actions Stalin has alienated the support of the toilers of the whole world. He makes it possible for the Finnish capitalists to pose as the defenders of freedom and to rally the Finnish masses behind their reactionary aims.

He has served very well the brigands, of world imperialism, who take advantage of the opportunity to discredit the idea of socialism. Thus he has endangered the safety of the Soviet Union. It was the support of the world working class which ended the war of intervention and saved the Soviet Union from the attacks of world capitalism. The international working class still remains the main bulwark of the Soviet system. The capture of a few islands and points of strategic importance are not worth sacrificing the support of the toilers of the entire globe.

But let us not while condemning Stalinism slacken for one moment our struggle against the capitalist class at home. They have dragged us again into an imperialist war. They try to justify and conceal their own reactionary aims by pointing at Stalin.

Attlee, Greenwood and other leaders of the Labour Party condemn Stalin's action only in order to justify their betrayal in supporting this war.

The Communist Party leaders represent nothing but the narrow interests of the Kremlin. Yesterday they supported the war. Today they are calling for an imperialist "peace" and are quite prepared to sacrifice the German, Czech and Polish workers to the rule of German fascism. Tomorrow, if Stalin makes a pact with Chamberlain they will again support the war. The working class can have nothing but contempt for such scoundrels.

The jackals of imperialism are howling with delight at Stalin's staining the ideas of Lenin. But against the bloodstained crimes of world imperialism, the endless slaughter and misery of capitalism, the workers can still look with hope towards the ideals expressed by the October Revolution. We will wrest the trampled banner of Leninism from under the feet of Stalin. In spite of the invasion of Finland we stand firmly for the defense of the Soviet Union; not by the methods of Stalin but by the methods of Lenin and Trotsky.

Only the overthrow of the Stalin regime by the Russian workers only the overthrow of decaying capitalism by the workers of the world, only the establishment of the Socialist United States of Europe can save the Soviet Union from destruction and banish forever the horrors of war. This is the road of the Fourth International.

NO SUPPORT FOR IMPERIALIST WAR
DOWN WITH STALINISM
FOR AN INDEPENDENT SOVIET FINLAND

Printed and Published for, **WORKERS' INTERNATIONAL NEWS** by B. French **87** Saffron Hill E.C.1.

WIL leaflet on the Winter War against Finland, end of 1939 [Ted Grant Archive]

Not for imperialist slaughter

By Ted Grant

[*Youth For Socialism*, Vol. 2 No. 6, March 1940]

With mingled dread and horror the masses of the people observe the ending of an exceptionally bitter winter and the coming of the thaw, for even worse lies in store for them. The war drags on; or rather the preparation for mass slaughter on both sides goes forward relentlessly and with gathering speed and momentum.

On February 24 Chamberlain and Hitler in their speeches both piously appeal to divine intervention as guarantees of victory for justice and right. Nevertheless Chamberlain not so piously echoes the Cromwellian advice "Trust in God but keep your powder dry" while Hitler zealously follows the doctrine of Bismarck: "God is always on the side of the big battalions," in his explanation of Nazi diplomacy and military preparations.

In despair, Chamberlain, with one eye on the British people and the other on the lookout for a miracle which will save British capitalism from its impending doom again reverses the "war aims" of the British government. Once again it is not the "German people" but "Nazism" which is the enemy. "We for our part should be ready to seek a settlement with any government that had subscribed to these aims [independence of Poland and Czechoslovakia, etc.] and given proof—proof that can be relied upon—of its sincerity." The campaign against the "Huns" has apparently not met with conspicuous success.

Hitler for his part, denying the charge by implication that Germany desires world domination states his humble aspirations:

> "I make Germany's claim modestly, I claim security for our living space—what has been economically developed by Germans in Central Europe. I also claim our German colonies, of which the plutocrats have robbed us."

To judge from the fine words and noble sentiments which ooze from every sentence of their speeches, it is all just a tragic misunderstanding. But even while they were talking, the ignorant tribesmen of the North-West frontier of India were being taught by British capitalism with planes and machine guns exactly what she means by the rights of nations to live their own lives, while German imperialism, too, on the backs of the enslaved Poles and Czechs was enlightening Europe as to the real meaning of *"Lebensraum."*

Reading these speeches the small neutrals can well shiver with apprehension as the giants look round for some battleground on which they can come to grips. The diplomatic tussles of the last few weeks have revealed in deeds the real desires of the participants in the war. Scandinavia has become one of the centres of the intrigues of London, Berlin and Paris.

For a long time now, Germany, for strategic reasons, in her desire to strike a blow against the Allies, has waged a cruel and merciless war on the shipping of Norway, Denmark and Sweden, in order to exert pressure on these little "neutrals" to force them to support Germany economically, and allow their waters to be an economic bridge between Germany and Russia, circumventing the control of the seas by the Allies.

This "brutal attitude" towards the "weak and defenceless" Northern states has sent the Allied press into paroxysms of rage and disgust which they contrast with the attitude of the "cowardly Nazi bully" towards those big and powerful neutrals who have the means to hit back: Japan, Italy, Russia and America, whose shipping and interests are treated with every consideration by the Germans.

Thus triumphantly was demonstrated the superiority of British and French democracy in its war methods and aims. But the last few weeks have laid bare the hypocrisy of the Allied camp as well. When they came into conflict with Japan over the arrest of German sailors in Japanese ships, despite the aggressive war of rape and brutality which Japan has been waging for three years against the Chinese people, we have the British bourgeoisie going on their hands and knees to conciliate and placate these inhuman "aggressors", says Chamberlain in a speech reported in the *Times* of February 1:

> "...And indeed nothing would more distress us than that there should be in the minds of the Japanese people or the Japanese government any idea that we had intentionally or deliberately exercised our belligerent rights as we see them with a want of courtesy or a want of consideration to the Japanese nation...The last thing that we want to do is to affront the self-respect of a friendly nation with whom we want to live in peace..."

With Italy so great has been their desire to exercise their belligerent rights with courtesy and consideration that this successful aggressor who grabbed Albania and Abyssinia not so very long ago is even allowed to break the Allied "blockade," by importing coal from Germany by sea, without let or hindrance from the Allies. Italian fascism, whose methods internally and externally are indistinguishable from Nazism, is thus tenderly treated in order to win Italy over to the struggle against "aggression" and for the "ending of Nazism forever."

The Nazis have always found reasons to justify their "aggression" on other nations by lying stories of "provocation", "intolerable oppression of Germans," etc. A technique which Chamberlain now claims the "apprentice Stalin" has learned from his mentor Hitler. But in this line of business the German imperialists can teach nothing to their British counterparts. The capitalist hypocrites can always find plausible reasons for their trampling on the rights of other nations. Chamberlain after indignantly explaining the Nazis crimes against the neutrals, airily dismissed the *Altmark* affair[1] as a "mere technical breach of neutrality."

The *Altmark* incident was a gift from heaven to the Allies. If there had been no *Altmark* it would have been necessary to invent one. The justification in the eyes of the British people for the turning of Britain into a "technical" aggressor was accomplished by lies and exaggerations about the "Nazi hell ship", "the dashing Nelson tradition", "gallant rescue of 300 seamen", etc.

The *Altmark*'s real significance does not lie in the rescue of the 300 sailors. For them the British imperialists would not stir a finger, for they will sacrifice any number of men in the interests of profit. But the incident was an ideal test for the reactions of the British people if and when Britain is compelled, for military and strategic reasons, to attack or coerce one of the small neutrals.

The experiment worked. The harrowing tales of the suffering of the seamen enabled the capitalists to gain the support of the British people in this minor deed of aggression. They can now go ahead with their blackmail and threatening of the small neutrals confident that they will be able to manufacture incidents and excuses to justify and mobilise British public opinion behind their acts. Already the *Daily Express*, least cautious of the yellow organs, has called for the British navy to operate in Norwegian territory against German ships using the shelter of the three-mile limit over which Norwegian sovereignty extends. They are blurting out crudely what Churchill threatened the neutrals with in veiled hints.

The Norwegians have offered to submit the dispute to arbitration. But the British imperialists who have always harped on Hitler's refusal to submit his "disputed' with his selected victims to "impartial judgment," show a lack of enthusiasm in exactly the same way when their own interests are at stake and when they too can settle the issue by the pressure of the overwhelming military

---

[1] The *Altmark* incident was a naval skirmish in neutral Norwegian waters between the UK and Nazi Germany, on February 16 1940.to Germany with 299 British merchant sailors on board, prisoners of war. *Altmark* was intercepted by the destroyer HMS Cossack and boarded, the ship's crew overwhelmed and the prisoners released. The incident boosted British morale but convinced Hitler to intensify the planning for Operation *Weserübung*, the occupation of Denmark and Norway, which eventually took place on April 9 1940.

force at their disposal.

Hitler has utilised these incidents to further draw the German people behind him. Hitler shows the German workers how the British people have rallied behind Chamberlain and the hypocrisy of the British capitalists' claim to be the champion of the small nations. In this, he has been assisted by the Labour leaders in Britain.

Utilising the crimes of Stalin, the Labour leaders have denounced the invasion of Finland in strident terms. "Poor little Finland," "the ending of aggression," the "rights of small nations to live their own lives," these have been the axioms on which labour policy was allegedly based. They even came out for the ending of imperialism, including British—after the war was over of course.

Here in the *Altmark* affair was a magnificent opportunity to show their mettle. No excuse whatever can justify aggression, they have told us. Norway is no bigger than Finland and even more defenceless. Britain has flagrantly violated Norwegian neutrality. And the Labour leaders have shamelessly added their applause to that of the jingoes for the "daring deeds" of the British navy. Chamberlain may plead like the girl who had an illegitimate child, that it was "only a little one." But what can the Labour leaders say? Hitler's gangsterism cannot extenuate the Allied violations in any way. Why have they not protested in Parliament and exposed the aims and deeds of the National government to the workers of Britain? They have betrayed the working class by supporting the war which is being fought for imperialist interests. Tomorrow they will support any aggression which the capitalists are compelled to launch as they have supported them over the *Altmark*. The propaganda machine of Goebbels explains to the German workers how the workers in Britain are supporting their capitalists and appeals to them to support "national unity." And Morrison, Citrine and Attlee render him the best aid possible.

The Communist Party is no better. They use this incident to suggest a "peace" which can only mean victory for Hitler. This the workers quite rightly reject as no solution to the problem.

Meanwhile the preparations proceed apace: victory for German imperialism or victory for British imperialism, neither can be in the interests of the workers of Britain, Germany or of the "small nations." And neither can gain victory soon. The misery and the slaughter will proceed endlessly once the war really begins.

The solution rests in the power of the working class. The war can only be ended and a real peace obtained by the victory of the German and the British workers against their real enemy, German and British capitalism. The socialist united states of Europe: that is our slogan. It is for this and not for the wars and the profiteering of capitalism that youth will make its sacrifice and lead the way.

How to win the class war

By Ted Grant

[*Youth For Socialism*, Vol. 2 No. 7, April 1940]

"The season for campaigning draws near." These ominous words in the leader columns of the *Times*, mouthpiece of British capitalism, herald the approach of real hostilities between the Allies and Germany. Until now only minor clashes in the air (even the bombing of Sylt and Scapa Flow[1] were not large scale operations) and isolated clashes of patrols on land have taken place. The war between the western powers has been mainly on the diplomatic and economic fronts. Here the Allies have suffered severe reverses in the first round of battle. The German destruction of Poland, along with the Russian invasion of Finland, was accomplished without serious opposition from the West.

For the present, Hitler's aim has been to pin the Allies down to fighting on one front while he builds up his military and economic power. He wishes to avoid the mistake of the last war, when Germany was compelled to fight on two fronts, thus lessening her military power; hence his pact with Russia and the efforts to come to an agreement with Italy and Russia to guarantee "peace in the Balkans". The meeting between Mussolini and Hitler was a setback for Britain and France, who have been trying to bribe Italy to desert the Axis and support, at least by benevolent neutrality, the British and French in the war.

Since the outbreak of war Britain has been trying to push Italy away from her national aspirations in the Mediterranean ("Tunis, Nice, Corsica!"), which bring her into violent conflict with France, and to guide her instead into the Balkans where she would collide with Germany and Russia. British newspapers ecstatically quoted the condemnation of the Italian press in the early days, and the material support given to the Finns by Mussolini, as proof of the consistent stand of Italian fascism against the forces of Bolshevism. The aggression of Russia, so piously condemned (and certainly Mussolini has set an example in recent years), was supposed to have united the whole of Christendom against the Red menace. But alas, the new knight of anti-Bolshevism, meant to replace Hitler, has tarnished his shield. Mussolini has refused to be drawn into the

---

[1] The German air force raided the British base of Scapa Flow on March 16 1940. In retaliation, British planes attacked the German seaplane base at Hornum on Sylt Island, north of the western end of the Kiel Canal.

Allied orbit, and the Italian press greeted with unconcealed delight the defeat which the British and French suffered in Scandinavia.

And the policy of the Allies in Scandinavia reveals their real aims in this war. For the present, Germany wishes to maintain nominal neutrality among the other nations in Europe, especially among those with whom she shares a common frontier. Britain, in order to strike at Germany, tries to spread the war as widely as possible. Neither is in the least concerned with the "rights of small nations". Both are only interested in the extension of their own power and influence, and in the retention of past gains.

That was the main reason for the attitude of Norway and Sweden to the allied request for facilities to aid Finland. They openly pointed out that Britain desired to "help" Finland in order, among other things, to weaken Russia strategically and economically, and to strike a blow at Germany, but mainly to open up a Scandinavian front at the expense of Norway and Sweden, thus creating another battlefield on which to come to grips with Germany. They were to be used as pawns in the game of power politics. "The military weakness of the Allies does not allow us to take these risks," they bluntly replied to the pressure.

Meanwhile, by offering Italy and Russia a share—a move which cuts the ground from under the Allied manoeuvres with Italy—Germany is striving to build up her economic domination of the Balkans by diplomacy; military force remains in the background as a final argument. Germany does this not from moral scruples (witness Poland and Czechoslovakia), but because peaceful domination is cheaper and, by ensuring supplies, would help in the war against the West. When the war is over, the Germans calculate that the Balkans will come under their sway as surely as if they were colonies conquered by military force.

The precipitation of hostilities against Germany was partly the result of its attempt to build an economic empire in the Balkans, preparatory to an attempt at world domination. Britain and France are straining every sinew to prevent German success in this sphere of operations. They are attempting to operate in the Balkans in such a way as to open up a South-Eastern battleground. For similar reasons Mr. Chamberlain assured the Scandinavian countries that the Finnish episode was not over, an assurance which has since been underlined by the systematic violation of Norwegian neutrality by the British Navy. These acts speak a thousand times louder than all the cant, of the real aims of British capitalism.

The French ambassador to the USA has stated that there will be large-scale fighting in the spring—not on the Western Front, but somewhere else! Where was not indicated, and it is uncertain. In the interests of their capitalist classes the belligerent powers coldly calculate the military possibilities. None are fighting for anything but the economic power of their own master class. For these ends they prepare to drag the people of all Europe, of the entire world if necessary, into the bloody massacre.

The people of Europe can look forward to a few months more or less of the present deadlock, then the sanguinary slaughter—there is no other prospect.

The mission of Sumner Welles was stillborn before it was attempted. There can be no peace between the warring powers until one has defeated the other; the antagonism between German and Allied imperialism is too great. There is room for only one group to dominate the greater part of the world—this, and only this, is the issue for which this war is being fought!

The offensives will begin soon. Hunger, misery, disease and death will be the lot of the masses. But already there are unmistakable signs of the answer the workers will give: the Admiralty trumpets forth the story of the mutiny of the *Graf Spee*[2], when the German sailors refused to go to their deaths for a cause which was not their own. Already, in the first naval engagement of the war, the instinctive reaction of the masses was demonstrated. Sailors have always been in the vanguard of such movements; the foot soldiers will not be far behind.

The workers of all lands will give their answer! War can be ended only by ending capitalism. Against the victory of both German and British imperialism! For a socialist united states of Europe! The youth of the *Graf Spee* have shown the way. The working youth of Britain salute them.

---

[2] *Admiral Graf Spee* was a German class cruiser. It entered the neutral port of Montevideo, Uruguay for repairs on December 14 1940 but was immediately cornered by the British navy. Having no way to escape, Captain Langsdorff decided to sink the ship rather than risking the life of his seamen.

No peace without socialism

By Ted Grant

[*Youth For Socialism*, Vol. 2 No. 8, May 1940]

With the invasion of Norway and Denmark the war has entered the stage of active hostilities. The allied press has made great play with the attack on these small countries' independence as further proof of the moral leprosy of the "German barbarians". From the purely strategic and economic implications involved, the calculation of the move fills the journalistic hacks with spurious indignation.

The virtuous fury displayed would have had a more genuine ring if the Allied mine laying in Norwegian territorial waters had not coincided with the German attack. *Then* the story was different. Said the Paris correspondent of *The Times* on April 9:

> "For the first time since the beginning of the war, in fact, it is seen that the Allies have got in a blow ahead of their enemies, and the result is a feeling of real encouragement, coupled with the belief that at last the conduct of the war is being tackled with the energy it deserves..."

From this point of view it can be seen that the Nazi coup in Norway meant merely that the German imperialists "got in a blow" ahead of the Allies. Both sides manoeuvred for the vantage point to strike hard at one another. The Germans, of course, following the familiar technique, announced that the Allies and Germany have found a battlefield, and that they had invaded Denmark and Norway "in order to protect them" from Allied action.

Whatever the results of the Norwegian conflict, the fighting is likely to be savage. Now Norwegian people are certain to be bitter; Norway will be blown to bits.

One reason for the immunity of London and Berlin, *up to the present*, is the fear that mass air-raids would engender reprisals, and the fear of the altered mood such havoc would bring in the minds of the British and German workers; plus the fact that such actions would mutually cancel each other out. If decisive advantage were to be obtained, neither side would hesitate before unleashing the most fearful slaughter of civilians. But in the case of Norway no such scruples will be taken into consideration. The belligerent powers will cheerfully tear

Norway to pieces. Already the Royal Air Force and the German Air Force in Norway are bombing each other's bases, sources of supply and occupied towns without mercy.

The cringing Norwegian capitalist class, sections of which desired to come to terms with Germany as agents in the exploitation of the Norwegian workers, and others who had accepted the support and, implicitly, the domination of the Allies, were not able to save Norway from becoming a slaughterhouse.

But the extension of the war will not stop at Norway. Norway is neither broad enough nor important enough to decide the issue. No matter who wins on this front, the war will not be ended. On some pretext or other Sweden will almost certainly be drawn into the conflict. But even the domination of all Scandinavia cannot mean victory for either side.

The Allies and Germany will look for new battlefronts; hence the impotent terror of all the small neutrals in Europe. Like rabbits caged with rattlesnakes fighting over their prospective prey, they search frantically for a means of escape from the doom which confronts them.

Already Holland and Belgium protest with monotonous regularity to both Allies and Germany against the violation of their territory by aeroplanes. Their protests will avail them little. They have nothing to gain and everything to lose by being involved in the war. But, in this battle of the great powers, the small nations have no alternative but to be forced one way or the other. Scant respect for their desires will be shown by either side under pressure of military necessity. In a matter of weeks, or months at most, the Low Countries will be in the war. The Balkans too cannot escape the holocaust. They can only crouch and manoeuvre desperately while the great powers prepare an extension of the war to South-East Europe.

The attempt to bribe Italy away from Germany apparently has failed. The Italian press once more conducts a virulent anti-British campaign. Simultaneously, the British capitalist press begins to remember the crimes of Italian fascism, which, after all, is twin brother to Nazism. Forgotten is the praise accorded to Mussolini in the leader columns of *The Times*, for instance, as a "consistent opponent of Bolshevism", a defender of civilization against the Red menace, during the course of the Finnish War, when a certain amount of support was given to Finland by Italy.

And alas, for the sacred duty of finishing with "aggression", proclaimed as the war aim of British "democracy", the British government has tentatively attempted, already, to arrive at a new agreement with Russia. "Poor little Finland" is quite forgotten in the needs and aims of British diplomacy.

Across the Atlantic the war clouds are gathering as Japan and America prepare to "protect" the Dutch East Indies when Holland becomes involved in the war. North and South, Pacific and Atlantic, over all Europe and the greater part of the globe, the shadow of Armageddon deepens. The world is one economic unit, and the fate of the world is being decided now.

An endless period of destruction and slaughter opens out before the peoples of the world. It can be ended, not by the victory of either imperialism, which would merely lay the basis for new wars and is not in the interests of the workers of any country, but by the victory of the workers over imperialism. Together with the German, French, Norwegian and European workers, the British workers must take their fate into their own hands. For an end to the interminable slaughter can only come with the victory of the workers over their oppressors. Not for the victory of either German or British imperialism, but for the socialist united states of Europe, and the world federation of socialist republics.

The workers' war is the class war!

By Ted Grant

[Youth For Socialism, Vol. 2 No. 10, June 1940]

The Allies and Germany have begun a war to the death, a ruthless war of extermination. The scale of the casualties can be judged by the fact that in the first few days one quarter of the Dutch army was wiped out. Mass air raids on Rotterdam, which according to the *News Chronicle* only lasted three days, destroyed one third of the city's buildings. Out of a population of half a million, according to the same source, 100,000 were killed or injured. That is the grim reality of totalitarian warfare.

Hitler has launched his threatened *blitzkrieg* in an effort to gain victory this year. He has staked everything on destroying France and Britain before they can use the tremendous potential reserves of material and the access to the whole world which control of the seas implies.

Meanwhile, Italy is also preparing to assure herself a "place in the sun" and to assume a role of active belligerency. While the world is being carved up once more, Italian capitalism, in the same impasse which led German imperialism to attempt to stave off the crisis of the regime of expansion, is compelled to prepare to enter the slaughter, with all its attendant risks, if it is to survive.

The Balkans and Switzerland watch with trembling horror the clash between the great imperialist powers which has already engulfed the Low Countries and Norway. No more than these can they escape the spreading of the world conflagration to their territories.

Meanwhile, diplomatic preparations for extending the war go on apace; preparations in which the struggling camps swing from one position to the opposite as fast as Hitler's *Panzer* divisions can penetrate enemy territory. Russia, which only a short time ago was being described as only one remove from Nazi Germany, is now being assiduously wooed by the Allies for a trade pact which cannot but have political repercussions. As a gesture of good will Stafford Cripps is being sent to Moscow as Britain's ambassador. The attempt is now being made to use Russia as a counterbalance to Germany and Italy in the Balkans. Until recently this role was reserved by the Allies for Italy in order to curb "Russian and German ambitions" which conflicted with the "interests of Italy" in South Eastern Europe.

More and more openly American imperialism prepares to intervene in order to destroy the menace of a German imperialist domination of Europe which could only lead to war within a limited time. The lightning speed of the German advance has upset all calculations and forced the American capitalists to disclose their aims sooner than they planned. Even before the American presidential elections, especially if Italy enters the war, it is likely that America will be drawn into the conflict. The speeches of Roosevelt, Hull, and other spokesmen of American capitalism, guarded as they are, reveal this clearly.

Armageddon is upon us. Millions will be crushed under the advancing tanks and warplanes. After five days of total war Holland was threatened with an epidemic of typhoid fever; the diseases which result from war will claim even more victims than the bombs, the gas, and all the instruments of destruction. Impartially, the germs will attack belligerents and neutrals alike—all humanity will suffer from the scourge of war!

Faced with the sudden shock of German occupation of the Channel ports, which brings the war to their doorsteps, there has been a slight resurgence of patriotism among British workers. Their lukewarm indifference has given way to a state of alarm. There seems to be no way out of the impasse except to continue the war to overthrow Hitler.

Advocates of the "stop the war" policy are attempting to educate the imperialist beasts of prey to live together peacefully when there is not enough meat to go round. The hopeless inadequacy of this stupid policy has been branded on mankind in letters of fire by flame-throwing tanks. There is not enough room in this world for both German and British-French imperialism to exist side by side. One side must destroy the other in an attempt to monopolise the whole globe.

The dilemma which faces the British and French workers is no different to that which faces the German workers. Victory for Hitler means a monstrous tyranny over all Europe. Victory for the Allies would mean a new and heavier Versailles Treaty being imposed upon the German workers which would enslave them to the victors. Faced with such an alternative they have no recourse but to support German imperialism.

Workers throughout the world are not interested in the victory of either imperialism. Herbert Morrison has already explained that after "we" (i.e. British capitalists) are victorious there will be 7 million unemployed in Britain. R.S. Hudson, minister for agriculture, has explained that the standard of living of the nation will be lower than for the past century. These are to be the glorious fruits of victory which Churchill has promised us are to come only after the ordeal of blood, toil, sweat and tears.

This war can be ended and the slaughter stopped only by striking at the cause of the conflict; capitalism has brought us to this fratricidal combat. The workers and soldiers of all lands must stretch the hand of friendship across the frontiers. Hateful though Hitler's fascism is to British workers, our enemy is not the German people, but the British capitalists at home. If we can carry on the struggle here we can leave the German workers to settle with Hitler.

The alternative is clear: already the British capitalists, now that the real fighting has started, are setting about the creation of a totalitarian state. As the war increases in intensity and the discontent of the workers grows, so the measures of repression will become harsher. Soon there will be little to choose between the regimes in Germany and England.

There can be no going back to the old days of democracy—win, lose, or draw! Capitalist democracy is finished. Not Hitler versus democracy is the issue, but totalitarianism against the working class.

The conquest of power by the workers and the establishment of a socialist united states of Europe is the sole way of banishing war and rebuilding shattered Europe.

It is by the youth of all lands, and not least of Britain, who are sacrificed to the Moloch* of capitalism, that there will be built up the revolutionary socialist leadership which can lead the workers to the accomplishment of this task.

---

* Moloch: a tyrannical power to be propitiated by human subservience or sacrifice; "the great Moloch of war"—God of the Ammonites and Phoenicians to whom parents sacrificed their children.

Workers must be armed against capitalism

By Ted Grant

[*Youth For Socialism*, Vol. 2 No. 10, July 1940]

The last few years have marked the end of an epoch in human history. The staggering and annihilating defeat of the armies of France by the Nazi war machine has left the continent of Europe under the bloody tyranny of German imperialism.

The empty boasts of Reynaud have been followed by the shameful surrender of Pétain and Weygand. The puffed up reputation which was built up around the military valour of these "heroes" stood the test while it was only concerned with the shooting down of the rebellious colonial masses of Algeria and Morocco, but was pitifully inadequate when faced with the monstrous military regime of Germany.

The ruling class of France, which had helped in the building up of reaction in Germany, showed itself completely incapable of offering any effective resistance to the Nazi legions. The capitalists paralysed the struggle against Hitler by their suppression of the French masses. Hitler could have been held up in North France, and again at the gates of Paris, if the whole population had been mobilised for resistance.

Why Paris was not defended

But for the ruling classes to have armed the workers would have meant that they were running the risk of these arms being used not only against Hitler, but also against the ruling classes themselves. Especially did they fear the revolutionary workers of Paris.

Once before, when the Prussians were at the gates of Paris in 1870, and the workers had been armed, they seized control in the first successful workers' uprising in history. The *Daily Telegraph* correspondent in France writes on June 17: "Danger of a communist uprising and civil war compelled the French government to sue for peace." They handed Paris intact to the Germans.

France was betrayed. The real fifth column was the capitulation government of financiers, manufacturers, millionaires and generals. It was they who sold the French people into the hands of Hitler. Rather than lose *all* their profits by a victory of the French masses, these "patriots" preferred to assure themselves of a few scraps from the tables of the Nazis.

And now the insatiable German imperialists are preparing for the destruction of Britain. The British government has announced that it is doing everything to counter this coming attack. But the ruling class of Britain is as rotten as that of France. The only real preparations they are making are those for use against their "main enemy" at home.

In France 20,000 police were left in Paris to "maintain order" and to hand over control to Himmler. A special civil guard was formed to keep order in the rear of the armies. Is there any guarantee that the British ruling class will not capitulate in the same manner as the French?

There is only one guarantee of a successful resistance to any attempt at invasion by Nazis: the arming of the working class in every street and every factory, and the control of this workers' militia by workers' committees.

This would render Britain completely impregnable. Parachute invaders and sea-borne troops alike would receive short shrift at the hands of the masses.

But the ruling-class cannot take this road for the same reason that the French rulers could not take it: it would present an even greater menace to their profit making and domination than even a victory of the Nazis.

Chamberlain, the Tory party, big business and the bankers of the City of London backed Hitler for years as a bulwark against socialism, and only fought him reluctantly when German imperialism threatened their empire and their profits. The contradictions between the two imperialisms gave them no alternative. But they are responsible for the disastrous position in which the British and European workers find themselves today. They have acted as Hitler's real fifth column for years. Their record, their very nature, and their position in society, renders them completely impotent to defend the workers against fascism. They must be swept aside, and the workers themselves must guide their own destinies.

Only socialism can defeat Hitler

For years the Labour leaders have allegedly been conducting a campaign against the pro-fascist policy of Chamberlain and the National government. But they now sit in that same government and assist it in a policy that is disastrous for the working-class.

Rank and file militants in the trade unions, Labour Party, and Leagues of Youth must demand that the Labour leaders must wage a struggle for full power immediately. Labour must take control on a programme which can mobilise all the toilers of Britain. And first on that programme must come the arming of the workers against their capitalist enemy at home and against the imperialist invader.

The resources of Britain cannot be utilised unless a great plan is undertaken which eliminates the waste and bureaucratic inefficiency of capitalism. The capitalist fifth column must be rendered completely impotent by the taking over of the banks, mines, land, railways and all big industries, without compensation and under control of the workers.

On a programme of socialism at home the masses of Britain could be mobilised for the death struggle against Nazism. But we must face the enemy with an unstained banner. British imperialism oppresses the masses in the colonies as viciously as Hitler does the people who are under his heel on the continent. Labour must immediately issue a declaration giving full self-determination to the peoples of the empire.

Then we could face the bombing planes and tanks of Hitler without fear of defeat. An appeal could be made to all the peoples of Europe, and especially those of Germany, to rally to our side. Hitler's support would crumble beneath his feet, and a mighty movement for liberation would spring up among the German soldiers and workers.

Only the slogans of genuine social and national liberation can find an echo among the oppressed masses of Europe. On this road alone can there be salvation for the working class.

The prospect of a British army advancing to the re-conquest of Europe under the rule of the imperialists after months and years of preparation opens up an endless vista of slaughter and destruction.

The choice before the working-class is clear. The road of Blum and Jouhaux led to the degradation and humiliation of the French masses, and their subjection to the Nazi exploiter. Attlee and Citrine are leading the British labour movement to the same disaster. Only a programme of socialism can save the workers of Britain and Europe.

But the sands of time are running out; action must be taken quickly. If the Labour leaders refuse to carry out this programme of socialism then they will be exposed to the masses as the traitors they are and it will be made clear that only the revolutionary socialists can lead the way forward to peace and socialism.

- Disarm the capitalists and arm the workers for the struggle against Nazism and the   capitalist fifth column at home.

- Take over the mines, banks, railways and big industry without compensation.

- Give freedom and self-determination to India and the colonies.

- Repeal all anti-working-class legislation.

- Appeal to the German, French and European workers to support the socialist struggle against Hitler.

LIFT THE 'DAILY WORKER' BAN!

COMRADES,

The "Daily Worker" has been suppressed. All workers irrespective of opinion must protest against this monstrous attack against working class liberties. We support the Communist Party in its protest because this is an attack on the working class as a whole and is the beginning of a period of savage repression to be opened against the workers of Britain. If it goes unchallenged it will mean the suppression not only of the Communist Party, but of the whole of the Left Wing of the workers' movement, including those sections of the Labour Party who raise a voice, however mild, against the policy of the Government in its attacks on the workers.

The Labour leaders claim that they are in the Government to wage a war against Hitlerism, yet they surrepticiously introduce measures of a totalitarian character at home. Nazism cannot be fought by such means and this policy can only end in the same disastrous consequences as did the policy of Blum, Jouhaux and Co. in France. The suppression of the Communist Party and other working class organisations in France was the necessary prelude to the capitulation of the French bourgeoisie to Hitler, and the setting up of the present caricature fascist regime in France. An essential safeguard against a repetition in Britain is the preservation of the rights of all working class organisations.

All left wing workers, whatever their differences, are threatened by this measure. This ban cannot be fought by linking it erroneously with the question of the " Peoples Government." The majority of the workers support the Labour leaders in the Government and if it is made clear to them that this is an attack on the rights of the whole of the working class, while not supporting the policy of the Communist Party, they could be won to the struggle of this specific issue. We appeal to the Communist Party members not to isolate themselves by a sectarian policy of making this an issue of support for the " Peoples Government ", but instead, to make an appeal for a united front of all workers' organisations on this issue of the defence of the democratic rights of the working class.

The Fourth International, although scurrilously attacked by the Communist Party, nevertheless is ready to stand shoulder to shoulder with the Communist Party in the fight against the repressive legislation of the ruling class.

FOR A UNITED FRONT OF ALL WORKING CLASS ORGANISATIONS IN THE DEFENCE OF DEMOCRATIC RIGHTS!
LIFT THE BAN ON THE " DAILY WORKER "!

Issued by " WORKERS INTERNATIONAL NEWS " (Trotskyist),
61 Northdown Street, London, N.1.

WIL leaflet opposing the January 1941 to September 1942 ban of the Communist Party newspaper, the *Daily Worker*, by Churchill's Labour Home Secretary, Herbert Morrison.

3 – The internal debate of WIL on revolutionary military policy [February-March 1941]

Introduction

The lead article published in *Youth For Socialism* and *Workers' International News* of February 1941 written by Andrew Scott on behalf of the EC Majority developed the approach already present in the July 1940 article by Ted Grant, reproducing the same slogans as a conclusion.

The approach towards the war provoked a differentiation within the leadership of the Workers' International League. The important change in the attitude of the WIL towards the war was a necessary step in the direction of the adoption and application in the conditions of Britain of Trotsky's "proletarian military policy". Different opinions arose within the EC of the WIL around the formulations contained in the articles that we reproduce in this section, and this provoked a sharp debate in the pages of the internal bulletin.

The debate was kicked off at the end of February by Millie Kahn and Sam Levy with a sharp criticism of the lead article of *Youth For Socialism*. This was soon followed by an article by Jock Haston that supported and developed the same line of argument. What these comrades feared was that the application of the military policy proposed by the EC Majority represented a capitulation to chauvinist pressure.

Although the documents reveal the tension of this debate and the arguments were raised in very sharp tones, we have to underline the extremely scrupulous attitude of the EC Majority in dealing with the arguments raised. Instead of weakening the cohesion of the WIL, this debate helped the organisation to grow politically and to develop an understanding of all the implications of the military policy.

The EC Majority around Ted Grant successfully argued their case, answering point by point the criticisms raised by the Minority, acknowledging some points where an agreement could be reached. In doing so, they managed to turn the League towards a successful intervention within the British army, forging an even greater degree of solidarity amongst the leading cadres of the organisation.

Arm the workers!
The only guarantee against Hitler's invasion

By Andrew Scott

[*Youth For Socialism*, Vol. 3 No. 4, February 1941]

Once more the campaigning season approaches. Spring is on its way, and the preparations of the rival imperialists for further redivisions of the earth are reaching fever pitch. Industrial production is being speeded up throughout the world; diplomacy is clearing roads for the advance of tanks, guns and soldiers; strategists are at work planning attacks, invasions, conquests.

The winter has been one of comparative military calm. It has been broken, certainly, by the nightly bombing of cities and by the advance of the British troops in Libya. But in spite of that it closely resembles the previous winter in the fact that there have been no major engagements between the British and German forces. It also resembles last winter in the fact that Germany has been making the same thorough preparations for attack, and the British leaders have been making almost exactly the same plans for defence.

A year ago, the Allied strategists sat comfortably behind their Maginot line waiting for Germany either to attack and batter itself to death against the "wall of steel" or to refrain from attacking and die an economic death through the blockade. Meantime, they were actually mad enough to make preparations to take on Russia too!

Today, the British generals are sitting comfortably behind their new Maginot line, the sea, boasting as they did a year ago that their defence is impregnable, and dreaming of their future invasion of the continent. How they are going to accomplish this with their maximum 4 million soldiers against the 10 million which the Berlin-Rome Axis has already trained and armed they do not reveal.

As the days pass, the similarity of the present position with that of a year ago becomes more pronounced. The principal preparation of the French ruling class for the alleged "war against Nazism" was the banning of working-class newspapers, the outlawing of the Communist Party, the Trotskyists, and other left wing groupings, the jailing of thousands of militants, the intensification of the exploitation of the workers.

Today in Britain, this process has already started, and the plans are ready for its extension on a gigantic scale. The *Daily Worker* has been banned and the next step will inevitably be the banning of the Communist Party. Then will follow the economic offensive against the workers' conditions and the arrest of every militant who protests. All the parties and groups of the left will be suppressed. The British ruling class, with the assistance of the Labour leaders, has set out on the road of totalitarian repression and there can be no going back for it.

In France the result of this method of "fighting Nazism" was that the German army simply walked into the country and took over Paris within a few days. The capitalists of France showed themselves more ready to fight the workers than to fight Hitler. The Labour and trade union leaders, who had actively supported the moves against the workers found themselves either in the dungeons of the Gestapo—or those of Pétain.

In Britain the results will be no different. The capitalist class is not fighting Hitler's fascism. They are only fighting his plans to relieve them of their Empire.

The only way in which Paris could have been defended and France saved from invading fascism was by the arming of the workers. Only an armed people, a nation in arms, could have held up Hitler's advance. If that had been done, then every town would have become a fortress, every village a tank trap, every house a front line trench. The masses would have rallied then to stop the advance of Hitler's machine. Willing hands would have been ready to make grenades and petrol bombs by the million and throw them under the tanks.

But the French capitalists dared not arm the workers. Certainly they armed that section which was under their own control—in the army. But to have armed the masses of the workers would have been to risk those arms being used against themselves. Rather surrender to Hitler, they thought, than take the risk of being defeated by the workers.

It was not the workers of France who left the way open for Hitler's advance. It was the Pétains and Weygands, who were more afraid of the workers having arms and control of them than they were of Hitler's conquering France. Until the very last moment they swore they would defend Paris street by street—only to hand it over intact to Hitler, together with a full police force to keep the workers in order.

The French ruling class revealed how lying were all their claims to be defending democracy against Hitler. The suppression of the workers, allegedly in the interests of conducting a struggle against Hitler led directly to his victory and to the possibility of the Pétain gang turning into agents of Hitler and imposing a [missing word] caricature of his regime on France.

So much for their love of democracy and freedom. Only the working class is willing to fight to the death against all forms of reaction both at home and abroad. As Bevin emphasised in a speech some months ago, the fifth column is not to be found among the workers—it is "higher up". But now Bevin finds himself supporting the "higher-ups" in their campaign against the alleged "fifth column" among the workers—a campaign which is in reality against the independence and rights of the entire working class.

Not by curtailing the power of the workers in the factory and the army—but by organising workers' control of industry and arms can [there] be a guarantee of victory not only over Hitler but over the fifth column gang of capitalists at home.

The workers of Britain must learn the lesson of France! Hitler is planning to invade this country just as he invaded France. The ruling class here has the same interests, the same fear of the workers, the same leaning towards fascism as the ruling class of France. And they are holding back arms and the control of arms from the workers in exactly the same way. They refuse to take the only step that can guarantee certain defeat for any attempt of Hitler to invade this country— the arming of the entire working class. The Home Guard, which they pretended for a time was a sort of arming of the nation, is being brought more and more under control of the chiefs of the regular army. Now that the Home Guard is to a certain extent armed, the government is bureaucratically imposing full-time officers from above. They must have complete control of all arms for their own purposes.

The workers of Britain support this war for the purpose of fighting fascism. But the ruling class will not allow them to do this. The ruling class is fighting German imperialist expansion—not fascism—and if in the course of the struggle it finds itself faced with the choice of defeat or the arming of the workers to avoid defeat, then it will choose defeat. For the arming of the workers would be the arming of the revolution, and that would be a hundred times more hateful to them than a Hitler victory.

Invasion is on the way. Yet we see the ruling class implacably refusing to arm and organise the working class in factories, streets and villages. This elementary measure would doom to extermination any force, however great, that Hitler might hurl against these islands. The easy victory of the *Panzer* divisions in France was made possible by the helplessness of the masses, unorganised and unarmed, who were compelled to flee in face of the Nazi advance.

An army can be destroyed, but it is impossible to fight a nation. Britain's island position, with a nation organised for resistance, would render any invasion threat ludicrous. Yet the ruling class has not armed and organised the workers for defence.

The Labour leaders have justified the terrible "sacrifices" made by the workers by the necessity of overthrowing the barbarism of the Nazis. Why have not the Labour leaders issued a call for the only measure which would not only paralyse any assault by Hitler, but would be a guarantee that "those in high places" with a hankering for Pétainism would be rendered completely powerless?

The working class is saturated through and through with a hatred of fascism. The arming of the workers would be a guarantee against any treacherous threat from within as well as from without. Yet the blind Labour leaders leave control to rest in the hands of those who would destroy them. The first need for a struggle against fascism is not even considered by the Labour leaders. The acid test for the bleatings of the ruling class that they are fighting Hitlerism, the acid test for the Labour leaders lies in this: are they prepared to organise, train and arm those who have always shown their unwavering determination to settle with Hitlerism forever?

The Labour leaders profess that they are eager to fight Hitler's fascism. But they do not press forward and fight for the only measures which can really defeat Nazism and really defend the "democracy" of the workers here. Bevin and company know all about the chaos in industry caused by capitalist anarchy and the struggle for profits, which is sabotaging production a million times more effectively than all the "agitators" in the country. But instead of struggling for workers' control, they are helping to increase capitalist control. They, as well as we, have seen the lesson of France—that the working class must be thoroughly armed and have control of those arms if Hitler is to be held up and defeated. But though they are willing to leave all the fighting to the workers, they are content to leave control in the hands of the ruling class. They claim to be leading a struggle for "democracy" but already the Statute Books of the government in which they are working are full of anti-working class, anti-democratic legislation which is already being used against the workers. They are fighting for the "rights of small nations". And yet they make no protest against the continued rule of Britain over a whole series of nations—small and large.

How can a real struggle against Hitler be waged under a banner so besmirched and tawdry? How can a genuine appeal be made to the masses of Europe to join in such a fake struggle. Their fear of another Versailles is great, and it is only when that fear is removed that they will feel free to turn their guns against Hitler and the German ruling class. Only the workers of Britain can free them of that fear. And they can only do that by turning the present imperialist brawl into a real struggle of the workers against Nazism.

Organised workers throughout the country must demand that the Labour leaders immediately wage a campaign for full power. They must take power on a programme which can mobilise the masses of Britain. The first point on that programme must be the arming of the workers against the threatened fascist invasion and against their capitalist enemy at home. Control of the army must be taken out of the hands of the reactionary officer class and put into those of the workers. The resources of the country, the land, mines, factories, railways, banks, etc. must be taken from the capitalists without compensation and controlled by the workers. The oppressed masses of India and the colonies must be freed. British imperialism grinds them under its heel as viciously as the Nazi jackboot tramples on the workers of the continent. Labour must give them full self-determination.

On such a programme of socialism the toilers of Britain could be mobilised for the struggle against Nazism. Hitler's bombers, his parachute troops, his sea-borne invaders would be beaten back by a nation which had not only arms but also something to fight for. And they could make a genuine appeal to the workers of Germany and all Europe to join them in the struggle against Hitler. The response to that appeal would be such as no appeal from Churchill can ever achieve. It would sweep Hitler into oblivion.

A victory for British imperialism in the war would be as harmful to the people of Europe and Britain as a Nazi victory itself. But how would this be obtained? Already the workers are being driven to incredible exertions and sacrifices while the big monopolies continue to pile up fabulous profits. The weariness and resentment of the masses when they see this contrast cannot but lead to explosions. In readiness for this, capitalism is making preparations to protect its profits.

The British capitalists did not want to fight Hitler; they only took up the cudgels regretfully when they found themselves compelled to safeguard their profits and empire. And already the thin end of the wedge of repression and dictatorship is being introduced even at a period when the capitalist class feel comparatively secure. But repression has a logic of its own. It cannot stop with the suppression of the *Daily Worker*. As the war proceeds the capitalists will turn more and more in a reactionary direction. A threat of overthrow from the workers—and they would call in Hitler tomorrow. The ruling clique of British bankers and generals are already preparing to install a reactionary dictatorship for Britain on the morrow. What they have in store for the continent has been hinted at by the Dean of St. Paul's. After the collapse of Germany, he has said, millions of British troops will have to hold down *all* Europe. The workers of Europe will have changed the yoke of Hitler for that of British imperialism.

But what will be happening at home? A continuation of what is already happening. Morrison is taking the road of Blum. He is sawing the very branch on which he is sitting. He is knocking away the very foundation on which he rests—the organised working class. Blum, too, was used by the French capitalists against the workers, and he attempted to justify himself by talking about "national unity". After he had helped to suppress the workers, he himself was put in jail by those with whom he had "national unity".

The victory of British imperialism would lead to fascism, not to its overthrow. There is only one road for the British working class. To fight Hitler we must take power into our own hands. The road of the Labour leaders is leading to destruction. If we do not wish to suffer the fate of our French comrades we must act in time.

We cannot fight Hitlerism under the control of the capitalist class. To attempt this is to make inevitable the victory either of Hitler or of some British Hitler. In order to wage a genuine revolutionary war for the liberation of the peoples of Europe and for the defence of the rights of the British working class, it is necessary that power should be in the hands of the workers.

The elementary immediate need for self-preservation demands that the workers should not be left helpless and unarmed in face of the coming Nazi onslaught. British "democracy" can be rendered impregnable against the attacks of Hitler or of a British Pétain if the working class is armed.

This is the only way for the masses. Any other way will lead to disaster. The road taken by Blum and Jouhaux led to catastrophe in France. Bevin and Morrison are at present leading the British workers at the same fearful position. If they refuse to carry out this programme of socialism they will be exposed to the masses as the same sort of traitors as their French counterparts, and it will be made clear that only the revolutionary socialists can lead the way to a future of socialism and peace.

Labour to power on the following programme:

- Disarm the capitalists and arm the workers for the struggle against Nazism and the capitalist fifth column at home.

- Take over the land, mines, factories, railways and banks without compensation.

- Give freedom and self-determination to India and the colonies.

- Repeal all anti-working class legislation.

- Appeal to the workers of Germany and all Europe to support the socialist struggle against Hitler.

Invasion: arm the workers!

By WIL EC Majority

[*Workers' International News*, Vol. 4 No. 2,
February 1941]

Germany has conquered Europe. The Channel bars her from the vista of adding Africa and Asia to the vast domains already conquered. But the German ruling class, no more than in the winter of last year, can afford to stand still. Despite the vast territorial conquests, they cannot say—"enough!" As thoroughly as they prepared the conquest of France, they are preparing to settle accounts with imperialist Britain which now bars the way. For the first time since 1066 the prospect of invasion has to be faced as a serious possibility. During the winter months the German military machine, as thorough and efficient as German industry, has been making its preparations down to the last detail. For Germany, a successful invasion of Britain would solve the immediate problems facing German imperialism. For British imperialism, of course, it is a question of fighting against being reduced to the position of another Poland from the previous heights of domination of half the world.

Under these conditions British imperialism is determined to resist to the very end. But the young brigand who so confidently and ruthlessly bludgeoned his way to overlordship of a great empire is now old and palsied. Basing itself on the profits gained from the exploitation of the colonial peoples the British ruling class has grown parasitic. There has been no incentive to greater efficiency and the improvement of industrial technique. This backwardness...[1]

The preparations which the British bourgeoisie is making to meet Hitler's invasion are little better than the preparations of Chamberlain and company last winter.

Their resistance will not be as feeble as that of the French bourgeoisie because of the advantages they possess—the morale of the people, an island position, a strong navy, etc. But as is now well known, the French ruling class surrendered not because it was impossible to defend the country, but because it was impossible to do so without placing the masses in a position, by arming them and mobilising, where they would not only have driven back the German

---

[1] Printing error; missing line in original.

invaders but could have easily ousted the French bourgeoisie as well. The spectre of the Commune hung over France in the days of June.

Churchill and the British capitalist class "sympathised" with the painful dilemma in which the French rulers were placed. They had no objection to Reynaud, Pétain, Weygand and company sending the French workers to the school of Hitler to teach them a lesson in obedience.

This was made quite clear by the fact that they were quite prepared to see the surrender of all France: all they demanded was that the French fleet should either be placed at their disposal or remain in a neutral port.

The howls that the whole of the British press set up against the traitors who had sold France into bondage were merely rage at the failure of this gang to come over to the side of British imperialism. The spurious indignation had its cause in this and this alone.

Although Churchill and the British bourgeoisie generally knew well the character of the Weygands and Pétains, they praised them to the end. How spurious was their rage is shown by their recent manoeuvres. Owing to the unexpected resistance of Britain the Vichy crew have had the possibility of manoeuvring for concessions between Hitler and the British government.

The spread of the war to the Mediterranean lends importance to the French ports, and the French fleet would be of great assistance in Germany's invasion plans. This allows the prostituted French capitalism to raise its fee to the German customer.

But the British ruling class is not above vieing with the Germans for the favours of Pétain. Forgotten are the recriminations. Pétain is no longer a traitor, but once more the "grand old man" of France. They are prepared to "overlook" the placing of the whole French nation into bondage to Hitler and the transformation of unoccupied France into a feeble imitation of Nazi Germany, with democracy officially declared dead. Churchill and company fawn upon this repulsive clique who have demonstrated before the eyes of the whole world that "democracy", "liberty", etc. at any rate have no place in their scheme of things.

As if to underline the hollow nature of the pretence that this is a war for the destruction of fascism, we have the appeal of Churchill to the ruling class of Italy to throw Mussolini overboard as a scapegoat and come over to the side of England. This single act of atonement would mean the ignoring of the crimes of Italian fascism which the British capitalists are willing to accept with equanimity since it serves their purpose. The fact that the Italian ruling class, and probably those of France and Spain, will be compelled to support Germany, will at a later stage lead to the revival of propaganda about the actual horrors and bestialities which fascism has perpetrated. The press, pulpit, wireless, etc. will be beside themselves with rage when cataloguing the crimes of the dictator and slave states.

But Churchill and the ruling class have revealed that they are anxious to do a deal with any fascist gang—on the terms of British ruling class supremacy. It is the fascist gangs which have refused the outstretched hand of friendship. In the case of Greece, this is clearly demonstrated by the attitude adopted to the regime of Metaxas which is as bloody and repressive as any to be found in Eastern Europe. We can look in vain in the columns of the British press or the speeches of the politicians, including the Labour leaders, for any remonstrance at the crimes of the Greek dictatorship.

The inevitable active intervention of American imperialism in the war—the war has resolved itself mainly into a conflict between Germany and America for world supremacy—forces the Germans to make haste. If Britain can hold out long enough, the inexhaustible resources of the American continent can be organised to build a military machine which will outstrip even the gargantuan efforts of Nazi Germany. But what is required for this is time: 12 to 24 months or so. This makes an invasion attempt to crush the British Isles even more urgent for German imperialism.

Everything is at stake for the British capitalists. The Empire, the very existence of Britain as a world power is placed in the balance. The British capitalist class is making as hurried and frantic preparations for resistance as it possibly can. We will suffer the fate of a modern Carthage if we are beaten—is their agonised appeal for resistance.

This is true. The fate of Ireland haunts the imagination of the British bourgeoisie. Ireland which was systematically despoiled and plundered and converted into an agricultural colony in the interests of British imperialism in the last century; Ireland where they deliberately organised famine and forced the emigration of a great part of the population—America has 20 million Irishmen, Eire only 3 million. It is the impossibility of reconciling the interests of British capitalism with those of German capitalism which compels that "fight to a finish" into which the war is resolving itself. For British imperialism there has been no other choice except that of acting as satellite of her mightier rival across the Atlantic.

But despite the tremendous jeopardy in which they are being placed—the speech of Hitler in which he boasted of the thorough preparations of the German army has probably a solid foundation—we see the British capitalist class refusing to take the one course which would doom any invasion, however formidable, to inevitable futility and defeat: the arming, mobilising, and organising of the entire working class for resistance, factory by factory, street by street, house by house.

No more than the French ruling class dare the ruling class of Britain place the working class in position where it would be possible for them to play an independent role. A thousand times rather accept the possibility of Hitler occupying Britain than risk a workers' revolution by arming the workers is the dominating thought of the ruling clique.

Nevertheless, in defending their imperialist loot they are compelled to appeal to the antifascist sentiments of the masses. The overwhelming majority of the working class hate fascism and do not wish to be placed under the heel of Hitler. They do not wish to be in the position of Poland, France, Holland and the other countries under the Nazi jackboot. This is the sentiment which the ruling class is using for its own ends.

Under these circumstances the position of the Labour leaders is quite clear. Utilising the hatred of the masses for Hitlerism, they have betrayed the interests of the workers by entering the government and justifying all attacks on the workers by the necessities of the conflict. But in spite of these attacks the working class for the time being continues to stand, albeit critically, behind their leaders.

By itself, all the propaganda in the world explaining the real aims of the ruling class could not move the working class one inch from this position. It is on this rock that the Communist Party has at the present time shattered itself. The working class, especially after the events of the last months is determined to resist to the uttermost any incursion from Nazi Germany.

This attitude of the masses must be the point of departure from our propaganda. The way to win them over is not by the sterile repetition of the Marxian axiom that only the socialist revolution can solve the problems of the working class. It is to convince the masses of this by their day to day experiences. The main task of the revolutionary socialist is to separate the workers from their leaders who place them behind the capitalists. This can only be done by showing them the absolute contradiction between their interests and those of their mortal enemy.

Taking the argument of the capitalists that every resource must be exploited in order to vanquish the coming invasion, we must emphasise that the capitalists have a greater hatred and fear of the working masses at home than of their imperialist enemy abroad. The damning fact stands out that the only advice given by the government as to any action to be taken by the broad masses in the event of invasion is to "stay put". This despite the experience of France where the terrified and helpless civilians materially assisted the Nazi invaders in their advance. This decisive fact must be burned into the consciousness of the masses.

The Labour leaders have used this antifascist sentiment of the masses to enter into a coalition with the capitalists in order to "wage war against Hitlerism." But the elementary precautions which would guarantee victory over a fascist invasion from abroad or a coup like that of Pétain at home are not being advocated or prepared by the Labour leaders. Taking them at their word, we demand that they immediately struggle for the putting into operation of the following measures: the arming and organising of the workers under their own control; the election of officers by the workers; control of production by the workers to end the chaos in the war industries; the immediate nationalisation of the armament industry, mines, banks, railways, and big industry; the granting of freedom and self-determination to India and the colonies; socialist appeal to the workers of Germany and Europe.

Only by measures such as these can the country really be defended in the interests of the masses. Launching a campaign on a programme of demands as outlined above cannot but get the Labour leaders the overwhelming support of the masses. The alternative policy is that of capitulation to British imperialism which is not in the least interested in the struggle against fascism, and which cannot but lead either to a victory for Hitler or that of a British Hitler.

We see steps in the direction of reaction being taken at the present time. Bevin as Minister of Labour, under the pressure of the bourgeoisie, has introduced the militarisation of labour, which works to the benefit of the bourgeoisie only as they draw colossal super profits at the expense of the workers. Morrison has introduced compulsory fire-fighting, and again the main burden is borne by the toilers. The rationing, high prices, etc. place the whole burden of the war on the shoulders of the workers and lower strata of the middle class. Naturally the masses, although passive at first through fear of doing anything that might aid Hitler, will sooner or later react violently against these monstrous impositions on the part of the ruling class.

If power continues to rest in the hands of the capitalists they will wage not a war against fascism but one in defence of their profits, a war waged with even greater ferocity against the workers than against their capitalist enemy. If capitalist control is to continue it must mean the speedy extension of the totalitarian methods, which can only end in a complete obliteration of all the rights of the working class. The suppression of the *Daily Worker* is the first significant step in this direction. It marks the twilight of bourgeois democracy in Britain. The methods of the Labour leaders in fighting "Hitlerism" lead directly to the destruction of the organisations of the working class and to concentration camps.

Nevertheless, the bourgeoisie has to move cautiously. Without the support of the Labour leaders they could not carry through such measures. But the Labour leaders themselves are in a contradictory position. They cannot destroy the foundations on which they rest without destroying themselves. British totalitarianism has not a solid foundation. While the trade unions, and especially the shop stewards, etc. continue to exist it is impossible to carry through anything but a military dictatorship. There is no mass support to back up anything else. With a big percentage of the workers called up in the army, and the main mass of the army stationed in Britain and in contact with the civil population, the army is in closer contact with the toilers than at any time in history. The big bourgeoisie, even more than in the last war, is dependent on the services of the Labour leaders to keep the masses in check. They rest primarily on the acceptance by the masses of the yoke of privations as an inescapable necessity in the cause of the "destruction of Hitlerism". The British bourgeoisie rules much more by deception than by force. Without the Labour bureaucracy they would be in a precarious position. The entire stock-in-trade of the Labour bureaucracy consists in the "fight against Hitlerism at all costs."

The road to the masses lies in showing them a real alternative, a genuine struggle against the danger of a victory of Hitlerism from abroad and at home. Accepting the argument of the Labour leaders that it is necessary to fight Hitlerism, we must point out that it is impossible to do this under the leadership of the capitalist class which must inevitably lead to the victory of Hitler or of a British Hitler or Pétain. The ground can be cut from under the feet of the Labour leaders by demanding that they take power on the programme of demands listed above. First on that list must come the arming of the workers against Hitler and the capitalist fifth column at home.

Accepting the coalition with the bourgeoisie leads the Labour bureaucracy naturally to the imposition of repression to force the masses to accept the privations which this involves. The position in which Blum, Johaux and company found themselves in France was almost identical. But suppression leads naturally to an enhancing of the power of the capitalist clique of bankers and generals. Blum helped to suppress the workers in the "sacred" cause of anti-fascism—only to find himself unceremoniously pitched into jail by his colleagues of yesterday who, incidentally, embraced the Nazis in the same act. Morrison-Bevin, despite tremors of anticipation (the speech in which Bevin denied that there could be a fifth column among the workers and asserted that it always came from the "higher-ups") are compelled by the inexorable logic of events to travel the same road as their French brethren. Collaboration with the capitalist class cannot mean anything else. This is the fatal path against which we must warn the workers. Hitlerism cannot be fought by a cowardly attempt to use homeopathic doses of Hitlerism at home. Moreover, once started, it would require bigger and bigger doses of the same medicine to keep the masses in check. If repression must be used, let it be used by the workers against the root of all Hitlerism and fifth columnism—big finance and big business.

Nevertheless, it is significant that the suppression of the *Daily Worker*, a preparation for the coming invasion and an onslaught on the working class, has been accepted by the masses of the workers, if not enthusiastically then passively. Morrison's whole argument was the accusation that the *Daily Worker* helped Hitler by the propaganda which it put forward.

This charge could not but meet with acquiescence by the masses owing to the propaganda developed by the Communist Party in the last few years. First the demand for a capitalist popular front government (Churchill, Attlee, Sinclair) to "stand up to Hitler". Then actual support for the war. Then "stop the war" on terms which would have meant victory for German imperialism. And now the vague, ambiguous "people's government" and "people's peace" which are meaningless to the main mass of the workers, who continue to support the Labour leaders. Previously they deceived the workers into believing that fascism could be fought under the leadership of a capitalist (popular front) government. Now they have no programme for the workers on how to fight invading fascism—or for that matter, fascism at home; the two problems are not separate but identical and simultaneous.

Now that the *Worker* is suppressed we find the Communist Party, in a desperate attempt to rally the workers, compelled to appeal for support on a caricature of the policy outlined above. There cannot be any other policy which would have the slightest hope of securing the support of the masses in their present mood. But the Communist Party appeals in a way which cannot lead to an independent mobilisation of the workers round their own programme and their own banner. It is of absolute significance that the slogan of the arming of the workers, which was put forward for an incautious fortnight last June by the *Daily Worker*, has never been revived in any form whatever. This demand is an elementary and fundamental one which goes right to the heart of the needs of the masses, especially with invasion but a few weeks or months ahead. The Communist Party leadership always sows demoralisation and confusion within the ranks of the working class.

With the programme of demands outlined above, the revolutionary socialists can raise the question of power in a way which can be easily understood and welcomed by the masses. The problem of a genuine revolutionary war against Hitlerism, which can only be solved by the working class conquest of power, will then appear in its correct perspective, as the only programme of salvation for our epoch. The Fourth International alone has such a banner and such a programme. Once they adopt it the masses will be unconquerable. For the struggle against Hitlerism only socialism can suffice!

"SUNDAY DISPATCH"

THEN ——— and ——— NOW

" The passionate sincerity of Hitler cried aloud. This was no cheap tub-thumping political firebrand, but a fervent patriot and a realist. . . ."

" It is monstrously untrue to say that the Storm Troops and Brown Shirts are a new German army in disguise. Germany does not want another war. . . ."

SUNDAY DISPATCH, 1933.

" The sort of Government which the Trotskyists would like to follow the present regime here, not only would not open a second front, but under the guise of alleged Left-Wing pacifism, would seek a compromise peace."

SUNDAY DISPATCH, 1942.

TROTSKYISM

THEN ——— and ——— NOW

"HITLER IS CHANCELLOR!
Workers, do you know what that means? It means complete starvation and loss of all rights, it means the destruction of all the active elements of the proletariat! After the speeches of the Nazi leader, there can be no doubt of this. HITLER'S PROGRAMME IS THE COMPLETE SMASHING OF ALL THE POLITICAL AND TRADE UNION ORGANISATIONS OF THE WORKING CLASS, to clear the way for a still more monstrous impoverishment of the working class. The aim of his foreign policy is WAR WITH SOVIET RUSSIA."

Manifesto of German Trotskyists, 1933.

"The only way in which the struggle against fascism can be successfully waged would be by taking the control of the army and industry by the working class. . . . If necessary, a Second Front would be established by the British workers to aid the German workers in over-throwing Hitler and giving real aid to the Soviet Union. . . ."

SOCIALIST APPEAL, 1942.

Socialist Appeal answers attacks by *Sunday Dispatch*, 1942

A reply to the lead article in *Youth For Socialism*, February issue, 1941

The interpretation of the EC majority

By Sam Levy and Millie Kahn

[WIL, *Internal Bulletin*, February 28 1941]

The article *Arm the workers—the only guarantee against Hitler's invasion* which is put forward as the Majority of the EC's interpretation of the military policy of the Fourth International, we consider to be incorrect in its emphasis and its glaring omissions, and an interpretation which cannot enhance the development of our group and indeed, serve to damage it.

On close examination of the article it is clear that the theme running through it is a mechanical identification of the French situation during the period of threatened invasion with the situation as exists in Britain today, both politically and militarily. This winter resembles last winter insofar as there have been no major engagements between Germany and Britain; Germany has been making the same thorough preparations for attack as the British have for defence; a year ago Allied strategists sat comfortably behind their Maginot line—today the British generals are sitting comfortably behind their new Maginot line, the sea; last year the repression against working class organisations in France commenced—today in Britain this process has started; in France the result of this method of "fighting Nazism" was that the German army simply walked into the country and took over Paris—in Britain the results will be no different; the French bourgeoisie capitulated to Hitler for fear of the workers—the British rulers have the same fear of the workers, they will do the same; the only guarantee for the defence of France would have been the arming of the workers—the only guarantee for the defence of Britain is the arming of the British workers.

Without going into the superficiality of the above in detail, we have tabled the outline of the article in order to show the mechanical foundation on which it is based. We propose therefore, to deal briefly with the background of the two countries as the necessary prerequisite to an understanding of the present situation in Britain. While France was, at that period, of the same basic political system—decadent bourgeois democracy—due to economic, political and national factors, her tempo of development was at a different stage, which necessitates a clear analysis of the demarcation between the British and French situations.

France

The French capitalist system of bourgeois democracy, with its relatively backward economy, was rapidly on the decline, a decline which was accelerated by the war. The general strikes of 1936 indicated that the French masses had taken the road of social revolution. The country was placed in a revolutionary situation, a situation which, as we know, was checked by the deliberate mis-leadership of the Communist and Socialist parties. The advent of the Popular Front acted as a brake on the further advancement of the French masses and a period of disintegration set in. By 1938 the masses were demoralised. The semi-Bonapartist regime of Daladier assumed power and the whole period following was analogous to the pre-Hitler period in Germany, that is the regimes of Bruning, Schleicher, von Papen. But the "war for democracy" (and the subsequent victory of Hitler) completely destroyed the French fascist organisations, thus leaving the French bourgeoisie in a precarious position insofar as they could not build up a French regime equivalent to Hitler's.

The attitude of the French masses to the war was apathetic in the defeatist sense due to the unprecedented lowering of the standards of life (the soldiers were receiving 1d[1] per day); they were fully conscious of the rottenness of their own bourgeoisie (they were still smarting under the defeats of 1936-38); the putrefaction of the army leadership was rapidly exposing itself. But there was no revolutionary leadership; the Socialist and Stalinist parties had betrayed them; the voice of the Fourth International, the only one which held the key to the situation, was too weak to have any effect.

One section of the bourgeoisie (Laval and company) went directly over to Hitler in the early period, and even before the outbreak of war. The Reynaud section, conscious of the fact that the masses were not behind them, hoped that they would last out long enough to place the French masses under the heel of American-British imperialism. But the sweeping victories of Hitler upset the

---

[1] Prior to decimalisation, the pound was divided into 20 shillings and each shilling into 12 pence, making 240 pence to the pound. The symbol for the shilling was "s"—not from the first letter of the word, but from the Latin *solidus*. The symbol for the penny was "d", from the French *denier*, from the Latin *denarius*. A mixed sum of shillings and pence such as 3 shillings and 6 pence was written as "3/6" or "3s 6d" and spoken as "three and six". 5 shillings was written as "5s" or "5/-".

applecart. After Reynaud's declaration that Paris would be defended "street by street", the French bourgeoisie, faced with the prospect of arming the Parisian proletariat who, together with a section of the army would have constituted a threat to their power and conducted a revolutionary war against Hitler, preferred to capitulate to Hitler. To understand the lesson of Pétain, to explain "Pétainism" we demonstrate this classic example of the defeatist character of the bourgeoisie (including Hitler) if it fears its working class at home.

England

Let us now compare the situation as it existed in France with that of present day England. Though on the decline, Britain is economically far stronger than France due to her mighty empire and the fact that she is predominantly an industrial country, over 66 percent of her population being proletarian. As distinct from the French masses, the British workers are not yet disillusioned with their own bourgeoisie and their labour leaders due to their past privileged economic position. Consequently the British masses are relatively far more backward politically than their French brothers. Of recent years they have not gone through a revolutionary period, or any form of mass strivings comparable to the French 1936-38 character. The "popular front" passed completely over the head of the British working class precisely because of the comparative economic stability of British capitalism.

Although the war has accelerated the political development of the working class by the rising cost of living, lengthening of working hours, wartime racketeering, industrial conscription, and the gradual filching of democratic rights, etc., this will not reach any proportions of mass opposition for some time—certainly not during the invasion period, or some little time following it. At the present moment we can say with regard to the question of war, the British masses, as distinct from the French, are apathetic in the defencist sense, insofar as they [see] no other alternative.

Throughout the article which purports to utilise the French experience there is no analysis of the differences in the situation in Britain today with that which existed in France, politically and economically, and which was the primary cause for the capitulation of the French bourgeoisie. The British bourgeoisie do not fear the working class in the present period. We cannot expect a turning of the masses to the left immediately. The proposition that faces the British bourgeoisie, therefore in the event of a successful German invasion is not—Hitler, i.e. German imperialism or Social revolution—but, Hitler or American imperialism, with more benefits accruing from America since Britain would be permitted to retain at least a large section of her Empire. Britain has already chosen the latter, and accepting the fact that a section of the bourgeoisie will back Hitler, as they are doing even today, in the event of a successful invasion Whitehall will be transferred to the White House. Arrangements have already been made for the transference of the British Navy to the USA. As we have so often repeated in our publications, Britain is rapidly being reduced to the status of "49th state of the USA." America is sending increasing amounts of war material to this country, even at the expense of her own defence, for she regards the British Isles as her front line. Britain in her turn, is dependent on aid from the USA for her very existence.

"Hitler" has become such a bogey that the role of American imperialism in relation to Britain is completely ignored. This is especially lacking in view of the recent visits of Willkie and Hopkins to evaluate the sincerity of the British bourgeoisie in the continuation of the struggle and the relations of Labour to the war. These emissaries of Wall Street were apparently satisfied that the British workers were not red and that the dominant section of the British bourgeoisie, headed by Churchill, are determined to continue the struggle against Hitler, firstly because they do not fear their own working class at the present stage, and secondly, because Hitler constitutes the immediate threat to their imperialist interests. This is no "fake" struggle, but is a struggle which will only be concluded after the wholesale destruction of millions of workers.

The only guarantee

The political proposition "Arm the workers—the only guarantee against Hitler's invasion" is incorrectly posed, flowing as it does from a military supposition, namely, that the British military machine is incapable of defeating a German invasion. What will happen to this argument if the British bourgeoisie, with American aid, *does* succeed in stemming an invasion, which possibility, although not guaranteed, at least cannot be excluded, and which Wall Street now seems to think it has a good chance of doing. Yet this hypothesis is implicit in the whole presentation of the question. For example:

> "In France the result of this method [suppression of workers] of 'fighting Nazism' was that the German army simply walked into the country and took over Paris within a few days. The capitalists of France showed themselves more ready to fight the workers than to fight Hitler. The Labour and trade union leaders, who had actively supported the moves against the workers, found themselves either in the dungeons of the Gestapo—or those of Pétain.

> "*In Britain the results will be no different.* The capitalist class is not fighting Hitler's fascism. They are only fighting his plans to relieve them of their Empire." (Our emphasis)

What is meant by "In Britain the results will be no different" if not that the British workers will lead, as it did in France, to the German army simply walking in and taking ever London? Totalitarian methods are being introduced precisely in order the better to face up to the German totalitarian war machine, and the adoption of those methods does not automatically lead to the inevitable defeat of British imperialism.

> "The elementary immediate need for self-preservation demands that the workers should not be left helpless and unarmed in face of the coming Nazi onslaught. British 'democracy' can be rendered impregnable against the attacks of Hitler or of a British Pétain if the working class is armed."

The posing of the question in this way presupposes the inevitable defeat, i.e. Hitler or a British Pétain.

We of course support the slogan "Arm the workers" but let us not confuse the working class by categorically stating that without the arming of the workers the British bourgeoisie is incapable of stemming the invasion of Hitler, as the title of the article does. Faced with the threat of invasion, as distinct from the way in which the *Youth* article reacts, i.e. "Invasion: arm the workers—the only guarantee against Hitler's invasion", we pose the question from a class angle, i.e. "Invasion: arm the workers under workers' control—the only guarantee for the defence of workers' democratic rights!" In other words, we approach the question from the interests of the working class and not from the angle of Wintringham[2]. The hypothesis of one comrade or another as to the fluctuating military potentialities of this or that imperialist army, while important as a means to present the relative transitional demand, must not be allowed to form the axis of our political slogans as exemplified in "Arm the workers—the only guarantee against Hitler's invasion".

While the article is based on the supposition that Britain cannot stem a German invasion, it has artificially grafted on it, the theoretical possibility, not merely of stemming the invasion but of an actual British victory! A possibility which appears somewhat incongruous side by side with the proposition of certain defeat by Hitler unless the workers are armed.

> "A victory for British imperialism in the war would be as harmful to the people of Europe and Britain as a Nazi victory itself. But how would this be obtained? Already the workers are being driven to incredible exertions and sacrifices while the big monopolies continue to pile up fabulous profits. The weariness and resentment of the masses when they see this contrast cannot but lead to explosions. In readiness for this, capitalism is making preparations to protect its profits."

---

[2] Thomas Henry Wintringham (1898 – 1949) joined the Communist Party of Great Britain in 1923. In 1925 he was one of twelve CPGB officers imprisoned for seditious activities in the army. In 1930 he founded the *Daily Worker* and was regarded as the expert on military matters of the CPGB. He was an important figure in the formation of the Home Guard during the Second World War, broke with the CP in 1938 and was one of the founders of the Common Wealth Party.

"What they have in store for the continent has been hinted at by the Dean of St. Paul's. After the collapse of Germany, he has said, millions of British troops will have to hold down all Europe. The workers of Europe will have changed the yoke of Hitler for that of British imperialism."

To prove that this proposition is not seriously considered we quote from the beginning of the same article:

"Today the British generals are sitting comfortably behind their new Maginot line, the sea, boasting as they did a year ago that their defence is impregnable, and dreaming of their future invasion of the continent. How they are going to accomplish this with their maximum 4 million soldiers against 10 million which the Berlin-Rome Axis has already trained and armed they do not reveal."

Let us examine another paragraph where the contradiction is glaring:

"The victory of British imperialism would lead to fascism not to its overthrow. There is only one road for the British working class. To fight Hitler we must take power into our own hands. The road of the Labour leaders is leading to destruction. If we do not wish to suffer the fate of our French comrades we must act in time."

In this paragraph alone is contained the following:

1) The possibility of victory for British imperialism.

2) The impossibility of victory for British imperialism.

3) The confusing of the question of stemming an invasion and the possibility of a British military victory over Germany.

4) Even when posing the question of a British victory which "would lead to fascism", the conclusion drawn is how to fight Hitler!

"Hitlerism"

Throughout, the article brings Hitler forward as the chief bugbear. The conclusions a reader could draw from it is that Hitler fascism is the main enemy of the British working class due to the threat of imminent invasion. Immediately after the capitulation of France, comrade Trotsky wrote:

"Hitler, the conqueror, has naturally day-dreams of becoming the chief executioner of the proletarian revolution in any part of Europe. But that does not at all mean that Hitler will be strong enough to deal with the proletarian revolution as he has been able to deal with imperialist democracy. It would be a fatal blunder, unworthy of a revolutionary party, to turn Hitler into a fetish, to exaggerate his power, to overlook the objective limits of his success and conquests. Hitler boastfully promises to establish the domination of the German people, at the expense of all

Europe and even of the whole world, 'for one thousand years'. But in all likelihood, this splendour will not endure even for ten years."

Comrade Trotsky was addressing himself to those comrades who depicted the coming of Hitler as the end of everything and seeing before them just a blank wall with no perspective. We believe that the article reflects this "fetishism" by its whole presentation. In order to justify this "fetishism", the majority characterise the mood of the masses as "we must at all costs fight and destroy Hitler." We disagree with this characterisation, but assuming it is correct, how does it fit in with the mood of the German masses which is anti-Churchill since he is the arch-representative of that imperialism which imposed the infamous Versailles treaty on the German people—and as they are fully aware, is preparing an even [more] infamous one in the event of a British victory.

Flowing from the article our traditional international appeal to the European working class is cast aside for an appeal to support the socialist struggle against Hitler. We consider that this slogan should have read: "Appeal to the workers of Europe and Germany for peace on the basis of the united socialist states of Europe." This would throw the onus for the continuation of the war onto Hitler and reveal to the German masses their enemy at home.

Similarly we take exception to the slogan: "Disarm the capitalists and arm the workers for the struggle against Nazism and the capitalist fifth column at home." While correctly pointing to the necessity of disarming the capitalists and arming the workers, the slogan, like the title of the article, does not mention under whose control the workers must be armed.

The second part of the slogan: "against Nazism and the capitalist fifth column at home", in the one hand is confusing since in the accepted sense of the term "fifth columnist" means the agent of the external enemy. On the other hand, if the *whole* of the British bourgeoisie is implied—are we to understand that the whole of the bourgeoisie is willing to sell out to Hitler? But most disturbing is the posing of the main enemy as the foreign one. This slogan should have read: "Disarm the capitalists and dissolve the Home Guard into workers' militia under workers' control. Trade union control of the army for the struggle against totalitarian oppression at home and abroad."

Defence of workers' democratic rights

With the coming of the Second World War, the process of decay of bourgeois democracy is accelerated. On the actual outbreak of the war, its death knell is already being sounded. In the present epoch of totalitarian war the luxury of "democracy" must be discarded by the bourgeoisie in order to face the totalitarian war machine of the adversary. Inevitably bourgeois democracy must eliminate its overhead expenses, i.e. the democratic rights of the workers, trade unions, the relatively high standard of living—all these must go. Totalitarianism can only be fought by totalitarianism.

In the forefront of our programme comes the fight for the democratic rights of the working class in the present period. These become revolutionary demands and assume tremendous importance in our transitional slogans. In the last two great remaining "democracies" the rights of the workers are being filched from them.

While these rights are threatened by a Hitler invasion, the immediate threat to the British working class comes directly from within. In the defence of democracy against "Hitlerism", the British bourgeoisie is rapidly destroying these very rights which we are supposed to be defending. Comrade Trotsky posed the question clearly in his last letters:

> "But we categorically refuse to defend civil liberties and democracy in the French manner; the workers and farmers to give their flesh and blood while the capitalists concentrate in their hands the command. The Pétain experiment should now form the centre of our war propaganda. It is important, of course, to explain to the advanced workers that the genuine fight against fascism is the socialist revolution. But it is more urgent, more imperative to explain to the millions of American workers that the defence of their 'democracy', cannot be delivered over to an American Marshall Pétain—and there are many candidates to such a role."

Again, comrade Trotsky under the title *Profound importance of French events*, wrote:

> "We must use the example of France to the very end. We must say, 'I warn you workers, that they (the bourgeoisie) will betray you! Look at Pétain, who is a friend of Hitler. Shall we have the same thing happening in this country? We must create our own machine, under workers' control.' We must be careful not to identify ourselves with the chauvinists, nor with the confused sentiments of self-preservation, but we must understand their feelings and adapt ourselves to these feelings critically, and prepare the masses for a better understanding of the situation, otherwise we will remain a sect, of which the pacifist variety is the most miserable."

In other words, we must defend our democratic rights, we are willing to give our flesh and blood for that which we find worth defending, *but we must be in command.* Our existing democracy must be defended and broadened into the army, etc., thus linking it up with full workers' democracy, i.e. the proletarian dictatorship. Now lot us examine how the article in *Youth* deals with the question:

> "The elementary need for self-preservation demands that the workers should not be left helpless and unarmed in the face of the coming Nazi onslaught. British 'democracy' can be rendered impregnable against

the attacks of Hitler or of a British Pétain if the working class is armed."

Is this adapting ourselves to the feelings of the masses critically? Is this preparing the masses for a better understanding of the situation? We say no, just the opposite. What is the meaning of "British 'democracy' can be rendered impregnable"? Does it mean decaying British bourgeois democracy—and since when are we prepared to render "British 'democracy' " impregnable against attacks? We presume that the above bases itself on the statements of comrade Trotsky on the defence of *workers' democracy*. But Trotsky is advocating that the only means of the working class defending their democratic rights is by taking control, by taking command in their own hands. Merely calling for arms for the workers as the elementary need for their self-preservation is to fall into these very errors against which Trotsky warns.

What the article omits: the military policy

Only the masses can take power and establish a socialist system, and in the present period the masses *in the military organisations* are destined to play the decisive role. The bourgeoisie are arming the masses—in their own way of course—to defend their imperialist interests. Already over three million are in the armed forces; two million are in the Home Guard; the age limit is being raised to 50 and lowered to 18—limits which in the last war were just being reached at the end of 1918; Bevin had declared that he hoped to call up a further million by raising the age limit in reserved occupations; working women are being mobilised and conscripted into the factories, just as in Germany. In other words, bourgeois democracy is giving way to the universal epoch of militarisation of the masses. The workers are being armed by the bourgeoisie. The military policy of the Fourth International is based on this historic fact—the universal militarisation of the proletariat—and not, as is implied in the article—on the withholding of arms from the workers.

While we naturally support the slogan "arms to the workers" the mechanical reiteration of this slogan in itself is not enough. The whole problem which poses itself before us is one of *control.*

Under the slogan "arm the workers" must flow a policy for the widening of the Home Guard from its present narrow reactionary basis under the Colonel Binghams, from its present composition of petty bourgeois, backward workers— we must demand its dissolution into workers' militia to include all sections of workers of both sexes. Where women are being conscripted to replace men in industry and indeed in every sphere of civil life, we must pose before them the necessity of demanding their incorporation in the workers' militias for the defence of their democratic rights—arms in hands—against whosoever attempted to destroy them.

A political position is determined by what is omitted as well as by what is stated. This article was put forward as the military policy yet so important a propaganda weapon as the Colonel Bingham affair[3], which could have served as a key point in exposing the utter reactionary and anti-working class nature of the existing officer caste and drawing the lesson of the French defeat from this, that is the necessity for workers' control in the armed forces, was not even mentioned in the article or in the whole issue of *Youth* for that matter.

The article misses the whole essence of the basis on which the military policy was developed by the American section—that is the present period of universal militarisation. Instead of posing a bold and clear policy for the armed workers it contents itself with moaning about the unwillingness of the British bourgeoisie to arm the workers against Hitler, to leave them helpless; etc. Where is our programme for the 4,000,000 soldiers *already under arms*, already trained and equipped in the arts of modern warfare? The entire personnel of our group, barring perhaps the women will soon be in the existing capitalist military organisations. Already many of our comrades are in the forces, selling our papers, *to workers in arms*. What policy does the article pose before them?

Let us give a few quotes to prove our contention that the article bases itself, not on the universal militarisation, but on the premise that the bourgeois are withholding arms from the masses.

"And they are holding back arms and control of arms from the workers in exactly the same way...

"For the arming of the workers would be the arming of the revolution...

"Yet we see the ruling class implacably refusing to arm and organise the working class in factories, streets and villages...

"Yet the ruling class has not armed and organised the workers for defence.

"The arming of the workers would be a guarantee against any treacherous threat from within as wall as from without...

"The first point in that programme must be the arming of the workers against the threat of fascist invasion...

"The elementary immediate need for self preservation demands that the workers should not be left helpless and unarmed in face of the com-

---

3 On January 15 1941 the *Times* published a letter from Lieutenant-Colonel R.C. Bingham. In it Bingham lamented that so many middle and lower class applicants were being granted access to officer training; these elements, Bingham argued, lacked the necessary *noblesse oblige* and the good breeding necessary to take charge of commanding troops. As a result of the protest letters and public outrage Bingham was dismissed from service.

ing onslaught. British 'democracy' can be rendered impregnable against the attacks of a British Pétain if the working class is armed...

"The working class is saturated through and through with a hatred of fascism. The arming of the workers would be a guarantee against any treacherous threat from within as well from without. Yet the blind labour leaders allow control to rest in the hands of those who would destroy them. The first need for the struggle against fascism is not even considered by the labour leaders. The acid test for the bleating of the ruling class that they are fighting Hitlerism, the acid test for the labour leaders is this: are they prepared to organise, train and arm those who have always shown their unwavering determination to settle with Hitlerism forever?"

To this we can only reply as Trotskysts and as "those who have always shown their unwavering determination to settle with Hitlerism forever", "*Yes*, they are organising, training and arming us in their military organisations." Revolutionary workers are not excluded from the universal conscription. We are learning this the hard way. Up to now the absence in our publications of any material relating to the armed forces has been most marked. But the adoption of the military policy of the proletariat must change this state of affairs. Linked with our demand for workers' militia must come the policy for the workers in arms. Serious attention must now be devoted to the structure of the bourgeois army. In close co-operation with the comrades in the armed forces, we must concretise our military policy for this country—a policy which will include the fight for democratic rights; for better conditions; for the right of the soldiers to elect their own officers; for trade union control of all training camps for privates as well as officers; for the abolition of the present brutal drill system; for the abolition of the present medieval system of court martial, punishment and military "justice"; for the control of the armed forces by the trade unions. We must include in our "Labour to power" demands that an armed forces trade union be formed which must be affiliated to the TUC—in this way we carry the class struggle into the army and flowing from this we pose the question of a revolutionary war against Hitler.

We have outlined above our criticism of the article which is the expression of the Majority of the EC's position on the military policy. We claim this is not an interpretation of the military policy of the Fourth International, but which has completely missed the essence of this policy. We hope that this will open the discussion within the organisation in which all members will participate, and which will therefore lead to a clearer understanding of the problem.

Ted in the early 1940s

A step towards capitulation

By Jock Haston

[WIL, *Internal bulletin*, March 21 1941]

The new policy of the Majority of the EC expressed in our press in February and proclaimed as an interpretation of the military policy of the Fourth International for this country, constitutes a radical shift in the orientation of our propaganda and is a misrepresentation of the basic ideas of Trotsky and Cannon on the military policy.

Bolsheviks base themselves on the axiom that the main enemy is at home. The popular form of expression this axiom takes depends on the objective clash of class forces on the one hand and the support of the revolutionary party among the working class, on the other. But the new conception expressed in the policy of the Majority is not, as they would have us believe, an extension and development of the policy of Lenin. Summed up the Majority position can be expressed in the slogan "For a revolutionary war against Hitler." That we would be opposed to this slogan under all circumstances is, of course, not correct. Should the working class achieve power in Britain, this could become the central slogan of a revolutionary workers' government. But to shift the axis of our propaganda at a period when the British bourgeoisie is defencist and has the support of the majority of the British working class, while our own tendency is hardly recognised within the labour movement, even by the advanced workers is, to say the least, a change in course. In the last issues of our publications the main emphasis of the material is directed against the invading army: *the foreign enemy.* Only in a secondary sense is the attack levelled against the British bourgeoisie.

Revolutionary wars: Lenin's position

Lenin has dealt with the question of revolutionary wars and the difficulties in presenting the policy of revolutionary defeatism to the masses, in a number of his works immediately following the February revolution in Russia in 1917. In his *Farewell letter to the Swiss workers* he wrote:

> "We do not close our eyes to the tremendous difficulties that face the international revolutionary vanguard of the proletariat of Russia. In

times like these sudden and swift changes are possible. In No. 47 of *Sotsial-Demokrat* we gave a clear and direct answer to the natural question: what would our party do if the revolution placed it in power *at this moment*? Our answer was: 1) we would forthwith propose peace to *all* the belligerent peoples; 2) we would announce our conditions of peace as being the immediate liberation of *all* colonies and *all* oppressed and non-sovereign peoples; 3) we would immediately begin to carry to its completion the liberation of all the peoples oppressed by the Great-Russians; 4) we do not deceive ourselves for one moment that such conditions would be unacceptable not only for the monarchist but also to the republican bourgeoisie of Germany , *and not only* to Germany, but also to the capitalist governments of England and France.

"We would be forced to wage a revolutionary war against the German bourgeoisie, and not the German bourgeoisie alone. And *we would wage this war*. We are not pacifists. We are opposed to imperialist wars for the division of spoils among the capitalists, but we have always declared it to be absurd for the revolutionary proletariat to renounce revolutionary wars that *may prove necessary in the interests of socialism*."

In *Tasks of the proletariat in the present revolution* Lenin wrote:

"1) In our attitude towards the war not the slightest concession must be made to 'revolutionary defencism', for even under the new government of Lvov and company, the war on Russia's part unquestionably remains a predatory imperialist war owing to the capitalist nature of that government.

"The class conscious proletariat can consent to a revolutionary war, which would really justify revolutionary defencism only on condition: a) that the power of the government pass to the proletariat and the poor sections of the peasantry bordering on the proletariat; b) that all annexations be renounced in deed as well as in words; c) that a complete and real break be made with all capitalist interests.

"*In view of the undoubted honesty of the mass of the rank-and-file believers in revolutionary defencism, who accept the war as a necessity only and not as a means of conquest; in view of the fact that they are being deceived by the bourgeoisie, it is necessary thoroughly, persistently and patiently to explain their error to them*, to explain the indissoluble connection between capital and the imperialist war, and to prove that it is impossible to end the war by a truly democratic, non-coercive peace without the overthrow of capital.

"The widespread propaganda of this view among the army on active service must be organised." (Our emphasis)

Again in *Tasks of the proletariat in the present revolution* we read:

"What is required of us is the *ability* to explain to the masses that the social and political character of the war is determined not by the 'good intentions' of individuals or groups or even peoples, but by the position of the class which conducts the war. To explain this to the masses skilfully and in a comprehensive way is not easy; none of us could do it at once without committing errors.

"...The slogan 'down with the war' is, of course, a correct one, but it fails to take into account the specific nature of the tasks at the present moment and the necessity of approaching the masses in a different way.

"...The rank and file believer in defencism regards the matter in a simple, matter-of-fact way. 'I don't want annexations but the German is after me, therefore I am defending a just cause and not imperialist interest'. It must be explained very patiently to a man like this that it is not a question of his personal wishes, but of mass, class, political relations and conditions of the connection between the war and the interests of capital, the international network of banks and so forth. Only such a serious struggle against defencism will be serious and promising of success—perhaps not a rapid success, but one which will be real and durable."

Finally let us quote from Lenin's *Report on the current situation*.

"The third point deals with the question of how to end the war. The Marxist point of view is well known: the difficulty is to present it to the masses in the clearest possible form. We are not pacifists and cannot renounce revolutionary war. Wherein does a revolutionary war differ from a capitalist war? Chiefly by the class that has an interest in the war...When we address the masses, we must give them concrete answers. First, then, how can one distinguish a revolutionary war from a capitalist war? The rank and file masses do not grasp the distinction, do not realise the distinction is one of classes. We must not confine ourselves to theory, but must demonstrate in practice that we can wage a truly revolutionary war only when the proletariat is in power. It seems to me that by putting the matter thus, we give a clearer answer to the question of what the nature of the war is and who is waging it."

The above quotations demonstrate that the problem of "approaching the masses" is not a new problem. Lenin was the greatest tactician that the revolutionary movement has had. His method undoubtedly led to the successful overthrow of the bourgeoisie. We hope to be able to demonstrate that the method of the Majority is not the method of Lenin—or of Trotsky. Even were the objective circumstances existent which necessitated the immediate posing of the proposition of the revolutionary war, we submit that the manner of their presentation is a negation of Lenin's directive...to patiently explain.

Lenin posed the question thus, at a period when Dual Power had been established in Russia; when there was a widespread feeling of "revolutionary defencism" implanted by the gains of the February revolution and the propaganda of the bourgeoisie; when the Bolsheviks had consolidated around themselves the most developed cadres of the revolutionary international movement; when they had a high standing among the best proletarian fighters in Russia; when all the forces for a genuine proletarian revolution were in the process of maturing—taking all these into consideration—it was in the clearest propagandist manner that the problem was posed. "It must be explained very patiently..."

Not a new policy

That the policy as presented by our Majority comrades is not new in British working class politics can be demonstrated by an examination of a pamphlet, *The workers' road to victory*, published by the left centrist grouping in the ILP, the Soccor, at the time of the invasion of Norway. When this pamphlet appeared, we, including the comrades of the Majority, proclaimed it a capitulation to anti-Hitlerism. The left centrists, capitulating to the mass pressure of bourgeois and petty bourgeois opinion, adopted this policy when the sphere of military operations had moved into the Baltic. Our comrades of the Majority waited till the Channel ports were occupied and the Germans moved somewhat closer to British shores.

Let us recapitulate the central slogans of the Soccor group as expressed in this pamphlet for purposes of comparison:

"Workers! You cannot trust your rulers to fight fascism! Only the workers can defeat fascism.

"The fight against fascism is:

"The fight for equality;

"The fight to jail the ruling class fifth columnists;

"The fight against profits;

"The fight to arm the people.

"Transform the imperialist war into a revolutionary war against Hitlerism."

Under the above slogans follow 22 demands which include: abolition of all profits in war industries; general arming of the people through their trade union and labour organisations; publication of secret treaties; the right of workers and shop stewards' committees to inspect the books of the capitalists; abolition of the national debt; press, broadcasting, etc. to be under the control of workers' committees; democratisation of the armed forces under the control of the workers; fullest use of revolutionary propaganda to the German and European workers, including appeals to them to desert and fight their tyrants; transfer of all big estates and combines to social ownerships; complete freedom to India and colonial peoples; abolition of anti-working class legislation.

Let us now compare these with the slogans of the Majority expressed in the February issue of *Youth For Socialism*:

"Labour to power on the following programme:

"Disarm the capitalists and arm the workers for the struggle against Nazism and the capitalist fifth column at home;

"Take over the land, mines, factories, railways and banks without compensation;

"Give freedom and self-determination to India and the colonies;

"Repeal all anti-working class legislation;

"Appeal to the workers of Germany and all Europe to support the socialist struggle against Hitler.

Apart from the demand of Labour to power, if anything, the class content expressed by the left centrists in their pamphlet is more explicit than it is in the journal of the fourth internationalists. If it is true that the policy expressed in the current issues of our press is an interpretation of the new policy evolved by comrade Trotsky, then we are forced to admit that the left centrists in Britain arrived at this before our comrades in the Majority—and even before comrade Trotsky! It does not follow, however, that if the centrists arrived at a policy before we did, that it is incorrect. But it can be stated, that despite the ambiguity here and there in the pamphlet *The workers' road to victory—the central aim is the same*, and we must ask ourselves why the Majority or the EC have not attempted to utilise this as a basis for an approach to Soccor.

The "mood of the masses"

One would expect to find some theoretical analysis of the change in basic objective circumstances as the background for the substitution of an entirely new orientation, for the central thesis of Bolshevism in the imperialist war. What circumstances have changed to motivate the shift from our former position of the "sterile repetition of the Marxist axiom that only the socialist revolution can solve the problems of the working class"? The answer we receive is the "mood of the masses" resulting from the threat of invasion.

There is no fundamental difference in the mood of the masses today to what it was at the commencement of the war. If anything their mood registers more sharply *against* the war than it did in 1939. This is demonstrated by the recent Dumbartonshire election where almost 4,000 workers voted for the Communist Party. The bulk of the 22,000 votes polled for the coalition Labour candidate undoubtedly came from elements who normally voted Tory. The bulk of the

Labour votes remained apathetic, while the best elements of the working class who normally voted Labour, cast their vote for the Communist Party *on the programme of the Peoples' Convention*. In the midst of a whipped-up campaign where the whole of the local bourgeois press directed its attack against the Communist Party as fifth columnists and agents of Hitler; this linked to a special series of articles on the threat of imminent invasion, the notion of these workers (1 in every 6.5 of those who voted) in registering their votes for peace on the basis of the Peoples' Convention programme, is indeed a significant register of the mood of the masses, and particularly its advanced strata.

A recent Gallup poll showed that 80 percent of the British population supported Churchill at the head of the government. Insofar as this is true, quite obviously our task is to patiently explain the nature of the struggle; the class who are carrying it out; the role of the leading politicians. But what of the remaining 20 percent who mainly registered *against* Churchill? A large percentage of these stand solidly *against* the war. Is the axis of our propaganda to be directed to the 80 percent who support the war under Churchill's leadership, or to the 20 percent who contain within its ranks the revolutionary anti-war elements?

The mood of the masses is registered in their confidence in Churchill. They are satisfied that Churchill is conducting the struggle in the best possible way. The defeat of the blitz last year; the successes of the British forces in Africa and in the Mediterranean; the rearming of the defeated legions of Dunkirk, plus the additions of the thousands of troops from the colonies—all these, added to the open support being given by American imperialism, have imbued the bulk of the workers with a quiet confidence in the Churchill administration. Under these circumstances they firmly believe that any invasion will be repulsed. There is no demand from the workers for arms from the government, and indeed, for those who wish to be armed, there are still avenues open through official channels. Flowing from the above, the sterile repetition "we want to fight Hitler" coincides with the high-power propaganda of the bourgeoisie and becomes merged with it; while the general slogan "arm the workers" remains a phrase, unrelated to the genuine "mood of the masses."

As a prelude to an approach to the "masses", it is necessary to have this concrete picture before us as to their real mood. The assertion, an implication that the government are making little or no genuine attempt to "defend the country" is categorically rejected by the masses; while the lack of a real analysis of the class content of what measures are being taken, and the exposition of a working class criticism and programme as an alternative, leaves the more advanced worker extremely confused—even within our own ranks.

The British working class, is still, unfortunately, the most chauvinistic working class in Europe, or for that matter in the world. What better proof of this is needed than their complete indifference to the attacks of the British Raj against Indian revolutionaries and nationalists? It is still necessary to patiently explain...

That this approach to the masses is not really the basis for this anti-Hitler fetishism was clearly demonstrated at the period of the Peoples' Convention held in London. Here were assembled over 2,000 people, the overwhelming bulk of whom were anti-war proletarian leaders in their particular districts and organisations. These workers had assembled together to discuss ways and means of struggling against their own capitalist class—their main enemy at home. The slogan our majority comrades proposed to approach them with was "how to really fight Hitler"! It was only when the Minority protested that this was withdrawn in favour of the Minority slogan "a fighting alternative for the working class." The whole sham of the "mood of the masses" was sharply revealed in this incident. Here was the most advanced strata of the British proletariat gathered together in a fighting mood to work out a policy of opposition to the present government, and our comrades proposed to approach them with a policy of "fighting Hitler"!

Again, in the drawing up of the *"Daily Worker* ban" leaflet—a leaflet putting forward the proposal of a united front—the Majority proposed the insertion of a clause that the reason there had been no protest among the masses of the workers against the ban, was that the Communist Party had no policy of fighting Hitler! Only on the insistence of the Minority, was this clause excluded.

Not only have the Majority comrades an incorrect evaluation as to the mood of the masses, but their characterisation is not even firmly based. We are at present discussing a document for the conference on "policy and perspectives" which characterises the mood of the masses in the following terms:

> "Notwithstanding the pressure of suffering and want, despite the murderous air-raids since the battle of Britain began, *despite the bitterness and scepticism, even to a certain extent, apathy and indifference of the toilers to the war,* there is no sign as yet of a mass movement developing..." (Our emphasis)

In a letter to the *Socialist Appeal* we read the following:

> "The Stalinists cannot fight the suppression of the *Daily Worker* because they have no programme to offer the workers. *'We must at all costs fight and destroy Hitler' is the mood of the masses,* and the bombing has strengthened, not weakened this. The Communist Party has not responded to this demand of the workers in the slightest degree. Their policy has been sectarian, pacifist and sterile. The Labour leaders and bourgeoisie are making much of the *Daily Worker* demand that every soldier should have a week's holiday at Christmas!" (Our emphasis)

In the February issue of *Workers' International News* the mood of the masses is characterised as follows:

"The working class, especially after the events of the last months, is determined to resist to the uttermost any incursion from Nazi Germany."

In the same issue of *Workers' International News* we read:

"The working class for the time being continues to stand, *albeit critically*, behind their leaders." (Our emphasis)

While in the letter to the *Socialist Appeal*:

"They [the workers] are still solidly behind the Labour leaders and the 'war against Hitler'."

We agree with the characterisation in the document on "policy and perspectives". We categorically reject the contradictions to this characterisation. But even were their evaluation correct, to attempt to base the military policy of the Fourth International on the "mood of the masses" would be to base ourselves on a fluctuating medium which is subject to intense and rapid changes. The military policy is not based on "moods" but on the objective historical phenomena "the universal militarisation of the working class."

The approach to the masses—A new departure

The core of the article in the February *Workers' International News*, which is in fact, an internal discussion directed against the Minority, is contained in the following:

"This attitude of the masses must be the point of departure for our propaganda. The way to win them over is not by the sterile repetition of the Marxian axiom that only the socialist revolution can solve the problems of the working class. It is to convince the masses of this by their day-to-day experiences. The main task of the revolutionary socialist is to separate the workers from their leaders. This can only be done by showing them the absolute contradiction between their interests and those of the mortal enemy."

But who in the Workers' International League has ever disagreed with this axiom of Leninist tactics? No one! This is an attempt to foist on the shoulders of the Minority the ideas of a sectarian clique, while covering themselves with the cloak of Leon Trotsky. However, in this very paragraph we find the key to the position of the Majority. The first proposition here is that the Minority merely favour the "sterile repetition of the Marxian axiom;" that the Minority reject the military policy of the Fourth International. This is not so. Where our disagreement lies, is precisely *what the military policy is*, and how to approach the workers with it. We claim that our first task is *the elaboration of and adoption of a military policy* to reach the advanced workers, and particularly those in the armed forces. The majority, on the other hand, claim that we can do so by shouting "wolf!" (Hitler!) louder even than the bourgeoisie. (In the *Youth* article

Hitlerism or Nazism is mentioned once in every sixty words!). We ask ourselves, has there at any time in the past appeared so many "sterile repetitions" as in the last issues of our publications? Paragraph after paragraph, the same refrain: Hitler is coming—The bourgeoisie won't let us fight him—Arm the workers!

Since the inception of Workers' International League we have based ourselves on an appeal to the *advanced* workers, because our task has been clearly posed before us—the training and educating of the initial cadres of the revolutionary party. We have considered our tasks to be those of a propaganda group, disseminating the fundamental ideas of revolutionary Marxism. For years we have adopted the standpoint that we are in the elementary stages of building cadres; *that we have absolutely no possibility of winning the masses until we have won the advanced workers.* The whole of our policy and perspective has been based on this. We have ruthlessly fought the sectarians who shouted "masses" from the housetops on the basis of general and abstract slogans. From this angle we adopted the tactic of entry and the programme of Labour to power, believing that by fighting side by side with the already politically conscious workers, we could train the necessary cadres for the revolutionary party. But the article in *Workers' International News* sets us new tasks: "The road to the masses lies in showing them a real alternative, a genuine struggle against a victory of Hitlerism from abroad and at home." It is in this gesture of despair that the key to our comrades' deviation lies. Having raised Hitler's invasion into a nightmare, they seek cover among the "masses". It is not so easy after all to "swim against the stream." Our organisation is now faced with an entirely new perspective—*we must now approach the masses.* But this new perspective fails to take into account "the specific nature of the tasks of the moment."

Comrade Trotsky elaborated the military policy which was based on the objective historical phenomena—the period of permanent war and universal militarism. Having elaborated this *policy* which is clearly and precisely formulated in the *Resolution on the military policy* it was adopted by the SWP convention. Flowing from the *policy* Trotsky and Cannon proceeded to explain the "mood of the masses" from which they can deduce a certain *approach* to place this policy before the workers; this, taken in conjunction with the status of the American Socialist Workers' Party.

The American working class are in a period similar to that of the British working class in 1910-14. The tide of militancy is rapidly rising and finds expression in the severest economic clashes. The American workers are groping for an independent labour political organisation. Concurrently with this movement on the part of the mass of the workers, the American party alone of all the Fourth Internationalist organisations has the prerequisites for an approach to the "masses". With a support among the advanced section of the American workers: witness their control of the largest trade union journal in circulation in America *The North West Organiser* organ of America's most militant workers; control of the teamsters of Minneapolis; Grace Carlson's successes at the recent election—all these must be taken into the picture. Our American comrades are equipped with developed and tested cadres; they are already in a position to influence broad sections of the most advanced workers. In fact we can state with confidence that they are in a position to challenge the existing working class organisations for the leadership of the American workers and the conquest of power.

We, on the other hand, have untrained and completely untested cadres. We have never been through the experience of having to give leadership, even on a local scale, to a movement among the workers. It is in the confused transportation of Trotsky's ideas in his discussions on the method of approach to the American workers that the Majority get bogged up. While we must reach the widest possible circles among the workers, nevertheless any approach must be cautioned by the status of our group in the working class arena.

On the slogan of arming the workers

The *Transitional Programme* of the Fourth International contains as one of its central planks the general slogan of arming the workers. In this document, drawn up in times of peace, the slogans arising from "arm the workers" are posed in a sharp and concrete manner: *the picket line—defence groups—workers' militia*. These slogans are crystallised and form the centre of our propaganda during periods of intense industrial strife or fascist attacks, and when the onslaught against the workers demands the necessary combat organisations for workers' defence. In the elaboration of these directives we see the method of presenting the slogan in a clear and concrete manner in times of peace which can be easily grasped by the advanced workers; while the slogans in relation to the armed forces are generalised and remain in the background: "military training and arming of workers and farmers under the direct control of workers' and farmers' committees; creation of military school for training of commanders among the toilers, chosen by the workers' organisations. Substitution for the standing army of a *people's militia* indissolubly linked up with the factories, mines, farms etc."

Without being presented in its concrete form, the slogan "arm the workers" remains a phrase. In view of the clear manner in which this question is dealt with in the *Transitional Programme*, we must ask ourselves why comrade Trotsky raised the question of a *military policy* with the American comrades and through them the International. Because the axis of life in the present period of the overwhelming majority of the workers of the world will be in the armed forces of the various nations, or directly affected by the armed forces. With this new perspective—the arming of millions of workers by the capitalist state—the slogan "arm the workers" assumes new and important emphasis. *From being a plank in our general programme, it now becomes the central question; from being posed in a general, propagandist sense in times of peace, it must now* become concretised.

It is for this reason that Trotsky raised the question in the manner that he did. The military policy is the elaboration of a programme of transitional demands which separates the workers from their class enemy and its agents in the all important *military* sphere. The resolution of the Socialist Workers Party is the elaborated programme for work in the armed forces; for the decisive military sphere.

A continuation, a deepening of Lenin's policy

In Trotsky's last article[1] published in February *Workers' International News*, he wrote the following under the heading, *We were caught unawares in 1914*:

"During the last war not only the proletariat as a whole but also its vanguard and, in a certain sense, the vanguard of this vanguard was caught unawares. The elaboration of the principles of revolutionary policy toward the war began at a time when the war was already in full blaze and the military machine exercised unlimited rule. One year after the outbreak of the war, the small revolutionary minority were compelled to accommodate itself to a centrist majority at the Zimmerwald conference. Prior to the February revolution and even afterwards the revolutionary elements felt themselves to be not contenders for power but the extreme left opposition. Even Lenin relegated the socialist revolution to a more or less distant future...

"This political position of the extreme left wing expressed itself most graphically on the question of the defence of the fatherland.

"In 1915 Lenin referred in his writings to revolutionary wars which the victorious proletariat would have to wage. But it was a question of an indefinite historical perspective and not of tomorrow's task. The attention of the revolutionary wing was centred on the question of the defence of the capitalist fatherland. The revolutionists naturally replied to this question in the negative. This was entirely correct. But this purely negative answer served as the basis for propaganda and for training the cadres but it could not win the masses who did not want a foreign conqueror. In Russia prior to the war the Bolsheviks constituted four-fifths of the proletarian vanguard, that is, of the workers participating in political life (newspapers, elections, etc). Following the February revolution the unlimited rule passed into the hands of the defencists, the Mensheviks and the Social-Revolutionaries. True enough, the Bolsheviks in the space of eight months conquered the overwhelming majority of the workers. But the decisive role in this conquest was played not by the

---

[1] Trotsky: *Bonapartism, fascism and war*, August 1940.

refusal to defend the bourgeois fatherland but by the slogan: 'All power to the soviets!' And only by this revolutionary slogan! The criticism of imperialism, its militarism, the renunciation of the defence of bourgeois democracy and so on could have never conquered the overwhelming majority of the people to the side of the Bolsheviks. In all other belligerent countries, with the exception of Russia the revolutionary wing toward the end of the war all...."[2]

Trotsky is drawing our attention to the situation at the beginning of the first imperialist war—how the question of *principle* was the paramount question of the period. He is also drawing our attention to the flexible tactics of Lenin during the course of the revolution. As late as the end of 1915 the Bolsheviks were forced to accommodate themselves to the centrists at Zimmerwald. Even as late as 1917 they had not yet elaborated their *tactics* in relation to the armed forces. This was true of the whole of the revolutionary left throughout the world. Karl Liebknecht captured the Kaiser's constituency at Potsdam in 1912 mainly on his anti-militarist policy. The first the socialist movement knew of his rejection of his pre-war pacifist position, was through a letter he sent to Zimmerwald, and even at the end of the war he had not worked out a *policy* or *tactic* for work in the armed forces. This was true of the best of the French socialists, Monatte, etc. The American revolutionaries took a similar stand to that of the SPGB[3] today. James Connolly, the only British socialist to organise a workers' army, supported the British conscientious objectors. In Britain John Maclean supported and adopted the same stand as hundreds of British socialists who were jailed as conscientious objectors. This was the attitude towards the war among the best of the British proletarian revolutionaries. Lenin characterised them in 1917 in the following terms: "They and they alone, are the internationalists in deed." The first years of the war were taken up with an ideological struggle in the elaboration of revolutionary *principles* and even at the end of the war, the revolutionary left had not laid down a programme, a *tactic*, in relation to the armed forces. Trotsky, in drawing our attention to the different situation in which the revolutionaries find themselves today, takes a step further.

The fourth internationalists enter the second imperialist war on an entirely different basis. We are not faced with the same ideological struggle within our ranks. Our *principles* have been defined and laid down in *War and the Fourth International* (1936). Far from congratulating the conscientious objectors, as Lenin did, we have consistently opposed their stand as utopian sectarianism, because it isolates the revolutionary from the workers in uniform.

When conscription was introduced in Britain we issued a *Manifesto* which

---

2 Quote ends abruptly.

3 Socialist Party of Great Britain, small socialist organisation founded in 1904 as a split from the Social Democratic Federation.

characterised the war as an imperialist war, criticised the opportunist and pacifist tendencies in British working class politics and advised the workers to take the gun which was placed in his hand and turn it against the real enemy at home. This was a correct general directive and was relatively more advanced than any manifesto issued in the British labour movement in this or the last imperialist war. But we had no alternative policy to offer the worker who acquiesced to conscription—*we lacked a military policy.*

Taking as the objective background for the new orientation, the fact that the entire world was being plunged into war and the working class had not overthrown their own capitalist class as a means of stopping the war; that we had entered what he characterised as a period of *universal militarisation of the working class*, comrade Trotsky conceived that since the axis of life would now revolve around the armed forces, it was necessary to have a *proletarian military policy* to face up to the changed situation—it was necessary to elaborate the *tactics* of a revolutionary opposition in the army. But this did not obviate the struggle *against* this war.

> "We must of course fight against the war, not only 'until the very last moment' but during the war itself when it begins. We must however, give to our fight against the war its fully revolutionary sense, opposing and pitilessly denouncing pacifism. The very simple and very great idea of our fight against war is: we are against the war but we will have the war if we are incapable of overthrowing the capitalists."[4]

While the American section outlined a series of concrete programmatic demands, this did not stop them from continuing a ruthless struggle against the war, crystallising the anti-war sentiment among the workers. This is not our war—we are against the class that conducts it—"not a man, not a penny, not a gun" for the imperialist war. While conducting this irreconcilable struggle *against the war*, we denounce and expose all forms of bourgeois and socialist pacifism. In his book *From October to Brest-Litovsk*, Trotsky explains why the peasants played so important a role in the February revolution: the bourgeoisie had *organised* the peasants, not as peasants, but as soldiers. Today he is explaining that the bourgeoisie is organising the proletariat, not as proletarians, but as soldiers: that the soldiers are destined to play the decisive role in the coming revolution. Consequently the programme of the party must base itself on this historic change.

How the Socialist Workers' Party tackled this question

In close conjunction with the Old Man, the Americans elaborated their military policy, their tactical approach to the workers about to be drafted into the army, which was published in the form of a resolution. Around this resolution they

4 Trotsky: *On conscription*, July 1940.

have directed their propaganda and agitation. In contradistinction to ourselves they outlined a complete programmatic alternative for the workers who were being conscripted. Instead of being in the background of our transitional demands in peace time, the slogans revolving around the arming of the workers were now thrust to the fore. These are summed up on the masthead of the editorial column of the *Socialist Appeal* and "constitute a military transitional programme supplementing the general political transitional programme of the party."

The American section carefully analysed the form and content of the bourgeois army; they have taken all the questions up, singly and collectively, affecting the workers in the armed forces. They have held a special party discussion and a convention, whose main task was to familiarise the membership from top to bottom with the new orientation. They have set themselves the task of hammering home the idea that the party must now base itself on war.

In case there is any doubt that the central question dealt with was the tactic for the armed forces, we propose to quote extensively from Cannon.

"...All great questions will be decided by military means. This was the great conclusion insisted upon by comrade Trotsky in his last few months of life. *In his letter, in his articles and in conversations he repeated this thesis over and over again. These are new times. The characteristic feature of our epoch is unceasing war and universal militarism. That imposes upon us as the first task, the task which dominates and shapes all others, the adoption of a military policy, an attitude of the proletarian party towards the solution of social problems during a time of universal militarism and war...*"

"Now, confronted with these facts of universal militarism and permanent war, *that the biggest industry of all now is going to be war, the army and preparation of things for the army—confronted with these facts, what shall the revolutionary party do?* Shall we stand aside and simply say we don't agree with the war, it is not our affair? No, we can't do that. We do not approve of this whole system of exploitation whereby private individuals can take possession of the means of production and enslave the masses. We are against that, but as long as we are not strong enough to put an end to capitalist exploitation in the factories, we adapt ourselves to reality. We don't abstain and go on individual strikes and separate ourselves from the working class. We go into the factories and try by working with the class to influence its development. We go with the workers and share all their experiences and try to influence them in a revolutionary direction.

"*The same logic applies to war. The great majority of the young generation will be dragged into the war.* The great majority of these young workers will think at first that they are doing a good thing. For a revolutionary party to stand by and say: 'we can tolerate exploitation in the factories, but not military exploitation,'—that is to be completely illogical. *To isolate ourselves from the mass of the proletariat which will be in the war is to lose all possibility to influence them.*

"We have got to be good soldiers. Our people must take upon themselves the task of defending the interests of the proletariat in the army in the same way as we try to protect their interests in the factory. As long as we can't take the factories away from the bosses we fight to improve the conditions there. Similarly, in the army. Adapting ourselves to the fact that the proletariat of this country is going to be the proletariat in arms we say, 'Very well, Mr. Capitalist, you have decided it so and we were not strong enough to prevent it. Your war is not our war, but so long as the mass of the proletariat goes with it, we will go too. We will raise our own independent programme in the army, in the military forces, in the same way as we raise it in the factories'..."

"We will fight all the time for the idea that the workers should have officers of their own choosing. That this great sum of money that is being appropriated out of the public treasury should be allocated in part to the trade unions for the setting up of their own military training camps under officers of their own selection; that we go into battle with the consciousness that the officer leading us is a man of our own flesh and blood who is not going to waste our lives, who is going to be true and loyal and who will represent our interests. And in that way, in the course of the development of the war, *we will build up in the army a great class-conscious movement of workers with arms in their hands* who will be absolutely invincible. Neither the German Hitler nor any other Hitler will be able to conquer them.

"We will never let anything happen as it did in France. These commanding officers from top to bottom turned out to be nothing but traitors and cowards crawling on their knees before Hitler, leaving the workers absolutely helpless..."

"We must remember all the time that the workers of this epoch are not only workers; they are soldiers. *These armies are no longer selected individuals; they are whole masses of the young proletarian youth who have been shifted from exploitation in the factories to exploitation in the military machine.* They will be imbued by the psychology of the proletariat from which they came. But they will have guns in their hand and they will learn how to shoot them. They will gain confidence in themselves. They will be fired with the conviction that the only man who counts in this time of history is a man who has a gun in his hand and knows how to use it."[5] (Our emphasis)

How the Majority tackle the question

Instead of basing themselves on a *policy*, a *programme*, for the proletariat in arms, the Majority relegate the *policy* to a minor position, while they raise the question of the *approach* to the status of a policy. The dispute on the EC crystallised around the proposition of the Majority that the leading article in July 1940 *Youth For Socialism* and in February 1941 *Workers' International News* and *Youth, were the correct interpretation of the military policy of the proletariat.* The Minority stated that the military policy was not based on the "mood of the masses" or on the particular occupations or reverses of the bourgeois armies, but was a formulation of a programme for the workers in arms in the present period of militarisation, and was aimed against all forms of pacifism in the labour movement.

The Majority comrades say: "You have missed the essence of Trotsky's ideas: the revolutionary war against Hitler. Cannon also said so!" To back this up they quote Cannon:

"We are willing to fight Hitler. No worker wants to see that gang of fascist barbarians overrun this country or any other country."

"The only thing we object to is the leadership of a class that we do not trust."

"The workers themselves must take charge of this fight against Hitler or anyone else who tries to invade their rights."

"We didn't visualise, nobody visualised, a world situation in which whole countries would be conquered by fascist armies. The workers don't want to be conquered by foreign invaders, above all by fascists. They require a programme of military struggle against foreign invaders which assures their class independence. That is the gist of the problem."

"This is why Trotsky advanced the military policy!" proclaim our comrades. No! *This is why you advance your policy, comrades!* Examine Cannon's speech, examine the material of our American section and we will see that these are references to the change in the outlook of the American working class consequent on the fall of France, as distinct from their anti-war, anti-militarist sentiment prior to the fall of France. The workers, because of this, did not want a foreign conqueror, and allowed themselves to be conscripted. Hence the urgent need for a policy which *separated the workers from the bosses* in the military sphere: anti-militarism was transformed into proletarian-militarism.

"Many times in the past we were put to a certain disadvantage; the demagogy of the social democrats against us was effective to a certain

---

5 Cannon: *Military policy of the proletariat*, October 1940.

extent. They said: 'you have no answer to the question of how to fight against Hitler from conquering France, Belgium, etc.' (Of course their programme was very simple—the suspension of the class struggle and complete subordination of the workers to the bourgeoisie. We have seen the results of this treacherous policy.) Well, we answered in a general way, the workers will first overthrow the bourgeoisie at home and then they will take care of invaders. That was a good programme. But the workers did not make the revolution in time. Now the two tasks must be telescoped and carried out simultaneously."

"...the two tasks must be telescoped and carried out simultaneously." Cannon's remarks are addressed to party delegates around a resolution which has been discussed in the party for two months. He is answering a query which the social democrats put to revolutionaries. In the past we answered in a general way. Now we answer in a concrete way. The resolution to which Cannon is speaking is the answer to the social democrats, the prosecution of which, as he put it, "will build up in the army a great class-conscious movement of workers with arms in their hands who will be absolutely invincible. Neither the German Hitler nor any other Hitler will be able to conquer them." This great class-conscious proletariat will overthrow their own bourgeoisie and at the same time, precisely because of the proletarian military policy, be in a position to defend the proletarian fatherland with the minimum of chaos. The two tasks are absolutely clear. The secondary task is prepared and carried out *within* the primary task; the one task slides into the other and operates at the same time.

But this is somewhat different to what the Majority say: "The Stalinists have no programme for the workers on how to fight invading fascism—or for that matter fascism at home; the two problems are not separate but identical and simultaneous." The Majority accuse the Stalinists of not having a programme against invading fascism (the primary enemy). What ought to be formulated "the main enemy at home" is presented: "or for that matter, fascism at home." By this means the question is reversed; it is not only reversed, it is distorted and confused. The British working class are not menaced by fascism. By saying something *similar* to Cannon they think they have said the same. In sharp contradistinction to Cannon, the tasks are posed by the Majority as "*identical*". Our own bourgeoisie becomes submerged in identity with the foreign invader. This according to the Majority is the continuation of the policy of Lenin. The main enemy at home recedes into the background because: we are fighting invading fascism! It is no accident that the question is formulated this way. Search in vain through their material for a single concrete directive to the 4 to 5 million armed workers, from which would flow the general policy of arming all the workers. With the raising of the invasion in the manner of the Majority, and the lack of a concrete policy for the workers in arms, there remains no alternative for the "masses" but to accept the very concrete directive of the bourgeoisie.

After the fall of France, Trotsky wrote in an article *We do not change our course*:

> "From the standpoint of the revolution in one's own country the defeat of one's own imperialist masters is undoubtedly the 'lesser evil.' Pseudo internationalists, however, refuse to apply this principle in relation to the defeated democratic countries. In return they interpret Hitler's victory not as a relative, but as an absolute obstacle in the way of a revolution in Germany. They lie in both instances."

These words were directed against the social democratic and centrist capitulators who were advocating various forms of tentative and open support for the "democratic bourgeoisie." Our comrades of the Majority, have not, of course, proposed that we support the bourgeoisie. Nevertheless the conception "*identical*" is, in our opinion, a step in this direction. This is further emphasised by the formulations of the less experienced comrades of the Majority in political discussions.

During the pre-October days Lenin remarked that to substitute the abstract for the concrete was one of the greatest sins of a revolutionary. This is also true, let us echo, in periods of apathy and reaction. This is what our comrades are doing at the present moment—substituting abstract "moods" for a concrete evaluation of these moods; substituting abstract phrases for concrete directives; proposing to win the "masses" instead of educating the cadres.

The army

Let us examine the material presented by the Majority insofar as it deals with the armed forces at all. As the *Internal Bulletin* [contribution] of SL-MK[6] correctly demonstrates, the emphasis in the article in *Youth For Socialism* is laid on the fact that the bourgeoisie are not arming the workers. In February *Youth* the army is referred to in the following passages:

> "How they are going to accomplish this with their maximum of 4 million soldiers against the 10 million which the Rome-Berlin axis has already trained and armed they do not reveal..."

> "Not by curtailing the power of the workers in the factory and in the army—but by organising workers control of industry and arms..."

> "Control of the army must be taken out of the hands of the reactionary officer class and put into those of the workers."

Assuming that this was due to error of omission, one would expect to find a deeper analysis in the *Workers' International News* article, particularly since our comrades state that *Youth* material is agitational and *Workers'*

---

6 See: Sam Levy and Millie Kahn, *The interpretation of the Majority of the executive committee of the military policy.*

International News is propaganda. In the *Workers' International News* article which has as its key "arm the workers", the Home Guard is not mentioned at all while the army is dismissed as follows:

> "With a big percentage of the workers called up in the army and the main mass of the soldiers stationed in Britain and in contact with the civil population, the army is in closer contact with the toilers than at any time in history. The bourgeoisie even more than in the last war, is dependent on the services of the labour leaders."

And what follows from the important observation that "the army is in closer contact with the toilers than at any time in history"? Will the army be more easily influenced by revolutionary ideas? Should we turn our attention to those workers with arms in their hands? Should we outline a programme of demands for the workers in arms? Why, no! "...The bourgeoisie, even more than in the last war, is dependent on the services of the labour leaders"! And this is presented as the military policy! Instead of a positive programme to the workers—we are served with a pious observation.

It is our duty to make a serious analysis of the problems facing the soldier workers and conduct a sustained propaganda towards workers in the army and link this up with the organised movement of the working class; to explain to the armed workers why it was possible for the French officer caste to sell out and what forms of organisation would stop a similar [thing] happening here; to explain the decisive role the armed proletariat are destined to play in the coming revolution. We must demand trade union wages and trade union rights; delegates from local barracks and battalions to trades councils; the right of soldiers to control the mess committee (the only legal channel in the army for expression at present); the right of assembly and full political rights for soldiers; the right to collective bargaining and deputation; the right to remove the reactionary officers; the right to elect their own officers; the right of the soldiers in the armed forces to give training in arms to workers in the trade unions and labour organisations; the abolition of court martial—these and many other problems must be hammered out in the form of a military programme for the armed forces and must be featured in our press and propaganda.

The experiences of the last war show that bourgeois military discipline tends to break down completely, particularly on the declaration of peace. Nevertheless in Britain, in spite of the widespread revolts in all sections of the forces, mainly on the question of demobilisation, the bourgeois were able, by making a concession to the soldiers in the introduction of the dole, to disarm the British army in France, and thus stave off any possibility of an armed movement on the part of the discontented returning soldiers. The pacifist and anti-militarist nature of the policy of the revolutionary left, the lack of sustained revolutionary activity in the armed forces—these facilitated the reactionary moves on the part of the bourgeoisie. This must not happen again—even if the war runs its course without the

British revolution, and the military policy must be the lever by which the same situation will be prevented.

The Majority have always maintained that revolutionaries and revolutionary parties in the past have had a programme for the army. We ask to be directed to where we can learn of this. We ask the Majority to show us that Lenin's general statement on conscription can in any way be compared to that of Trotsky; if at any time the Bolsheviks or any other revolutionary party outlined so comprehensive a programme for the armed forces as the American SWP. Or is it, as we have always maintained, precisely in the concrete manner in which Trotsky deals with the question, that distinguishes him from Lenin and constitutes the "deepening, the continuation" of Lenin's policy?

The Home Guard

While in *Workers' International News* the Home Guard is not even mentioned, the February issue of *Youth* deals with this question in the following manner:

> "The Home Guard, which they pretended for a time was a sort of arming of the nation, is being brought more and more under the control of the chiefs of the regular army. Now that the Home Guard is to a certain extent armed, the government is bureaucratically imposing full time officers from above. They must have complete control of all arms for their own purposes."

What arises from the proposition that "now that the Home Guard is to a certain extent armed, the government is bureaucratically imposing full time officers from above"? Shall the workers in the Home Guard conduct a struggle for democratic control? Should the workers oppose the setting up of the Home Guard and organise a separate working class militia? No! "They [the capitalists] must have complete control of all arms for their own purposes." A brilliant deduction! One which must have taken a great deal of thought. But how does it bring the ideas of the workingmen who have joined the Home Guard "to fight Hitler" into conflict with those of the capitalist class? How does it teach the proletarian who has grasped at the idea "arm the workers" what his class interests are? Every petty bourgeois trend in British working class politics has said what the Majority say. The task of the revolutionary is not to make pious observations such as the *New Statesman and Nation* or the *Spectator* are wont to do. *It is to develop a programme of revolutionary demands which separates the workers from their class enemy.* Instead of shouting "Hitler is coming—Arm the workers" and shouting even more loudly than the boss class press at that, it is necessary to show the worker where his true interests lie.

The Majority adopt the standpoint that the Home Guard was a concession by the bourgeoisie to the demand on the part of the workers to be armed. In other words: the workers were surging forward for arms to "fight Hitler" and the bosses were holding them back; an "emasculated concession" it is now termed. We do not agree with this proposition. We believe that the initiative for the Home Guard came from the bourgeoisie. The LDV[7] was formed when the first parachutists descended on Norway. This was accompanied by a tremendous press campaign on the part of the bourgeoisie, a campaign which was intensified when the bulge in the allied lines took place, which finally culminated in editorials in the Beaverbrook press "Arm the workers." The most patriotic and politically backward section of the workers joined the Home Guard together with a section of the petit bourgeois staff and a small number of advanced workers, mainly under Stalinist influence. While there was an undoubted influx into the Home Guard as the result of the fall of France, this was stimulated by bourgeois propaganda, and many of these who joined have since dropped out. Nevertheless the fact that there are a large number of workers—even backward workers, though the great majority are in the Home Guard—means that when a movement among the workers takes place, the Home Guard will be vitally affected. An elementary task for the revolutionary party is to develop a programme for these workers. And how much more necessary is such a programme if the viewpoint of the Majority is correct?

The Home Guard will reflect the mood of the workers much more rapidly than the army because it is in closer contact with them. The development of the struggle will burst the Home Guard asunder; one section will go directly over to the counter-revolution, the other will rally to the side of the proletariat. The outcome of this process will be determined by the actions and policy of the revolutionary proletarian party. For this reason it is necessary to have a programme for the Home Guard.

We approach the workers in the Home Guard and in the factories as follows: the capitalists have got us into this war, which is *their* war and not ours. They ask us to join the Home Guard to defend Britain. You fellow workers accept this proposition that we must be armed. You believe and we agree with you, that a successful invasion would smash our standards of life, our trade unions, our Labour parties, and all the civil rights which we have won by years of struggle. We agree with this. But who is going to protect these rights? Is it going to be the reactionary boss class stooges from the managerial staff who control the factory Home Guard? Why, all our lives we have to fight these people to retain what few rights and privileges we have. Day in, day out there is a constant struggle between them and us because they try to grind our conditions down. Look how the bosses keep the best militants out of the Home Guard; how they use the Home Guard in such and such a factory to intimidate the shop stewards, the strikers, etc. No! These people are not interested in defending *our* rights, they are only interested in defending the property of the boss—the factory. That is what *they* mean by the "defence of Britain." We want to defend *our* rights to the

---

7 Local Defence Volunteers, former denomination of the Home Guard.

very end against anyone who attempts to attack them. We are aware that in the present period this can only be done with arms in our hands. Who better to give us a lead on this question than the shop stewards and the trade union militants who spend their lives struggling for this end, who are victimised, attacked because they genuinely desire to defend *our* rights. We demand the rejection of the reactionary managerial staff and the election of our own officers under the control of the shop stewards' and factory committees. We demand that every worker in the factory—*not only those who the boss elects*—should have access to arms. Side by side with the demand for the election of worker officers in the Home Guard, we demand the dissolution of the Home Guard into the *workers' militia*. We don't trust these people to defend us. Look what they did in France; look how Marshall Pétain was able to wipe out our organisation in unoccupied France by a stroke of the pen because the French workers relied on the bourgeoisie and the Blums.

With this, or a similar approach, the ideas of a workers' militia can be easily grasped and we will be able to raise the class consciousness of the worker who already has a gun in his hand. At the same time these elements in the factory, the militants who have been suspicious of the Home Guard from the very inception, will be drawn along the road to a genuine understanding of a working class military attitude towards war. "Arm the workers" from being a phrase, becomes a clear and concrete revolutionary slogan of struggle. With such a programme we will be able to build a great class conscious movement of workers with arms in their hands who will never permit the same thing to happen here as happened in France.

Another aspect of our propaganda which needs to be sharply corrected is the abstract method of presenting our ideas, and the loose and slipshod phraseology which hides the loose and slipshod ideas. In the February article in *Youth*, the democratic rights of the workers are dealt with in very general terms. At the same time we get phrases such as "the workers support the war for the purpose of fighting fascism." No mention of any opposition to the war at all. With this general and abstract way of saying that the workers support the war, the directives are similarly of a general and abstract character. The workers do not support the war for the purpose of fighting fascism, no more than the German workers support the war for the purpose of fighting "pluto-democracy" as Haw-Haw puts it. The workers support the war in the belief that they will retain the primary things in life: family, living standards, trade unions etc. Put this way—the way of the *Transitional Programme*—it becomes simple to develop concrete demands. Arming the workers becomes directly linked to these primary needs of the workers and not to the abstract defence of the country.

In the past we have always attempted to harden out any *opposition* of the advanced workers to the war, seeking out any manifestation, however slight, and attempting to crystallise it into defeatist channels. In the March 1940 issue of *Workers' International News* we published an article—*The ballot box test*:

> "But does not the vote for the Stop-the-war candidate mean a vote for Hitler? Yes. Nevertheless those workers who record such a vote do not thereby try to make a pro-Hitler gesture. They vote that way because it is one way open to them to express their abomination of the war. And in the absence of a revolutionary socialist candidate, we advise all workers to do the same, voting not *for* the policy of the Stop-the-war candidate, but against the war."

But today our attitude is different. On receiving the report of the Dumbartonshire election, instead of seizing upon it as an anti-war manifestation, the reaction of the Majority was that the Stalinists must have obtained the 4,000 votes on an anti-Hitler ticket—on a "caricature of the military policy", as they put it.

And in the present material in *Workers' International News* and *Youth*, we adopt an entirely different standpoint. We now attempt to show that the workers *want* to fight, but the bourgeoisie refuse to let them. For example in *Youth*: "The workers of Britain support this war for the purpose of fighting fascism, but the ruling class will not allow them to do this." In the document sent to the *Socialist Appeal*, the mood of the masses is characterised in exactly the same terms as the "entire stock in trade of the labour bureaucracy"—they want "to fight against Hitlerism at all costs." No mention of the anti-war sentiments of the advanced workers.

In these lines we see a sharp switch in our propaganda. In the past we said: "this is not our war; the best workers are fighting against it." Today we say: "we want to fight Hitler; but the bourgeoisie won't let us." Whereas in the past we attacked the Stalinist anti-war policy from a critical standpoint, explaining how it plays into the hands of the bourgeoisie, now we wail: "You haven't got a policy to fight Hitler!"

This is carried out to extreme lengths. In the February issue of *Youth*, on the subject of the *Daily Worker* ban, we read:

> "The reason the masses have passively accepted the ban on the *Daily Worker* without any real movement of protest can be laid at the door of the Communist Party policy...And today they do not offer the masses any way of fighting invading fascism."

In the letter to the *Socialist Appeal*:

> "The Stalinists cannot fight the suppression of the *Daily Worker* because they have no program to offer the workers. 'We must at all costs fight and destroy Hitler' is the mood of the masses, and the bombing has strengthened, not weakened this. The Communist Party has not responded to this demand of the workers in the slightest degree. Their

policy has been sectarian, pacifist and sterile. The Labour leaders and the bourgeoisie are making much of the *Daily Worker* demand that every soldier should have a week's holiday at Christmas!

"But the main body of workers has not been roused on this issue. They are still solidly behind the labour leaders and the war against Hitler, and since Morrison accused the *Daily Worker* of helping Hitler, workers have accepted its suppression."

We have always maintained that the Communist Party had not a mass following among the working class, because generally speaking their policy was sectarian as well as opportunist and the workers barely raised their heads to see what they were doing. Now we find that the masses supported Morrison in the banning of the *Daily Worker* because the Communist Party did not have a policy of fighting invading fascism!

The reports from all Labour Party constituencies show that the Stalinists are making headway among the advanced sections of the Labour Party membership. The Scottish Labour Party reports show that in the decisive area of the Clydeside—the storm centre of the British revolutionary movement—the membership are turning to the Stalinists for leadership on the basis of their anti-war platform. The sell out of the Labour and trade union bureaucracy is being sharply demonstrated to the advanced workers in the labour and trade union movement. In their hostility to the attacks the bourgeoisie is levelling against them, the advanced workers are becoming more and more antagonistic to the war. The Stalinists, masquerading under the banner of the October revolution, appear to them to be the only alternative. This movement on the part of the workers is slow (yes comrades, because of the fear of invasion which the capitalists are whipping up) but its tempo will rapidly quicken, depending of course to a large degree, on Stalin's foreign policy.

The ILP, the Victor Gollanczs, the "lefts" in the Labour Party—all these are distorting the thesis of Lenin on revolutionary defeatism. The Stalinists are being labelled "Leninist defeatists" and are basking in the reflected glory of the Leninist policy. They will reap to the full the benefits of the inevitable turn of the masses towards defeatism unless we pose in the clearest possible manner, the true policy of Lenin. Our task is to conduct a sharp ideological struggle with the various distortions if we are to keep the banner of defeatism alive.

Military policy—or confusion

By WIL EC Majority

[WIL, *Internal Bulletin*, March 20 1941]

Reading through the criticism of the article "Arm the workers—The only guarantee against Hitler's invasion" which has appeared in *Youth for Socialism* can only leave one wondering what the comrades are trying to say. What on earth are they criticising? What are they trying to put in its place? Even the criticism of Shachtman of the military policy in America has at least a clearly motivated, if negatively and passively pacifist, point of view.

The comrades of the Minority "accept" the slogans of the Americans, alas, "mechanically" (one of their favourite and groundless assertions against the *Youth* article) and dump them on the British scene without adopting the *general principles and ideas* which these slogans are intended to concretise.

But before dealing with this, let us examine the tangled skein into which the strips of this article are wound and get some order out of the chaos into which it has been strung. We will first of all deal with one by one with the points raised in order not to leave any basis for any further confusion on the part of the comrades concerned, and then attempt to raise the questions as they were clearly and simply explained by Trotsky and Cannon.

First we must counterpose a correct outline of the *Youth* article to the incorrect summary given in the criticism.

A descriptive outline of the military-political situation.

An application of the lessons of France to Britain.

An exposure of the bourgeois lie that they are fighting Hitlerism.

The posing of the question of invasion—and giving the workers a concrete and positive alternative.

This leading to the posing of the problem of power and a revolutionary war against fascism.

The first argument is that the article is "superficial" and has a "mechanical foundation" in that it draws a parallel between the position in France and that in Britain. And then the criticism in a pedantic, lifeless, eclectic way proceeds to give a formal and mechanical counterposing of the French situation with the British. Analysing France, they finish with a correct proposition:

> "After Reynaud's declaration that Paris would be defended 'street by street' the French bourgeoisie, faced with the prospect of arming the Paris proletariat who, together with a section of the army, would have constituted a threat to their own power and conducted a revolutionary war against Hitler, preferred to capitulate to Hitler. To understand the lesson of Pétain, to explain "Pétainism" is to demonstrate this classic example of the defeatist character of the bourgeoisie (including Hitler) if it fears its working class at home."

We will not quarrel with the outline of the situation in France and Britain (we do not wish the argument to be sidetracked on the side issues which do not concern the question under discussion). But they say regarding Britain:

> "At the present moment we can say with regard to the question of war, the British masses, as distinct from the French, *are apathetic in the defencist sense, insofar as they see no other alternative...*Throughout the article which purports to utilise the French experience, there is no analysis of the differences in the situation in Britain today with that which existed in France, politically and economically and which was the primary cause for the capitulation of the French bourgeoisie. The British bourgeoisie do not fear their working class in the present period..." (Our emphasis)

Let us cut through this by one single fact which destroys their interpretation as a landmine destroys a building, without leaving a single brick. So well do the comrades "interpret" the military policy that they have not even noticed it: the military policy was originally put forward not *before* the fall of France, but *after* it, not for France and not even for Britain, but for...America!!

The military policy was developed as a result of the new situation in the world. "The old principles, which remained unchanged, must be applied correctly to the new conditions of permanent war and universal militarism." Trotsky and Cannon utilising the lesson of France show the American workers that they can't leave the "defence against fascist invasion" in the hands of the ruling class. To do so means inevitable defeat and the victory of fascism whether of the German or American variety. That is the meaning of the "military policy." To explain this they utilise to the full the lesson of France. They do not go into long involved explanations as to the "different" situation of the French and American bourgeoisie. They utilise this experience to demonstrate that "...the victories of the fascist war machine of Hitler have destroyed ever plausible basis for the illusion that a serious struggle against fascism can be conducted under the leadership of a bourgeois democratic regime."

They compare *imperialist America*, [the] mightiest capitalist power that has ever existed, with rotting enfeebled France.

Let us hear the author of the policy, Trotsky:

> "The American workers do not want to be conquered by Hitler, and to those who say 'Let us have a peace programme,' the worker will reply, 'But Hitler does not want a peace programme.' Therefore we say: 'We will defend the United States with a workers' army, with workers' officers, with a workers' government, etc'."

Let us also see how Cannon understands this problem. Dealing with the inevitable participation of America in the war, he says, in explaining the military policy:

> "We will never let anything happen as it did in France. These commanding officers from top to bottom turned out to be nothing but traitors and cowards crawling on their knees before Hitler, leaving the workers absolutely helpless. They were far more concerned to save a part of their property than to fight the fascist invader. The myth about the war of 'democracy against fascism' was exploded most shamefully and disgracefully. We must shout at the top of our voices that this is precisely what that gang in Washington will do because they are made of the same stuff as the French, Belgian and Norwegian bourgeoisie. The French example is the great warning that the officers from the class of bourgeois democrats can lead the workers only to useless slaughter, defeat and betrayal."

Does the Minority consider that Cannon is "mechanically" comparing the situation in America with that in Norway? Does he not know the difference in the situation of the Norwegian, French, Belgian and American bourgeoisie?

In order to clarify further we quote an article in the *Socialist Appeal*, December 28 1940.

> "The chief feature of the December 7 issue of the *Saturday Evening Post* is the diary of a British staff officer during the Battle of France. The details he gives constitute an annihilating indictment of the French bourgeoisie and its general staff. Blind, fatuous, complacent, stupid, lacking intelligence and imagination, cowardly—the bourgeois 'democracy' of France emerges from this officer's diary shorn of every claim to any stature.
>
> "But the picture is too damning. The bourgeois 'democracy' of France was exactly the same kind of ruling class which still rules in Britain and the United States. Therefore the author—perhaps at the suggestion of his publisher—casts about to find a striking detail which will enable him to

make the situation of the French rulers different from that in Britain and the United States. He cannot find it because it does not exist…whereupon he invents it…"

Does the American bourgeoisie, which is far stronger than the British, "fear the working class in the present period"? America today dominates Britain and is preparing the greatest imperialist bid for world supremacy that the blood-stained history of imperialism has witnessed. But the Minority, instead of approaching this question from the angle of the American comrades, spend pages analysing the differences in the French and British situations.

Instead of analysing the mood of the masses and helping them to draw revolutionary conclusions from what is progressive in this; they fall into exactly the fatal error against which Trotsky warned. "We do not oppose to events and to the feelings of the masses an abstract affirmation of our sanctity." The workers feel themselves threatened by an immediate invasion from Hitler…so these comrades explain, like a lawyer arguing about some abstract legal quibble, that after all America as well as Germany intends to dominate England. Nevertheless, the workers do not see American troops just across the Channel getting ready to pounce for conquest: and if they did, it would be to welcome them as "allies" in the struggle against what they consider to be a "common menace." Is here any difference in the two situations?

The Minority says: "At the present moment we can say with regard to the question of war, the British masses, as distinct from the French, are apathetic in the defencist sense, *insofar as they have no other alternative.*" Precisely! And here is the whole aim of the military policy—to give them a *positive* alternative to accepting the control and leadership of the capitalist class in fending off a danger which they dread. It was to face a situation like this that the military policy was developed and put forward. As Cannon expresses it:

> "We didn't visualise, nobody visualised, a world situation in which whole countries would be conquered by fascist armies. The workers don't want to be conquered by foreign invaders above all by fascists. They require a programme of military struggle against foreign invaders which assures their class independence."

But the Minority refuse to face up to this situation and while "accepting" the slogans put forward as the "military policy" refuse to concretise them as a way out of the dilemma with which the masses are faced. Incredible as it may seem, the Minority attempt to operate the "new" slogans on the basis of the old *negative* policy. Here is the *real difference* between the Majority and the Minority.

We may remark, in parenthesis, that the comrades calmly repeat the analysis of America's role written for the press over a period by the Majority. Still, we ask, what has this got to do with the issue in dispute? The article doesn't deal with Japan in the Pacific, nor the economic crisis in Brazil, nor the political regime in Portugal. All "very important" of course, and "serious omissions"—but not dealing directly with the problem at issue: invasion. The question of America has been dealt with in our press and will be dealt with again in its due time and place.

In concluding their section headed "England" the comrades say:

> "This is no 'fake' struggle, but is a struggle which will only be concluded after the wholesale destruction of millions of workers."

That the imperialist struggle of the British capitalist class isn't a "fake" struggle nobody would disagree, and the article in *Youth* does not suggest this. *It points out that it is their claim to be fighting fascism that is fake.* To quote *Youth*: "The capitalist class is not fighting Hitler's fascism. They are only fighting his plans to relieve them of their Empire." It is our job to explain, as we have done in this and other articles, for what and in what way the British bourgeoisie is "fighting Hitler" and to prepare the overthrow of the ruling class and a genuine revolutionary war against Hitler.

Do the critics believe that America is threatened with invasion? The mightiest power on earth is preparing the most powerful murder machine in history, dwarfing even that of Germany, in order to battle for domination of the world; and yet our American comrades make full use of the argument of the bourgeoisie that German fascism is threatening to invade America. They say in the *Socialist Appeal*:

> "The government tells us that fascism, the mortal enemy of the Labour movement is threatening to invade our shores? Then let the government also provide technical instructors to teach the unions the military arts...And we can predict in advance that if the organised workers of this country were thus armed and trained, what happened in France could never happen here. No 'democratic' government could ever turn fascist with impunity."

Is there any analysis here of the differences between the situations in America and France, the different "tempo of development" and so on? No! But there is full use made of one of the greatest political lessons of our time—the betrayal of France to Hitler and its overnight transformation into a caricature of a fascist state.

> "The political proposition 'Arm the workers—The only guarantee against Hitler's invasion' is incorrectly posed, flowing as it does, from a military supposition, namely, that the British military machine is incapable of defeating a German invasion. What will happen to this argument if the British bourgeoisie, with American aid, *does* succeed in stemming the invasion, which possibility, although not guaranteed, at least cannot be excluded, and which Wall Street now seems to think it has a good chance of doing? Yet this hypothesis is implicit in the whole presentation

of the question."

A mere detail has escaped our critics' notice. A *guarantee* that something will happen does not at all preclude the same thing happening without the guarantee. The comrades, in their usual confused way, appreciate this, as is shown in the following paragraph from their criticism where they use the word "guarantee" in its proper sense. "What will happen to this argument if the British bourgeoisie, with American aid, *does* succeed in stemming invasion, which possibility, although *not guaranteed*, at least cannot be excluded."

Not only is it not excluded that invasion will be beaten off in spite of the fact that the masses are not armed, but in the opinion of the Majority this is the most likely course of events. But, and here the whole "essence" of the question is missed by the Minority—both militarily and politically the conclusion is indisputable that an arming, organising and training of the whole working class *would make inevitable* a defeat of invasion. Our critics carefully explain that "the British bourgeoisie do not fear their working class in the present period." But they do not draw the conclusion—that *in spite of this they do not arm and organise the whole "people" for resistance*; they prefer to risk the success of an invasion. And even these comrades do not deny that the success of invasion under the present circumstances is "not excluded." Isn't it necessary to draw the conclusion and explain to the masses why the "only guarantee" is not put into force?

Really, one cannot take seriously the infantile arguments into which their petty, quibbling attitude has led these comrades. Instead of the slogan in *Youth* they suggest:

> "We pose the question from a class angle, i.e. 'Invasion: arm the workers under workers' control—the only guarantee for the defence of workers' democratic rights'; in other words we approach the question from the interests of the working class, and not from the angle of a Wintringham."

In other words, these comrades fall precisely into the error of which they characterise the article. They regard the situation from the "Wintringham" angle. We, on the contrary, draw precisely the *class* angle from the *way* in which the capitalists are fighting German imperialism at the present time—in other words, the class lesson flows from this. As to the "under workers' control" the whole *Youth* article points the lesson. We quote:

> "But instead of struggling for workers' control they [the Labour leaders] are helping to increase capitalist control."

> "They, as well as we, have seen the lesson of France—that the working class must be thoroughly armed and have control of those arms if Hitler is to be held up and be defeated. But though they are willing to leave all the fighting to the workers, they are content to leave the control

in the hands of the ruling class."

The critics then quote *Youth*:

> "In Britain the results will be no different. The capitalist class is not fighting Hitler's fascism. They are only fighting his plans of relieving them of their Empire."

And they ask, "What is meant by 'In Britain the results will be no different' if not that the suppression of the British workers will lead, as it did in France, to the German army simply walking in and taking over London?"

What is meant by "In Britain the results will be no different" is quite clearly explained in the article. The "totalitarian" preparations of the ruling class are examined and it is explained, in the same way as Trotsky has explained, that if the masses link their fate with the bourgeois democratic regime of Churchill and the British ruling class it can only result in the victory of Hitler or of a British Pétain or Hitler. In other words it is impossible to fight Hitler's fascism under the control of the capitalist class. To attempt to do so can only lead to fascism in Britain. As Cannon says "The workers themselves have to take charge of this fight against Hitler and anybody else who tries to invade their rights."

Now we quote from the criticism:

> "The hypothesis of one comrade or another as to the fluctuating military potentialities of this or that imperialist army, while important as a means to present the relative transitional demand, must not be allowed to form the axis of our political slogans as exemplified in 'Arm the workers—the only guarantee against Hitler's invasion'."

But this is precisely the pitfall into which our critics stumble. In analysing "the only guarantee" they give precisely a *Wintringham* interpretation of the possibility of a defeat for invasion. For them the problem ends where for us it just begins. We explain (we would refer the comrades to the February issue of *Workers' International News*) that despite the fact that the bourgeoisie is *risking* the major part of its plunder and risking a possible defeat ("not excluded" the critics admit) they prefer this rather than arming and organising of the whole of the "people"—not just under workers' control—*but even under their own control*. And all this, even accepting for the moment the academic, false and incredibly formalistic approach of the comrades, "the British workers are not red"; "the British bourgeoisie is not afraid of the working class in the present period."

For the benefit of the authors we will let them into the "secret" (to them anyway) of how the dialectic of this process works. Is it necessary to reiterate here that the capitalist class has been systematically preparing for a bloody settlement with the workers and civil war for the last number of years? Army manoeuvres on the assumption of civil war, placing machine guns at strategic points in government buildings, the formation of the Civil Guard, arming of the police, etc. But the facts are well known to the comrades. We presume that these are preparations springing, not out of fear of the workers, but out of a desire to celebrate the fraternity and goodwill between the bourgeoisie and the workers which the Minority points out that Wilkie discovered on his visit to Britain.

What happens if a working class armed and organised under the control of their own committees and trade unions beats off invasion? What then? It would not be so easy to disarm them once the danger had passed. Once the workers go on the move against the exploiters on the economic field, the danger to the ruling class, which previously has been potential and dormant, would become active and acute. Here is the key to the question—why under all conditions the bourgeoisie is against the organisation and the arming of the broad masses.

Today the class struggle is not at an extreme point of tension; tomorrow it will inevitably be so. The bourgeoisie, more far-sighted than our critics, do not look at events from a static point of view, and inevitably their policy flows from this perspective. That is why, in contradistinction to the slogans of the Minority, which merely tend to further befuddlement of the masses—not to speak of themselves—we can emphasise what Marx called the bourgeois fraud of "national defence" and expose the naked class calculations underlying the policy of the bourgeoisie—at the same time offering a positive and concrete alternative which the workers cannot but see is the means to their salvation. Accepting the argument of the bourgeoisie (and more important of the labour leaders) that it is necessary to fight Hitlerism—*the problem of power* is raised in the minds of the masses—the proposition "how to defend ourselves against Hitler" or invasion, etc. leads direct to the question which in a blurred and distorted fashion the opposition sees (correctly) as our task, the problem of overthrowing the bourgeoisie—taking power into our own hands and waging a genuine revolutionary war against fascism.

And then our critics go on to give still another quotation together with their comment:

> "The victory of British imperialism would lead to fascism not to its overthrow. There is only one road for the British working class. To fight Hitler we must take power into our own hands. The road of the Labour leaders is leading to destruction. If we do not wish to suffer the fate of our French comrades we must act in time."

In this paragraph, they claim is contained the following:

- The possibility of victory of British imperialism.

- The impossibility of victory of British imperialism.

- The confusing of the question of stemming the invasion and the possibility of a British military victory over Germany.

- Even when posing the question of a British military victory which "would lead to fascism" the conclusion drawn is how to fight Hitler.

But just read this paragraph in context with the preceding three paragraphs, and the only conclusion that one can come to is that the comrades have become blinded by prejudice and completely incapable of understanding the meaning of words or ideas:

> "A victory of British imperialism in the war would be as harmful to the people of Europe and Britain as a Nazi victory itself...

> "...If we do not wish to suffer the fate of our French comrades we must act in time."

The paragraph, especially when taken in context, but even without this, explains that *in order to fight fascism it is necessary to take power*. Victory for British imperialism would not lead to an overthrow of fascism (even in Germany) but to the establishment ultimately of fascism in Britain as well. Therefore, to support British imperialism as the Labour leaders are doing would lead to the destruction of the labour organisations, just as they have been destroyed in France. Therefore if we wish to fight Hitlerism it is necessary to take power into our own hands—to entrust this to the hands of British imperialism is to lead to the victory of fascism.

From what sentence in the first paragraph quoted does the "impossibility of victory for British imperialism" arise? You can search in this paragraph, both on the lines and between them: not even by implication is any such suggestion made. It only arises out of the lack of clarity of thought of our comrades.

From what sentence in the paragraph quoted do they deduce their second conclusion? Have we to explain what every schoolboy writing an essay knows: that, having dealt with a question (invasion) one can then turn to another question? The article deals primarily with the immediate question of invasion. But that does not at all exclude the question of a military victory for British imperialism being dealt with. Where does this "confusing" etc. come in? All the "confusing" that is being done is by the comrades of the Minority. This particular paragraph does not deal with the question of invasion from the point of view of stemming it or anything else; but alas, it apparently fails lamentably in "stemming" the confusion in the minds of our critics.

> "Even when posing the question of a British victory which 'would lead to fascism' the conclusion drawn is how to fight Hitler!"

Exactly! And that conclusion is? The workers must take power! Along with Cannon we say:

> "The workers themselves must take charge of this fight against Hitler and anybody else who tries to invade their rights. That is the whole prin-

ciple of the new policy that has been elaborated for us by comrade Trotsky."[1]

In other words, it is necessary for the workers to take power in order to fight Hitler. It is the complete incapacity of the comrades to understand this that is the source of all their errors and confusion and their inability to criticise the articles from the point of view of a difference in principles.

In their efforts to discredit the policy as put forward by the Majority, the comrades attempt to "graft" an argument onto us which is not ours. Giving the brilliant quotation from Trotsky which forms the basis of our international strategy, they surreptitiously, cautiously and confusedly attempt to use this quotation against us and smuggle in the idea that we are defencists and social patriots.

We ask the comrades point blank: Do you accuse us of defencism? If so, state it openly instead of approaching it cautiously like a mouse approaching a particularly delectable piece of cheese, but afraid to nibble it for fear of the cat (the real military policy of Trotsky and Cannon) which is waiting round the corner to spring on it.

Is Trotsky being defencist and "bringing forward Hitler as the chief bugbear" when he says:

> "That is why we must try to separate the workers from the others by a programme of education of workers' schools, of workers' officers, devoted to the welfare of the workers' army, etc. We cannot escape from their militarisation but inside the machine we can observe the class line. *The American workers do not want to be conquered by Hitler, and to those who say, 'Let us have a peace programme', the workers will reply, 'But Hitler does not want a peace programme.'* Therefore we say: 'we will defend the United States with a workers' army, with workers' officers, with a workers' government, etc.' "

Is Cannon being defencist and "bringing forward Hitler as the chief bugbear" when he says:

> "No worker wants to see that gang of fascist barbarians over-run this country or any country. But we want to fight fascism under a leadership we can trust."

Is the Majority being defencist and "bringing forward Hitler as the chief bugbear" when it says:

---

[1] This refers to the manifesto written by Trotsky, *Imperialist war and the world proletarian revolution*, approved by the emergency conference of the Fourth International, May 19 to 26 1940.

> "We cannot fight Hitlerism under the control of the capitalist class. To attempt this is to make inevitable the victory either of Hitler or of some British Hitler. In order to wage a genuine revolutionary war for the liberation of the people of Europe and for the defence of the rights of the British working class, it is necessary that power should be in the hands of the workers."

On the contrary there is no trace of defencism here, but a clear expression of the military policy of the proletariat.

The Minority then quotes the following passage from Trotsky's article, *We do not change our course*:

> "Hitler the conqueror has naturally day dreams of becoming the chief executioner of the proletarian revolution in any part of Europe. But that does not at all mean that Hitler will be strong enough to deal with the proletarian revolution, as he has been able to deal with imperialist democracy. It would be a fatal blunder, unworthy of a revolutionary party, to turn Hitler into a fetish, to exaggerate his power, to overlook the objective limits of his successes and conquests. Hitler boastfully promises to establish the domination of the German people, at the expense of all Europe and even of the whole world, 'for one thousand years.' But in all likelihood, this splendour will not endure even for ten years."

The confusion of the Minority is eloquently illustrated by their attempt to utilise this quotation against us. They have not understood what "fetishism" Trotsky was warning the Fourth International against. This will appear clearly when we show what Trotsky was really dealing with in the article quoted.

Trotsky is saying that under no circumstances and no conditions must the fate of the working class, and principally of the vanguard, be linked up with the fate of rotting bourgeois democracy. He points out, as the comrades say quite correctly, that Hitler's day dream of becoming the chief executioner of the proletarian revolution in any part of Europe is, of course, false. But the point that Trotsky was making they have completely missed. He is arguing this against the social patriots who, on the basis of Hitler's victories demand that the proletariat subordinate themselves to the imperialist bourgeoisie of Britain and America because the victory of Hitler "would mean the end of everything and...just a blank wall with no perspective." In other words, that no support should be given to Churchill, Roosevelt, etc.

This is clearly expressed not only in the article in question but also in a very compact form in the manifesto *War and the world revolution*[1].

> *"By his victories and bestialities Hitler provokes naturally the sharp hatred of workers the world over. But between this legitimate hatred of workers and the helping of his weaker but not less reactionary enemies*

is an unbridgeable gulf. The victory of the imperialists of Great Britain and France would be not less frightful for the ultimate fate of mankind than that of Hitler and Mussolini. Bourgeois democracy cannot be saved. *By helping our bourgeoisie against foreign fascism the workers would only accelerate the victory of fascism in their own country. The task which is posed by history is not to support one part of the imperialist system against another, but to make an end of the system as a whole."* (Our emphasis)

But between this and the sectarian refusal to base ourselves on the "legitimate hatred of the workers of Hitler, his victories and bestialities", there exists indeed an "unbridgeable gulf" into which the Minority has fallen and until it is clearly understood by the members of our organisation we will not be able to move forward a single inch.

The criticism proceeds:

"Comrade Trotsky was addressing himself to these comrades [which comrades?—EG] who depicted the coming of Hitler as the end of everything and seeing before them just a blank wall with no perspective. We believe that the article reflects this 'fetishism' by its whole presentation. In order to justify this 'fetishism', the Majority characterise the mood of the masses as 'We must at all costs fight and destroy Hitler.' We disagree with this characterisation, but assuming it is correct, how does this fit in with the mood of the German masses which is anti-Churchill since he is the arch representative of that imperialism which imposed the infamous Versailles Treaty on the German people—and they are fully aware, is preparing an even more infamous one in the event of a British victory."

Once more let us see who and what Trotsky was attacking. He polemicises in the article against the conceptions held in this country by Strachey, Gollancz, C. A. Smith, "left" Labour leaders, etc. (We intend dealing with these in our publications in due course.) Here is a quotation from this same article of Trotsky:

"In the wake of a number of other and smaller European states, France is being transformed into an oppressed nation. German imperialism has risen to unprecedented military heights, with all the ensuing opportunities for world plunder.

"What then follows?

"From the side of all sorts of semi-internationalists one may expect approximately the following line of argumentation: successful uprisings in conquered countries, under the Nazi heel, are impossible, because every revolutionary movement will be immediately drowned in blood by the conquerors. There is even less reason to expect a successful uprising in the camp of the totalitarian victors. Favourable conditions for revolution could be created only by the defeat of Hitler and Mussolini.

Therefore, nothing remains except to aid England and the United States. Should the Soviet Union join us it would be possible not only to halt Germany's military successes but to deal her heavy military and economic defeats. The further development of the revolution is possible only on this road. And so forth and so on."

"This argumentation which appears on the surface to be inspired by the new map of Europe is in reality only an adaptation to the new map of Europe of the *old arguments of social patriotism, i.e. class betrayal.* Hitler's victory over France has revealed completely the corruption of imperialist democracy, even in the sphere of its own tasks. It cannot be 'saved' from fascism. It can only be replaced by proletarian democracy. *Should the working class tie up its fate in the present war with the fate of imperialist democracy, it would only assure itself a new series of defeats.*

"'For victory's sake' England has already found herself obliged to introduce the methods of dictatorship, the primary pre-requisite for which was the renunciation by the Labour Party of *any political independence whatsoever. If the international proletariat, in the form of all its organisations and tendencies, were to take to the same road, then this would only facilitate and hasten the victory of the totalitarian regime on a world scale.* Under the conditions of the world proletariat renouncing independent politics, an alliance between the USSR and the imperialist democracies would signify the growth of the omnipotence of the Moscow bureaucracy, its further transformation into an agency of imperialism, and its inevitably making concessions to imperialism in the economic sphere. In all likelihood the military position of the various imperialist countries on the world arena would be greatly changed thereby; but the position of the world proletariat, from the standpoint of the tasks of the socialist revolution, would be changed very little." (Our emphasis)

Isn't it clear what Trotsky is dealing with here? He is warning the cadres of the Fourth International that the social patriots of all descriptions will attempt to use Hitler's victories for the purpose of justifying their collaboration with the capitalist class. Do the comrades of the Minority accuse us of this? They cannot! On the contrary, we use Hitler's victories and the mood of the masses in regard to them for the purpose of *separating* the workers from the bourgeoisie, and not advocating collaboration; we use Hitler's victories and the betrayals of the bourgeoisie of France, Belgium, Norway, etc. to *increase* working class independence, and not to decrease it. If we in any way indicate that we support Churchill and British imperialism in the conflict, let the comrades give one single quotation from the article to prove it.

No! The mood of the masses is to find a way out of the impasse in which they find themselves, and in this article we give them the only real alternative to fighting Hitler under Churchill and company—that of fighting Hitler under their own independent working class banner.

In this we stand on the same ground as Trotsky and Cannon:

> "The American workers do not want to be conquered by Hitler, and to those who say, 'Let us have a peace programme', the worker will reply, 'But Hitler does not want a peace programme.' Therefore we say: 'We will defend the United States with a workers' army, with workers' officers, with a workers' government, etc.' "

Does the Minority agree with Trotsky's characterisation of the mood of the masses in America—3,000 miles from the scene of the conflict? And not even openly in the war? If so, do they characterise the mood of the British workers differently? And then, most important of all, if the workers do not want to be conquered by Hitler—what flows from this? Do we simply give "an affirmative of our sanctity"? Do we just turn to the workers and say, as do the Minority, "The immediate threat (to your democratic rights) comes directly from within"? Or basing ourselves on the mood of the masses, do we say, "If you want really to fight Hitler, you must take the fight into your own hands? If you don't, you will have either the victory of Hitler or of British Hitlerism." That is how the Majority poses the question. This way leads directly to the struggle against "the main enemy at home"—but it is raised in a way which cannot but appeal to the masses, and not in the formal, scholastic manner of the Minority.

Another question is put to us by the Minority:

> "...how does this fit in with the mood of the German masses which is anti-Churchill since he is the arch-representative of that imperialism which imposed the infamous Versailles Treaty on the German people— and as they are fully aware, is preparing an even more infamous one in the event of a British victory?"

An adequate understanding of the military policy would have answered this puerile objection in advance; and indeed the fear of the German masses of another Versailles is dealt with in an article in *Youth*, though from the point of view of the British workers. But "how does this fit in with the mood of the German masses..." The answer is quite simple. We are not in any way, by hint, implication or innuendo giving the slightest political support to Churchill or any imperialist politician or class at any time or any place whatsoever. We are not for the victory of Churchill and infamous Versailles treaties, etc., etc. Is not that sufficiently clear? From the point of view of the German revolutionaries the answer is that they can agree on the struggle against Churchill and British imperialism (assuming that that is the "mood of the masses")—*but not under the leadership and control of Hitler and the German capitalists*. The rest of the propaganda would follow from this. The taking of power by the workers in order to wage a *real* fight against Churchill and his imperialism, etc. Surely, it is easy to understand this? The whole argument against us falls away of itself.

In the following paragraph the comrades say:

> "Flowing from the article our traditional international appeal to the European working class is cast aside for an appeal to support the socialist struggle against Hitler."

This attempt to contrast the "socialist struggle against Hitler" with our "traditional international appeal to the European working class" can only arise out of confusion. It would certainly be interesting, if the Minority insists that there is a difference, to hear them explain it. But we notice that, while asserting that there *is* a difference, they make no attempt to contrast the two; and for the very good reason that it would be impossible to do so.

The last paragraph of the section on "Hitlerism" says: "...the slogan, like the title of the article, does not mention under whose control the workers must be armed." We have already quoted the passage from the *Youth* article which calls for workers' control, etc. But instead of recognising this and dealing with the *principle* involved, we get this attempt to seize on and exaggerate minor points.

But in their zeal the comrades have overlooked a trifle! Are they suggesting that we demand that the capitalists be disarmed—and then that we suggest that the workers should be placed under capitalist control? The mere posing of the question shows to what an absurd position the comrades have been reduced. Obviously if the bourgeoisie is to be disarmed they cannot be left in the control of the workers, as the quotation shows. If it will help to relieve their anxiety, we will accept the correction in all humility. (Incidentally the article in *Workers' International News* gives exactly this slogan.)

The second part of the criticism in this paragraph is "most disturbing", seeing that it contradicts itself.

> "On the other hand, if the *whole* of the British bourgeoisie is implied—are we to understand that the whole bourgeoisie is willing to sell out to Hitler? But *most disturbing* is the posing of the main enemy as the foreign one. This slogan should have read: 'Disarm the capitalists and dissolve the Home Guard into workers' militia under workers' control. Trade union control of the army for the struggle against totalitarian oppression at home and abroad.' " (Our emphasis)

These two criticisms are mutually exclusive. If the *whole bourgeoisie* is going to sell out then obviously the "main enemy" is the treacherous ruling class within the gates. But aside from this, actually all the slogan implies is that in order to fight Hitler it is necessary to overthrow the ruling class. "The whole principle" of the new policy, as Cannon has stated, is that "the workers themselves must take charge of this fight against Hitler and anybody else who tries to invade their rights." In other words, the disturbance in the minds of the comrades can subside. The axis around which the new policy revolves is precisely what the comrades have completely and hopelessly missed. That out of the posing of a struggle against "Hitler and anybody else who tries to invade their rights" precisely flows the question of the "main enemy at home." The question of whether the *whole* of the bourgeoisie will sell out or whether 90 percent or 10 percent, is something which entirely misses the mark. When Cannon says: "The French example is the great warning that officers from the class of bourgeois democrats can lead the workers only to useless slaughter, defeat and betrayal" we could ask him in the same scandalised way—"does Cannon think that *all* the bourgeois officers will lead the workers to useless slaughter? That *all* the bourgeois officers will betray?"

But the whole question cannot be considered in this way at all. This slogan cannot be separated from the rest. Do the comrades agree that the threat of putting into operation the expropriation of the mines, banks, industry, etc. would immediately turn the overwhelming majority of the ruling class into fifth columnists?

As is usual with sectarians, the Minority fall headlong into opportunism when attempting to face the problems concretely. The slogan "Trade union control of the army for the struggle against totalitarian oppression both at home and abroad" is a dangerous one, which we can search through the pages of the *Socialist Appeal* in vain to find. As a matter of fact Shachtman bases his whole criticism of Cannon's position on the allegation that this is his policy. It flies in the face of the Marxian attitude towards the state as developed by Lenin. But we do not desire to go into a long and involved argument on this side issue. If the comrades insist on maintaining a wrong position on this fundamental question we shall return to it again. Soldiers' committees in the army would be the correct way to pose this question if a slogan is issued. The other slogan is quite good and possibly ought to be accepted, "Disarm the capitalists and dissolve the Home Guard into workers' militia under workers' control," but requires further study.

"Defence of workers' democratic rights"

"With the coming of the Second World War, the process of decay and destruction of bourgeois democracy is accelerated. On the actual outbreak of the war, its death knell is already being sounded. In the present epoch of totalitarian war the luxury of 'democracy' must be discarded by the bourgeoisie in order to face the totalitarian war machine of the adversary. Inevitably bourgeois democracy must eliminate its overhead expenses, i.e. the democratic rights of the workers, trade unions, the relatively high standard of living—all these must go. Totalitarianism can only be fought by totalitarianism."

This is correct. But here again the whole fundamental change in the tactic which the military policy implies is missed. What the comrades say above has always been said by us Trotskyists in the past in the same negative—although not so formalistic and lifeless way as the comrades are doing. But now *we pose the problem in a different—in a positive way*, although the essence of the question remains the same. Instead of saying, "totalitarianism can only be fought by totalitarianism", *we say totalitarianism can only be fought by the taking of power by the working class*. Any other way means it will end in bourgeois democracy becoming totalitarian. This is how the question is raised in *Youth*:

> "We cannot fight Hitlerism under the control of the capitalist class. To attempt this is to make inevitable the victory of either Hitler or of some British Hitler. In order to wage a genuine revolutionary war for the liberation of the peoples of Europe and for the defence of the rights of the British working class, it is necessary that power should be in the hands of the workers."

And this is how it is posed by Trotsky and Cannon:

> "The workers themselves must take charge of this fight against Hitler and anybody else who tries to invade their rights..."

> "...We must use the example of France to the very end. We must say, 'I warn you, workers, that they, (the bourgeoisie) will betray you! Look at Pétain, who is a friend of Hitler. Shall we have the same thing happen in this country? We must create our own machine under workers' control."

This simple posing of the fundamental problems of our epoch—the question of the regime, the question of power, the question of the military policy—how clear, how simple it emerges from the posing of the problem in the way the Old Man[2] poses it. Compare this with the tortuous confused, one-sided, mechanical way in which the Minority attempt to grapple with the problem.

> "In the forefront of our programme comes the fight for the democratic rights of the working class in the present period. These become revolutionary demands and assume tremendous importance in our transitional slogans. In the last two great remaining 'democracies' the rights of the workers are being filched from them. *While these rights are threatened by a Hitler invasion the immediate threat to the British working class comes directly from within.* In the defence of 'democracy against Hitlerism', the British bourgeoisie is rapidly destroying the very rights which we are supposed to be defending. Comrade Trotsky posed the question clearly in his last letters." (Our emphasis)

---

2 Within the Fourth Internationalist movement, Trotsky was frequently referred to as the "Old Man".

But here exactly is the whole heart of the problem. How to explain to the masses that the "immediate threat" comes "directly from within"? The workers "don't want to be conquered by foreign invaders" and the Minority falls exactly into that *negative* attitude which is condemned by Cannon. They attempt to operate on the basis we have always done in the past.

> "Many times in the past we were put at a certain disadvantage, the demagogy of the social democrats against us was effective to a certain extent. They said 'You have no answer to the question of *how to fight against Hitler*, how to prevent Hitler from conquering France, Belgium, etc.' (Of course, their programme was very simple—the suspension of the class struggle and complete subordination of the workers to the bourgeoisie. We have seen the results of this treacherous policy). *Well, we answered in a general way the workers will first overthrow the bourgeoisie at home and then they will take care of the invaders*. That was a good programme, but the workers did not make the revolution in time. *Now the two tasks must be telescoped and carried out simultaneously*." (Our emphasis)

The Minority wishes to carry on under the new conditions the old abstract propaganda which is completely sterile at the present time—whereas by posing the question of "how to fight Hitler" we immediately expose the bourgeoisie and *what is more important the Labour leaders*. The Labour and trade union leaders justify their collaboration with the bourgeoisie in the government and—the "rapid destroying of those very rights which we are supposed to be defending", by the necessity to make "sacrifices" in order to win victory over Hitler. You would be a thousand times worse off if Hitler were to conquer you, they tell the workers. And by these means they have been enabled (temporarily of course) to paralyse the movement of the masses. The masses tolerate their treachery because they do not see any alternative.

Now merely to denounce Churchill as a more "immediate threat" to Hitler is useless and barren. But to point out that the "destroying of these very rights which we are supposed to be defending", is not necessary to fight Hitler, that is the way to "find an approach to the masses." By posing the question of how to fight Hitler we lead the masses to the conclusion that it is necessary to wage a struggle against Churchill. By posing the way of waging war against the fascist enemy without, flows directly the question of waging struggle against the enemy within. That is the whole theme of the article in *Youth*.

In the Minority's bulletin, the struggle against "Hitlerism" at home and abroad are entirely *separated* and two distinct problems. But let us see how Trotsky and Cannon (and with them the Majority) really posed the problem and examine the confused way in which the Minority distorts it. They give two quotations from Trotsky:

"But we categorically refuse to defend civil liberties and democracy in the French manner; the workers and farmers to give their flesh and blood while the capitalists concentrate in their hands the command. The Pétain experiment should now form the centre of our war propaganda. It is important, of course, to explain to the advanced workers that the genuine fight against fascism is the socialist revolution. But it is more urgent, more imperative to explain to the millions of American workers that the defence of their 'democracy' cannot be delivered over to an American Marshall Pétain—and there are many candidates for such a role."

"We must use the example of France to the very end. We must say, 'I warn you workers, that they (the bourgeoisie) will betray you! Look at Pétain, who is a friend of Hitler, shall we have the same thing happen in this country? We must create our own machine, under workers' control.' We must be careful not to identify ourselves with the chauvinists, nor with the confused sentiments of self-preservation, but we must understand their feelings and adapt ourselves to those feelings critically, and prepare the masses for a better understanding of the situation, otherwise we will remain a sect, of which the pacifist variety is the most miserable."

The first quotation, despite the attempt of the Minority to distort and confuse the issue, has a crystal-clear meaning. The bourgeoisie, and with them the Labour leaders, argue that we must "defend civil liberties and democracy" *against the attacks of Hitler*. Trotsky replies—"Yes. But this cannot be done under your leadership, Messrs Bourgeoisie!" "The Pétain experiment should now form the centre of our war propaganda." Cannon makes this quite clear in his speech expounding the military policy.

"We will never let anything happen as it did in France. These commanding officers from top to bottom turned out to be nothing but traitors and cowards crawling *on their knees before Hitler*, leaving the workers *absolutely helpless. They were far more concerned to save part of their property than to fight the fascist invader.* The myth about the war of 'democracy against fascism' was exploded most shamefully and disgracefully. *We must shout at the top of our voices that this is precisely what this gang in Washington will do because they are made of the same stuff as the French, Belgian and Norwegian bourgeoisie.* The French example is the great warning that officers from the class of bourgeois democrats can lead the workers only to useless slaughter, defeat and betrayal." (Our emphasis)

Isn't it clear here that the question of the enemy "within" is raised by explaining that the enemy "without" cannot be fought except by dealing with the enemy at home? The second quotation from Trotsky makes the position even clearer, despite the frantic efforts of the Minority to "graft" a different meaning and interpretation on it. The bourgeoisie will *betray* the workers. Trotsky makes this clear despite the attempt to confuse the issue. "Look at Pétain who is a friend of Hitler." The quotation just as it stands annihilates the distortion that is attempted.

Cannon says:

"The workers themselves must take charge of this fight against Hitler and anybody else who tries to invade their rights. That is the whole principle of the new policy that has been elaborated for us by comrade Trotsky."

And again:

"We must shout at the top of our voices that this is precisely what that gang in Washington will do because they are made of the same stuff as the French, Belgian and Norwegian bourgeoisie."

But the Minority is shouting at the top of their voices to prevent the membership understanding this problem clearly.

We quote the preceding paragraph to Trotsky's second quotation which has been "glaringly omitted."

"That is why it would be doubly stupid to present a purely abstract pacifist position today; the feeling the masses have is that it is necessary to defend themselves. We must say: 'Roosevelt (or Willkie) says it is necessary to defend the country; Good! Only it must be *our* country, not that of the 60 families and their Wall Street. The army must be under our own command; we must have our own officers, who will be loyal to us.' In this way we can find an approach to the masses that will not push them away from us, and thus to prepare for the second step—a more revolutionary one."

Let us look a little further up the page:

"Now the national feeling is for a tremendous army, navy and airforce. This is the psychological atmosphere for the creation of a military machine, and you will see it becoming stronger and stronger every day and every week. You will have military schools etc., and a Prussianisation of the United States will take place. The sons of the bourgeois families will become imbued with Prussian feelings and ideals, and their parents will be proud that their sons look like Prussian lieutenants. *To some extent this will be also true of the workers.*

"That is why we must try to *separate the workers from the others* by a programme of education, of workers' schools, of workers' officers, devoted to the welfare of the worker army, etc. We cannot escape from the militarisation but inside the machine we can observe the class line.

The American workers do not want to be conquered by Hitler, and to those who say 'Let us have a peace programme', the worker will reply, 'But Hitler does not want a peace programme'. Therefore we say: 'We will defend the United States with a workers' army, with workers' officers, with a workers' government, etc. If we are not pacifists, who wait for a better future and if we are active revolutionists, our job is to penetrate into the whole military machine'." (Our emphasis)

The whole of these "Questions on American problems" are devoted to the inevitable participation of America in the war, and the tactics of the revolutionaries towards this.

Trotsky in dealing with the problems clearly explains our tasks *in the war* despite all the efforts of the Minority who will not or cannot see the task in front of us..."Let us have an organised workers' programme for the war..."

"...They should provoke in the workers a mistrust of the old traditions, the military plans of the bourgeois class and officers, and should insist upon the necessity of educating workers' officers who will be absolutely loyal to the proletariat. *In this epoch every great question national or international will be resolved with arms*—not by peaceful means." (Our emphasis)

Now let us look a little further *down* the page and see the paragraph which *follows* the Minority's quotation:

"We must also say that the war has a tendency toward totalitarian dictatorship. War develops a centralisation, and during war the bourgeois class cannot allow the workers any new concessions. The trade unions will therefore become a kind of Red Cross for the workers, a sort of philanthropic institution. The bosses themselves will be under control by the state, everything will be sacrificed to the army, and the trade union influence will become zero. And we must say of this now: '*If you don't place yourselves on a workers' military basis, with workers' schools workers' officers, etc., and go to war on the old style military basis you will be doomed.*' And this in its own way will preserve the trade unions themselves." (Our emphasis)

Isn't it clear what Trotsky is talking about? He is dealing with *war against Hitler and/or Japan.* Having pointed out that the war is inevitable, he says: "If we have war *we must have a programme for war.*" But the Minority refuse to "find an approach to the masses that will not push them away from us, and thus [to] prepare for the second step—a more revolutionary one."

We notice that Trotsky generalises the question of defending *the country*—but it must be *our* country, etc. He proceeds in the whole of the passages quoted, from the "defence of the country" *which the bourgeois will betray.* "Shall we have the same thing happen in this country?"

But let us return to the Minority:

> "In other words, we must defend our democratic rights, we are willing to give our flesh and blood for that which we find worth defending, but we must be in command."

So far so good! We entirely agree with this! But then once more the sectarians fall blindly into opportunism.

> "Our existing democracy must be defended and broadened into the army, etc., thus linking it up with full workers' democracy, i.e. the proletarian dictatorship."

On the contrary, the "defence of democratic rights" against Hitler or the bourgeoisie at home leads to the posing of the problem of *seizing power*.

"Now," say our critics, "let us examine how the article in *Youth* deals with the question" and they quote from *Youth*:

> "The elementary need for self preservation demands that the workers should not be left helpless and unarmed in face of the coming Nazi onslaught. British 'democracy' can be rendered impregnable against the attacks of Hitler or of a British Pétain if the working class is armed."

And their comment:

> "Is this adapting ourselves to the feelings of the masses critically? Is this preparing the masses for a better understanding of a situation? We say no, just the opposite. What is the meaning of 'British 'democracy' can be rendered impregnable'? Does it mean that decaying British bourgeois democracy—and since when are we prepared to render 'British democracy' impregnable against attacks? We presume that the above bases itself on the statements of comrade Trotsky on the defence of *workers' democracy*. But Trotsky is advocating that the only means of the working class defending their democratic rights is by taking control, by taking command in their own hands. Merely calling for arms for the workers as the elementary need for their preservation is to fall into those very errors against which Trotsky warns."

It is intensely aggravating to find wilful misunderstanding of your position by your opponent. "Merely calling for arms for the workers as the elementary need for their self preservation is to fall into those very errors against which Trotsky warned." Certainly! But did these comrades read the *Youth* article or not?! From wading through this criticism one would come to the conclusion that they imagine that every paragraph is a separate and independent article by itself!

The preceding paragraph to the one quoted says:

"We cannot fight Hitlerism under the control of the capitalist class. To attempt this is to make inevitable either the victory of Hitler or of some British Hitler. In order to wage a genuine revolutionary war for the liberation of Europe and for the defence of the rights of the British working class, it is necessary that power should be in the hands of the workers."

"Is this adapting ourselves to the feelings of the masses critically?" *Yes!* "Is this preparing the masses for a better understanding of the situation?" *Yes!* "But Trotsky is advocating that the only means of the working class defending their democratic rights is by taking control, by taking command in their own hands." Does the paragraph advocate this? *Yes!*

Let us see how the *Socialist Appeal* deals with the same question. In the issue of August 3 1940, there is a leading article with the heading *Arming the workers*. The whole article is given in full at the end of this bulletin. Here is one paragraph.

"It [an article in the *New York Times*] tells that a miners' convention at Blackpool unanimously adopted a resolution asking that miners be armed to meet a possible invasion.

"We should like to see every union in this country adopt a similar resolution. The government tells us that fascism, the mortal enemy of the labour movement is threatening to invade our shores? Then let the government provide arms for the mortal enemies of fascism everywhere—the trade unions.

"...And we can also predict in advance that, if the organised workers of this country were thus armed and trained what happened in France could never happen here. No 'democratic' government could ever turn fascist with impunity."

Our critics ask us—"What is the meaning of 'British 'democracy' can be rendered impregnable'?" It means that all the workers' rights which are summed up in "democracy" can only be safeguarded if the working class is armed to resist any incursions by Hitler or a British Hitler. The immediate problem is invasion. See how the *Socialist Appeal* deals with this question, although invasion of America is at the moment an abstract and almost fantastic conception.

What the criticism confuses—the military policy

"*The workers are being armed by the bourgeoisie.* The military policy of the Fourth International is based on this historic fact—the universal militarisation of the proletariat—and not, as is implied in the article on the withholding of arms from the workers."

"While we naturally support the slogan 'Arm the workers', mechanical interpretation of this slogan in itself is not enough. The whole problem which poses itself before us is one of *control*." (Our emphasis)

The unconscious contradiction of this criticism is really humorous. In their anxiety to criticise the article the comrades of the Minority land themselves in an absurd position. While correctly stating that we must base ourselves on the arming of the proletariat by the bourgeoisie, which in the end will prove their undoing and stating that the "military policy" bases itself on this, they calmly proceed to call for...the "arming of the workers, under workers' control, etc.". Coming straight after their one sided criticism in the preceding paragraph this contradiction is really "glaring." They do not notice that the bottom is knocked out of their criticism. That calling for the arming of the workers *who are not armed* in no way contradicts having a policy for the workers who are already in the army. The bourgeoisie is compelled by the contradictions of world imperialism to place arms in the hands of the workers in the army. But this does not mean to say that we "mechanically" ignore the problem of the workers who are not armed. What is "mechanical" is to attempt to counterpose the one to the other as if they mutually excluded one another. In reality both flow from the same basic policy. Nowhere, indeed it is fantastic to assume this, can it be "implied" that the Majority believe the military policy is based on "the withholding of arms from the workers."

That the military policy is based on the arming of the workers is correct. Yes. But it is only one side of the medal. The bourgeoisie arms the workers in the army and even a special section under their own control in the Home Guard. But between this and the levee en mass for which *Youth* called, not only in February but also in July of last year, there is a decisive difference. The fact that the comrades confusedly recognise the difference is revealed by their "naturally" supporting the slogan "Arm the workers." If the military policy is based *only* on the fact that the "workers are being armed by the bourgeoisie" why do the comrades call for the "arming of the workers"? If it is a question only of *control* and not of arming, then they should not call for "Arm the workers" but "change bourgeois control of the armed workers for workers' control." These comrades who quibble about whether *all* of the bourgeoisie will betray to Hitler fail to notice that *all* (not even a majority) of the workers are not armed, organised and trained for resistance to "the foreign invaders."

The Minority complains that we did not deal with the Colonel Bingham affair. But there are other aspects of the military policy which we did not deal with. And for the simple reason that it is not possible to deal with every aspect in one article—or even one issue of *Youth*. It is necessary to apply the policy to the most burning issues with which the workers are faced at any particular time. In any case, an article on Bingham was wrritten for that issue of *Youth*, [but] as the comrades of the Minority are well aware, it was withheld for the next month's issue. We considered, and still consider that the question of invasion enabled us to put the military policy forward better than the Colonel Bingham affair. The "gist of the problem" was to give the workers "a programme of military struggle against foreign invaders which assures their class independence."

The comrades give "a few quotes" from the *Youth* article to prove their contention that "the article bases itself, not on the universal militarisation, but on the premise that the bourgeois are withholding arms from the masses." But if we are to believe that they are taking seriously their own slogan of "Invasion: arm the workers…, etc." from what does their slogan arise if the military policy is based *only* on the fact that the bourgeoisie are "organising, training and arming us in their military organisations"? Or has the slogan "Invasion: arm the workers…, etc." got nothing to do with the military policy?

We presume that the SWP "interprets" the military policy correctly. And we see that they make use, of the (to them) almost abstract question of invasion—*as a problem of arming the workers*! Have they failed too to understand that the bourgeoisie is "organising, training and arming us in their military organisations"? Here is what they say:

> "…a miners' convention at Blackpool unanimously adopted a resolution asking that miners be armed to meet a possible invasion.

> "We should like to see every union in this country adopt a similar resolution. The government tells us that fascism, the mortal enemy of the labour movement is threatening to invade our shores? Then let the government provide arms for the mortal enemies of fascism everywhere—the trade unions."

We notice two points in the lead article. First the SWP takes it for granted that the revolutionaries in England would raise the issue of arming the workers in connection with repelling invading fascism. Secondly, that they consider this as part of the application of the military policy in England—and in America. Thirdly, the heading of the article, "Arming the workers" does not mention under whose control!

And a last point—is the *Socialist Appeal* "moaning" about the unwillingness of [the] bourgeoisie to arm the workers against Hitler?

We agree that "up to now the absence in our publications of any material relating to the armed forces has not been marked." We are only too willing to see this remedied, and if these comrades or any others submit material or articles we shall be only too pleased to consider them for publication. The absence of material relating to industrial questions has also been "most marked". When comrades correctly deplored this, we together with the Minority pointed out that it was an expression of our weakness. But we agree wholeheartedly that this state of affairs must be remedied—and "in close co-operation with the comrades in the armed forces, we must concretise our military policy for this country." But it must be remembered that a policy and the concretisation of that policy are not one and the same thing.

With most of the demands in relation to the armed forces we can agree. But there are two or three which are completely wrong, un-Marxian and dangerous to our tendency. But we will not argue about those here. If the comrades persist in putting them forward we shall deal with them fully.

Even the demands which are correct, however, are not the "new" military policy. As a matter of fact, most of these that are correct are put forward in the *Transitional Programme* of the Fourth International, published in 1938. But even in the *Transitional Programme* they were not new. All of the correct demands were put forward by Lenin during the last imperialist war. And indeed, most were to be found in the programme of Social Democracy before 1914.

Wherein, then, is the difference between the "new" policy and the old? This, the comrades have not indicated in any way. That it is necessary to enter and work in the armed forces is something that is taken for granted. Shachtmanites, Stalinists and other pacifists in the labour movement are also agreed on the necessity of work in the armed forces and, as a matter of fact, the Stalinists have tabled a series of reformist demands for the soldiers.

What *is* new in the military policy is the posing of the problem of *proletarian militarism*. In other words, the problem in an epoch of universal war and militarism is the fact that we must have an "organised workers' programme for war." Instead of negatively putting forward the idea that we must struggle against imperialist war, we put forward the positive idea of transforming the war into a revolutionary war—by taking control out of the hands of the imperialists and into the hands of the workers. As Cannon puts it:

> "The workers don't want to be conquered by foreign invaders, above all by fascists. They require a programme of military struggle against foreign invaders which assures their class independence. That is the gist of the problem."

The comrades have not noticed the difference between the old policy and the new as applied in America. The old policy was—to oppose tooth and nail all war preparations of the bourgeoisie to defend and extend their imperialist loot. The war was in the interests of the finance-capitalist clique and not in the interests of the workers. But this, while correct both then and now, was a negative approach in a period of universal militarism and war.

Instead of this negative way of putting the problem, we now put forward a positive programme—"an organised workers' programme for war." Instead of opposing all war preparations for what the capitalists call the defence of the country against Hitler, we now say—Yes! Military training, etc., but *under the control* of the workers! Defend America—*but a workers' America!*

In Britain we have already reached a more advanced stage than in America.

Britain has been at war for eighteen months. We have to have a programme for the workers inside and outside the armed forces which gives them a method of fighting foreign invaders while preserving their class independence. Cannon describes how:

> "The demagogy of the social democrats against us was effective to a certain extent. They said, 'You have no answer to the question of how to fight against Hitler, how to prevent Hitler from conquering France, Belgium, etc.' (Of course their programme was very simple—the suspension of the class struggle and complete subordination of the workers to the bourgeoisie. We have seen the results of this treacherous policy.) Well, we answered in a general way, the workers will first overthrow the bourgeoisie at home and then they will take care of the invaders. That was a good programme, but the workers did not make the revolution in time. Now the two tasks must be carried out simultaneously."

Cannon then tells us how:

> "We cannot avoid the new circumstances; we must adapt our tactics to them."

But that is exactly what the Minority refuses to do. They continue to pose the problem in the old way: "the workers will first overthrow the bourgeoisie at home and then they will take care of the invaders" or, to quote from their bulletin, "while these rights are threatened by a Hitler invasion, the immediate threat to the British working class comes directly from within." The Majority, on the other hand, has adapted its tactics to the new circumstances, and poses the question thus: "In order really to fight Hitler and his invasion it is necessary for the workers to struggle against Churchill and take power into their own hands."

It is only the "mechanical" dumping of the *slogans* from America on to Britain, without realising the *policy* they are expressing which could lead the comrades to the military policy to the article in *Youth*. None of the slogans developed in America (or for that matter, even the slogans correct and incorrect put forward in the criticism) invalidates the conclusions, ideas and policy on which the article in *Youth* is based. Indeed the slogans (those of the SWP and *Youth*) flow consciously from the necessity of posing a revolutionary defence against invasion, a defence which will ensure the "class independence" of the proletariat. This is done, on the one hand, by exposing the naked class calculations of the bourgeoisie in their "defence", and on the other, by the posing of alternative revolutionary means. Precisely here is the whole "essence" of the military policy.

The article in *Youth* stands as a correct interpretation of the military policy. (So also does the article in the February number of *Workers' International News*. Despite the fact that they were written about the same time we notice that the comrades do not criticise the *Workers' International News* article. The only difference between them is that one is agitational, the other propagandist.) It is only the confusion as to what the policy implies, and the "new" idea (new to them only) that it is necessary to work in the army which leads the comrades to reject the ideas expressed in the article.

The "new policy" is a method of working among the masses both in and out of uniform. Just as on the economic field we put forward our transitional programme, now linked up through the "new policy" with the question of taking power and *transforming* the imperialist war into a revolutionary war; so on the military field we put forward these "military transitional" demands which *supplement* and round out our *general* transitional demands. But what is *new in both cases is not the slogans themselves. It is the method of posing the problem.* (Although in parenthesis Lenin posed the problem in a similar way in Russia in 1917, *Threatening catastrophe*). We do not *negatively* refuse merely to defend the *bourgeois fatherland,* we positively raise the question of *workers' power* and the defence of the *proletarian fatherland.* In this way both on the economic and military fields we defend the interests of the working masses and in indissoluble connection with this pose the problem of the conquest of power and a revolutionary war against fascism. In this way the task of overthrowing the bourgeoisie at home and that of fighting the invaders become "telescoped and carried out simultaneously." This is the meaning of Trotsky's position, incorrectly used by the Minority. The "new policy" links these demands as a means of "fighting foreign invaders" as an "organised workers' programme for war" with the struggle against the main enemy at home—the seizure of power by the working class and the waging of a genuine revolutionary war.

We would like to point out that the slogans put forward as the military policy are not unfamiliar to the Majority comrades as well as the Minority. We can read the material which appears regularly every week at the head of the *Socialist Appeal.* But as we have pointed out, these slogans were already developed in the *Transitional Programme.* We quote from page 10 of the *Transitional Programme*:

> "Once and for all we must tear from the hands of the greedy and merciless imperialist clique, scheming behind the backs of the people, the disposition of the peoples' fate. In accordance with this we demand: military training and arming of the workers and farmers under direct control of workers' and farmers' committees; creation of military schools for the training of commanders among the toilers, chosen by workers' organisations; substitution for the standing army of *peoples' militia* indissolubly linked up with factories, mines, farms, etc."

As early as June of last year in a draft pamphlet on the lessons of France these slogans were developed and put forward as the only programme for the masses in Britain. And indeed with the *Transitional Programme* as a programme which we accepted as a guide to action to be applied concretely, how could it be different?

In conclusion we issue a challenge to the Minority to write an article of 2,000 words or so to the internal bulletin *positively* giving a lead to the workers on the issue of invasion instead of *negatively* criticising the articles of the Majority. They have given us the heading, they have given us the slogans—now let us see the article. It would certainly be a peculiar concoction if it contained all the points put forward in the criticism. We await the article with interest. Comrades would then be able to compare the two and make their own judgment as to which dealt adequately with the problem with which we are faced.

It is unfortunate that the reply to the criticism is so lengthy. But we believe that the criticism is so confused that it was necessary to deal with it at length. A brief theoretical exposition expounding the view of the Majority on what is the military policy will follow very shortly and should be read in conjunction with this reply.

In conclusion we would appeal to the comrades to read the articles in *Workers' International News* and *Youth*, the article appended to this bulletin and the material of Trotsky and Cannon. When they have read these we have no doubt that they will realise that the position of the Majority is the position of Trotsky, Cannon and the Fourth International.

4 – A turning point:
the attack on the USSR
[July 1941 – December 1942]

Introduction

In June 1941 operation "Barbarossa" began the Nazi attack on the USSR. The treacherous policies of Stalin enforced in the August 1939 non-aggression pact with Hitler were swept away overnight and the Soviet bureaucracy was thrown into panic. Caught by surprise, the Communist International had to hastily change its policy from one of opposition to imperialist war to one of collaboration with the "democratic" nations in the war against fascism.

The effect in the British labour movement of this sudden turn was an equally sudden change of policy of the Communist Party, from one of conducting an agitation against the "imperialist" war in order to reach peace on Hitler's terms to one of joining the national unity hysteria. All the efforts of the party were now geared towards supporting Churchill's war plans against the German Nazi enemy. Overnight the CPGB leaders turned into a powerful strike-breaking force in the heart of the British working class at the service of the war effort.

This sudden turn provoked a crisis in the CPGB with many workers questioning the new policy. At the same time there was growing unrest within the working class leading to a wave of strikes for better conditions, especially amongst the miners in Yorkshire and other areas, traditionally a constituency of the CPGB. The Workers' International League showed a high degree of flexibility in its tactics and immediately turned its attention towards the Communist Party, including the development of fractional work within its ranks, as is stated in the internal circular of September 1941 that we publish in this section.

The ideological offensive of the WIL in defence of a principled internationalist stand against Nazism, without concessions to the British bourgeoisie, managed to make a breakthrough both amongst the communist rank and file and in the working class, leading to important growth of the organisation. Due to the development of the war the WIL had abandoned entry work within the Labour League of Youth and the Labour Party, emptied out by conscription and the treacherous policies of the Labour leaders, and had consequently increased their profile as an independent organisation. To reflect the new orientation the name of the paper was changed to *Socialist Appeal.*

At the same time as orientating towards the communist workers, the WIL increased its work towards the Independent Labour Party which, as a consequence of the betrayal of the Stalinist leaders and of the class-collaboration policies of the Labour Party, was left alone in opposition to the war. In this section we also publish some interesting documents and articles relating to the ILP that reveal the extremely complex political environment in which the WIL had to orient itself.

The growth of the WIL did not pass unnoticed by the Stalinist leadership, provoking increasingly vicious attacks against the Trotskyists, but it also attracted the attention of the government. Thanks to the hysterical campaign of the Stalinists and, significantly, with the ardent support of the former pro-Nazi press like the *Sunday Dispatch,* or the mouthpiece of the coal owners, the *Daily Telegraph,* the question of banning the WIL and its organ, the *Socialist Appeal,* was posed in a Parliamentary debate. The fact that the WIL supported the CP campaign against the ban imposed on the *Daily Worker* between January 1941 and September 1942 did not prevent the Stalinist leaders from demanding that a similar ban should be imposed on the *Socialist Appeal.*

The counteroffensive of the WIL demonstrated a bold approach and also a good sense of humour. The articles and leaflets dealing with the attacks from the Stalinists (mainly written by Ted Grant and Jock Haston) expose in a humorous way all the contradictions of the policies of Stalinism and were successful in reaching the communist workers.

In this section we also have included a few important contributions by Ted Grant on the heated question of the colonial revolution and in particular about India. The internationalist work was an integral part of the activities of the WIL, as its decisive contribution in developing a Trotskyist movement in the subcontinent testifies.

Defend the Soviet Union—
Fascism can only be defeated by
international socialism

By Ted Grant

[*Socialist Appeal*, Vol. 3 No. 9, July 1941]

The war has taken a new turn with the attack by German imperialism on the Soviet Union. A terrible danger now threatens the first workers' state with destruction. The greatest clash in the history of the world on a 1,800-mile front has thrown the whole international situation into a state of flux. The assault of world imperialism on the first workers' state is no longer a Marxist perspective, but a grim reality.

The fruits of "socialism in one country"

Ever since they usurped power in 1923, the Kremlin bureaucracy and its transformed appendage, the Communist International, have laid all their hopes on "neutralising" the world bourgeoisie while they pursued the utopian mirage of "socialism in one country." It was with his "theory" that the bureaucracy in Russia was enabled to consolidate its power and amass its privileges. In every country in the world, the policy of the Communist International was conditioned by the episodic and shifting needs of Soviet foreign policy and not on the course of the class struggle. It was this which led to the victory of Hitler, in the first place, with all its disastrous consequences.

While Trotsky was demanding an international campaign by the Communist International, warning the workers of the world of the consequences [of] the coming to power of fascism in Germany; demanding a united front between socialists and communists in Germany to prepare for civil war to prevent it, demanding in the last resort the mobilisation of the Red Army to actively come to the assistance of the German workers, if necessary. While Trotsky was urging this, the Soviet bureaucracy and the German Communist Party complacently paralysed the resistance of the German workers and allowed this "super-Wrangel"[1] (as Trotsky called Hitler) to take power without lifting a finger.

---

[1] Baron Pyotr Nikolayevich Wrangel (1878 – 1928) was an officer in the imperial Russian army and later commanding general of the anti-Bolshevik White Army in Southern Russia in the later stages of the Russian Civil War.

For the Leninist tactic of the united front of socialists and communists against Hitler, they substituted the disastrous policy of "social-fascism"—the theory that in Germany the main danger was not Hitler but social democracy. Thus the door was left open for Hitler to take power. Civil war in Germany and its inevitable repercussions would disturb the rhythm of the five-year plans. Moreover, "Hitler would be too preoccupied with breaking the chains imposed on Germany by the Versailles victors to constitute an immediate threat to the Soviet Union", was the short-sighted reasoning of these "Marxist" epigones.

With the victory of Hitler and the fear that the Western powers would orientate themselves on the programme he then put forward of "liberating Europe from the menace of Bolshevism", the Kremlin and the Comintern threw overboard the last vestiges of Marxism inherited from Lenin. Instead of explaining to the masses that war could only be avoided by the overthrow of capitalism, they relied upon an agreement with Britain, France and America and the League of Nations to "protect" the workers' state from imperialist attack. This was the policy which led to the stabbing in the back of the Spanish and French revolutions.

Those were the halcyon days of "popular frontism", "collective security", "pacts to stop the aggressor", etc., which disoriented and confused the masses of the world working class who, feeling themselves threatened by German fascism, turned; under the influence or these slogans, to the support of their own bourgeois governments. It was during this period that Churchill established his reputation for "anti-fascism", not without the zealous assistance of the Communist Party in Britain, who appealed to him to form a government of "Churchill, Attlee and Sinclair" to stand up to Hitler.

World fascism or the extension of October

This period was ended by the pact of August 1939 between Germany and Russia which shocked and disgusted the masses throughout the world and discredited the Soviet Union and the ideas of socialism among hundreds of millions. Stalin and the Communist International oriented their policy on the pact with Hitler and demanded that the "war be stopped" by negotiated peace, which meant victory for Hitler. So indifferent were they to the fate of the workers under his heel!

Hitler could allow himself the luxury of striking against the Western rivals of German imperialism first, only because of the counter-revolutionary role which the Kremlin bureaucracy and the Comintern had played in the last period. Freed from the threat of revolution by Stalinism, Hitler marched ahead with confidence. He was able to unleash the full fury of the German war machine with the knowledge that the German masses were disoriented by the pact, and that the proletariat in the Western democracies, particularly in France, had been rendered completely apathetic and indifferent by the swift change of front by the Kremlin. It was in this soil that the astounding victories of Hitler were achieved.

But after the lightning collapse of France the Comintern rediscovered the imperialist character of the war and impartially thundered against both sets of belligerents. But all the twists and turns and squirmings of the bureaucracy, caught in the iron vice of the contradictions of world economy and the conflicting interests of world imperialism, could not isolate the Soviet state from the fate of the rest of the world. History has now inexorably presented its bill for the crimes, lies, treachery and stupidity of the Kremlin bureaucracy. The theory of socialism for Russia alone has borne its inevitable fruit.

In the light of these events how miserable are the justifications of the sycophants of the Kremlin—the Dutts, the Pollitts, the Gallachers. "The strength of the Soviet Union assured its socialist neutrality", they chorused only yesterday. The Soviet Union was a citadel of peace while war raged over the greater part of the world. A fifteen-year plan was inaugurated on the basis of a peaceful co-existence of the capitalist world with the Soviet Union. But today it is clear that socialism is indivisible; the cause of the workers in all countries is one. The harvest is now being reaped by the policies of the bureaucracy over the last eighteen years, who wished only to be left alone to enjoy their privileges unmolested by the march of events.

This review of the developments of the past years is necessary if we are to have a clear perspective and guide to the development of forces in Europe and the world in the immediate future.

Molotov's nationalist appeal

The attack of Germany upon Russia could lead to the complete smashing not only of Hitler but of world imperialism, had we at the present time in the Kremlin, a leadership which based itself firmly on the masses of Russian workers and peasants, and had the perspective of the international revolution as the sole means of salvation. The supreme test is here and already the Bonapartist clique which holds the reigns of power in Moscow, has revealed its complete worthlessness. Trembling before their own masses—and with contempt and fear of the revolutionary possibilities of the world proletariat, above all the German and European proletariat—these contemptible flunkeys are clutching at the coat tails of Roosevelt and Churchill to save them.

The appeal they issued to the Russian and German people is almost incredible. It contained all the old outworn liberal phrases regarding the "aggressor", the "megalomaniac" Hitler, etc. Bloody Tsar Nicholas could have appended his signature to this disgraceful appeal without altering a single word. Corroded through and through with nationalism, not a trace of revolutionary socialism or internationalism even by implication pervaded this speech.

So corrupt, so degenerate have this perfidious Bonapartist clique become, that in their appeal to the Russian masses to rally in defence against the invader, they can go back only to the "magnificent" example of the defeat of Napoleon by reactionary feudal tsarism! It were as though the October revolution and the revolutionary war against intervention had never taken place. They dare not, they cannot appeal to the traditions dearest to the hearts of the Russian and international proletariat—to the tradition of the Red Army of Lenin and Trotsky, the army which was the child of October.

The Red Army has a tradition of courage, sacrifice and heroism unexampled in history. Ragged, ill-equipped, starving and militarily unskilled masses succeeded in beating back, despite the ruined and exhausted condition of Russia, the armies of intervention of twenty one different capitalist countries, as well as the traitor armies of Russian capitalism. They emerged victorious because they were inspired by the consciousness that they were fighting for a better world; for the cause of international socialism. It is this tradition which is deliberately avoided by Molotov. Decisively they have turned their backs on the internationalist mould from which the Soviet Union emerged and substituted for it bankrupt nationalism.

Stalin is doing this for reasons of self-preservation. A revolution in Europe would soon lead to the Russian proletariat settling accounts with the bureaucracy. It will not be long before their agents of the Communist International will attempt to pacify the uneasiness among their members by pointing to the need to keep Britain and America from joining with the Nazis against the Soviet Union.

Having led the proletariat to disaster in one country after another, the fate of the Soviet Union and their own heads is now at stake, and all they can do is to look for succour from the Western powers. While loud in offers of assistance and protestations of sympathy, the British and American imperialists offer "clothes and shoes" in place of planes and vital equipment in the decisive period. The bombing of Germany by the RAF is not of decisive importance.

Stalin's foreign policy has succeeded in isolating his Western frontiers from the Western powers. Every German plane, tank and soldier is being thrown in full force from the Black Sea to the Baltic. Aid from Britain and America, even in the best case, could not come till the decisive battles had been fought. Moreover, even a military victory under these conditions will not save the Soviet state. It is a significant fact that the Moscow radio, in transmitting Churchill's speech, omitted the passage in which he referred to his hatred of communism. Instead of unequivocally pointing to the nature of their "ally", the bureaucracy hopes to deceive the Soviet people.

The first successes of the Red Army which threatened to destroy completely the power of German imperialism would result in an immediate agreement of all the imperialist powers, including Britain and America, to crush the Soviet Union. If imperialism emerges from this war intact, the Soviet Union is doomed.

The revolutionary potentialities

Yet the revolutionary possibilities inherent in the situation have never been greater. The German people have suffered under the iron heel of Nazi totalitarianism for nearly nine years. The peoples of Europe are being oppressed with unexampled horror. Hitler retains his stronghold only because of the fear of the German masses of an even worse fate under a super Versailles if British imperialism were to emerge victorious. From reports appearing in the snore sober bourgeois papers (*Times* and *Telegraph*) it is clear that there is universal detestation of the Nazi regime and the victories occasion no enthusiasm. But the masses, fearing the consequences of a Churchill victory, grimly fight on. The "Communist" Party press has correctly pointed out that this alone has paralysed the German workers' struggle against Hitler.

Suddenly and without ideological preparation among the German masses Hitler has executed another reversal of policy and ordered the armies to march. This will reveal to even the most fanatical Nazi youth, the lie that they are waging a socialist crusade against "capitalist pluto-democracy," and it cannot fail to have caused deep consternation in the minds of the German people. Only yesterday Ribbentrop had acclaimed Molotov's assurance that the interests of the German and Russian peoples were "cemented in blood". Without a shadow of doubt the German proletariat were waiting a revolutionary message from the Soviet government. The German workers are the most educated and culturally advanced in Europe and have a Marxian tradition extending over seventy-five years. Over 8 million socialists and 6 million communists recorded their votes before Hitler came to power. Thus, one in every two of Hitler's soldiers must have been either a socialist or a communist. It therefore becomes clear that a fraternal socialist appeal from Moscow could not fail to arouse this latent might of the German toilers, groaning under the Nazi yoke, and transform the entire picture. Given such a lead, the entire European continent would be aflame with revolution.

As long ago as 1927 Trotsky warned of the incapacity of the Stalin bureaucracy to wage a revolutionary war. This prediction is now confirmed by events.

But despite the treacherous role of the degenerate and corrupt ruling clique, the Soviet Union has tremendous potentialities. The workers and peasants of Russia will fight with a fervour and enthusiasm unparalleled by any other of the armies ranged against Hitler. In spite of the policies of Stalin, it is probable that the *Blitzkrieg* will this time fail. Should the Nazi machine, composed of soldiers with heavy hearts, batter itself on the resistance of the Soviet masses, and fail to make headway against the defenders of what remains of Lenin's heritage, revolution must inevitably follow the demoralisation thus engendered. Given a leadership, it would open out the perspective of a socialist Europe and a socialist world. A wave of revolutionary fervour would paralyse the imperialists of America, Britain and Japan against any possibility of attack. That is why the abandonment of the class struggle by Stalin is so suicidal. By demoralising the workers of Germany and Europe, by befuddling the Soviet and Anglo-American masses, that aid can be given to the workers' struggle against German fascism by British and American imperialism only assists Hitler and serves the interests of Anglo-American imperialism. If on the other hand, the Ukraine and the Caucasus should fall, through the failure of the Kremlin to wage a revolutionary war, this would not be the end. The war would go on and plunge mankind into complete chaos and barbarism. Only complete destruction of capitalism can prevent this.

In Britain our course is clear. The Communist Party will accept the leadership of the capitalist class under the guise of the demand for a "peoples' government." They will sabotage the struggles of the workers, as they did in France (and as the Labour leaders are doing today) with the treacherous cry that they would help Hitler. Instead of raising the consciousness of the workers by exposing the real aims of the capitalists, they will do everything to camouflage their imperialist aims. Such a policy will lead to disaster, to the defeat of the Soviet Union and the world proletariat, and to the victory of world fascism and reaction.

The policy of the *Socialist Appeal* alone defends the USSR and fights for the destruction of Hitlerism by the only possible method: the method of Lenin. Only by means of the conquest of power by the proletariat, can fascism be defeated, not only in Germany but in the world, and the Soviet Union be saved from destruction.

Dark days lie ahead, but the events of our epoch are ruthlessly destroying the programmes of reformism and Stalinism. Reaction is a force—but the programme of revolution, of world socialism, is an even mightier force.

The indispensable means of defending the Soviet Union and defeating fascism is:

1. The overthrow of the Kremlin bureaucracy and the restoration of the workers' democracy of Lenin and Trotsky.

2. The struggle for the overthrow of the British capitalist class and the conquest of power by the workers.

An analysis of the social basis of the Soviet Union— and why we defend it

By Ted Grant

[*Workers' International News*, Vol. 4 No. 8, August 1941]

The Russo-German war is now entering its second month, and this gives us the opportunity to measure the relation of forces. It is clear that the heroic resistance of the workers and peasants has for the first time stemmed the blows of the German *Blitzkrieg* machine. The bitter resistance of Soviet soldiers has completely upset the Nazi timetable. Already the German soldiery have had to pay the price for their territorial gains in such measure that the Soviet claim to have inflicted a million casualties on the German army cannot be far short of the mark.

In addition to this the "scorched earth" policy announced by Stalin completely deprives the Nazis of any immediate economic gains in the territory occupied by their troops. They conquer only blackened ruins and desolation. Banking on the experience of the campaigns in the West, Hitler had anticipated a relatively cheap and easy victory. Moreover the experience of the Finnish war which had been decidedly unpopular among the masses of the Russian people had led the German imperialists to completely underestimate the powers of resistance of the masses when defending themselves against imperialist attack. Napoleon, whom Hitler has desired to render a tyro in the field of world conquest, could have explained in advance to his would-be imitator that the moral factor stands as to the physical in the relation of three to one.

Basing themselves on the oppression of the Russian workers and peasants by the uncontrolled bureaucracy, the German capitalists, and for that matter world imperialism, deluded themselves into the belief that the Russian people could be overwhelmed without too costly an effort. Trotsky had predicted that the idea of the Japanese militarists and German fascists, that the Russian people were only waiting for the armies of the Mikado and Hitler to "liberate" them, was fantastic delirium. The capitulations of Stalin in the past two years encouraged this belief in the minds of the German military clique. In spite of the ravages of the bureaucracy, the basic conquests of the October revolution still remain: the capitalist class has never regained its possessions and private ownership in the means of production has never been restored. It is this that the masses, despite their aversion for the bureaucracy, have rallied to defend, just as the British workers would rally to the defence of their trade unions against capitalist attack, in spite of their aversion for the Bevins and Citrines.

Up to now the Nazi army has not had a serious test to face. In France the bourgeoisie were concerned only with saving their property, and the moment the Germans had broken through, they capitulated. The French soldiers and workers had been demoralised by the Stalinists and the actions of the bourgeoisie, and rendered morally prostrate, which resulted in only half-hearted resistance. Likewise in the other countries the bourgeoisie sold out, and the German military machine marched over Europe as if on military manoeuvres. It was this which gave the Nazis the illusion of invincibility.

But today Goebbels is forced to admit that the Russian soldier fights to the death. "When the machine guns are knocked out by tanks, the Mongol soldier does not surrender; he fights on with a revolver." And behind the German lines of advance the population remains bitterly hostile, and conducts guerrilla warfare. It is this wave of enthusiasm and self-sacrifice that has served to stem the German advance. And with a correct policy would guarantee the victory of the Russian workers and peasants over the Nazi military machine and the establishment of a socialist Europe. But as was foreseen, Stalin cannot wage a revolutionary war.

The bureaucracy in Russia is fighting Hitler because he leaves them no alternative, and thus, they do, in a distorted bureaucratic fashion defend the Soviet Union. The Soviet bureaucracy—the army officers, managers, technicians, artists and higher officials, numbering about 10,000,000, intend to continue to devour four-fifths of the goods produced for consumption, while the rest of the population consume one-fifth, and this is what they are fighting for. But in spite of the fact that Stalin desires the defeat of Hitler, he does not wish for a proletarian revolution in Germany, because a socialist revolution in Germany would mean a socialist Europe. And a socialist Europe would mean that the victorious Russian workers and peasants, imbued with self-confidence by their victory, would return home and soon settle accounts with the Kremlin usurpers by immediately restoring control into their own hands. Stalinism only came to power on the basis of the defeats of the world working class. A victory of such titanic proportions as the seizure of power by the German proletariat would sweep Stalinism aside!

The organic needs of the bureaucracy in internal policy find expression in the foreign policy of Stalin. If they had placed their confidence in the European and world working class, by consistent day in and day out leaflets and radio appeals to the German workers, explaining the real character of the war on the part of their Nazi rulers, urging them in fraternal collaboration to establish a socialist Germany—this, coupled with the unyielding resistance of the Russian workers and peasants, would have been the signal for transforming the whole world situation and would have sounded the death knell of world capitalism. Instead of this irrefutable Leninist position, we see the reliance upon Churchill and Roosevelt, the "democratic" imperialists. Not only is the Comintern deceiving the Russian masses as to the nature of the voracious imperialists of Britain and America, but is spreading the illusion among the entire world working class that they are fighting for the liberty of all nations. On the Moscow wireless we hear:

> "When the German fascist hordes appeared on the shores on the Straits of Dover and the English Channel, and prematurely celebrated their victory over democratic Britain, the British showed in the moment of mortal danger that they were capable, under the leadership of their far-sighted statesmen, of developing the gigantic strength latent within them."

In the *Times* of July 17 we read:

> "As happened during the lesser crises of recent years, resolutions have come pouring into Moscow from factories and farms throughout the Union. A word from Moscow can usually bring such resolutions at any time. In the past they have not been wholly spontaneous: but their wording is now significant. The Anglo-Soviet alliance is applauded not merely in the Moscow newspapers; it is being welcomed and praised in all these resolutions, proof that the Soviet government is not afraid of letting even the most isolated centres know that it has joined forces with the power which until lately was denounced as imperialist and capitalist."

And we are told by Stalin in his speech:

> "In this connection the historic utterances of the British Prime Minister, Churchill, regarding aid to the Soviet Union, and the declaration of the United States government, signifies readiness to render aid to our country, which can only evoke a feeling of gratitude in the hearts of the peoples of the Soviet Union, are fully comprehensible and symptomatic."

Thus we see the deliberate deception of the masses in the Soviet Union as to the real aims of Anglo-American imperialism, the aims of world domination for the continued exploitation of the people of the entire globe and, above all as a long-term perspective, the re-introduction of capitalism in the Soviet Union.

On the other hand, Churchill and the bourgeois statesmen have openly proclaimed their detestation of communism and by innuendo have made it clear to the class they represent that they intend to settle this account at a more propitious time. Mr. Churchill does not withdraw a word of what he has said about communism in the past. And Churchill has expressed his preference for Hitler's Nazism to Bolshevism. The support which Churchill will give is based only on the knowledge of the world bourgeoisie on the counter-revolutionary role of Stalinism, which the nationalist charlatanism emanating from Moscow has wholly justified. Were it not for this, Churchill would be clutching at Hitler as a saviour from the menace of Bolshevism.

Confident of the role of the Stalinist bureaucracy within and without Russia, Churchill and Roosevelt are calculating on the mutual exhaustion of Germany and Russia. As a Turkish journalist expressed it: "Wouldn't it be fine if Hitler and Stalin would knock each other out?" Anglo-American imperialism will then be enabled to destroy the Soviet regime and emerge masters of the world. The resistance of Russia has been as much of a surprise to them as to Germany. A protracted resistance and its inevitable threat of revolution in Europe would compel Hitler to seek terms at the expense of Russia, and Hitler would be compelled to play the role originally allotted him by world finance.

The internal development of the Soviet Union

But what will take place within Soviet society? To save himself Stalin must appeal to the revolutionary energies of the masses and arm once again tens of millions of workers and peasants. Not for long will these masses be fobbed off by the crimes and stupidities of the bureaucracy. The baneful effects of mismanagement, inefficiency, and corruption which are characteristic of the ignorant and uncontrolled bureaucracy will be even more glaring under the stress of the war. Meanwhile, war will impose a terrible strain on the industry and transport of the Soviet Union, and the privations of the masses will inevitably become worsened, in the interests of "everything for the front". This policy can only be carried through without provoking sharp legitimate dissatisfaction, if, as was the case in Lenin's day, the sacrifices are more or less spread equally over the entire population.

In the course of the war the wasteful extravagance and corruption of the generals, admirals and other high bureaucrats will arouse extreme resentment and hostility among the masses. This is the reason for the unparalleled chauvinist appeals on the basis of "national unity." Lenin taught us always to look beneath formulae and slogans for the *social content*. In capitalist states the appeal for "national unity", "union sacrée", in time of war, is a cloak to gloss over the antagonism of interests in the given society. Of course, in Russia today it is correct to appeal for the defence of the fatherland—but in Lenin's day the emphasis, as always, would be the workers' fatherland. The defence of the Russian workers' state would be the defence of the entire world working class, especially of the workers in Europe and Germany!

Under the fire of British guns in the wars of intervention, both in the internal and external propaganda, the Bolsheviks appealed to the Russian soldiers fighting against the British: "We never forget while English guns and English bombs and English soldiers are raining death upon us that there are two Englands, the England of the workers, and the England of finance capitalists." The reason why the Soviet bureaucracy cannot make this simple and true call, internally and externally, is because of the profound gulf which has opened out between the people and the avaricious officialdom. This is the social content of the appeal for "national unity" within the Soviet Union

If, as we hope, the Nazis fail to score a decisive success—which is the best that can be hoped for with Stalinism in control, the war will become a bloody war of attrition and exhaustion, and the contradictions within Soviet society will reach their extreme limit, beyond which there must be an explosion.

Like all doomed regimes, Stalin's preoccupation with preserving his position is shown by the measures which he has dictated for the army. The splitting of the front into three commands is not dictated by the military needs of the Soviet Union. In war a unified command is obviously the best means of conducting operations on the fronts as a planned whole. Stalin's reduction of Timoshenko from Commander in Chief is dictated by fear that the reins of power will slip out of the hands of the civil bureaucracy into the hands of the army caste. After the Finnish war the abolition of the control of the political commissars, which were in reality the GPU guards of the civil bureaucracy, was a victory for the army caste. Stalin was compelled, by the disastrous consequences of the GPU control and purges which led to military reverses, to give a freer hand to the generals. But now fearful of his position, even in the face of the mightiest foe in world history, Stalin once again has introduced the GPU in order to ensure his control, from below as well as above, in the army. But in any event, this will not prevent at a later stage power passing into the hands of the military bureaucracy as in all Bonapartist regimes.

In industry and transport, through the disruption of economy, the heads of the trust will be compelled more and more to act as if they were the owners of the enterprises. Planned economy, which pre-supposes the conscious co-operation, activity, and control by the masses, managed in spite of the bureaucratic straight-jacket, to maintain a semblance of unified progress in time of peace. In time of war, the bureaucratic strangulation means that planned economy as a whole must crumble. The "fifteen year plan" of 1941 is automatically scrapped. Under the aggravation of these contradictions, the processes speeded up by the war, a section of the bureaucratic tops will tend to seek the assistance of the capitalist "allies" to solve the contradictions by the restoration of capitalism.

On the other hand the workers and peasants who bear the main brunt of the war will now be armed and organised (it is true under the control of the GPU), and while they have tolerated in the past the Old Man of the Sea[1] on their backs for fear of a worse alternative in the form of capitalist intervention, they will not look with any too indulgent an eye on the excesses and inefficiencies of the bureaucracy. As time passes it will become more and more evident that the bureaucratic control is paralysing the organisation of the defence of the Soviet Union. It will become apparent that only restoration of workers' control in the factories, the restoration of Soviets and Soviet democracy can save the workers' state from disaster. At that time the programme of Lenin and Trotsky will be rejuvenated.

The utopian character of the dream of "socialism in one country" has been destroyed, in passing, by the Nazi attack. Whatever the outcome of the struggle it is obvious that the economy of the Soviet Union will be terribly shattered and weakened. The policy of "scorched earth", with a revolutionary perspective, is, of course, the only correct one. Nevertheless it is a policy of desperation. Tens of millions of people will flee to the interior of the Soviet Union and the devastated regions will require years to build up again. Even a victory would find Soviet economy more and more dependent upon the rich and mighty "democracies" of the West.

Even under tsarism the bourgeois democracies bled Russia white in man power and economically. In the salons of St. Petersburg the bourgeois joked that "England is prepared to fight to the last drop of blood of the Russian soldier." At that period, while fighting German imperialism in alliance with Russia, the allied bourgeoisie were not loath to try and transform Russia into an Anglo-French colony. This at a time when they were propping up Russian tsarism as a bulwark of European reaction. Today it is clear that Washington and London regard the attack of Hitler as a gift of providence to simultaneously bleed their mighty German rival and at the same time obtain an advantageous position for the throttling of the workers' state. The antagonisms between collective ownership in Russia and the capitalist world *is the most fundamental of all antagonisms within present-day society.*

That is why, in spite of all the concessions and cringing of the bureaucracy, the Soviet regime, even in its emasculated form, cannot be saved unless the intervention of the workers in the capitalist states takes place. If world capitalism manages to survive the present bloody conflagration it has let loose on mankind, regardless of the victors, Russia will not escape the engulfment like the rest of the world, of fascist barbarism, and the bourgeois counter-revolution in Russia will be heralded.

---

[1] A figure in Greek and Persian mythology. The Old Man of the Sea enslaved Sinbad the sailor; Sinbad managed to free himself, by making his oppressor drunk with wine, and killed him.

The end of the Comintern as an international

This austere, but sober, calculation of the development of events plays its part with the Churchills and Roosevelts. Stalin is assisting them with all his might to transform their calculations into reality. The prostituted Comintern, from being sold together with oil and manganese to placate Hitler, is now bartered for promises of machine tools and Spitfires. Not only in the allied countries, but in the occupied territories too, the Comintern is dancing to the tune of Churchill. In France and Czechoslovakia, where the communist parties probably have the support of the majority of the working class, they are now placing their followers under the banner of de Gaulle and Benes, who represent London, and nothing else.

But the calculations of world imperialism are built on quicksand. In Germany and Europe, far more than in the Soviet Union itself, the contradictions between the Nazi bureaucracy and the German imperialists on the one side, and the German workers and peasants on the other, and the contradiction between German imperialism and the oppressed workers and peasants of the conquered nations, are being strained to breaking point. The development of the war will bring all five continents into the harvest of "blood, toil, tears and sweat" which capitalism has sown. The violent reaction of the masses to this bloody and senseless slaughter will come with absolute certainty. And on this optimistic perspective the Trotskyists base their programme.

In Britain the bourgeoisie is chuckling at the exorcising of the "red menace" by the betrayal of the Communist Party. The *Times* notes with satisfaction that Hitler's move into Russia has "placed the dissident communist minority behind the national effort." This, it is to be hoped, will be the final turn of the already dizzy Comintern. The revolutionary element within the Communist Party will not for long allow themselves to be dragooned into support for Churchill. Perhaps it has been fortunate that the Comintern has not managed to penetrate and corrupt the decisive section of the British working class. In Europe the lash of fascism is the price which the working class has paid for the crimes of social democracy and Stalinism. But we in Britain have the opportunity to profit from the lessons of the past decades. The British working class can play a decisive role in the destruction of the European reaction and salvage and regenerate what remains of the October revolution, but only by waging an ever more implacable and irreconcilable struggle against the government of finance capital. The programme of the Fourth International alone advocates such a path and the revolutionary elements of the Communist Party, who are already voting with their feet, must be drawn to our banner.

The fate of the workers of Europe and the world has been tied in one knot by the imperialist war. Either a socialist Britain and a socialist Europe, or a fascist Britain and Europe and the destruction of the USSR as a workers' state.

Daily Herald—
A public statement,
not a private admission

By Ted Grant

[*Workers' International News*, Vol. 4 No. 8, August 1941]

We print below the correspondence between ourselves and the *Daily Herald* arising from a report which appeared in the issue of July 16 on the arrest of our American comrades. In the past it has been the prerogative of the Stalinists to slander and vilify the internationalist wing of the labour movement by amalgams and frame-ups. Now we see the defenders of "democracy", who held up their hands in horror at the methods of Stalin in the Moscow trials, descending to the same level. The refusal to publish our refutation, even accepting that this report was "included accidentally", shows what will be the position of the internationalists in the coming period. It is the duty of all Labour Party members, socialists and trade unionists to fight against such methods of political struggle in the labour movement—Editor.

Workers' International League—Fourth International

Publication: *Workers' International News*

61 Northdown Street, London N1
21 July 1941

To the editor, *Daily Herald*

Dear Sir,

It has been brought to our notice that the issue of the *Daily Herald* dated July 16 1941, features a report of the trial of 33 German spies. In this report is contained an amalgam of another, an entirely separate trial, which is in no way connected with this spy case.

This may be accidental or otherwise, but it gives a slanderous impression that the trial of the American leaders of the Minneapolis General Drivers' Union, Local 554, also leaders and supporters of the Socialist Workers' Party (Fourth International), is linked together with the spy trial.

With the trial of the Nazi spies, who will receive their deserts, we are not concerned. But whatever one's opinions of the politics of the revolutionary socialists, they cannot in any way be tarred with the dirty brush of Nazism. They stand for international socialism, "...accepting as an ideal formula the Russian Revolution of 1917", and are implacable opponents of Hitler and what he represents. To link them up in this manner is on a par with the slander against Lenin of being a German spy.

This libellous report damages and casts credit not only on these 29 trade union leaders and the thousands of workers they represent, but also reflects on the whole international socialist movement of the Fourth International, including its British followers who stand irreconcilably for the overthrow of Hitlerism and for the defence of the Soviet Union, and advocate that only a workers' government in Britain can achieve those ends.

We trust that the official organ of the British Labour Party will take immediate steps to dispel the false impression which the report, whether deliberately or accidentally, conveys to the British working class. In the interests of political honesty we demand the unabridged publication of this letter. Failure to comply with this will brand the *Daily Herald* as a dishonest and slanderous journal.

E. Grant, for the Executive Committee, Workers' International League.

Copy of reply from the *Daily Herald*, July 23 1941:

Daily Herald Editorial Office,
2-12 Endell Street, Long Acre, London, WC2
PC/DMS
E. Grant,
Workers' International League,
61 Northdown Street, N1

Dear Sir,

I have made a full enquiry into the matter raised in your letter of July 21, and I find that the indictment against 29 leaders of the Minneapolis General Drivers' Union was included accidentally in our report of the trial of alleged Nazi spies.

I cannot agree with you that this is in anyway damaging to the Minneapolis union leaders, since they were not mentioned at all in the report.

In these circumstances I see no point in drawing further attention to the matter by publication of your letter.

Yours faithfully, Percy Cudlipp, Editor

The next steps forward—Towards the rank and file of the Communist Party

By Executive Committee of WIL

[WIL, *Internal Bulletin*, September 21 1941]

Three months ago our organisation decided to launch a campaign for new members and an increased circulation of the press. The Nazi invasion of the Soviet Union threw the labour movement into a ferment. The introduction of the *Socialist Appeal* provided us with an invaluable weapon to tackle the new situation. Throughout the country the rank and file of the Communist Party were thrown into confusion by the "about turn" in party policy. To the best of our ability we reacted to the situation through the press and dealt with the many problems confronting the workers. Our membership was quick to realise our opportunities and the circulation of our press was trebled with comparative ease. Locals, which before were selling only a few dozen copies per month now order their supplies in hundreds, and the general tone of their reports is that they hope before long to transform this into thousands.

This is excellent and amply justifies the transformation of *Youth For Socialism* to the *Socialist Appeal*. But it must be stated at the outset, that this is *not enough*. Increased circulation by itself is only one of the many aspects of group activity. Unless we can harness this to the general development of the group as a whole, and particularly towards an increase in membership and contacts, a valuable opportunity will be lost.

Let us pose the question bluntly. The bewilderment of the CP rank and file should have provided us with a glorious opportunity to make wide inroads into their ranks. Our study circles should have become the centre of a well planned propaganda campaign to expound our political position as well as clear up all doubts that may exist. Our members should have gone out of their way to contact as many CP comrades as possible. They should not have been content to confine themselves to the areas in which they operate, but should have attended all the meetings possible in outside districts in order to circulate our literature and make new contacts. In the trade union branches and in the workshops we should have sought out all members and sympathisers of the CP and acquainted them with our position. Yet there is no record in the reports from locals that this was done to any great extent.

We do not mean to imply that our members shirked their responsibilities and were lacking. On the contrary, we know that everyone put what they had into it. The magnificent sale of our literature testifies to this. No other revolutionary grouping with such small resources could have accomplished what ours has. We also know that a large number of CP'ers were contacted. The main question, however, was not one of activity alone, but on *how* the activity was conducted.

The bulk of the study circles are still attended by the same contacts who have attended since before the opening up of the Nazi-Soviet conflict. In a number of cases lack of initiative in popularising these classes has been largely responsible for this. But what has been perturbing is the failure of those of our members who have responsible positions in industry, in the trade unions and in labour organisations, to sharply counterpose our position to Stalinism and reformism. Apart from the building workers' conference in London and the ETU[1] shop stewards' conference in the Merseyside and the Nottingham area, nothing worth noting has been carried out.

It is necessary, here and now, to come to grips with the root causes of these shortcomings, the remedy for which is to be found in relentless self-criticism and discussion.

How to tackle the new situation

There are in the main, two reasons for our failure to measure up to the new situation. The first is the failure of the majority of our comrades to effectively advance the positive policy of our organisation and the Fourth International. We have to bear in mind, of course, that our weakness at the present time is directly related to the political immaturity and inexperience of our members and leading cadres. The efforts to raise the all round theoretical level of the group coupled with the active participation of our members in the working class movement, must be intensified in order to effectively arm us for the events ahead. We cling to the old abstract theoretical approach and become known as "theorists" rather than active militants with a fighting programme for all the problems which confront the workers. Secondly, we have not yet completely broken from [the] stranglehold of the reformist organisations. Their poisonous atmosphere, intermixed with Stalinist propaganda, subdues the voice and activities of our comrades to the extent that they often keep their mouths shut and lapse into passive acceptance of procedure. They become overawed by the speech-making of local bureaucrats on such issues on the USSR, and not having confidence in themselves, are lulled into support of these most reactionary aims. This is the truth, bitter as it may seem.

---

[1] Electrical Trades Union.

Almost immediately after the outbreak of the conflict on the Eastern front, a general members' meeting in the London area was called and a circular was issued by the EC on the organisational steps to be taken in the new situation. It was stated that the main task before the organisation was "the turn towards the CP rank and file." This necessitated a change in our organisational outlook. Instead of directing CP contacts towards the Labour Party to carry on activity as we do normally with new contacts, we were to appeal to them as an organisation of the Fourth International: in other words we were to devote a section of the group towards the carrying out of independent activity, whilst the remaining portion of our membership carried out work in the mass political organisations.

It is absolutely necessary to be clear as to what this means. It does not mean that the leadership of the group is succumbing to the old "independent party" bogey. Nothing of the sort. In fact we intensify our campaign of "Labour to power" on a programme of revolutionary demands. And every available member is required to be inside the mass organisations. The difference between ourselves and the old sectarians is that we evaluate the real role of the Labour Party leaders in relation to their hold over the rank and file, whereas they were content to ignore this and compete as an independent force for the leadership of the masses, without putting forward the necessary transitional demands. Neither does it mean that we indulge in adventurism, such as getting up in mass organisations and proclaiming that we are disciples of the Fourth International. We carry out our programme as members of these organisations, and not as outsiders. The workers will only see the correctness of our policy by careful preparation and consistent activity on the part of our members. When we work in mass organisations, it means that we must be the best workers as well as the best political leaders. It means that we have to sell the literature of these organisations, whilst we rigidly adhere to our criticisms and policy. Anything short of this will lead to sectarianism and isolation.

We know that it is easier to change group policy in words than in deeds. The new words may be on our lips while the old habits continue to dominate our actions. The new organisational turn also demands a new outlook on the part of our members. The previous "small group", sect outlook must go, and the atmosphere of the offensive introduced. This does not mean that we visualise a mushroom rate of growth overnight at this stage. On the contrary, we fully realise that in the main, for a long time to come, we shall recruit members on a one here and one there basis. What it does mean is that by correct application of our programme and ideas to the given situations we shall grow more rapidly in influence and contacts. Let us give one example of this. One of our comrades in a factory employing a considerable number of workers was working as a rank and file trade unionist eighteen months ago. Today, not only is he the convenor of his factory, but has won several valuable contacts to the organisation. This is the result not only of correct fraction work, but above all, of a correct political position.

We know that the situation was never more favourable than it is today. We are the only revolutionary Leninist grouping with a correct and tested policy for every issue confronting the workers. Every member of the group should be proud that they are members of the Fourth International, and of that group which has done more to put Trotskyism on the map in Britain than all the others put together. When we enter mass organisations it should be as leaders and officers of the new revolutionary army, because we alone can tell the whole truth to the working class. It is absolutely unthinkable that comrades can go along to trade union branches and meetings of other working class organisations and refrain from advancing the real programme of Bolshevism. We are well aware of the oppositionists. But we thrive on opposition. Our motto is "Let them all come"; we can handle every trend of thought in the working class movement. Politically we fear no one. That is why we must rivet the attention of the whole organisation towards the advancement of our programme in all organisations where our members participate. Nothing short of this will suffice. There is absolutely no use in carrying out fraction work if it is not carried out around our programme. If this is not done, then we are simply wasting our time and holding back the growth of our movement. Our programme is summed up in the ten point mast-head of the *Socialist Appeal*. Every member must push forward and concretise these demands among his workmates and contacts. Henceforth we must cease to exist as rank and file back stair theorists. We must emerge as responsible leaders of the working class. And for this, half hearted activity will not do. Each one of our members must drive home our positive policy, must win the confidence of his fellow workers and by this means, enrol them into the ranks of the new revolutionary party. It has been done. It can be done. It will be done.

The future of our work among the CP members

Some comrades may wonder if we have lost our opportunity insofar as the CP is concerned. Nothing could [be] further from the truth. The opportunity is just opening up. We have entered but the first rounds and in the coming months we must intensify our efforts to obtain as many contacts as possible amongst the rank and file of the CP. A recent EC directive sketched the perspective for such work in stating that we must prepare for a prolonged struggle inside the ranks. Building and operating a fraction is a long and tedious job. It requires thorough preparation and discussion in each local group and an all-embracing grasp of the situation on the part of every comrade. The need for a clear method of exposition of what we mean by the "defence of the Soviet Union" as well as a positive answer to the war itself is vital if such work is to progress.

We must therefore get down to building a national fraction in the CP as the rank and file have but entered the first phase of their crisis.

The group press

Never in the history of the working class movement, has so much depended upon the voice of the revolutionary workers' press. The vast awakening of hundreds and thousands of fresh militant workers and members of left wing political parties, demands a Herculean effort on the part of our members and sympathisers, to strengthen and develop the group press.

It is of the utmost importance that we should understand what is expected from us insofar as this is concerned. The small quantity of theoretical material crossing the Atlantic is insufficient to whet the political appetites of our own membership, much less our growing list of press subscribers, contacts and sympathisers. Month after month we have to witness well thumbed copies of American publications being passed from hand to hand throughout the group. Members write to us from the provinces pleading for back copies. We are of course sorry to have to disappoint them, but in most cases the material is simply not available. And this brings us to the crux of the matter. We must be prepared for the complete cutting off of postal supplies from America. The demand for revolutionary literature, and in particular the works of comrade Trotsky, is going to increase. With the developing upsurge of working class struggles the need for Marxian classics becomes greater. We have got to answer to this new demand. Upon our shoulders rests the future not only of the fate of the forty three million British toilers but upon the crystallisation and rejuvenation of the voice of our movement on the continent. For this purpose we need an immediate press fund of £200; we need a plant capable of meeting the demands of the hour: i.e. a fortnightly *Socialist Appeal*, a monthly theoretical organ, up to the minute policy and theoretical pamphlets and the reproduction of the most essential works of comrade Trotsky.

This is no day dreaming. The magnitude of the approaching conflict demands that we now redouble our efforts to set the wheel in motion of the most important of all publication jobs, our group press—the popular organiser of the new revolutionary party.

Why USSR is suffering reverses—
Internationalism
has been abandoned

By Ted Grant

[*Socialist Appeal*, Vol. 4, No. 1, October 1941]

Kiev has fallen to the legions of German imperialism. The Donetz basin is threatened. Leningrad and Odessa are besieged. Even the bourgeois press speaks of the seriousness of the military situation in which the Soviet Union finds itself and is already preparing an alibi for the failure to send substantial aid.

The German armies are blasting their way inch by inch into Soviet territory, paying a bloody price in casualties, it is true. Already the regions conquered are twice the area of greater Germany. The bitterly contested but triumphant advance of the German troops is due, of course, to the superiority of German technique, organisation, industry and military skill over that of Russia.

But in war, morale is the decisive factor. Even these victories would not be of vital importance if the armies of German imperialism had their morale shattered. The German soldier today is apathetic and indifferent. Insofar as Russian propaganda has any effect, it serves only to drive him, in despair, into support of Hitler. At the time of the wars of intervention almost the whole of Russia was at one time in the hands of imperialism. All that was left to the Bolsheviks at one period were the two towns Petrograd and Moscow and one province. An overwhelming superiority in military equipment was in the hands of the armies of intervention. Annihilation of the young Soviet Republic seemed certain. And if it had been allowed to remain a purely military question, annihilation would have been the result. But that was a revolutionary war, led by Lenin and Trotsky.

What are the methods of waging a revolutionary war for which the *Socialist Appeal* calls—the methods which would avert the disasters now facing the workers' state?

First: the reintroduction of complete workers' democracy within the Soviet Union, and the re-establishment of Soviets.

Second: a clear explanation to the peoples of the Soviet Union, Germany and the world, of the real nature and causes of the war. Not the lying and meaningless statements of the capitalist politicians that it is due to the blood lust and megalomania of Adolph Hitler. But the simple truth that it is in the interests of finance capital and the preservation of the capitalist system. Above all, it is the duty of Stalin to clearly differentiate to the German workers between the war being fought by the Soviet Union and that being waged by capitalist Britain under Churchill.

Third: instead of the chauvinist appeal, an international socialist call to the German and European workers and soldiers for the extension of the socialist revolution to all Europe: this would be the only means of awakening the class solidarity of the once proud and mighty German working class.

Necessary conditions for workers' democracy

Stalin and the Soviet bureaucracy will not and cannot make use of these revolutionary methods. Why? Workers have often asked us—"If you are in favour of the Soviet Union why do you attack the leaders in Russia?"

Russia is a workers' state because the land, mines, banks, factories, railways have been taken out of the hands of the capitalists and have been nationalised. That is why, in spite of all the crimes of Stalin, the Soviet Union must be defended by every class-conscious worker to the fullest extent.

Lenin laid down certain conditions for the existence of a workers' state which can be summed up as follows:

1. All officials to be elected with right of recall through workers' councils (soviets).

2. The abolition of the standing army and its substitution by the armed people.

3. No official to receive a wage higher than that of a skilled worker.

4. Administrative posts to be filled gradually in rotation so that no permanent officialdom could be formed.

What is the "Stalinist bureaucracy"?

But a similar process has taken place in Russia to that which took place in the labour and trade union movement in Britain. The trade union movement here was formed as a weapon of struggle against capitalism. But the officials—the Citrines and Bevins—gradually took over control and operated the trade unions in their own interests. Every trade unionist knows this from his own experience. But this does not mean to say we reject trade unionism. What it does mean is that we must conduct a struggle to get rid of the Citrines and Bevins and the whole strata of bureaucrats in order to transform the trade unions into fighting instruments of the working class.

In Russia, likewise, because of the backward development of the country and the defeats of the world working class, power has been seized out of the hands of the workers by the officialdom, the bureaucracy. In this case the officials not of a trade union, but of a state. The 11 million government officials, managers, heads of industry, etcetera, are now utilising the workers' state in their own interests instead of those of the workers. All the conditions laid down by Lenin are being eradicated. The soviets no longer exist. The officials are arbitrarily appointed and removed from above with the workers having no control over them. In place of the armed people, we have the old reactionary caste system restored in the army and the privileged officer strata. The law that the wages of officials do not exceed those of the skilled workers was abolished years ago.

This privileged caste defends its power and privileges against the working class, just as Morrison and his ilk do. To understand this is to understand the destruction of the entire old Bolshevik guard, the destruction of the rights of the working class, of the officer cadres of the Red Army when 90 percent of the general staff were murdered and three quarters of the officers executed[1]. The representative of this bureaucracy is Stalin, who has organised nothing but defeats for the workers.

Internationalism is the only salvation

The victories under Lenin and Trotsky were obtained, not only by the response of the Allied and German working class to their international calls, but by relying on the democratic organisations of the workers. Lenin based his power on the workers, placed his trust on their initiative and self-sacrifice, and made his first rule to tell the workers the truth. At every crisis in the wars of intervention, the Bolsheviks made an open, worldwide appeal to the masses, never misinforming them or sowing illusions. But the incompetent and venal bureaucracy dare not do this. One of the principal factors in the demoralisation of the French nation was the vicious censorship. In Russia today we see the contempt and panic with which the bureaucracy regards the masses in an even more rigid stifling of news. According to the *News Chronicle* Moscow correspondent, the destruction of the Dnieprostroy dam was not known to the masses of the people in the capital. The correspondent himself was not aware of it until he heard it on the British wireless.

---

[1] The Stalinist purges literally beheaded the Red Army. As a result of a secret trial (for alleged collaboration with the Nazi enemy) in June 1937 there were removed three of five marshals (including the Civil War hero Marshal Tukhachevsky), 13 of 15 army commanders, 8 of 9 admirals, 50 of 57 army corps commanders, 154 out of 186 division commanders, 16 of 16 army commissars, and 25 of 28 army corps commissars. Most of them were executed or sent to labour camps.

The acceptance by Stalin of the Atlantic Charter deception is a betrayal of the workers of Russia and the world. Churchill and Roosevelt are despatching carefully calculated aid to Russia. But behind the scenes, the policy which Moore-Brabazon indiscreetly blurted out is the policy of the ruling class. They wish to see the Soviet Union destroyed—but only after Germany has been sufficiently weakened to collapse under the offensive of Anglo-American imperialism. By relying on them, Stalin has placed the workers' state in the gravest danger of destruction. The capitalists will turn the flow of supplies on and off as it suits them.

Under the most favourable conditions, the production of war materials within the Soviet Union is only half that of Germany and occupied Europe. But with the occupation of some of the main industrial areas of the USSR, this disparity is now even greater. From this point of view, apart from the superiority of German military technique and organisation, if Hitler retains the support of the German people and his armies and if the peoples in occupied Europe do not rise (and these two conditions are largely interdependent), then Russia is doomed.

Reliance upon the capitalist democracies means inevitable disaster. Churchill and Roosevelt are not out to smash fascism or defend the conquests of October. The ruling class is taking advantage of the sentiment among the workers for support of the Soviet Union for their own ends. That is what lies behind the "tanks for Russia week" which was launched by Beaverbrook. Every worker would like to see the greatest possible material support sent to the gallant defenders of the USSR. But while control of these supplies remains in the hands of the ruling class there is no guarantee that these will be sent when most needed, or even that they will be sent at all. To trust the promises of aid given by Mr. Moore-Brabazon and his ilk, who control the government, would be suicidal.

The USSR will be defended our way

Russia must be defended in spite of the fact that Stalin and the bureaucracy are in control, in the same way as we defend the trade unions from capitalist attack even though the labour bureaucrats control them. The defeat of Russia would signal the most terrible setback for the working class for the past two decades. Because of this, we dare not sow illusions among the workers. The only guarantee that real aid will be despatched to our Russian brothers in sufficient quantities to affect the issue of the great battles, is when the shop stewards' and trade union committees control the despatch of supplies.

The tasks of the British workers are clear: full support for the fight of the Soviet Union against the onslaught of German imperialism. But to rally behind Churchill and the British ruling class would be to make certain the ultimate destruction of the Soviet Union and the victory of fascism. Only a workers' government in Britain could impel the German masses to overthrow Hitler and together with the Russian and British workers, establish a socialist Europe.

Statement on policy and perspectives

By Political Bureau of WIL

[Original draft document, autumn 1941]

For discussion in local groups

The first national conference of our organisation—the first genuinely national organisation covering a great part of the country—of the Fourth International tendency in Britain, is a great step forward in the history of our movement[1]. It is perhaps symbolic that it should take place to the drone of bombers and the sound of anti-aircraft guns; a fitting and grim reminder of the tasks which history has placed squarely on the shoulders of the British proletariat, and not least of all, of the historic responsibility which rests on the delegates to measure up to the working out of a solution of the problem to which our movement alone can provide the key.

It is not necessary to reiterate time and again what has become a commonplace within our ranks during the past fifteen years; that the building of a new revolutionary party is the only road to salvation. We accept as a starting point the basic documents of the Fourth International including the *Transitional Programme* and *Imperialist war and the world proletarian revolution*. The purpose of this statement on perspective is not and cannot be merely the mechanical repetition of these ideas and resolutions which we accept as axiomatic, but an attempt to understand the conditions in which Britain and the British labour movement are functioning today and of the probable trend of events.

We meet when the second year of the imperialist world war is in full swing and when the shadows which threatened to darken over the Empire upon which "the sun never sets", have imperceptibly gathered and the aged lion has gazed his last upon the era of world domination, ironically, precisely at the time when he has gathered his failing powers for a desperate resistance to the challenge of his younger and hungrier rivals.

---

[1] The document refers to an imminent conference which was postponed.

The decline of Britain as the invincible mistress of half the world is best seen in the loss of her position of paramountcy on the seven seas. Britannia has ceased to be the ruler of the waves. The classic emphasis by British military strategists on the decisive nature of sea power in this war caused by the island position of Britain, coupled with her complete dependence on overseas supplies, is a further reminder of the secondary role to which Britain has been reduced. Before firing a shot in either hemisphere, while preparing the cataclysmic destruction of Germany and Japan, America has announced a programme of naval expansion which alone will assure her unchallengeable superiority in a sphere which Britain has for centuries considered her own exclusive preserve; a sphere in which the loss of first position exposes Britain to particular vulnerability in the event of a conflict with the new master. So that not only has Britain lost her former vantage point of detachment from the European continent, but her former advantages on a world scale threaten to turn into mortal disadvantages. She is at the mercy of her trans-Atlantic "saviour". This humiliating dependence is underscored by the bases-destroyer deal, where America has helped herself to vital strategic positions in the Atlantic; by the preparation for a similar deal in the Pacific; by the consultations with Britain's dominions in the Western hemisphere more as dominions of her own than those of another country. All this with the enthusiastic plaudits (public at any rate) of the British bourgeoisie and their man of the hour, Churchill. Of course there is nothing else they can do. Defeat in the present war means annihilation for the British bourgeoisie, victory will mean a less spectacular decline to a second rate position. This is the best outcome that the British bourgeoisie can hope for. The shattering blows of German imperialism have been the means of revealing in the relationship of forces on a world scale, the decline and decay of the economic power of British capitalism—changes in economic power and world position only now beginning to assume correspondence. The glory of Empire is tarnished. Britain must stand humbly as a servitor of the new aspirant to world mastership in Wall Street.

This is the background to the internal and external politics of the British bourgeoisie. The almost complete destruction of the European labour movement in the last seven years has seen an apparently inexplicable strengthening of the position and power of the British Labour and trade union bureaucracy. Alone on the European continent, with the unimportant exception of Switzerland and Sweden (existing by the gracious tolerance of Hitler) the British labour organisations have remained intact. This is explained by the fact that while her rivals were preoccupied with internal social conflict or the intensive preparation for the coming war, Britain managed, for the last time perhaps, to increase her trade to nearly all her markets. By these means she was enabled to grant slight illusory concessions to the working masses by increasing output by approximately 20 percent while increasing the standard of living by 3 or 4 percent. The result was that the few years preceding the war was one of the most peaceful in the history of British capitalism. The class struggle suffered a lull with far fewer and less bitter strikes on the industrial field. The Labour and trade union bureaucracy became more than ever associated with the interests of the employers as obedient and interested servants.

Immediately after the declaration of war, the cloven hoof of the bourgeoisie was revealed. Draconic legislation, which, when carried out will turn Britain into a totalitarian state on the approved model, was placed on the statute book with the more or less tacit support of the Labour leaders. Nevertheless, in contradistinction to the "democratic" ally, France, no immediate attempt was made to put these laws into exclusive effect. The French bourgeoisie was compelled by the severity of the social crisis and the bitter mood of the workers to carry their repressive legislation into immediate effect, and, in the last analysis, to surrender to Hitler at the decisive moment partly as the result of this crisis—as a safeguard against their own masses.

The same military crisis which has seen the obliteration of Blum, Jouhaux and company, in France has seen the Labour leaders in Britain more firmly placed in ministerial positions. Much more than in the last war, the capitalists lean heavily for support upon their Labour agents. The course of the struggle upon the continent, the chains which German imperialism has riveted upon the conquered and subject peoples has led to the possibility of the Labour bureaucracy to move more confidently and surely to the open path of surrender to the bourgeoisie. The working class, not without some murmuring, faced with no other alternative that it could see than Nazi totalitarianism, which they instinctively regard with abhorrence and hatred, or support for their "own" government, supported the entry and consolidation of the Labour ministers in the government. Thus the worsened international position and the difficulties of British imperialism strengthened the role of the Labour bureaucracy in the internal calculations of the bourgeoisie. Morrison and Bevin have been placed in those posts where the bourgeoisie expected there would be the most pressure from the masses—Labour and Home Security. Under the sign-post "against Hitlerism" the Labour leaders have called for the utmost exertion on the part of the workers as exemplified by the inspiring "Go for it" slogan of Morrison.

The blows which Britain has suffered compel her to draw on her last resources. The accumulated plunder of centuries has to be used up; the very existence of the bourgeoisie is at stake; all must be thrown to the Moloch of war, of course at the expenses of the working masses and colonial peoples from whom the last ounce of tribute must be exhorted. In Germany this has been done by the iron heel of the Nazis grinding down the German workers and stripping bare the conquered nations. In the Empire, with the craven assistance of the native bourgeoisie, the screw has been drawn tighter by open measures of repression. In Britain the bourgeoisie, compelled to move cautiously, have relied upon trickery and the assistance of the Labour leaders to achieve their ends— giving minor concessions with the left hand, while taking away bigger "sacrifices" with the right.

The new taxes and increased prices have laid all the major burdens of the war on the back of the poorest section of the population. But while compelling key sections of the workers in the arms trade to work long hours of overtime, the bourgeoisie has been careful to pay them overtime at the traditional rates, a concession which is of course partly cancelled out by the rise in prices. This rise in prices, however, has placed even heavier burdens on that section of the workers which has not received increased pay. Notwithstanding the cruel pressure of suffering and want, despite the murderous air raids since the Battle of Britain began, despite the bitterness and scepticism, even to a certain extent, apathy and indifference of the toilers to the war, there is no sign as yet of a mass movement developing against the treachery of the Labour leaders, against the war, or even a mass movement in the workshops in favour of increases in pay. Hardly, in fact, have isolated strike struggles of major importance developed during the last period.

With great difficulty, much muddle and inefficiency, the bourgeoisie prepares that "total" effort which is necessary to defeat Germany. A total effort not rendered any less salutary by the inevitable active intervention of her more powerful ally, America, who will impose vigorous and stringent conditions for her credits and supplies. There are limits to the amount which can be squeezed out of the colonial masses. A great part will have to be contributed by the British masses. Further and unprecedented "sacrifices" will be demanded.

The blind self confidence of the ruling class in face of this perspective, declaimed through the mouth of Churchill, indicates the twilight of British capitalism. Like all doomed regimes, the British capitalists, in their mad careering to destruction cannot and do not wish to see the path into the future. Nero fiddled while Rome burned; Churchill airily announces the prospect of offensive campaigns in 1943 and 1944. While London is threatened with systematic destruction, with all its attendant miseries, he tosses forward the indecent slogan "It's a great life if you don't weaken." For the bourgeoisie, safe, comfortable and well fed, even in the ruin which their system has wrought, this slogan is befitting. Out of the very havoc and destruction even as they lose their position of world power, the golden rain continues to shower upon them. Super profits are being coined by the small group of monopolies, utilising the war to further enhance and tighten their complete domination over all fields of industry. The war accelerates enormously the increase in their profits. From this angle, for them it certainly is "a great life."

Still, this feverish confidence of the bourgeoisie rests on an uneasy basis. They are watching the pulse of the mass movement very carefully. The situation is charged with social dynamite and they proceed cautiously. The strangling grip of the bureaucracy of the labour movement on the masses is their chief social prop—a grip which might be broken once the masses are aroused. This caution is indicated by the retreat which the government has had to make on a number of issues: the opening of the tubes as air raids shelters; the niggardly concessions on the notorious Means Test[2], symbol of social degradation and humiliation to the masses for years; the emasculation and canalising in a reactionary direction, the striving of the masses to be armed, by the formation of the Home Guard.

In the last war the ministerial coalition of Labour with the bourgeoisie which commenced in 1915, was ended in 1917 through the pressure of the disillusioned masses, exasperated by the privations at home and the predatory imperialist policy abroad. A tremendous effect was created by the Russian Revolution which had immediate repercussions in Britain. The immediate and widespread swing to the left was reflected in the attitude of the Labour leaders, who, scenting danger, were compelled to put forward pseudo-revolutionary speeches to maintain their hold on the rank and file.

The revolutionary left, which later crystallised into the Communist Party of Great Britain, destroyed its chance of winning a mass basis precisely because it did not understand the necessity of keeping in close touch the unclear feelings and aspirations of the masses, which in their beginnings could not but be in the direction of the Labour Party. As Lenin had the occasion to lecture the ultra-lefts "it is very useful to chronicle the crimes of the Labour bureaucracy but that is not sufficient to win the masses." This was the key to the weakness of the revolutionary forces in the first years. It is the key to all the subsequent developments, coupled of course, with the betrayal of Stalinism. The present weakness of the Independent Labour Party, apart from the fatal sterility which issues from the policies of centrism, also comes from their incapacity to face towards the Labour Party masses.

The revolutionary wave of 1917-1920 reached its culmination in this country in the "Hands off Russia" movement among the masses. The "councils of action" which were formed through the length and breadth of Britain, correspond to the soviets formed in Russia and Germany. Under pressure of the masses, MacDonald, Snowden and company[3] made speeches in order to pacify the

---

[2] Investigative process undertaken to determine whether or not an individual or family is eligible to qualify for help from the government. In 1921 the abolition of the Means Test was one of the main demands of the National Unemployed Workers' Movement set up by members of the CPGB.

[3] James Ramsay MacDonald (1866 – 1937) rose from humble origins to become the first Labour Prime Minister in 1924. His first government lasted less than one year. Labour returned to power in 1929, but in 1931 MacDonald split the Labour Party forming a "national government" supported by a Tory majority. Philip Snowden (1864 – 1937) was among the founders of the Labour Party, Chancellor of the Exchequer in the first Labour government of 1924. He followed MacDonald's trajectory and ended up expelled from the Labour Party.

workers, threatening the ruling class with general strike and civil war if they persisted in their intention of making war on Russia—a threat sufficiently dangerous to paralyse the hand of Lloyd George and Churchill. Nevertheless the leadership of this movement was retained by the Labour bureaucracy which utilised its position to render innocuous the revolutionary enthusiasm and ardour of the masses. It is interesting to note that the year 1920 marks the peak of membership in the trade unions, reaching 8 million, the highest figure ever recorded, thus showing that the revolutionary movement of the masses is reflected in the traditional organisations, without coming into conflict with them immediately. MacDonald and Snowden even played, in words, with the idea of British soviets and the present Minister of Labour, Mr. Bevin, threatened the rulers in the last war with civil war if it was necessary to win socialism. Incidentally, he solemnly assured the well fed bourgeois Rotarians in a recent speech that he was "not against revolution" if, as he happily expressed it, it was well led! That is, a revolution which broke out and in which Bevin and his ilk could thrust themselves forward to "lead" in order the better to betray and emasculate it. The revolution will come, but the crux of our problem consists in preparing and organising ourselves so that the Bevins and their brothers under the skin, the Pollitts, will not strangle it.

The experience of the Labour government of 1924 once again demonstrated the strong roots which reformism has within the working class. The Communist Party, at that time not yet completely degenerated, failed to gain a mass support, despite the fact that Labour had shown itself utterly incapable of producing even one major reform in the interests of the masses. The embittered toilers turned from the political field to the industrial. A revolutionary radicalisation of the masses began. It reached its culmination and greatest expression in the general strike of 1926. The Labour bureaucracy—the trade union wing this time—were compelled by the upward swing to place themselves at the head of the movement which thay hated and dreaded, if that movement was not to get completely out of their control. In order to cloak their activities they utilised the Russian trade unions through the Anglo-Russian Committee. It is true to say that the major responsibility for the rout and demoralisation rests on the shoulders of Stalinism and in particular on its fount[ain]head in Moscow.

The defeat of the general strike, owing of course to the incapacity of the Stalinists to offer an alternative, led to the reinforcement of the Labour bureaucracy. The strivings of the masses found its outlet in the formation of the second Labour government. The debacle of 1931 soon followed when the leadership revealed its true colours and went openly over to the camp of the enemy class. Despite this, the masses of workers, with ranks almost intact, remained behind the banner of Labour. Not of course without inner convulsions; the pressure from within forced a split of the left wing—the Independent Labour Party broke away from the Labour Party.

The developments as outlined above, are not only not excluded during the course of this war, but are most likely. Under the impact of the masses certain demagogic lefts together with some sincere elements, together with a section of members of Parliament, will form a "left" opposition within the Labour Party, or even break away, perhaps combining with the ILP to form a new centrist or left-reformist organisation. A movement of opinions among the masses will inevitably provoke reactions within the Labour Party—even in its upper crust.

The years which have intervened since this period have witnessed the rising of the power of the Labour and trade union bureaucracy to new heights. Since the war, membership of the trade unions, continuing the trend of developments prior to the outbreak, has reached new heights and is approaching the record figure of 1920. Correspondingly the membership of the Labour Party increases through affiliation. Before the outbreak of the war the working class, recovering from the defeats of 1926 and 1931, once again began to press forward. The strikes of the railwaymen in London began to overstep the bounds of trade union "legality". In the teeth of the opposition of the trade union leaders, under the leadership of their factory committees, the workers took direct action and sought support from their fellow workers on a national scale. The bourgeoisie immediately sounded a note of alarm. Threatening articles appeared in the *Times, Telegraph* and other capitalist organs, demanding that the "leaders" of the trade union restore "control" over their members and keep them from "unconstitutional acts" against the legally established machinery; if this was not done they would have to adopt other methods—fascist methods were plainly hinted at. The workers began to move against their own leaders but simultaneously they moved in the direction of the Labour Party. This was evidenced by the increased Labour vote in the elections, and in the increase of membership in the trade union and Labour Party.

The whole policy of the bourgeoisie in the few years before the war was in the main, preoccupied with the possibility of civil war in Britain. The military manoeuvres of the army in 1937 and 1938 were conducted for the first time in English history, on the basis of civil war. The construction of a Civil Guard composed of upper middle class elements who were taught the use of aeroplanes, locomotive engines, lorries, ground staff work of aeroplanes, and in the placing of machine gun emplacements at strategic points and in government buildings was obviously thought of with an eye to civil war. The bourgeoisie expected explosions and prepared for them.

Although these developments will not be avoided, the war temporarily cut across them, and gave them a new direction and tempo. Even with these movements in embryo, the masses turned in the direction of the Labour Party. During the first period of the war a certain opposition, or at least a feeling of uneasiness manifested itself among the masses. A critical attitude of distrust for the war was apparent. The Stalinists attempted to divert it into their channels. In South

Wales, where they controlled the Miners' Federation, they attempted to canalise their support by organising a referendum vote on the war question. The Labour bureaucracy neatly side-tracked the issue by posing the question as "against the war" or "for the war but with a Labour government to carry it out." Even at that period, this latter motion was carried by a majority of three to one. The fact that at a moment of danger this slogan had to be thrust forward by the Labour leaders is an indication of the likely trend of developments. This does not contradict the fact that now when the developments of the war have swept the working class solidly behind the war, that at a later stage the masses will find themselves compelled to turn to industrial action through their own shop and factory committees. Nor does this latter inevitable stage mean that the slogan for a Labour government will not find an expression among the masses.

After the February revolution in Russia, the agitation of the Bolsheviks demanded the calling of the constituent assembly. But this did not at all prevent them from fighting round the slogan of "All power to the soviets" at the same time. There is no contradiction here. In the same way there is no contradiction between the agitation for the slogan of Labour to power and the development of factory committees. It is necessary only to understand the contradictions of development as expressed in the daily life of the toilers, taking into consideration their mood, and taking this as a starting point.

The ultra-lefts of the present war base their stand on the ideas that the Labour leaders, by entering the government, have written finis to their hold on the working class. They had better read their Lenin once again: "Without the support of the Labour bureaucracy and its support among the aristocracy of labour, the English bourgeoisie could not rule for a single day", he tells us. This elementary Marxian proposition is not invalidated by the outbreak of the imperialist war. War is the continuation of politics by other means, including the politics of the labour organisations. It is unfortunate, but the course of events does not automatically reveal the role of the Labour bureaucrats to the workers. Because Bevin and company stand exposed before the eyes of a small section of advanced workers it does not follow that the working class as a whole have become aware of their true role. If this were so, the most difficult part of our task would have been accomplished. The very existence of a broad democracy in the war is rendered possible only because of the leaning of the bourgeoisie on the Labour bureaucracy, and through them indirectly on the mass of the organised workers.

The bourgeoisie sees things much more clearly than the ultra-lefts. They well understand that the Labour Party is far from played out as the instrument of their rule. The main stream of development of the workers' movement in Britain must be, and cannot be otherwise, than in the direction of the Labour Party. The argument sometimes put forward that the Labour Party and trade unions do not comprise the whole of the working class does not invalidate this process in the least. The inevitable awakening of all strata of the masses to political life will lead to their active participation in the organised working class movement. Exactly these strata require the active experience of the role of the Labour leaders before they can be won for the revolution. We cannot expect that the more backward, even if more exploited sections of the toilers, can be in advance of their organised brothers. So that here too our propaganda cannot but be in the direction of the tested ideas of Bolshevism. There are no short cuts to the revolution.

We cannot expect a turning of the masses to the left immediately. There will be ebbs and flows before a decisive break takes place. Even on the Clyde and in South Wales, storm centres of the workers' movement in the last war, the break has not come as yet. Incipient signs are there. The workers are preparing to measure their strength against the bosses in the coming struggles. But such is the mood of the workers at present that there have been no large strikes as yet on the scale of those in the second year of the last war. But the development of events promises even more stormy and bitter struggles. The workers will turn to their shop and factory committees in masses, as organs of struggle most directly representing their interests. And when the struggle really begins to assume mass forms, the pressure on the labour organisations will be increased. In one way or another, just as in the last war, the Labour leaders will reflect this pressure.

In Russia, despite the long traditions of Bolshevism, the experience of the revolution of 1905, and the fact that the Bolsheviks had the support of the overwhelming majority of the organised workers in the years preceding the war, after the February revolution the vast majority of the population awakening to political life rallied to the Mensheviks and Social Revolutionaries.

The fact that the German Social Democracy had betrayed the masses for four years, had entered the Kaiser's government, did not prevent a swing in their direction when the revolution of 1918 took place—a revolution they had attempted to prevent by all means in their power. This despite the inspiring example of the Russian October which was fresh before their eyes. Despite the fine work of the Spartacists led by Liebknecht and Luxemburg, the first step of the broad masses entering actively on the political arena was in the direction of social democracy.

The outbreak of the war compelled the bourgeoisie to liquidate the organisation of Mosley fascists, which in any case had failed to penetrate the working class to any extent, or even a considerable section of the middle class, and which now became completely discredited. For the present the bourgeoisie clings to the Labour leaders as the sheet anchor of their rule, relying more on the deception of the masses by lying demagogy than upon the smashing of the ♦ labour organisations forcibly. But this situation opens up the prospect of mortal danger for the decaying ruling class. All their attempts to operate a policy of repression will meet with the opposition of the workers. Without a mass basis, like that of the Nazis in Germany, the reaction will cling in the first stages to the coat tails of the Labour leaders. If we separate ourselves from the workers we will isolate ourselves without in any way helping, instructing and learning from the workers themselves, through their own experiences. The mainstream of development lies through the Labour organisations. Our own weakness dictates the necessity for us to fight for influence among the advanced workers. This does not hamper certain independent activity where it is not conducted in a vacuum divorced from the masses. The mass movement will attain a broad sweep, but it will pass us by unnoticed if we isolate ourselves from the inevitable, unclear strivings of the workers.

Those who imagine that the surging forward of the masses in strike struggles and the development of the industrial conflict to extreme pitches of bitterness, even the development of factory committees into soviets, will herald the doom of the Labour bureaucracy within the working class, fail to understand the lessons and traditions of history. On the contrary, to isolate the revolutionaries by an incorrect tactical approach in the preparatory period, will lead to fatal consequences for the development and organisation of the Fourth International in Britain. It is exactly in this period that the role of the Labour leaders will be most dangerous to the working class. By the correct application of the transitional programme counterposing it to the privileges of the bourgeoisie—by demanding the expropriation of the land, mines, banks, railways and industry; the arming of the working class; freedom for India and the colonies and the issuing of a socialist appeal to the workers of Europe on the basis of the overthrow of British imperialism, the most advanced elements will be won over to the banner of the revolution and the path will be cleared for the construction of the revolutionary party. The party is not formed merely by the desire or the objective necessity for it, but is indissolubly linked with the day to day life of the workers and their reactions to events. A party cannot be "imposed" upon the workers. Under present conditions, for a small section of revolutionaries to place themselves as an immediate alternative to the government is to make themselves ludicrous in the eyes of the workers, who can but dismiss them as utopian dreamers. But a Labour government, which could only be achieved by the active mobilisation of the masses, round the demand that the Labour leaders break with the boss class—this is a formidable means of awakening the masses to the consciousness of the role of the Labour traitors in their active refusal and mortal terror to assume full responsibility of government. By the flexible use of transitional slogans as rallying points for the broad issues which confront the masses, linking them with the question of power in a form which can be immediately understood, they can be converted from lifeless abstractions and be seen as living realities by the toilers.

The general perspective of the Labour Party does not invalidate in the least the necessity to follow the developments within the Independent Labour Party and the Communist Party and to work within these organisations. The tactic of the revolutionaries must be flexible. The one pre-requisite is to remain rooted within the mass organisations of the working class. With a lack of a real alternative the Communist Party with its powerful organisational apparatus, will make extensive gains, among whom will be found the most self-sacrificing and most militant sections of the workers. The Communist Party has retained its hold on an important number of key militants in industry. These act as points of support within the broad strata of trade union workers. Even at the height of the unpopular Finnish episode[4], the Communist Party managed, perhaps with a certain loosening, to retain its grip on these workers—a grip which has tightened during recent events. The Communist Party is far from being discredited. On the rise of the mass movement their unexcelled demagogy will exploit the revolutionary sentiments of the masses in the direction most favourable to Soviet diplomacy. The Peoples' Convention was formed to divert the revolutionary energy of the masses into harmless popular front channels. With no other alternative the genuine militants will be diverted onto this path. Wherever possible we must fight side by side with the rank and file of the Communist Party on the day to day issues on which we have common ground, thus creating a healthy basis for drawing the lessons home to these militants of the fallacy of the "people's government" and the only road to the solution of their problems—the struggle for workers' power.

The Independent Labour Party offers a field to certain elements within the working class movement, who disgusted with the Labour Party and repelled by the Communist Party, turn to what appears [to be] a party with a different and even "revolutionary" approach. These elements must be reached and diverted from the path of semi-pacifism, semi-patriotism onto the road of the revolution. The differences of opinion now raised so sharply within the ILP affords a revolutionary nucleus, an opportunity to contrast the lucid line of Marxism to the muddled, confused currents of social patriotism and pacifism held together in an unprincipled bloc within its framework. A revolutionary wing within the ILP could not only expose the opportunism and reactionary nature of the contending factions, but also their sectarianism. The left wing in the ILP, composed of comparatively advanced workers, must turn its face towards the left wing in the Labour Party and on the basis of a revolutionary programme, attempt to link up its policy and activities, thus drawing the two sections together. But here again, this cannot detract from, but merely enhance the slogan of "full strength at the

---

4 Also known as the Winter War, the Finnish episode revealed the weaknesses of the USSR. On November 30 1939 Stalin launched an attack on Finland. The Red Army—badly trained and equipped and serverly debilitated by the Stalinist purges—encountered a fierce resistance from the Finnish troops and population. The Red Army finally managed to overcome the resistance only thanks to the large amount of troops and resources poured into the campaign.

point of attack". The main axis of our activity remains in the Labour Party and trade unions.

Expressive of the tendency of our epoch, it is mainly the youth who have been attracted to the banner of the Fourth International. Amid the demoralisation wrought by defeats for the international proletariat, we can look with pride to the grouping gathered around Workers' International League. The weakness of the organisation theoretically and organisationally gives no cause for despair. During the last war the revolutionary wing in Britain stood on a much lower level of theoretical understanding of the problems of the workers' movement. We have the experience not only of the British workers, but of the international working class since the last world war, the theoretical lessons of which have been worked out by our tendency internationally. The British working class, organised for the revolution, possesses a crushing social weight. The main obstacle on the road of the revolution remains the Labour bureaucracy. But the development of the class struggle will put them to far sterner tests than they have ever experienced in the past. The fate of the bourgeois regime is going to be measured, not in words, but in battles on the streets, and all the attempts on part of the Labour leaders to prevent this will be of no avail. The coming struggles of the British workers on a new historical basis will equal and surpass by far those of the Chartists and of the post-war period, including the general strike.

Events are crowding on one another—our resources are slender, we are weak politically, organisationally and in experience. Whether we will be able to build the party in time to face up to coming events is a question that history alone will answer. If Stalinism and reformism retain their hold on the workers the consequences can only be, from the most dazzling of possibilities, the most ghastly of defeats. We have faith in our party and our future—the key to which is held by the Fourth International alone. Whatever the immediate vicissitudes, in the end our ideas must triumph, but our work has always been guided by the necessity of building cadres capable of upholding, in face of all obstacles, this banner. Our policy is dominated by the conception elaborated in *Imperialist war and the world proletarian revolution* by comrade Trotsky:

"Naturally, this or that uprising will end in defeat owing to the immaturity of the revolutionary leadership. But it is not a question of a single uprising. It is a question of an entire revolutionary epoch.

"The capitalist world has no way out, unless a prolonged death agony is so considered. It is necessary to prepare for long years, if not decades, of war, uprisings, brief interludes of truce, new wars and new uprisings. A young revolutionary party must base itself on this perspective. History will provide it with enough opportunities and possibilities to test itself, accumulate experience and to mature. The swifter the ranks of the vanguard are fused the more the epoch of bloody convulsions will be shortened, the less destruction will our planet suffer. But the great historical problem will not be solved in any case until a revolutionary party stands at the head of the proletariat. The question of tempos and time interludes is of enormous importance; but it alters neither the general historical perspective nor the direction of our policy. The conclusion is a simple one: it is necessary to carry on the work of educating and organising the proletarian vanguard with tenfold energy. Precisely in this lies the task of the Fourth International."

For us there can be no easy road to success. Our main task consists in strengthening, extending and building the organisation by education, selection and the hardening of cadres. The favourable conditions of work which exist at present in Britain offer opportunities for this. And principally our task is to gain the ear of the advanced workers. The military successes of Hitler have once again demonstrated the efficacy of the slogan "full strength at the point of attack." In the present relation of forces, the small revolutionary group must retain this maxim—concentration of work within the mass organisations of the working class.

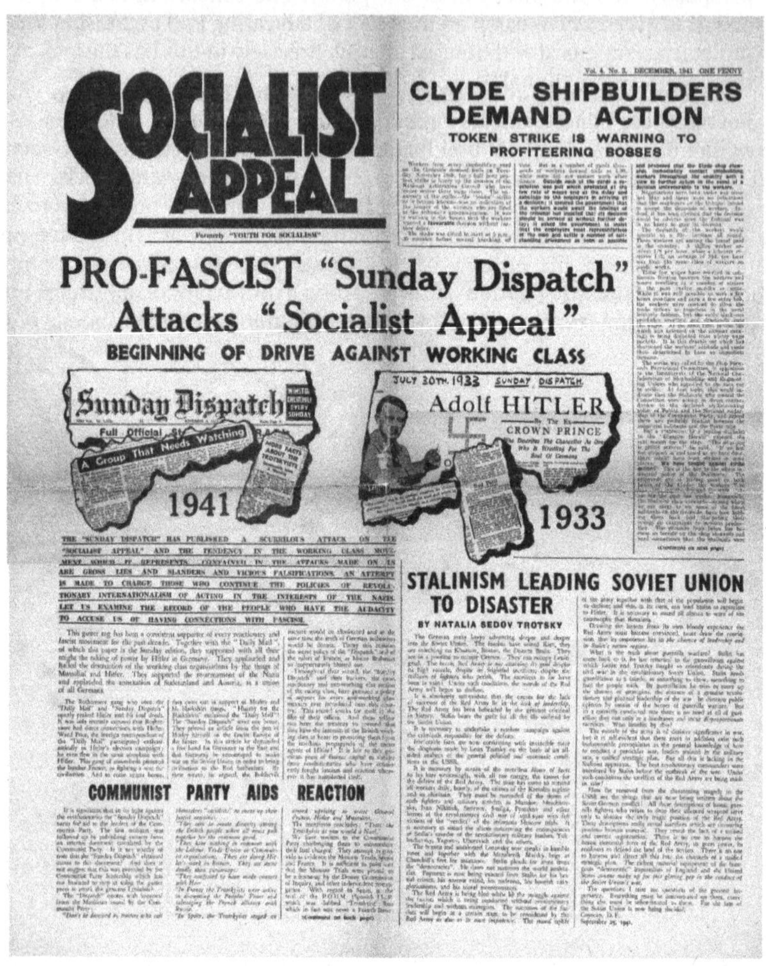

Socialist Appeal, Vol. 4 No. 3, December 1941 (Ted Grant Archive)

A challenge to the Communist Party

By Ted Grant

[*Socialist Appeal*, Vol. 4 No. 3, December 1941]

November 25 1941

To the Secretary of the Communist Party

Your leading body has recently issued a slanderous statement to branch secretaries regarding the *Socialist Appeal* and the fourth internationalists in Britain. We denounce your assertions that the Trotskyists are, or ever have been, agents or supporters of Nazism or fascism. Further, we challenge you to substantiate this document in public debate before the members of your Party and the workers of Britain.

The *Sunday Dispatch* has already made use of your document as justification for its attacks against worker militants in general and against the *Socialist Appeal* in particular. The manner in which it is presented, proves that your present policy closely coincides with that of the most reactionary clique in British capitalist newspaper publications. Tomorrow, these very people will be clamouring for the suppression of the Communist Party.

Your document indicates that the Communist Party of Great Britain is preparing to play the role of strike-breaker-in-chief and police agent for Churchill and his government. It is an invitation to the government to suppress the *Socialist Appeal* and ban our organisation. But it also contains a directive to Communist Party members to commit acts of physical violence against fourth internationalists and salesmen of the *Socialist Appeal*. In your statement to the Young Communist League secretaries you state:

> "We are too tolerant of these people. They are allowed to sell their paper *Socialist Appeal* outside meetings. They have even become members of the Communist Party and YCL. We must be utterly ruthless with these people. They spread confusion amongst the working class and do serious harm to our party."

These are methods of fascist reaction and cannot but harm the working class movement. You cannot answer our policy in open discussion because this would result in the exposure of the falsity of CP policy and the correctness of the programme of the Fourth International. Fearing the ideas of Marx and Lenin which we represent, you resort to anti-working class methods of slander and violence. We appeal to the rank and file members of the CP and YCL not to be misled, but to conduct polemics on working class policy on the basis of open and comradely argument and discussion, and by these means find a way to the correct policy for the workers. We will not be intimidated by methods of hooliganism but will protect our right to distribute our propaganda among the workers.

In recent months, since the capitulation of the Communist Party to the Churchill government, many members of the party have joined the ranks of the Fourth International. Your statement that Trotskyists have joined the party would appear to be a reply to this reaction of party militants and a preparation for the intensified expulsions from the party of all who oppose your present reactionary policy.

We are holding a meeting on December 21 at the Holborn Hall at 6.30 pm to expose the slanders of the pro-fascist *Sunday Dispatch* and of the Communist Party. An opportunity will be given to any spokesmen of the Communist Party whom you would like to nominate to justify your statements. Failure to avail yourself of this opportunity will brand you as slanderers and deceivers of the working class.

E. Grant, For the Editorial Board of the *Socialist Appeal*

December 21 1941 meeting announcement

ILP and the Stalinist slander

[Socialist Appeal, Vol. 4 No. 4, January 1942]

Below we publish the letters exchanged between the ILP and ourselves on the question of a united front against Stalinist provocation and slander. These letters were exchanged following on a discussion between comrades Atkinson and Brockway.

The leaders of the ILP do not believe it necessary to hold "special" meetings to combat the Stalinist campaign; that such meetings would assist rather than deter the Stalinists in their provocations. At the same time they refer to the fate which befell their brother party—the POUM—in Spain! But it is precisely because the POUM carried out the same ostrich policy as is now being carried out by the ILP that attacks were facilitated against it, culminating in the murder of its leaders by the Stalinists.

Already the campaign has reached the stage of physical assault, not only of the Trotskyists, but of workers selling the *New Leader* at Communist Party meetings. And the campaign is still in its early stages. As the war proceeds and the workers turn towards the left, the Stalinists will, in desperation turn to more violent methods. Under these circumstances it is an elementary precaution of self-preservation that a vigorous campaign of exposure be waged against these degrading methods of organised hooliganism.

The Central Committee of the Communist Party have issued instructions that the names and addresses of all Trotskyists should be secured. This undoubtedly applies to members of the ILP as well. In Spain and in France this action was a prelude to Stalinist assistance to police reaction. In the Nazi occupied countries the names and addresses of revolutionaries opposed to CP policy were handed over to the Gestapo.

This is not a question of a merely incidental character. It concerns the very existence of workers' organisations which operate a policy opposed to Churchill and the Communist Party. If the ILP refuses to carry the struggle against the Stalinist pogroms, how will they face up to the far stronger blows of the capitalists when they really start to suppress the left wing, particularly since they will have the active assistance of the Stalinists?

Comrades of the ILP! Remember the fate of the workers in Spain! We appeal to the leadership of the ILP to reverse its present disastrously negative policy and enter a united front.

We appeal to the members of the ILP to force their leadership to change its present policy and conduct a vigorous united front campaign which will expose the Stalinists before the whole labour movement, as well as protect our organisations from their gangster assaults.

Workers' International League

61, Northdown Street, London, N1

December 3 1941

Secretary, ILP

Dear comrade,

Following the recent attacks on the *Socialist Appeal* by the *Sunday Dispatch* and the Communist Party, we have issued a challenge to the latter to an open debate in order to substantiate their accusations. In confirmation of our verbal request, through comrade Harold Atkinson, we again ask that you delegate a speaker to this meeting in order to put the case of the ILP which is also being attacked by the Communist Party.

We believe that this method of thrashing out differences between sections of the organised working class complies with the best traditions of the British labour movement. We would be grateful if you will publish our letter to the Communist Party in the *New Leader*.

Yours fraternally,

E. Grant,

for the Editorial Board of the *Socialist Appeal*.

Independent Labour Party

National Administrative Council

318 Regents Park Road, Finchley, London, N3

December 8 1941

Mr. Atkinson,

61, Northdown Street, London, N1

Dear comrade Atkinson,

I promised to let you have a note about the decision against my coming to your meeting on December 21.

We are well aware that the Communist Party will adopt any tactics against ourselves, as well as against you, including demands as the situation develops for the suppression of our paper and of all our activities. Already they are beginning tactics here which are similar to those they adopted against the POUM in Spain.

We take the view, however, that if we hold or participate in special meetings dealing with this matter, it will assist rather than deter their purpose. We shall meet vigorously their tactics, as we are now doing in the bye-election at Central Edinburgh, but to over-emphasise the importance of their attack will only play into their own hands.

It was for this reason that we felt it inadvisable that we should accept your invitation to send a speaker to your meeting.

Fraternally yours,

Fenner Brockway

Stalin threatens new turn Anglo-USA imperialists fear Soviet victory

By Ted Grant

[*Socialist Appeal*, Vol. 4 No. 6, March 1942]

A world already astonished at the dizzying turns of Stalin's policies, witnessed a new threatened orientation in Stalin's order of the day, no. 55, on the occasion of the 24th anniversary of the Red Army. In it, Stalin seems to have made the discovery that there is a difference between the German people and Hitler.

"It would be ridiculous," he said, "to identify Hitler's clique with the German people and the German state. The experience of history shows that Hitlers come and go whereas the German people and the German state remain."

This is in striking contrast to what Stalin and his supporters have been saying in their propaganda in the last few months. Whereas in the beginning of the war between Germany and Russia, the Kremlin leaders, although not issuing a call to internationalism, did make a distinction between the Nazi gang and the German people. Gradually, however, the propaganda of Stalin became more and more indistinguishable from that of his "democratic allies". Indeed it became even worse, arousing protests from even the liberals and Labour lefts. Stalin's national chauvinism was epitomised in the symbolic replacement of the words "workers of the world unite!" on the heading of the Red Army paper, the *Red Star* with the words "Death to the German invaders." Innumerable examples appeared in the press, such as the one we reproduce, whose authenticity is guaranteed by its appearance in the official Communist Party publication *World News and Views*.

"How can the German people not be held to pay for these terrible crimes? And if one states: the German people have nothing in common with these murderers, then the question arises, what proof of this can the German people present? After all these are not isolated cases of men ravaging Russia like Huns. Hundreds of thousands are involved."

No international appeal

Has Stalin dimly remembered the traditions of Lenin by his newly voiced discrimination between the Nazis and the German people? Nothing could be further from the truth. For there is no mention of socialism or internationalism in the whole speech; there is no appeal to the German workers and soldiers to unite to establish a socialist Europe and world. Under these circumstances, the assurances of Stalin that German soldiers who surrender will be spared their lives do not carry much weight. The British imperialists and the American imperialists have done no more and no less to their adversaries. What effect can this be expected to have on the Germans, who have been led to believe by Stalin's propaganda that they are fighting for the preservation of Germany against another Versailles? Turns cannot be made overnight and expect to reap response. The mischief rendered by previous propaganda has resulted in a desperate resistance of the German soldiers against the advances of the Red Army—even in the face of complete annihilation.

Destruction of fascism—not Stalin's war aim

Veiled behind Stalin's speech is contained a threat to the democracies of a peace with the German state—another Soviet-German alliance—this time not necessarily with Hitler, but if need be with the German militarists.

Stalin did everything possible to avoid the conflict with Hitler and would just as readily return to the policy of German-Russian collaboration. Any terms, any pacts, any alliances—Stalin's sole concern is the preservation of the privileges and power of the Russian ruling caste.

Stalin's war aims, as outlined by himself, are no longer the destruction of Germany, or even the destruction of German fascism, but merely the restoration of Russia's 1940 frontiers. In the course of achieving these aims, he states,

> "It is very likely that the war for the liberation of our Soviet land will result in the busting or destruction of Hitler's clique. We would welcome such an outcome..."

We would welcome such an outcome, mark you! Not that the overthrow of German fascism is an intrinsic part of the fight for freedom of the peoples of the world!

The more sober capitalist press has seen the warning and understood its meaning, unfortunately, better than the majority of the advanced workers. They have understood that Stalin is concerned only with the preservation of the borders of Russia and the maintenance of the ruling clique in its present position of power. *The Economist,* of February 28 1942, states:

> "...the spectacle of the leader of the socialist Mecca rousing his people to 'a war of patriotism, of liberation, a just war', without a single ref-

erence to internationalism, the world-wide solidarity of the workers, and the inevitability of communist revolution, must be rather like hearing the angel Gabriel sounding the Last Trump on a swanee whistle. Stalin has restated in the most uncompromising terms the war aims of the Soviet people. They are: to liberate Soviet soil, Soviet lands, from the foreign invader—and the Soviet lands are carefully enumerated: White Russia, the Ukraine, Lithuania, Latvia, Estonia and Karelia. If in the course of ridding the country of the foreign invader, the Russians should drive out the 'fascist clique' in Germany, all the better—but Stalin does not raise this point to the dignity of war aim. For the rest neither he nor the Russian people have any quarrel with the German people or with the German state".

Imperialists fear Soviet victory—Stalin silent on aid from Allies

It is noteworthy that not a single mention was made of the democratic "allies" throughout the speech. No felicitations were exchanged with the "grand old warrior Churchill," no reference to the gallant war of the united nations against the worst menace of mankind. Last November on the occasion of the twenty-fourth anniversary of the October revolution, Stalin boasted: "We now have allies forming a united front with us against the German invaders." Last November Stalin promised the Soviet masses that his foreign policy would assure not only material aid, but a second front. He stated then:

> "But neither can there be any doubt that the appearance of a second front on the Continent of Europe—*and it must appear in the nearest future*—will render substantially easier the opposition of the Red Army to the detriment of the German army."

But in his last speech there were no boasts of the benefits of the alliance with the imperialists of Britain and America; instead of a warning to the Soviet masses that they rely only upon their own resources to overcome the invader.

> "The German fascist army" says Stalin, "is directly supported at the front by the troops of Italy, Rumania and Finland. The Red Army, so far, has no such support."

As we have consistently pointed out, Churchill and Roosevelt have rendered small aid to the Soviet Union. Compared to the Herculean expenditure of Russian men and material, their aid has been derisory and insulting. The whole policy of the British and American ruling class has been to seek the destruction of the Soviet Union and the simultaneous exhaustion of Germany, to the point where Anglo-American imperialism could overcome Germany with ease. In pursuance of this policy the Soviet Union has been left to bear the brunt of the most terrible war machine in history.

It is admitted even by the Communist Party that the "United States has failed to deliver more than 50 percent of its commitments to the Soviet Union during the past three months."

Coupled with this, the recent statement of Wendell Wilkie bears the greatest significance that he has "no confidence that Russia could really win this war in a definite way. And I have every confidence that the Americans would not like the peace very much if she did."

Their calculations have been upset by the unparalleled heroism of the Russian workers and peasants, and Hitler has failed in his objective. Meanwhile the British and American capitalists, while building up their forces for the crushing of Germany in 1943, have looked on with complacency; shedding crocodile tears at the sufferings of the Russian people while Russia was being systematically weakened.

SOCIALIST APPEAL

ORGAN OF WORKERS INTERNATIONAL LEAGUE
FOURTH INTERNATIONAL

Vol. 4 No. 6 MARCH, 1942. ONE PENNY

JOINT PRODUCTION COMMITTEES— 'BOSSES' TOOLS

Swanson Puts Bosses' Case

AT A TIME WHEN THE GOVERNMENT IS CONTEMPLATING THE ESTABLISHMENT OF COMPULSORY JOINT PRODUCTION COMMITTEES BETWEEN THE WORKERS AND MANAGEMENTS IN ALL ENGINEERING ESTABLISHMENTS, IT IS OF EXTREME IMPORTANCE TO STUDY THE ACTUAL WORKINGS OF ONE OF THESE COMMITTEES, TO SEE WHAT FUNCTIONS THEY ACTUALLY PERFORM, AND WHOSE INTERESTS THEY ARE INTENDED TO SERVE.

A Joint Production Committee has been in existence at Napier's, Acton, for a period of some months now. It was formed on the initiative of the convenor, Bro. Swanson and other Stalinist Shop Stewards, who have suddenly discovered the great merits to be accrued from "friendship and collaboration" with the bosses since Russia was attacked.

By AJIT ROY

STALIN THREATENS NEW TURN

Anglo—U.S.A. Imperialists Fear Soviet Victory

By E. GRANT

A WORLD, ALREADY ASTONISHED AT THE DIZZYING TURNS OF STALIN'S POLICIES, WITNESSED A NEW THREATENED ORIENTATION IN STALIN'S ORDER OF THE DAY, NO. 55 ON THE OCCASION OF THE 24TH ANNIVERSARY OF THE RED ARMY.

In it Stalin seems to have made the discovery that there is a difference between the German people and Hitler. "It would be ridiculous," he said, "to identify Hitler's clique with the German people and the German state. The experience of history shows that Hitlers come and go whereas the German people and the German state remain."

This is in striking contrast to what Stalin and his supporters have been saying in their propaganda in the last few months. [...]

NO INTERNATIONAL APPEAL

Has Stalin dimly remembered the traditions of Lenin by his newly voiced discrimination between the Nazis and the German people? Nothing could be further from the truth. For there is no mention of socialism or internationalism in the whole speech; there is no appeal to the German workers and soldiers to unite to establish a socialist Europe and world. [...]

DESTRUCTION OF FASCISM— NOT STALIN'S WAR AIM

Veiled behind Stalin's speech is contained a threat to the democracies of a peace with the German state—another Soviet-German alliance—this time not necessarily with Hitler, but if need be with the German militarists. [...]

TROTSKY'S ROLE IN THE RED ARMY

Why the Press was Silent

In the entire course of the war, there is nothing that has sent so much enthusiasm through the ranks of the British workers as the mighty and inspiring resistance of the Red Army. Against the advancing tide of Hitler's fascism the Red Army has set a world, a fighting morale and a self-sacrificing heroism that have lit up the dark ages like a beacon. [...]

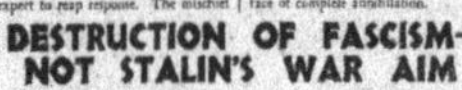

TROTSKY REVIEWING THE RED ARMY WITH HIS STAFF IN 1918

FOR A SOCIALIST BRITAIN—

Demand Labour Leaders End Truce and Take Power

On the basis of the campaign for a Socialist Britain Now, the I.L.P. is increasing its support throughout the country. But the programme and the campaign suffer from the weaknesses in all the methods and ideas of centrism.

Fatal Weakness in I.L.P. Campaign

It does not take as its starting point a Marxist analysis always does, the existing consciousness of the working class. At the present, the overwhelming majority of the workers are passively accepting the collaboration of the Labour leaders with the Tories in the Government because they cannot see any alternative. [...]

An open letter to [ILP] national conference

By WIL (Fourth International)

[Leaflet, Easter 1942]

Comrades,

The annual conference of the ILP meets at a time when revolutionary possibilities are already opening up. The confidence of the British working class in the leadership of the ruling class is daily being stricken by the heavy blow of events. In industry, in the army and in the government of the country, the ruling class is being increasingly exposed in its utter incompetence to offer the workers any solution to their problems. The increasing votes cast for ILP candidates, the result of the Grantham bye-election, the strikes in the mines, all point to one thing: the working class in Britain is in the process of breaking with the capitalist class, all it needs is an alternative lead and an alternative policy.

The members of the ILP are looking up to the leadership for a policy and a programme which would enable the party to mobilise this growing radical tendency in the working class for a decisive struggle against capitalism and for workers' power.

For a workers' military policy

The campaign for a "Socialist Britain Now" and the programme associated with it, is the answer to this demand. But look at the programme from whichever aspect you like, it offers no solution to any one of the fateful issues which history has placed before the workers.

The programme could well have been formulated in the years of peace for all the account it takes of the war; surely it is not a programme for 1942! If the working class is to fight for power in war as well as in peace, then it must have a programme for war. We cannot merely denounce the war as an imperialist war and say, as the pacifists do, that we shall have nothing to do with this foul thing. The workers do not want a foreign conqueror, least of all a fascist one. They want to see fascism destroyed, and they know that all the issues in our epoch will be settled by military means. That is why they continue to support the war, not from enthusiasm but for lack of an alternative. Only a working class policy for war which would separate the workers from the capitalists and at the same time guarantee success against all foreign capitalist aggression could mobilise the masses for the struggle for power.

Instead of regarding the war and the universal militarization of the masses with tragic contemplation, the ILP leadership should have faced up to these facts. But even yet they cannot break with pacifism; even yet they cannot tell their members that conscientious objection is no answer to imperialist wars. The need for a class programme for workers in uniform is not even realised. The demand for the universal arming of the working class under the control of trade unions and shop committees, trade union schools, for providing military training for workers, the ejection of the pro-fascist officer class from the armed forces and the election of officers by the soldiers are not even mentioned. And yet without such an independent military policy it is impossible for the workers to fight fascism whether from within or without. Maxton, Brockway and the rest of the leadership have demonstrated that the only break they have made with pacifism is in phrases. The demand for peace with Hitler may have been dropped, but pacifism still remains the dominant note.

Need to expose Labour leaders

Most members of the ILP will concede that the campaign for a socialist Britain has remained on the level of pious generalities. And this is no accident, for it lacks the one essential element of a real socialist campaign for power, viz, a concrete programme for action. There is no hint as to what we have to do now and in the immediate future to bring about socialism in Britain. There is the necessity for going to the meetings and taking friends along to hear Maxton. There is the duty of voting for party candidates. But beyond that, what else? Nobody knows the answer. Without any concrete programme for action, the campaign hangs in the air. It remains a campaign of leaders without any real relationship with the masses.

The mass of the organised workers, unfortunate though it is, accept the leadership of the Labour and the trade union bureaucracy in the belief that they are waging a real war in defence of their rights against fascism and for the defence of the Soviet Union. Without conducting a campaign to expose the labour bureaucracy it is impossible to convince the masses of the need for a new and revolutionary leadership. The tie-up of the organised working class movement through its official leadership with the ruling class is mainly responsible for the present inertia and immobility in the movement. To mobilise the rank and file of the trade unionists against this coalition in a nation-wide agitation round the demand that the Labour and ILP lenders should take power on a socialist programme and wage a genuine war against fascism is the immediate task. Smash the coalition. Labour to power on a socialist programme—these are the only slogans which could rouse the working class to immediate action, including that immense mass which is only beginning to attain political consciousness.

Brockway may argue that to demand that the Labour leaders take power is to deceive the workers into the belief that Morrison, Bevin and their associates can defend the interests of the workers. This is a dull and pedantic argument. How could anyone imagine that a campaign under present circumstances, demanding that the Labour leaders break with the capitalists and fight for power on a socialist programme, can be anything but the most effective method of educating the workers as to the bankruptcy of the Labour leaders and into an understanding of the need for a revolutionary party? When Lenin was demanding a break on the part of the socialist ministers from the capitalists in the provisional government, was he deceiving the Russian masses as to Kerensky and his friends?

But the real reason why Brockway and the leaders of the ILP refuse to raise this concrete slogan and are content to leave the socialist Britain [campaign] on the level of pious generalities, is because they themselves are not convinced of the need for a complete break with the Labour leaders but in reality they are still their allies. Brockway scoffs at the Labour leaders and yet refuses to put up candidates in bye-election against Labour nominees. His excuse at a recent conference that the party cannot afford the money is contradicted by the fact that the party has raised the money to put up two candidates simultaneously—in Cardiff and Cathcart, against Tories.

Left wing attacked—right wing tolerated

This refusal to undertake the task of exposing the Labour leaders in the eyes of the workers arises at the bottom from the absence of all revolutionary perspectives and their desire to remain on the friendliest term with the reformist leaders. Tom Colyer said at a recent meeting in London that he did not believe that the Labour leadership had deliberately betrayed the socialist cause; they have made a grievous blunder. The truth is that the ILP leaders are thinking in terms of parliamentary alliances and combinations and socialism through bye-elections. This opportunistic tendency expresses itself not only in the programme but also on questions of organisation and party discipline. Extreme toleration and friendliness continues to be shown towards C.A. Smith and Jennie Lee whose policies and utterances stand in open contradiction to the official party policy. But the process of ferreting out and isolating Trotskyist sympathisers is never allowed to flag. The centrists have always fought the revolutionaries within their own ranks with far more vigour and consistency than the reactionaries. Of late this hatred of Trotskyism on the part of Brockway, Padley and the other leaders has reached such a stage that no amendments were allowed to be put at socialist Britain conferences, thus reducing them to a farce.

The need to combat Stalinism

Equally typical of this centrism is your leadership's failure to offer intransigent opposition to the criminal policies of Stalin. Their refusal to face up to the implications of the campaign of intimidation which accompanies the present Stalinist line flows logically from their refusal to offer political opposition to the Stalinist bureaucracy—its abandonment of internationalism, its persecution of the revolutionaries inside Russia as well as outside. The belated article *They disgrace the name of communism* hastily published in the pre-conference *New Leader* in an attempt to anticipate this criticism, will not deceive the revolutionaries in the ILP.

Brockway states (December 8 1941) that he does not believe it necessary to hold "special" meetings to combat the Stalinist campaign; that such meetings would assist rather than deter the Stalinists in their provocations. At the same time he refers to the tactics they used against the ILP's brother party—the POUM—in Spain. But it was precisely because the POUM carried out the same ostrich policy as is now being carried out by the ILP, that facilitated the attacks against it, culminating in the murder of its leaders by the Stalinists.

Already the campaign has reached the stage of physical assault, not only of Trotskyists but of members of the ILP. As the war proceeds and the workers turn towards the left, the Stalinists will in desperation turn to more violent methods. Under these circumstances it is an elementary precaution of self-preservation that a vigorous campaign of exposure be waged against these degrading methods of organised hooliganism. The Central Committee of the Communist Party has issued instructions that the names and addresses of all Trotskyists should be secured. This undoubtedly applies to members of the ILP as well. In Spain and in France this action was a prelude to Stalinist assistance to police reaction. In the Nazi occupied countries the names and address of revolutionaries opposed to CP policy were handed over to the Gestapo. This is not a question of a merely incidental character. It concerns the very existence of workers' organisations which operate a policy opposed to Churchill and the Communist Party. If the ILP refuses to carry the struggle against the Stalinist pogroms, how will they face up to the far stronger blows of the capitalists when they really start to suppress the left wing? Particularly since they will have the active assistance of the Stalinists.

We appeal to the members of the ILP to force its leadership to reverse its present disastrously negative policy and to conduct a vigorous united front campaign with other working class bodies which will expose the Stalinists before the whole labour movement, as well as protect our organisations from their gangster assaults.

In this conference a great responsibility rests on the shoulders of the revolutionary elements in the ILP. It is time to wage a relentless struggle against the unreal opportunistic pacifist policy of the leadership. If they genuinely believe that the ILP can be transformed into a revolutionary party, they must fight for a revolutionary policy. In this task they will have the full support of the Workers' International League and the revolutionary workers gathered under the banner of the Fourth International, the banner of Marx, Engels, Lenin and Trotsky.

Labour leaders hold workers back

By Ted Grant
[*Socialist Appeal*, Vol. 4 No. 8, May 1942]

The recent bye-elections have been the means of demonstrating the present mood and feelings of the British masses. Rugby, Wallasey, Grantham, Cathcart, and Cardiff—all these present a broad cross-section of the mood among the people—not only the workers, but the middle class as well.

What is striking about these elections is the clarity with which they reveal the change in outlook of the working people. All of these constituencies were previously represented by Tories—some with big majorities. Now we have the situation where, for the first time since the outbreak of the war, the government is suffering defeats, while a substantial vote is recorded for the ILP in the constituencies which they have contested.

Coupled with the growing restlessness in industry, as evidenced by the growing strikes among the miners, dockers and engineers, the defeats underline the rapidly developing distrust of the masses of the people in the rule of the capitalist class. The reasons for their disillusionment are becoming clearer daily: the military defeats, the incompetence and bungling of the military officer caste; the profiteering, chaos and mismanagement in production; the pauperisation of the small businessmen—all these have played their part in developing an anti-capitalist sentiment among the working class and the general radicalisation of the masses as a whole.

Despite all the attempts of the labour and trade union leadership to drive the Labour supporters into the camp of the Tory candidates, the elections show that only a negligible proportion of Labour supporters have allowed themselves to be led in this direction. As a matter of fact, a substantial proportion of the former Tory voters are steadily moving to the left by voting against the official government candidates, while large numbers have become apathetic and indifferent.

The feeling prevailing in the country is demonstrated by events in Rugby where a large number of workers—socialists, trade union militants, and shop-stewards, Labour Party and members of the Trades Council—came together to discuss the putting up of an independent "socialist" candidate to fight the official government candidate. They went so far as to elect their nominee. The intervention of W. J. Brown, on a fake left programme, caused their nominee to withdraw. Despite the particularly vituperative attacks of Transport House, Brown was enabled to win the seat by a narrow majority. In Grantham, on a pretence of supporting a "labour" programme, the independent candidate was elected.

But the clearest and most decisive indication of all was given by the result of the Wallasey election. On a programme of "common ownership of the means of production", the former Labour Party member Alderman Reakes was elected by a large majority! This in a constituency with a strong middle class vote and formerly a fairly safe Tory seat. Cripps' brother, who intervened on a "non-party" independent platform, did not even succeed in retaining his deposit.

In the areas which the ILP contested, they received a substantial proportion of the Labour vote but did not win the majority of working class supporters, primarily because of their pacifist or semi-pacifist position and their negative sectarian approach.

A particularly pernicious role in these elections was played by the so-called Communist Party. In all the elections, they attempted to influence the voters to support the government candidate. These "communists" attempted to utilise the stirring resistance of the Red Army in their appeals to the electorate to support the representatives of big business! Despite all their propaganda, the decisive majority of the workers refused to be diverted from expressing their growing opposition and mistrust of the capitalists and bankers who control the policy of the Churchill government.

The capitalists and their representatives have realised clearly the lesson of these elections. Commenting on Sir Stafford Cripps' speech appealing for "economic democracy" after the war, the *Times* comments:

> "The country is in a mood to respond to such a programme. Recent bye-elections are among many symptoms which show that the challenge of a positive appeal will bring fresh heart and fresh enthusiasm to the ordinary citizen bearing without complaint [!] the burden and the drabness of war on the home front. The candidate who can offer such an appeal will in the long run win the suffrages of the electorate."

The ruling class has seen the striking fact that all the anti-government candidates achieved victory on the basis of left demagogy; of an anti-capitalist, anti-profiteering appeal on the basis of a more efficient organisation of production to "prosecute the struggle against Hitlerism"; and lastly, on the basis of more help for the Soviet Union.

Unmistakably, despite all the efforts of the Labour leaders, despite all the efforts of the Communist Party leaders, to hold the masses in check, the war itself is pushing them irresistibly in the direction of socialism. The only thing holding this development back is the betrayal of the Labour, trade union and CP leadership. The verdict of the working class electorate is clear. They are demanding by their votes an end to the electoral truce. They have given a vote of no confidence in the policy of the official labour leaders.

Comrades of the Labour Party and trade unions, comrades of the co-op, comrades of the factory committees, comrades of the whole labour movement!

Is it not clear that the policy of the labour and trade union leadership is false and shameful? They claim to be in the government in the interests of waging a war against fascism in the interests of the working class. But they have entered into a truce with those elements who represent the bankers and financiers who subsidised, armed and helped to organise Hitler and his gangsters. They talk about "equality of sacrifice" while the big monopolies continue to pile up profits at the expense of the toilers. They ask the workers to accept lower rations, while the rich live well. They shout for increased production by greater strain and effort on the part of the workers, while the profits and greed of the bosses impedes and sabotages production. And they persist in remaining with the capitalists as their obedient tools and lackeys.

They tell us "national unity" is necessary to defeat fascism! But the feeling among the people is that "national unity" with the ruling class is leading the people to major disaster, both on the home front and the military front; that "national unity" is leading to the strengthening of reaction at home and fascism abroad. In reality, the reason is that these "leaders" are content with the present line up—they are content to remain tied to the millionaire combines and banks. If the labour leaders would end the so-called political truce and fight for a general election on a fighting Socialist policy—on the programme of the *Socialist Appeal*—they would obtain an overwhelming majority throughout the country. In the past, the Labour leaders have always used the excuse that the workers were not ready for a "full socialist case". Today that excuse is shown to be completely exposed. It is these so-called leaders who are holding the struggle back. The workers are only waiting for an enthusiastic, positive lead. They are looking for a way out of the impasse in which they have found themselves.

Shame on those who have no faith and no confidence in the working class. These bye-elections have been a means of demonstrating the correct class instincts of the workers. Their progressive aspirations are being utilised and misdirected by these fake left opportunists. Now is the time to harness this feeling in the interests of socialism.

Workers' International League believes that the solution of the problems which confront the working class can only be solved by the workers taking power into their own hands. But the first step in this direction must be re-establishment of the independence of the organisations of the working class from subordination to the bosses. While the workers still have faith and trust in their leaders we will fight side by side with them to put these leaders to the test. In this way we believe that the correctness of our ideas will become apparent to the whole of the working class.

The Labour leaders claim to represent the interests and aspirations of the workers: the workers have demonstrated their desires! The coalition must be ended! Labour must take power! Put into force the programme of the *Socialist Appeal*!

British refuse arms to Indians "Live more frugally" says Lord Linlithgow!

By Ted Grant

[Socialist Appeal, Vol. 4 No. 9, June 1942]

The threatened invasion of India by Japanese imperialism has brought the question of India as a burning issue before the working class of this country.

The policy of British imperialism, and the present mood among the Indian masses, can best be understood if the conditions under which the Indian workers and peasants are compelled to exist under British imperialist rule are known.

The British imperialists squeeze £150,000,000 a year out of the Indian people in tribute. This is obtained at the expense of the misery and suffering of the masses of the people. After 150 years of British rule 90 percent of the people cannot read or write. The average income of the masses of the peasants amounts to less than two pence a day. The conditions of the workers are not much better. Crowded five, ten, and even twenty people living in one room, compelled to live on a diet which in 1927-28 (since then the conditions have if anything worsened) the Medical Officer of Health in Bengal recorded in the following terms: "The present peasantry of Bengal are in a very large proportion taking to a diet on which even rats could not live for more than five weeks." Tens of millions die every year from diseases of malnutrition and starvation, malaria and other diseases which could be prevented by decent food, proper sanitation and drainage.

The peasants' income is so low that the average peasant family is five years' income in debt to the moneylenders and landlords. The peasants pay land revenue while the landlords' incomes are exempt from income tax. They are born, they live, and they die in debt. The industrial workers are more "fortunate". They are merely in debt to the extent of 6 months' wages.

Upon all these burdens is superimposed the burden of taxation. Today when the British workers have legitimate cause for complaint and feel the exactions of income tax, they can well imagine the position of their Indian brothers who do not receive more than one shilling a day on the average and who are paying more than a third of their income on taxes.

Due to these terrible conditions the dissatisfaction and unrest among the Indian masses is intense. The Japanese imperialists have been playing on this in their propaganda to the Indians in attempting to win the Indians over to their side. Subhas Bose, former Congress leader who went over to the Japanese, is using this skilfully in his wireless broadcasts from Japan.

The British press has time and again pointed to the measures which Hitler and his quislings in the occupied territories have taken to prevent news from the outside reaching the occupied countries. Among the desperate measures resorted to was the prohibition of listening to foreign broadcasts and the confiscation of wireless sets.

Great play has been made of the fact that such prohibition was not necessary in the "democracies" where complete freedom of thought was permitted. But in India the reply to Japanese propaganda—the imperialists cannot make any other reply—has been the same as that of all oppressors: wireless sets have been confiscated.

The real position in India has been underlined by a speech of the Viceroy in Delhi at the beginning of May on the question of arming the population to resist the Japanese.

"I have often heard it said lately: 'We are unarmed. What can we do? What can we do? Let the government put arms in our hands and we will spring to the defence of India like one man!' Here is my answer to that:

"Were the people of Great Britain armed in June 1940? Were the people of Russia armed on June 9 1941? During the long agony of China have the ordinary men had arms in their hands?

"The answer is 'no'. The mass of the people have never carried arms in any country or in any modern campaign..."

Lord Linlithgow ended with an appeal to the Indian masses to "use less of everything and to lead more frugal lives"!

This speech is the only answer the imperialists have to the demand of the Indians for arms. It is of course, untrue, because to a large extent the resistance of Russia and China has been due to the arming and organising of large sections of the masses of the people. Even in Britain, at least one in ten is in the armed forces. In the same proportion this would mean the arming of 40,000,000 or more of the Indian people. Yet only a million Indians or less are even organised into the regular Indian army.

The farce of "defence of India's freedom" is underlined by the fact that the Viceroy is compelled to resort to such arguments to bolster up the refusal of the ruling class to arm the Indian masses. Point is given to this inability by the importing of tens of thousands of British and American troops who have been pouring into India. Now news comes that native troops from East Africa are being sent to India! That it would be technically possible to arm millions upon millions of Indian workers has been demonstrated by Tom Wintringham in an article written in *Picture Post* where he points out that in the last three to six months enough tommy-guns and munitions could have been produced to arm such a force without any difficulty whatsoever. The industrial capacity to produce the machines is there. But the political question is what determines the position of British imperialism.

The Viceroy's speech is an indication of the insolence and arrogance of the ruling class. To ask the workers and peasants who are not even able to get one decent meal a day, to live more frugally is to add insult to injury. This from the Viceroy who has spent thousands of pounds on 100 lavatories for his palace.

This is the real reason for the refusal to place arms in the hands of the masses. They dare not do so. The contrast between the squalor and misery of the workers and peasants and the huge tribute of £150,000,000 a year drained from these poor workers and peasants is too great. It is clear that the masses would not stop at throwing out the Japanese invaders but would throw out the British invaders as well. It is clear that rather than arm the Indian people and risk India falling into the hands of the Indians, the British imperialists would prefer it to fall, temporarily, into the hands of the Japanese.

The Indian capitalists are not much better than the British rulers themselves. The Congress has refused to wage a struggle against British imperialism despite the pressure of the masses. For fear of the repercussions among the masses, they have been compelled to reject the proposals of the British government brought by Cripps. In their treachery they are only surpassed by the Indian "Communist" Party which, though formally illegal, has completely capitulated to British imperialism. Its activities are openly carried out and tolerated by the police. Their campaign for a "national government" of landlords and capitalists, imperialists and workers and peasants, of Congress, the princes and the Moslem League is a craven capitulation to British imperialism which even the Congress leaders were not prepared to do.

India's freedom can only be obtained and the terrible conditions of the masses alleviated by the workers of India taking power into their own hands and assisting the peasants to seize the land. This would be the means of rendering India impregnable to any foreign invader. It would shatter Japanese and world imperialism and the Indian and British workers could march together on the road to socialism and freedom.

WORKERS' INTERNATIONAL NEWS, Vol. 5 Nos. 3 & 4

THE
ROAD TO INDIA'S FREEDOM

THE PERMANENT REVOLUTION IN INDIA
AND THE TASK OF THE
BRITISH WORKING-CLASS

by E. GRANT and A. SCOTT

---

also

THESIS OF INDIAN
FOURTH INTERNATIONALISTS
1941

PRICE 3d.

Published by WORKERS' INTERNATIONAL LEAGUE
FOURTH INTERNATIONAL

The road to India's freedom
The permanent revolution in India and the tasks of the British working class

By Ted Grant and Andrew Scott

[*Workers' International News*, Vol. 5 Nos. 3&4,
presumably June 1942]

Like a giant awakening after the sleep of centuries, India is stirring. The gaze of the whole world is being transferred from Europe, a continent which has just been locked in the chains of fascism, to India, a sub-continent which for two centuries has endured the chains of democratic imperialism. With Japanese imperialism advancing, with British imperialism doped and semi-paralysed, with the Indian masses stirring to their very depths, mighty questions are serving notice on humanity that they must be solved one way or another—and without delay.

For the British workers in particular the question of freedom for India is no empty abstraction. It is bound up closely with their own problems and particularly the problems raised by the war.

The masses of the workers have supported the ruling class in the war because they believe it was being fought for the liberation of oppressed peoples throughout the world, and for the "four freedoms". The British workers in the past have jogged along comfortably with the illusion that British domination of India was being imposed for the benefit of the Indian people. But today they are beginning to realise that the Indian people regard the British not as liberators but as alien invaders and oppressors.

In Burma and Malaya[1] the masses demonstrated by their indifference and apathy that they made no distinction between the Japanese and the British. For

---

[1] "Burma" was the modern Myanmar. "British Malaya" defined a set of states on the Malay Peninsula that were colonised by the British. Before the formation of the Malayan Union in 1946, the colonies were not placed under a single unified administration. Malaya became independent on August 31 1957. A larger federation was later formed called Malaysia.

them the struggle was one to decide which of two contenders was to dominate them.

The whole colonial policy of British imperialism has been summed up by Sir William Joynson-Hicks:

> "We did not conquer India for the benefit of the Indians. I know that it is said at missionary meetings that we have conquered India to raise the level of the Indians. That is cant. We conquered India by the sword, and by the sword we shall hold it...We hold it as the finest outlet for British goods."

This is, as it always has been, the policy of British imperialism in her colonial empire. India and China, together with the rest of Asia constitute the richest prize in the struggle for the redistribution of the world now being fought out on the world battlefield. The only difference today is that the British sword has lost its sharp edge, has become rusty and for this reason the bourgeoisie have been forced to resort to other methods—empty promises, fake "concessions", "national independence"—all to be implemented, of course at some future date.

Prime Minister Winston Churchill has always maintained a consistent policy towards India. Even when the Tories were willing to concede minor concessions in the past to the Indian capitalists, Churchill has stood on the policy of extreme opposition to any concessions to the Indian bourgeoisie and Congress. The mere possibility of an independent India evinced from him the prophecy that it would lead to "anarchy" and the "dull roar or scream of carnage and confusion". That he did not change his policy after he became Prime Minister is testified by the fact that—by July 1941—12,129 Indians were imprisoned for political reasons, including 28 ex-ministers, and 290 members of the provincial legislatures. Today, the large majority of these, particularly those who stand for complete and unconditional freedom of the Indian people, are still languishing in British jails.

If the Indians gain their independence, or even a measure of control, the palace of Empire will crash to the ground. In the eyes of the British ruling class the road of "anarchy", that is the road of socialist revolution, will have opened up. Of what use would be the defeat of the Axis if it meant the certain destruction of not only British, but world imperialism? For the repercussions of Indian freedom would not be limited by the boundaries of India.

The British capitalist class would far rather lose India to the Japanese than grant her independence, reasoning that, with the aid of America and at the cost of countless British and American soldiers, they would regain it, even if it took years and years of bloody slaughter. The affinity between the imperialists of Japan and Britain was eloquently demonstrated at the fall of Singapore, where the British scrupulously kept to the letter of their agreement with Japan to "keep law and order" by means of British bayonets until the Japanese, took over. This precaution against the masses taking matters into their own hands predominates in the policy of imperialism—even in its most critical hour.

The policy of divide and rule

The farce of a "war for freedom" while hundreds of millions are in chains is fast becoming evident to the working class. In their arguments, the bourgeoisie emphasise the "lack of tranquillity" within India, the "disunity" of the Indian people. But the so-called problem of Indian "disorder" is in reality a creation of British imperialism—deliberately fostered, in order through their age-old policy of "divide-and-rule" to maintain their hold on the Indian masses.

In this policy one of the principal weapons in the armoury of the British are the communal organisations which are the direct agents of, paid and subsidised by, British imperialism itself. These are the "minorities" about whom the capitalist class and their lackeys the Labour leaders are displaying so much concern in their negotiations. The most important of these organisations is the Moslem League, which is in reality supported by only a small proportion of Moslems. In the elections of 1937 the Moslem League—only secured 4.6 percent of the total Moslem vote—321,772 out of the total of 7,319,445. Of the 80 million Moslems 20 percent are Shias, who have their own organisation, having disowned the Moslem League, and support Congress. The Momins[2], who number about 45 million, also repudiate the claim of the Moslem League to represent the Moslems, and support the demand for a constituent assembly. In the North West Frontier province which contains a large majority of Moslems—Congress was returned with a big Majority.

The Hindu Mahasabha[3]—another tool of the British imperialists—is the representative of the richest section of the population and naturally, in its attempt to secure a disguise, it cloaks itself in the reactionary covering of rigid Hindu orthodoxy. It acts as a foil and a supplement to the reactionism of the Moslem League.

An example of the deliberate policy of fostering division in Indian society, which is described by the imperialists as the "Hindu-Moslem problem", is provided by a strike in a sugar mill in Bihar in 1939. The strike was caused by the management granting the workers' demand for a holiday *to the Hindu employees only*. The object was, of course, to divide the workers on communal lines. *But both Hindu and Moslem workers replied to this provocation by united strike action.* They won the strike.

Cripps' "horror" at the suggestion of what he calls a "dictatorship" of India

---

2 Literally, believers.

3 The all-Indian Hindu Assembly, a Hindu nationalist organization, was originally founded in 1915 to counter the Muslim League and the secular Indian National Congress.

by the overwhelming majority represented by Congress over the "unprotected minorities" can be seen for what it is worth. It is a horror at the prospect of the British capitalists losing control through the decayed and outlived Indian princes and privileged minorities losing their grip over the oppressed masses. His protest on behalf of "democracy" is in fact made on behalf of an oligarchy of 285,000 British capitalists and their lackeys who dictate and decide the fate of 400 million people.

With the armies of Nippon hammering at the gates of India, and a rising ferment not only in India but among the British working class, the British capitalist class has been compelled to feign a policy of so-called "concessions". As a token of their "sincerity" they sent Sir Stafford Cripps, a left labour representative with a reputation as a "friend of India" with promises of "freedom" *but after the war*. Returning empty-handed, Cripps has confessed the failure of the plan to gain the enthusiastic support of the Indians in the British war effort against Japan. Before dealing with the fundamental reasons for the failure of his mission, let us examine the epoch-making proposals with which this dove set forth from its Downing Street Ark.

During the last war, too, India was promised "dominion status". But after the crisis was over, it was discovered that political conditions were not sufficiently "tranquil" and the Indian people were not sufficiently "ripe" for this to be granted immediately. Nearly 25 years have elapsed since that promise. And once again, with World War Two well in progress, and not going so well for the British rulers, the old promises "after the war" are refurbished with a Crippsian veneer. It is self evident that after the experience of Britain's methods for the last three centuries, promises of this nature leave the masses completely indifferent.

If the imperialists genuinely desired to grant freedom to India, they would grant it now. If freedom can be given after the war, why not now? The answer to this is provided in the manifesto of our Indian comrades which is republished in this pamphlet[4]. Real independence for India means above all *the agrarian revolution*—land for the peasants; the cleansing of India of the relics of barbaric feudalism represented by the princes and landlords.

The farce of representative government

It is proposed that the constitution-making body to be elected be a college of all the provincial legislatures, where not one in ten of the Indian people have the vote, and those who do have it belong to the better-off strata. Such an assembly, to say the least, would be completely unrepresentative. Besides this, the princes of the Indian states are to nominate a third of the members of the Electoral College. These princes who rule over 25 percent of the population, only contin-

---

4 This refers to the 1941 thesis of the Indian Fourth Internationalists, published as Appendix IV.

ue their corrupt and autocratic domination by the direct aid of British bayonets. The 90 million people under the domination of the princes are to have no voice, but are to be "represented" by these despots. Time and again, uprisings in one or another of the Indian states have been brutally suppressed through the intervention of troop from British India. Without the support of British imperialism the princes - these obsolete and senile survivals of a by-gone age of Asiatic feudalism - could not continue to crush the peasants for longer than 24 hours.

The representatives in the provincial legislatures are not selected on the basis of an ordinary electoral role, but are artificially divided into communities of Moslems, Sikhs, Brahmins, etc. They are thus even more unrepresentative because the number of representatives between the various denominations (especially Hindus and Moslems) is not according to proportion of population. By the division of the communities into classes—workers, peasants, landlords, merchants, etc., the representation of the mass of the Indian people becomes completely unreal.

British imperialism, by manipulating kept agents, is enabled to promote disruption and disunity in India.

It was the deliberate intention of the British government so to frame the promised constitution as to provoke sanguinary conflicts and bloody civil war. The British Raj would then step in and proclaim that only Britain could keep peace between the warring factions and "preserve order". Inherent in the whole plan is the fundamental proposition that the real power was to rest in the hands of the Viceroy through the continuation of his power of veto. The farce of "representative government" has been demonstrated in the past where provincial governments passed measures with which the Viceroy disagreed...so he simply vetoed them! Furthermore, it must be pointed out, that the provincial governments ceased to function when the war broke out, and the control reverted openly to the Viceroy and his council.

British to control armed forces

When the mass of verbiage concealing the real aims and intentions of the British rulers is thrust aside, it is clearly observed that all power, the decisive power, *control of arms and the armed forces*, shall remain in the hands of British imperialism.

If the 400 million Indian workers and peasants were granted their freedom and supplied with arms and equipment, it would not be necessary to send a single British soldier to the Far East to stem a threat of Japanese invasion. India could provide an inexhaustible army of 50 million. But the British dare not arm their slaves, any more than they dared in Burma, Malaya and Java. Far from this, legislation has been passed during the course of the war forbidding in India "unlawful drilling with or without arms and the wearing of unofficial uniforms which bear a colourable resemblance to military or other official uniforms by non-official volunteer organisations."

Control was the issue around which the discussions took place. Under pressure, the British agreed to the appointment of an Indian Defence Minister, but he was to be without power to decide policy or strategy; all decisions were to remain finally in the hands of the Commander in Chief—an appointee of Britain, such as General Wavell.

"During the critical period which now faces India, and until the new constitution can be framed His Majesty's government must inevitably bear the responsibility for and retain control and direction of India as part of their world war effort, but the task of organising to the full the military, moral and material resources of India must be the responsibility of the government of India..."

In other words, *control* was to be retained by Britain, while *responsibility* was to fall on the shoulders of Congress.

In the final analysis all power rests with those in control of the armed forces. Lenin and before him Marx and Engels pointed out that this is the decisive touchstone of the question of power. The British have not the slightest intention of relaxing their iron grip by relinquishing control of the armed forces. When has it ever happened in history that the capitalists, voluntarily and without bitter and violent struggle, give up their possessions?

It was on this decisive issue that the talks broke down. Congress, while willing to capitulate to British imperialism, desired at least a semblance of control in order to delude their followers that the British had given them some real concessions, otherwise they could expect to lose all support among the Indian masses. The Congress position can be summed up in the words of Mr. Rajagopalachari:

"At the present moment defence is practically the whole government, and if, as repeatedly declared by Sir Stafford Cripps so far, defence is to be strictly reserved, the leaders of the people feel that they cannot hope to overcome the popular attitude of apathy, if not hostility, towards the British.

"The leaders of the people should be enabled to honestly shout to the masses that the war is a peoples' war, and the government a peoples' government."

In these lines is contained the reason why Congress was reluctantly compelled to reject the plan.

Cripps may once again be sent on his errand; this time with some face-saving formula which will enable the Indian capitalists to show some pretence that power has really been turned over to the Indian people...while in reality it will remain in the hand of Whitehall.

Despite the breakdown of negotiations, Nehru, in the name of Congress, has appealed for the organising of the utmost resistance to the Japanese advance. The reason for this is their belief that a greater share of the exploitation of the Indian people will be their lot under British domination than under Japanese. They understand that only with the aid of one great imperialistic power or another can the weak Indian bourgeoisie maintain its parasitic role in India. They have the example of China in the last few years as a warning. The Chinese capitalists, through Chiang Kai-Shek, tried ceaselessly to arrive at a compromise with the Japanese. During the seizure of Manchuria and North China, they offered no resistance to Japanese encroachments. Only when it became clear that the Japanese, as at Shanghai, were destroying Chinese factories which competed with Japan and sending the machinery to Japan as scrap for armaments production, were they compelled to offer resistance.

The Japanese industrialists compete very keenly with those of India. It is fear for their investments, plus the links with British and American capital, which compels Congress to choose the British rather than the Japanese exploiters.

Background of the present crisis—the economic conditions of Indian masses

According to the estimate made by Sir James Grigg, the present War Minister, the average income in all India is £4 4s 0d *a year*. This includes the fabulously wealthy Maharajahs and the millionaire mill-owners, as well as the humble worker and peasant. Yet even so, it amounts to about 1s 7d a week, or a little less than 3d a day[5]. This is the fruit of 200 years of British "protection" of India. The standard of living of the masses is even lower than at the time of the East India Company.

To give some idea of what it means to the Indian masses to exist on such an income, this can be gauged from the following extract from a report by two Indian bourgeois economists:

> "The average Indian income is just enough either to feed two men in every three of the population, or give them all two in place of every three meals they need, on condition that they all consent to go naked, live out of doors all the year round, have no amusement or recreation, and want nothing else but food, and that the lowest, the coarsest, the least nutritious."

The housing situation is no better than nutrition. The Bombay labour office inquiry into working class budgets found that 97 percent of the working class

---

5 See previous note on British currency system prior to decimalisation, p. 102.

families in Bombay were living in one room tenements, often containing two and even up to eight families in one room. One third of the population were living more than 5 persons in a room; 256,379 from 6 to 9 in a room; 8,133 from 10 to 19 persons in a room, 15,490 were living 20 persons and over in one room.

Under the beneficent auspices of British imperialism, the average length of life in India has gone down from 24.75 years in 1921 to 23 years in 1931. Even V. Anstey, a writer sympathetic to imperialism, has reckoned that 3 deaths out of 4 in India are due to diseases of poverty. The Bengal Officer of Health stated in his report for 1927-28 that "the present peasantry of Bengal are in a very large proportion taking to a diet on which even rats could not live for more than five weeks." Illiteracy, which amounted to 94 percent of the population in 1911, had been reduced by 1931 to 92 percent! Truly a great achievement and a testimony to the civilising influence of British imperialism.

These few figures serve to give some indication of the "horror without end" to which the rule of British imperialism has condemned a quarter of the world's population.

The agrarian problem

The basis of existence of the peasants has been taken away from them. Driven off the land, they have been forced into the status of village proletarians. Between the years 1921 and 1931 the number of agricultural labourers increased from 21.7 million to 33.5 million. These are the most miserable and poverty-stricken strata in the villages. But to them must be added at least 50 million more who earn only a bare pittance from their small plots of land, and have to supplement this by working for a big landlord. The amount of land held by these millions, and the standard of life it can afford them, can be seen from a report of the situation in the presidency of Bombay. In that area 48 percent of all the agricultural holdings consisted of less than 5 acres of cultivated land, and this 48 percent of small peasant holders possessed together only 2.4 percent of the total area. It is estimated by some experts that these two classes of landless and semi-landless peasants form more than half the population of the villages.

The vast majority of the peasants live in debt to the moneylender. The total income of the peasantry (this includes the rich peasants) has been estimated at 42 rupees (£2 13s 0d) a year. From this there is taken in rent and taxes 20 rupees. When to this are added the exactions of the moneylender (whose rate, remember is 75 percent) the total paid out is more than two-thirds of the income. This was confirmed by an investigation conducted by a Congress representative: "Of the net total income more than two thirds goes out of the village by way of land revenue and excise taxes, interest charges and rents to non-resident owners." After all the vultures have had their pick, the peasant is left with an *average* of 13 rupees a year, that is, 19s.

The peasants are permanently in debt. The obliging moneylenders charge a mere Anna per rupee per month[6]—that is 75 percent! The total debt of the peasants in 1921 was £400 million. By 1937 it had increased to £1,350 million. This means that on an average every peasant is in debt to the extent of at least 5 years income! With the combined burden of the British imperialists, the moneylenders and the landlords, the slavery of the masses is growing steadily worse.

These figures constitute, as Trotsky remarked of similar statistics in tsarist Russia, "the finished programme of a peasant war." The difference is that in India the problem is even more intense than it was in Russia; the poverty, the landlessness of the peasants is even worse, the exactions and extortions of landlords and imperialists, even greater. It may be added that the links between the landlords and the Indian bourgeoisie are even more firmly united than they were in Russia. It is this that dictates the inevitable betrayal of the movement against imperialism by the organisations of the bourgeoisie, of which the Congress Party has the largest support.

The role of Congress

The Congress Party is the representative of the Indian capitalist class. But it has the support of the overwhelming majority of the Indian people—Hindus and Moslems, workers and peasants—in their aspirations for national liberation from British imperialism. But the capitalists in Congress are not really desirous of waging a struggle to the end against the British Raj.

The big capitalists in India who control the Congress are linked by many ties with the imperialists on the one side and the landlords, moneylenders and princes on the other. The bankers and big capitalists spring from the landlord class and have simultaneous interests in both land and industry.

In the Indian states the capitalists have investments which link them to the princes, and British imperialism has the controlling interest in the banks. Large sections of industry in India are jointly controlled by British and Indian capital. The financial structure of India is directly linked with the City of London. Thus, the landlords, capitalists, princes and imperialists, although they may quarrel as to the division of the spoils squeezed out of the Indian workers and peasants, are united as one against any encroachment on this surplus by the Indian people.

Striking proof of this was provided in the mass struggles against British imperialism in 1922 and 1929-31. The moment the movement threatened to rouse the peasantry into action, the bourgeoisie, through Congress, made haste to capitulate to British imperialism. In his book *India today*, written during the recent phase of the Comintern when Britain was the "most reactionary" imperi-

---

[6] In the old Indian currency system, before decimalisation in 1957, 16 Anna made a rupee.

alism, Palme Dutt writes* in describing the betrayal of the mass movement by Congress:

> "On a word of command from the Congress centre this process (refusal to pay taxes: not 5 percent were collected in Guntur) could undoubtedly be unleashed throughout the country, and would have turned into a universal refusal of *land revenue and rent*. But this process would have meant the sweeping away, not only of imperialism, *but also of landlordism*. The Bardoli resolution instructed the local Congress committees to advise the cultivators to pay land revenue and other taxes due to the government...The working committee advises Congress workers and organisations to inform the *ryots* (peasants) that *withholding of rent payment to the* zamindars (landlords) *is contrary to the Congress' resolutions and injurious to the best interests of the country...The working committee assures the* zamindars *that the Congress movement is in no way intended to attack their legal rights*, and that even where the *ryots* have grievances the committee desires that redress be sought by mutual consultation and arbitration."

Here can be seen the essence of the betrayal of the national struggle by the Congress in 1930-34: fear of arousing the pent-up feelings of the peasants, which would express itself in a struggle not only against the British government (the visible symbol of which is the tax collector) but also against the native exploiters. In the struggle for emancipation the peasant would be as little concerned with the fine distinction between landlords, tax-collectors and moneylenders as he is with the distinction between the other vermin—the lice, fleas and bugs—which prey upon him.

The striving of the peasants to rid themselves of their terrible burdens has resulted in organs of struggle being developed in the countryside to lead this movement. These organs have been the peasant committees which have arisen independent of the bourgeois national Congress. The first all-India peasant organisation was formed in 1936—the *all-India Kisan Sabha*. By 1939 the membership was already 800,000. Included in their programme was the demand for complete national independence and a democratic state of the Indian people, leading ultimately to a "peasants' and workers' rule".

The leadership, for lack of a different perspective, have subordinated these

---

* Dutt provides invaluable material in describing the betrayal of the mass movement by the native bourgeoisie. But blinded by the ignorant and reactionary school of Stalinism, he is incapable of drawing the correct conclusion—which is the theory of the permanent rev-olution. His conclusions demanding a national united front are completely contradicted by the data he presents. Duty bound in the struggle against "Trotskyism" he shuts his eyes to the theory of the permanent revolution which flows inexorably out of the actual relation of forces.

independent organisations to the Congress, although increasingly coming into collision with it. If the movement is not to suffer the fate of the peasant movement in China, it must find leadership in the industrial proletariat. These peasant committees which have already reached a stage far in advance of the organisation of the Russian peasants before the Revolution of 1917, are no doubt an expression of the pressure of the rural proletariat. Tomorrow, linked with the committees of action of the workers in the towns, that is, soviets, they must inevitably play a great role in the mobilising of the Indian people in the struggle for freedom. Subordination to the bourgeoisie would mean inevitable disaster. Only by organising the peasants round their own committees and in their own interests, in co-operation with the leadership of the workers in the cities, will the agrarian revolution be successfully carried out. Subhas Bose, the radical petty bourgeois on the left wing of Congress, after despairing of India receiving freedom from the British, has now landed up in the camp of the ravishers of the Chinese people—the camp of military-feudal Japanese imperialism. Wang Ching-Wei, who could be described as the Chinese Bose, also betrayed the masses and ended up as the head of the puppet government of Japan. This is an instructive lesson of the blind alley in which not only the bourgeoisie, but the radical petty bourgeoisie find themselves. These elements must inevitably end up in one or another camp of imperialism if they fail to base themselves on the progressive programme of a workers' and peasants' government.

The role of the Indian proletariat

Owing to the stringent censorship, news of the Indian working class struggles is indeed scant. From individual reports of visiting seamen and Indian workers it is clear that there has been no suspension of the class struggle—rather an intensification.

The rapid growth of the proletariat can be seen from the fact that between the years 1921 and 1931 the number of industrial workers employed in establishments of more than 10 workers rose from 2.6 million to 3.5 million. In the intervening decade, and especially in the last two and a half years of the war with the large increase in heavy war industry, this number has rocketed by leaps and bounds. Even taking the term in the narrowest sense the industrial proletariat numbers today far more than the 5 million estimate of 1931. To this core of true industrial workers must be added about 20 million handicraft workers who work in places employing less than 10 people. These are wage workers and constitute a reserve for the industrial working class. They will follow the lead of the decisive section of the conscious proletariat. In addition to this there is an agricultural proletariat which is now estimated to number about half the peasantry—that is approximately 130 million.

In the ten biggest cities the population has increased during the last decade from 5,309,000 to 8,183,000. Calcutta has increased its population by 85 percent and Bombay by 28 percent. About a dozen other cities not including the above have increased their population by from 50 to 100 percent. This tremendous rise in the numbers of the proletariat increases its specific weight in Indian society enormously.

From the scanty government statistics, biased and incomplete as they are, it is nevertheless possible to gain some idea of the dynamic of events in India. In the last few years, despite the increase in industry, the only industries which showed a decrease were rice, cotton-ginning and cotton-baling. These are Indian consumption industries and therefore their decline is a measure of the worsening conditions of the masses. A government report, confirming this decline, has estimated an average indebtedness of working class families of four months wages. This in 1939, when the effects of the war were just beginning to be felt.

The workers have been replying to the attacks on their living standards. This awakening is to be observed from the government reports of the different provinces, where bitter strikes against both British and Indian owned factories are recorded. In March 1940, 160,000 textile workers came out on strike for "dearness" allowance; that is for a rise of wages to meet the increased cost of living. Three leaders were arrested. The council of action of the Bombay TUC called for a general strike in sympathy. The majority of cases tell the same story—strike after strike, leading to outbreaks of violence and pitched battles between police and strikers, and arrests. Most of the strikes, according to the reports began as strikes against personal assault, ill-treatment and victimisation of workers, strikes for the dismissal of foremen and managers, and strikes in sympathy with other workers. Once begun, however, wage demands were invariably put forward, revealing the continual underlying economic discontent.

The high level of consciousness and militancy of the Indian working class was seen in the sugar-mill strike in Bihar in 1939. Beginning as a solidarity strike, it developed to a point where demands were put forward in the course of the struggle for increased supply of fuel, bedding and better housing. But significant are the words of the official government report of the strike: "All the demands were conceded *except the formation of a committee to manage the concern* and the immediate increase of pay." Here we see the expression of the elemental strivings of the workers to take control of industry—and through this the fate of the nation—into their own hands.

The militant movement among the workers must inevitably take an anticapitalist as well as anti-imperialist form. The workers in the towns interpret the struggle against the hated domination into a collision with the Indian bourgeoisie. The elemental striving of the working class to assume leadership will throw up a new layer of fighting leaders, which will be hammered out and tempered in the fire of struggle. Before the outbreak of the war, the Bihar government recognised the ominous portents of the rise of the workers' movement. Their report states:

> "The year 1938 continues to be characterised by general restlessness. As reported last year this was due to *the expectations raised by the emergence of political leaders amongst the labouring classes*...there were 16 strikes including one lockout in 1938 as compared with 11 in 1937."

The elemental striving of the working class to assume leadership, and its preponderance in the struggle, was shown in the movement of 1929-31, which was ushered in by a strike movement of colossal dimensions. At the Calcutta Congress held just prior to this upsurge, 50,000 workers demonstrated with the slogan *"An independent socialist republic of India!"* This tendency towards independent working class leadership of the national struggle manifested itself again at the outbreak of the war in a *political anti-war strike* of 80,000 workers of Bombay.

Under the exceptional conditions, with the awakening of the workers and peasants throughout India, this layer will find itself at the head of the whole nation. All they require is a policy which will make conscious in them the role which instinctively they are striving to play. The continuous reverses and defeats of the British will imbue the oppressed masses of India with a new confidence to face their imperialist masters. As an Indian student expressed it after the fall of Singapore: "Good God! For years we have imagined these fellows were so strong, but look at them! We have been afraid of a phantom!"

The failure of the bourgeoisie to conduct a struggle for the emancipation of the masses, due to the same reasons as in Russia, gives the young proletariat the possibility of victoriously accomplishing the tasks which in the past had been carried out by the national bourgeoisie, and of laying the path for the new development of society. In India the proletariat is the only class which can solve the problems of the masses and lead the nation consistently in the struggle against imperialism, feudalism and landlordism. The small, but rapidly growing class, can lead the scattered peasantry, and by taking power into its own hands, proceed first of all to carry out the tasks of the bourgeois democratic revolution. From there, by the logic of its position it will advance inevitably to the socialist tasks. This in a nutshell is the sole solution to the Indian revolution which is now begun—this is the permanent revolution.

The Indian proletariat is not isolated. Like the proletariat of Russia it springs directly from the peasantry. The vast majority have been peasants themselves, or have relatives in the villages. The workers have direct connection with the peasants, and above all, with the scores of millions of rural proletarians and rural semi-proletarians.

Coupled with the rise in militancy has emerged the awakening of tens of millions by the war crisis. The masses do not want the victory of Japan; they have seen the terrible exploitation and suppression of the Chinese and Korean masses at the hands of Japanese imperialism. Their critical attitude not only towards British imperialism, but towards the traitors of the bourgeois national Congress, drives them irresistibly towards attempting to organise on an independent class basis. The bitter struggle the workers have waged against their employers, and the struggle of the peasants against the landlords, drives into their consciousness the need for independent class organisation.

The permanent revolution as applied to India

The theory of the permanent revolution is based on the incapacity of the bourgeoisie in backward countries to solve the tasks of the bourgeois revolution; the national liberation from the shackles of imperialism, the ending of the feudal division of the country into separate provinces and its unification into a single whole, the dividing of the land among the peasantry, and the adoption of the democratic constituent assembly. In the past these tasks were solved, as in France and Britain, by the young and vigorous bourgeoisie. But now under the conditions of world imperialism, the colonial bourgeoisie is no longer capable of carrying through these progressive tasks. It is this that makes it imperative, if the struggle for liberation is to be successful, that the proletariat should assume the leadership of the entire nation, weak in numbers though it is. It is only thus that the tasks of India can be solved. The rebellious peasantry must find an ally and a leader in the city workers.

But in order to accomplish this it will be necessary for the proletariat to take power. Once having done this, they will advance not merely to the solution of the bourgeois tasks, but to the socialist tasks. In this they will need the support of the international working class, that is, by the extension of the proletarian revolution to other parts of the world.

In analysing the *Tragedy of the Chinese Revolution*, comrade Trotsky wrote:

> "Not a single one of the tasks of the 'bourgeois' revolution can be solved in these backward countries under the leadership of the 'national' bourgeoisie, because the latter emerges at once with foreign support as a class alien or hostile to the people. Every stage in its development binds it only the more closely to the foreign finance capital of which it is essentially the agency. The petty bourgeoisie of the colonies, that of handicrafts and trade, is the first to fall victim in the unequal struggle with foreign capital, declining into economic insignificance, becoming declassed and pauperised. It cannot even conceive of playing an independent political role. The peasantry, the largest numerically and the most atomised, backward and oppressed class, is capable of local uprisings and partisan warfare, but requires the leadership of a more advanced and centralised class

in order for this struggle to be elevated to an all-national level. The task of such leadership falls in the nature of things upon the colonial proletariat, which, from its very first steps, stands opposed not only to the foreign but also to its own national bourgeoisie." (L. Trotsky, *Introduction* to *Tragedy of the Chinese Revolution*, by H. Isaacs)

In China the revolution of 1925-27 could quite easily have achieved success. If the colonial bourgeoisie could play a progressive role this would surely be the case more so in China than in India, where the native capitalists were at least nominally independent of imperialism. But as in India, the Chinese bourgeoisie placed itself at the head of the mass movement in order to extract concessions from imperialism. But as soon as the peasants began to move in the direction of the agrarian revolution and the workers strove to take control of industry, the alarmed bourgeois, led by Chiang Kai-Shek, betrayed the Chinese revolution and arrived at a compromise with imperialism. They were compelled to capitulate to imperialism because they could not solve a single major problem due to their links with the landowners and militarists.

It was in justification of their unconditional support for the Chinese bourgeoisie (Stalin's "bloc of four classes") that Trotsky's "permanent revolution" was attacked by the Comintern. This support led to the defeat of the Chinese revolution, and betrayed the Chinese workers and peasants to the mercies of the counter-revolution. By the end of 1930 the Red Aid estimated that no less than 140,000 Chinese workers and peasants had been killed or died in the prisons of the Kuomintang under the leadership of Chiang Kai-Shek.

In Russia, the bourgeoisie was incapable of conducting a struggle against tsarist feudalism, the Church and the landlords due to the self-same ties as in China and India. This gave the young proletariat the possibility of victoriously accomplishing the tasks which in the past had been carried out by the bourgeoisie and of laying the path for a new and higher development of Russian society. In his *Thesis on the colonial question* adopted by the second congress [of the Communist International], Lenin wrote:

"There are to be found in the dependent countries two distinct movements which every day grow farther and farther apart from each other. One is the bourgeois democratic nationalist movement, with a programme of political independence under the bourgeois order, and the other is the mass action of the poor and ignorant peasants and workers for their liberation from all sorts of exploitation. The former endeavour to control the latter, and often succeed to a certain extent, but the Communist International and the parties affected must struggle against such control and help to develop class consciousness in the working masses of the colonies. For the overthrow of foreign capitalists, which is the first step towards revolution in the colonies, the co-operation of the bourgeois nationalist revolutionary elements is useful. But the foremost and necessary task is the formation of communist parties which will organise the peasants and workers and lead them to the revolution and to the establishment of soviet republics. Thus the masses in the backward countries may reach communism, not through capitalist development, but led by the class-conscious proletariat of the advanced capitalist countries.

"The revolution in the colonies is not going to be a communist revolution in its first stages. But if from the outset the leadership is in the hands of a communist vanguard, the revolutionary masses will not be led astray, but will go ahead through the successive periods of development of revolutionary experience...In the first stages the revolution in the colonies must be carried on with a programme which will include many petty bourgeois reform clauses, such as division of land, etc. But from this it does not follow at all that the leadership of the revolution will have to be surrendered to the bourgeois democrats. On the contrary, the proletarian parties must carry on vigorous and systematic propaganda for the Soviet idea and organise the peasants' and workers' soviets as soon as possible..."

Armed with this policy the Russian proletariat were led to victory; with this policy alone will the Indian proletariat be led to victory. But what a far cry this is from the present policies of Stalin and the Comintern! Today Stalinism is crowning its ignominious record with an even more base betrayal. From the struggle against imperialism for which they stood in words, they have now advanced into the position of agents of British imperialism since the attacks on Soviet Russia.

At a time when the mass struggle was rising, they subordinated the struggle to the demands of the bourgeois national Congress, and remained inside that organisation as a *loyal* opposition. Instead of fighting for the leadership of the working class through the building of the Communist Party, independent of the capitalists, they organised so-called worker-peasant parties which appeared out of the ground as mysteriously as they vanished. Having burned their fingers thus, they advanced to the ultra-left policy in the period of mass upsurge 1929-32; they denounced Congress as "fascist" and succeeded by these methods in isolating themselves from the mass movement, and at the same time lowered the class consciousness of the Indian masses.

At the present period they are supporting, as far as they dare without completely discrediting themselves, the position taken by Congress. They differ from Congress principally in being more servile towards the imperialists, whom they now claim are fighting a progressive anti-fascist war. Like their fellow-compatriots in Malaya, Singapore, Java and Burma, they demand "unity" with British imperialism against Japan. But such a policy can only have the same results as in these countries.

The call for a "national government" in India is the call for an agreement on the part of the Indian capitalists and landlords with the British imperialists, which would be directed against the masses.

Stalinism merely demoralises and confuses the vanguard of the working class. Their policy of collaboration with the oppressor cannot gain the support of the downtrodden masses in the colonial countries against any invader. This road leads only to the continued rule of one imperialism or another, and to the inevitable defeat of the masses in their struggle for both national and social emancipation. Far from weakening the power of the Axis, insofar as they have any effect at all, these policies serve only to assist Japan's advance by spreading disillusionment and demoralisation among the masses. Far from aiding the Soviet Union, they are helping its enemies.

For a constituent assembly

The Indian Trotskyists, the vanguard of the Indian working class, basing themselves on the teachings of Lenin, are putting forward the demand for the immediate convening of a constituent assembly. This is the elementary democratic demand—the right of the people to elect their own representatives by means of universal suffrage. The struggle for a constituent assembly involves the struggle for elementary human rights which are denied to the Indian people by Churchill and his government: the right of free speech and organisation; the release of thousands of political prisoners languishing in Indian jails; an election throughout the country to be held on the basis of universal adult suffrage from the age of 18 without property or other restrictions; land to the peasants; living wages for the proletariat including the 8 hour day; the prohibition of child labour; expropriation of war profits.

This slogan will immediately receive support from the workers' organisations: from the unions, from the councils set up in the factories, from the strike committees and the area committees. It will evoke an immediate response from the peasants' councils which have been set up as organs of struggle against the landlords and tax collectors, and which still continue to function despite all repressions. In the course of the struggle for the constituent assembly the masses will become convinced by their own experience that the solution to their problems lies in their own hands. Only by the dictatorship of the proletariat supported by the peasantry—that is, only by basing themselves on Lenin's formula—can the liberation of India be achieved.

The complete incapacity of Congress and the Indian capitalists to wage a struggle for freedom is demonstrated by their failure to conduct a consistent agitation for the convening of a constituent assembly. We say "consistent" because from time to time the issue has been raised by sections of Congress. But at a time when British imperialism is at her weakest and posing as a great "democrat", they dare not put forward the demand for the constituent assembly because of their fear of the Indian masses. This alone reveals, more than anything else, the role of the Indian bourgeoisie as agents of British imperialism. Even if they were to put forward the slogan, they could not carry the matter beyond words and into action.

In Russia in 1917 the capitalists were forced to "accept" the slogan in words, but vigorously sabotaged and resisted all attempts to convene the constituent assembly. In India the capitalists have not even gone to that length. Instead of the present position being utilised by Congress to wage a struggle against British domination, it resorts to a desperate attempt to arrive at agreement with Whitehall. The main struggle in Congress has been for the different sections to out-do each other in grovelling at the feet of British imperialism.

In the first place the struggle in India must be waged against *all* imperialisms—and above all the treachery of the Congress as the tool of imperialism must be ruthlessly exposed. Had Congress so desired, the difficulties of the British imperialists position, coupled with the reawakening of political life of the Indian masses, could have served to lay the way for the complete victory over the forces of British domination. The taking of power by Congress, and the mobilisation of the workers and peasants—arms in hand—would render the threat of Japanese invasion impossible. No army in the world could conquer and hold down the peoples of an entire sub-continent who were thus genuinely fighting for their freedom. The arming of the workers and peasants for the struggle against all imperialisms; the giving of the land to the peasants; the destruction of the power of the princes; the taking over of industry by the workers—these would sound the death-knell of all imperialisms and would immediately topple the Japanese militarists from their throne, for the Japanese soldiers, mostly peasants themselves, would respond to the slogan of "land to the peasants". The Indian revolution would spread to Japan and light up the whole of Asia.

Policies of British working class organisations

In this situation it is necessary to analyse carefully the policies of the organisations which claim to represent the interests of the British working class. For, as Lenin once remarked, the acid test for those who claim to be socialists in the metropolitan countries, especially Britain, is their attitude to the colonial question; the road to the liberation of the workers of Britain lay through India; the test was not merely that of opposing in words the iniquities of imperialism but systematically clarifying the workers of Britain and assisting the workers and peasants of India to fight against the same oppressor.

The Labour Party

The Labour and trade union bureaucracy have shown clearly that they stand as watch-dogs in the interests of British imperialism. They are even more zealous in defending the vultures' grip on India than the imperialists themselves. The loss of India would mean for them the end of the privileges enjoyed by the Labour and trade union upper crust and the better paid stratum of the workers, which have fallen to them as the crumbs from the table of the bourgeoisie, only because of the super-exploitation of the Indian and colonial masses. The only difference between the Labour leaders and Churchill on this question is that the former are more hypocritical and dishonest.

In a recent speech Bevin came out in defence of India's "underdogs". Shedding crocodile tears, he vowed that the labour movement would not be prepared to leave the 50 million untouchables to the mercies of the majority of the Indian people—that is to the mercies of the Indian workers and peasants! Apparently he wishes to convey that the British have subjugated India for the past 200 years merely to safeguard the interests of the unprotected "minorities". During the entire period of their domination, the British imperialists have succeeded in perpetuating the most abominable slavery—especially of the untouchable caste—on the pretext that they could not interfere with Indian customs!

Bevin and his *confrères* had the opportunity to demonstrate the sincerity of their concern for the welfare of the Indian "underdog" in the Labour governments of 1924 and 1929-31. But they were too busy jailing, suppressing and shooting those Indians who demanded that they should put into effect Labour's promises of freedom to India. No less than 60,000 Indians were imprisoned by the second Labour government.

The Labour "lefts" gathered under the banner of the *Tribune* play an even more dangerous role. They "reason" with Churchill and Bevin, pointing to the benefits which would accrue to Britain by granting of concessions to India. It is a classic expression of the role of the "left" wing of the Labour Party, that the British bourgeoisie should have entrusted their dirty work in India to one of them—Sir Stafford Cripps. Beneath the left sounding phrases which cover the policy of the *Tribune* like a coating of inferior varnish, can be seen the same old stains of official Labour.

> "What is now at issue is a different question. It is the participation of India in the struggle to defeat the common enemy. If the Japs win, self-government for India will cease to have even academic interest. Therefore we repeat: what now requires to be done is to agree on the amount of immediate self-government which will enable that first object to be achieved. If the Indian leaders press their claims beyond that necessity they will betray their own cause. If the British terms fall short of that they will miss the target."

"Give the Indian masses just enough to create the illusion that they have something to fight the Japanese for"—that is the policy of the Labour lefts. "Loosen the chains of the Indian people in order that the master can gain their services in his hour of need."

The Communist Party

The Communist Party instead of explaining why the vultures of British imperialist will not release their chains and exposing the fraudulency of their claim to be fighting a war against fascism, the Communist Party covers up the real imperialist aims of the war. In the party declaration issued after the failure of the Cripps' mission[7] they state:

> "The negotiations broke down because the British government will not agree to the formation of an Indian national government, which alone can rally the peoples of India and organise all their resources in the struggle against fascism."

In actuality the talks broke down because the British are not prepared to give even the Indian bourgeoisie—never mind the Indian people—the pretence of national independence. The statement goes on:

> "The British government has not yet learnt the lessons of its defeats in Hong Kong, Malaya, Singapore and Burma where we failed to win the peoples for the fight alongside Britain against Japan."

They have not yet learnt the lessons! As if the ruling class could operate any other policy. To get the enthusiastic support of the masses in the fight against Japan the first prerequisite is that they have something to fight for. To plead piteously to the ruling class for a change of heart is to ask the vampires of imperialism to kindly leave off sucking the blood of the colonial masses on humanitarian grounds.

Contrast this with Dutt's statements at the beginning of the war, when the role of Britain was correctly characterised as imperialist.

> "Nothing could be more dangerous than for the new tone of official utterance to give rise to any illusions as to the iron realities of imperialist policy and power, or as to the intention of imperialism by every means at its command to maintain that power."

It is not possible to reach any conclusion other than that Palme Dutt and the leaders of the Communist Party, fully schooled in the Marxist characterisation of imperialism and its colonial policy and aims, are deliberately deceiving the British workers.

In *World News and Views*, April 25 1942, Ben Bradley writes:

---

7 The Cripps' mission was an attempt by the British government in late March 1942 to secure Indian cooperation and support for their efforts in the Second World War. Sir Stafford Cripps, senior left wing politician and minister in the war cabinet of Winston Churchill, headed the mission.

"The Congress proposal, that a national government be set up which commands the confidence of the people, was rejected by the British government, but is receiving widespread support in India, even from such British official newspapers as the Calcutta *Statesman*. All sections are agreed on the postponement of major issues until after the war."

All sections, including the Communist Party. The demand for a "national government in India now" does not deceive the Indian masses and it will not deceive the British working class. What is this so-called "national government"? Is it to be a coalition government of the princes, Congress, Moslem League, liberals, Hindu Mahasaba, communists and others? We know that the slogan of a "national government" has always been used to deceive the masses into believing their interests are being catered for, when in actuality it is a cover for the continued rule of the oppressors. The Communist Party are well aware that the only method whereby the Indian masses will be led to the path of freedom is by the calling of a constituent assembly on the basis of universal suffrage. But freedom for India—that is freedom for the workers and peasants—would cut across the policy of the Stalinist bureaucracy in appeasing Churchill.

The CP leaders attempt to justify this false policy by saying that it is part of the policy of defending the Soviet Union. But far from doing this, such a policy can only result in disaster for the Soviet Union as well as for the British and Indian workers.

The Independent Labour Party

Instead of attempting to reach the Indian workers and help them organise their own independent party, the ILP graciously advised them to seek salvation in Nehru. The role of the bourgeois national Congress hasd been clearly foreseen by the Fourth International long in advance, especially the role of that section which, under the pressure of the aspirations of the masses, adopted a "socialist" coloration. Nehru, who was on the left wing of Congress and claiming to be a supporter of socialism, has become the most zealous advocate of capitulation to the niggardly concessions offered by Britain.

For years Brockway and the other centrist leaders of the ILP pictured Nehru, both to the British and Indian workers, as the genuine leader of the struggle, not only for national but for social freedom in India. We consistently pointed out that Nehru was interested in neither. The logic of his position would lead him into the open camp of imperialism. The *New Leader* published articles and pictures of Nehru as their "socialist" comrade. Brockway will no doubt shake his head sadly at this "unfortunate" betrayal, or will plead "exceptional circumstances" to justify Nehru's treachery, as Cripps is even today being justified. At an election speech their candidate deplores the fact that Cripps—"an honest man"—is being used by the capitalist class!

As always the centrists are led by the nose by the radical bourgeoisie and middle class. The position of the ILP on India is the inevitable fruit of the entire centrist position over the past period. Such a party is incapable of leading a genuine struggle for Indian freedom, and therefore cannot lead the struggle for workers' power in Britain, for the two are indissolubly bound together.

Tasks of the British workers

By extending the war over the entire planet, the imperialists have given a more profound significance to the permanent revolution. By drawing the whole of the colonial world into the conflict, they have placed their very existence in jeopardy. The last war and its repercussions in the Russian revolution provoked a whole series of colonial uprisings and revolutions: Turkey, Persia, India, Arabia, etc. By drawing these areas *directly* into the struggle they have linked the colonial struggle for national freedom and independence directly with the struggle of the British workers for power.

It has been a truism of revolutionary politics that the fate of the workers in Britain was irrevocably bound with that of the colonial peoples—especially with the Indian revolution. The events of the war have tied in one knot the destiny of the Indian and British workers and unless the working class of this country understands the urgent need to break with their capitalist class and their imperialist politics, and extend the fraternal hand to the oppressed colonial workers and peasants, they will rapidly find themselves reduced to the status of their colonial brothers.

If the British workers want to win as allies the Indian and colonial masses in a genuine struggle against oppression they must take the road, not of supporting the British imperialist oppressors, but of struggling against them and taking power into their own hands.

Only when the Indian people see a genuine war of liberation being waged by the British workers, and not the present imperialist war for world domination, will they be won as enthusiastic allies.

An unprecedented opportunity confronts the British workers today—and an opportunity which, if missed will not recur under such favourable circumstances. A real alliance between the toilers of India and Britain can be brought about today by a complete break with their common exploiters, British imperialism, and the establishment of a workers' government. Only such a government which can point to the expropriation of British capitalism, which can point to a complete break with their brutal and age-old exploiters, can win the friendship of the masses of India for the common struggle against capitalist reaction everywhere. The programme on which we appeal to the organised British labour movement, a programme of minimum democratic demands for India, is one which every British worker will support. As a first step towards unifying the toilers of India with the British workers, it is essential that they fight for power in Britain and put the following programme into operation:

1) Freedom for India.

2) A constituent assembly and full democratic rights.

3) Arming of the free Indian people to fight for their freedom.

4) Supplying of India with all the necessary arms and equipment.

5) Release all political prisoners.

Ajit Roy speaking in Hyde Park, late 1942

Labour lefts rehearsed debate with Tories!
Right wing Tories want military dictatorship

By Ted Grant

[*Socialist Appeal*, Vol. 4 No. 10, July 1942]

Coming after three years of uninterrupted defeats, the events in Libya and Egypt have aroused a profound disquiet within the British people. The debate on this latest crisis is a warning and a portent to the working class.

The workers are becoming critical and disgusted at the continued incompetence of their rulers in the military and industrial spheres. After three years of war industry is still not producing the type of equipment to match that of the Germans, and the officer caste reveals itself to be utterly stupid and incompetent.

Nothing but anarchy and chaos faces the workers everywhere. The feeling in the workshops and in the army is one of exasperation and frustration.

It is this which has compelled the ruling class to stage a debate, as a lightning conductor to the anger of the masses.

One section of the ruling class is already beginning to think of desperate measures to be used against the working class, whose eyes are being opened to the necessity for a change. This was demonstrated by the censure motion of Sir John Wardlaw Milne and the extreme right wing of the Tory Party. This right wing Tory utilised the obvious inefficiency of the generals to make a "brilliant" suggestion of changes in the military leadership. He proposed that the situation could be retrieved by appointing as commander in chief...the Duke of Gloucester! Even in the House of Commons this was greeted with loud groans. No matter the qualities of the noble Duke, it is obvious that as a military leader he would be a joke. But the sinister implication of this proposal is all too clear. The last reserve of the ruling class, the royal family, was to be brought forward as a cover for a military dictatorship to keep the masses down by force.

Sir Roger Keyes reflected this tendency when he contemptuously attacked the Labour leaders—Bevin, Morrison and Alexander—suggesting that their services in the government were no longer required. He clearly indicated that they could not hold the masses in check. They could not prevent strikes or other manifestations of unrest, and were therefore no longer of any use to the ruling class. They see too that the Churchill myth is ending.

Today, of course, their programme is not taken seriously by the decisive section of ruling class. Such a programme is not needed as yet. But the fact that, at the first signs of disgust on the part of the workers, already such a tendency has been manifested within their ranks is an indication of what will happen among the basic section when a real movement begins among the masses.

In as guarded and veiled a way as possible, Churchill, in self-defence, indicated what the right wing Tories were after:

> "The mover of the vote of censure has proposed that I be stripped of my responsibilities for defence in order that some military figure or unnamed personage should assume the general conduct of the war, that he should have under him a royal duke as commander in chief of the army...

> "This is a system very different from the parliamentary system under which we have lived. It might easily amount to, or be converted into, a dictatorship."

This section of the ruling class could quite easily don the robes of Pétain.

And Churchill's protestations that he would not participate in such a regime are worth no more and no less than the protestations of Reynaud and Daladier in France. They too held their hands to their black hearts and proclaimed undying devotion to "democracy". But in the hour of crisis they handed over to the Pétains and Lavals who sold out to Hitler.

The writing is on the wall. If the workers do not realise the danger, they could find themselves under a British "Vichy". There are already candidates for this post! For the time being they lurk and plot in the background, but in times of crisis they will thrust themselves forward. Already they are cautiously airing their programme in Parliament. What are they saying and preparing behind the scenes? And what alternative has Churchill to offer? The not very consoling prospect of a long and bloody war.

> "I have never shared the view," he assured us in his reply, "that this would be a short war or that it would end in 1942. It is far more likely to be a long war. There is no reason to suppose that it will stop when the final result has become obvious."

Churchill offers a programme of interminable slaughter and misery. He admits that even when there will be no hope of victory for Hitler, that the German people will continue a desperate resistance to the end. The reason for this is not far to seek. They have good reason to fear a Churchill victory.

In face of this exposure, the Labour leaders maintained their allegiance with Churchill and his class, which tomorrow will turn on the workers, as did Pétain. They insisted on giving full support to a system of utter corruption which can only lead the workers to ruin and disaster.

How Labour "lefts" fool the workers

The profound disquiet among the working class has had its effect not only in alarming the ruling-class right-wing of the Tory party to prepare measures against it, but has had its repercussions in the Labour Party as well. One section of the Labour "left" led by Shinwell abstained from voting—this was the most cowardly position of all. Other "left" labour leaders found themselves following in the wake of the leftward moving masses in order to retain some support. It was only yesterday that Aneurin Bevan and the other "left" leaders were fawning on Churchill and pleading with this arch representative of the capitalist class to introduce socialism in the interests of the war. But no more realistic and not one whit better than this is their present policy.

Debate was staged

Aneurin Bevan launched a slashing attack on Churchill and the ruling class. But all this fiery speechifying, as well as the other Labour "lefts", was so much hot air! The whole thing was staged from beginning to end for the purpose of fooling the workers. Alfred Edwards, Labour MP for Middlesbrough East has blown the gaff!

Speeches by Labour MPs attacking cabinet ministers were rehearsed and agreed to beforehand by the ministers themselves! Mr. Alfred Edwards, described it as: "This shadow boxing which will bring us and Parliament into contempt." Thus reported the *News Chronicle* on July 7.

What could more clearly demonstrate the shameful hypocrisy and cynicism of the Bevans and Shinwells. Their sham statements are meant to act as a safety valve for the accumulated anger and discontent of the working class. In this sense, they play an even more despicable and contemptible role than the Labour leaders themselves. Their phrases are not meant as a means of organising and giving a fighting lead to the working class. But they are given for the purpose of preventing the exasperation getting an organised outlet.

They did not even differentiate themselves from the Tory right wing gang of reactionaries, going to the length of signing the motion of censure together with them. They offered no alternative whatsoever. Although Bevan and the left were compelled to castigate the reactionary officer caste and the inefficiency in production, they did not demand a break with these evils. They did not offer the only practicable alternative in the interests of the working class—an end to the disastrous coalition. The reason for this is that they have no desire to break from their capitalist masters, and in this they are no different to the rest of the Labour leaders.

End the truce!

All these staged debates cannot hold the working class in check for long.

The British workers are moving left and what they are seeking is a fighting lead on the road to independence from their exploiters—the road of class struggle.

Workers! Exert pressure on the Labour leaders to break the coalition and take power on the programme of the *Socialist Appeal*. This fighting policy of socialism is the only answer to all problems confronting the workers—the defence of the Soviet Union—the defeat of fascism abroad as well as at home—to a future of a world of peace, run by the workers for the workers.

By fighting side by side with the workers on this programme, we can convince them by their own experience that the Labour leaders do not represent their interests and that only the Fourth International can lead to the victory of the working class against the sinister forces which the ruling class is preparing to crush the workers of this and other lands.

An open letter to the Yorkshire Miners' Association

Our answer to the slanders of the President, Mr. Joseph Hall

By Ted Grant

[*Socialist Appeal*, Vol. 4 No. 11, August 1942]

July 18 1942

To the Secretary,

Yorkshire Miners' Association,

2 Huddersfield Road, Barnsley, Yorks.

Dear Sir and Brother,

Our Executive Committee has had under consideration the recent statements of the President of your organisation, Mr. Joseph Hall, regarding the *Socialist Appeal* and the people who support it. Mr. Hall has lent authority to his pronouncements by stating that he intends to have an official pronouncement from your Council at the earliest opportunity.

In view of the irresponsible and slanderous character of these allegations and of the wide publicity which has been given to his statements in the press, and in Parliament, it is in the interest of the working class and therefore of your Council, that it investigates the question seriously as a representative working class body, and have before it all the available evidence, before making such a pronouncement.

We propose to deal briefly with the following four outstanding allegations made by Mr. Hall to the press:

1. "I am convinced in my own mind unrest in the coalfield has been fostered by subversive influences outside the miners' organisation."

2. "These influences are definitely subversive and pro-Nazi. Their object is to hinder production and thereby cripple the war effort."

3. "The effort to lead these boys away and to destroy their faith in the trade

union movement has gone too far already."

4. "Young men between 25 and 30 were being paid £10 a week for distributing the *Socialist Appeal*."

Bad conditions cause strikes—not "subversive" propaganda

The assertion by Mr. Hall that the recent strike wave has arisen as the result of, and has been fostered by, "subversive" influence outside the miners' organisation, is not only untrue, it is a direct insult to the miners whom he claims to represent. Miners are forced to resort to strike action only because they have no other method of redressing their legitimate grievances of bad conditions, low wages etc., and not at all because elements outside their ranks surreptitiously foster discontent. This is true not only for the miners, but for the working class as a whole, and it certainly cannot be refuted by your Council or any other representative working class body. Each delegate who now plays a leading role in the Yorkshire Miners' Association, including Mr. Hall, has at one time or another in the past been accused by the mine owners as "subversive." Coming from the lips of a "leader" of the miners, the term smacks of that "MacDonaldism" which dealt such a savage blow to the labour movement in the past decade or two.

Coal owners are the real pro-Nazis

Mr. Hall's statement that our organisation and propaganda is "pro-Nazi" and "aims to hold up production" is a gross slander. We challenge Mr. Hall to prove that our sympathies and aims are in any way pro-Nazi. Our tendency has consistently fought fascism in every phase of its existence, nationally and internationally. We claim that only our programme can lead to the defeat of fascism in the Nazi or any other form. If Mr. Hall suggests that to continue the fight for the minimum demands of the miners and working peoples is "pro-Nazi"; or to demand from the miners' leaders a fight to implement the declared programme of the unions for the nationalisation and democratic control of the mines—is pro-Nazi, then he has travelled into the camp of the class enemy. He has consciously or unconsciously gone over to the camp of the coal owners. The real pro-Nazis in Britain are the coal owners who aided Hitler in his rise against the German workers; who today sabotage production in the interest of profits; who wish to introduce Nazi methods against the British working class; and whose extreme representatives, the right wing Tories, as Mr. Churchill so recently exposed in Parliament, are even now in favour of a military dictatorship in Britain.

We believe that the task of a serious working class body today is to expose this capitalist sabotage and anarchy which holds up production, and to counterpose a clear alternative programme for the workers. Far from being interested in holding up production, we consider that the situation is too serious to allow the capitalists to retain control. We believe that our programme of nationalisation of the mines, and their operation under the unified and democratic control of the miners and technicians, will achieve the maximum productive results, and is the only policy consistent with the interests of our class.

It is the trade union leaders who undermine trade unionism

Mr. Hall's assertion that our propaganda has "undermined the faith of the workers in their trade unions" is completely false. It is an attempt to identify the Yorkshire Miners' Association with himself and his friends who are in a similar position, and thus to identify his own interests with those of the miners. This conception was developed by J. H. Thomas before he passed finally into the camp of the ruling class. Far from being identical, the interests of the trade union bureaucracy as represented by Mr. Hall, and of the rank and file, are antagonistic. Each day the trade union leaders become more and more interlocked with the capitalist state machine instead of breaking sharply and reasserting the independence of the trade union movement. This is becoming more sharply exposed with each successive struggle of the miners to maintain their conditions of life, where the leaders are to be found, not with the miners, but on the side of the coal owners. It is the present policy and actions of Joseph Hall and his colleagues which is succeeding in undermining the confidence of the miners in their unions. This is particularly true of the younger workers who are impatient to see a fighting union which backs them up in their economic demands. Disgusted at the treatment at the hands of their officials, many in the Wombwell district proposed to tear up their union cards in the recent dispute! Our comrades patiently explained the false and incorrect character of such action and proposed instead to these young workers that they set up a school through the National Council of Labour Colleges to study the history of the trade union movement and to prepare to take over the functions of the trade unions themselves; in this way to convert their unions once more into fighting organisations.

Mr. Hall's "£10 a week" lie can only discredit your Association

The assertion of Mr. Hall that "young men between the ages of 25 and 30 are receiving £10 a week for distributing the *Socialist Appeal*" cannot be other than a deliberate and premeditated lie. His object is to discredit the distributors and policy of the paper in the eyes of the miners. By suggesting that the *Socialist Appeal* is financed by sources where money is no object, he hoped to lend his statements a sinister ring. However, Mr. Hall attempted to afford himself some cover. He claims that he received the story second hand! May we inquire who told him that the distributors of the *Socialist Appeal* received £10 a week for the job? Was it someone who had connections with the labour movement or with the *Socialist Appeal* and its management? Or is it, as we assume, some fanciful individual concocted by Mr. Hall to give his story sonic little credence? Let us assume that some person with whom Mr. Hall is not well acquainted, did impart such information to him: is he so gullible that he accepts such a statement for public distribution without checking on it? If so, his conduct is, to say the least, irresponsible and he deserves to be censured. This question is one that your organisation cannot afford to let go unanswered. Mr. Sorenson, a Labour MP, and Mr. Morrison, the Labour Home Secretary, have now asked the question in the highest public body in the country: what evidence Mr. Hall has to back up his assertion. It can only bring discredit on your Council if Mr. Hall is without an answer.

The object of Mr. Hall's irresponsible and reactionary attack was to draw the attention of the government to the *Socialist Appeal* in order to get it suppressed. In this he had the full support of those newspapers which, in the past, had the closest sympathy for and connections with German and British fascism. Moreover, the paper which clamours most insistently for our suppression is the voice of the coal owners, the *Daily Telegraph*. By this gesture, Mr. Hall has thrown overboard all pretence of being a democrat himself. He proposes to adopt and implement the methods of fascism in Britain.

Demand a public inquiry

If Mr. Hall were some backward rank and file member of your union, it would be your task to re-educate him in the democratic ideology of the labour movement. But he is your president, and as such his every action is a public gesture in your name. The publicity given to Mr. Hall's reactionary proclamations have already, we believe, rebounded to the discredit of your organisation. Your Council cannot assume the responsibility of demanding the suppression of another working class body, or its press, by the capitalist class. It is your duty to establish a public enquiry into the whole matter, and we feel confident that the thousands of members of the Yorkshire Miners' Association would welcome such an inquiry. We propose therefore to your Council:

1. The immediate setting up by your Council of a special committee to investigate the allegations of Mr. Hall.

2. The investigations of this committee should be conducted in public. Our organization, Workers' International League, will place a complete file of our political documents for the last 10 years as well as our books and files of correspondence at the disposal of such a committee.

3. At the conclusion of the investigation, a mass meeting of Yorkshire miners should be called at Barnsley or Wombwell to which the committee will make its report. Present at the meeting will be Mr. Hall, the Editor of the *Socialist Appeal*, and Mr. J. Haston, the contributor of the articles of which Mr. Hall

complains.

If there is the slightest semblance of truth in any one of the allegations of Mr. Hall, there can be no doubt that such a procedure would establish the facts, and the Yorkshire Miners' Association Council could thus completely destroy any faith which local miners might have in the policy of the *Socialist Appeal*. The miners would themselves run the distributors of the *Socialist Appeal* out of the district whenever or wherever they appeared in the future. On the other hand, if Mr. Hall is shown to be guilty, as we are confident he will be, of falsehood and misrepresentation, the exposure should be sufficient to drive him out of public life.

Yours fraternally,

E. Grant, Editor *Socialist Appeal*

Socialist Appeal

CORTONWOOD SUPPLEMENT — ONE PENNY

Solidarity With Cortonwood
IT MAY BE YOUR PIT NEXT
Send Donations to:
T. Byrd,
Secretary Cortonwood Branch Y.M.A.,
21, Jardine Street,
Wombwell, Barnsley.
UNITY CAN BEAT THE BOSSES

Cortonwood Owners Provoke Pit Strike
Hall Helps Bosses in Wage Slash
BY JOCK HASTON

A wall of silence has been erected by the Yellow Press around a strike which is taking place at the Cortonwood Colliery, Wombwell, Yorkshire. This voluntary censorship by the capitalist press as well as that of the Labour and "Communist" Party, is imposed to cover up the most vicious wage attack to be made against a section of the working class for many years. The people who control these papers are well aware that if the true facts of this dispute were publicised, the workers everywhere would immediately be in sympathy with the Cortonwood Colliers in their present struggle.

In the December issue of the "Socialist Appeal," miner correspondents from another pit in the same village issued a warning through our columns, that the mood of the workers at Cortonwood was bitter, and that there would be an immediate down tools if the proposed cut was imposed. The correctness of their estimation is demonstrated by the bitterness of the struggle which meant very lean Christmas dinners for the families of the striking miners.

1,500 miners have been on strike for several weeks as a reply to a cut in the wages of about 150 fillers on the Silkstone Seam by approximately 30/- per week. The reduction is the result of a slash in the price list for the Silkstone Seam from 1/7 a ton to 1/3 a ton. This unjustifiable wage cut has infuriated all the workers at the Colliery, welding their ranks into a solid body in defence of the standards of the few who have been directly attacked.

Sharp friction has existed at this colliery for more than 18 months owing to the previous attempts by the employers to cut the price list. In November of 1941, Joe Hall, President (referred to in Wombwell as the Mussolini of Barnsley), along with Tom Oakey, another official of the Yorkshire Miners Association, signed a new price list with the management without consulting the workers who would be thus affected, and indeed in direct contradiction to their expressed desires with which the officials were familiar. By this act, Hall and Oakey demonstrated that they were not guided by the wishes of the miners who employ them, but on the contrary, they undertook to **dictate** terms to the miners. This they were enabled to do as the result of their control of the Yorkshire Miners Association.

When the management attempted to put the new price list into operation in May 1942, the pit struck work, the workers returning to work only when the new price list was suspended and negotiations reopened through the intervention of the then Ministry of Mines, headed by Dai Grenfel.

The Arbitration Board, which met on November 20th to finally decide on the price list, was a farce from beginning to end. The employers were represented by their most conscious agent, Mr. Furness, **who ruthlessly and loyally presented the coalowners' case;** the workers were represented by Mr. J. Hall, **who did not, indeed could not honestly or loyally put the case for the miners,** since he had already agreed to the owners' terms **in advance.** Under these circumstances he could only act as a stooge for Furness. With the workers' "representative" already in agreement with the bosses, the decisions of this Board were a foregone conclusion. The miners at Cortonwood knew that this would be so in advance, and warned the employers and Government that they would not stand for a reduction and would strike if necessary in defence of their existing standards.

COALOWNERS INTERESTED IN PROFITS NOT IN COAL OUTPUT

The price list at this Colliery has been in force for several years— "peace" years, but the employers must slash the price list in the middle of the war when they are fully aware that this would upset the "normal" trend at the pit and provoke a strike in defence of the already meagre conditions of the miners. **By this action the coalowners demonstrate clearly the motive of capitalist control of the mines as maximum profit and not at all maximum production.**

The workers at this seam have increased their output of coal from 4.41 tons per shift in 1938 to 6.61 tons in 1941. Instead of welcoming this increase of tonnage and consequent increase in wages, the coalowners set out to break the price list down so that the wages of the colliers would remain static in spite of the 50 per cent increased output. All the capitalist propaganda for "increased output" is seen to be lies and fakery—all the owners are interested in is profits, and more profits.

Continued on next page.

Socialist Appeal, Cortonwood supplement

Right wing Tories fear our programme

By Ted Grant

[*Socialist Appeal*, Vol. 4 No.11, August 1942]

The attack on the *Socialist Appeal* last month by the entire national and provincial press, the right wing Tories, the Communist Party, the Liberals, the miners' misleaders—was launched with one object—to get the *Socialist Appeal* suppressed.

So farcical were the charges, so irresponsible were the allegations of the miners' officials that the campaign collapsed—for the moment. But this is by no means the end of the matter. It serves as a warning of the most serious nature to the entire working class.

For it was not merely the *Socialist Appeal* that was under fire: it was the struggle of the miners for the betterment of their lot; it was the right to the working class to organise independently, to seek its own solution to the tremendous problems of today; to fight for power. This is what was being attacked. The *Socialist Appeal* bore the brunt, because through it is expressed the true aspirations of the workers; through it is offered the road of independence and hope for the workers—and doom for the capitalist class.

The campaign in the press went hand in hand with the campaign in Parliament. The right wing Tories advanced to the attack from every possible angle: paper supplies, personnel, internment under 18B[1], and suppression of the paper. These reactionaries, who stand for the method of force and suppression against the working class at the present time, gladly seized the opportunity of attacking the most conscious representatives of the working class. They are longing for the time when they will be able to use the methods of fascism in Britain. Today it is the Trotskyists, tomorrow it could be the ILP, and finally they would be after the scalps of Morrison, Bevin and the Labour leaders themselves. But at the moment they would have it seem that in this attack on the *Socialist Appeal*, these ultra-reactionaries were motivated solely by their disinterested

---

[1] Rule 18B of the Emergency Powers Act (1939) was part of the Defence Regulations used by the British government during the Second World War. It allowed for the internment of people suspected of being Nazi sympathisers

love for the labour movement and the Soviet Union.

This newfound love for the organisations of the workers and the Soviet Union ill-befits them. The impudence of these people posing as friends of the Soviet Union against us, when it was but yesterday that they were preparing for war against Russia at the time of the Finnish events, and who have always fought and conspired against the Soviet Union and the labour movement, while we have consistently fought and defended the Soviet Union and the labour movement against all attacks. All this is typical of the brazen hypocrisy of the ruling class.

The attitude of the press and of the reactionary MPs is a commentary on the situation in "democratic" Britain today. What capitalist paper or political party would have questions of this character asked about their reporters, paper supplies etc? The pro-Nazi *Daily Mail* for instance? It is taken for granted that the capitalist press and organisations should have the right to conduct its normal functions without interference by the state. But when it comes to a socialist newspaper, in which the downtrodden and oppressed find a voice, then no inquisition or persecution is too severe.

The paper which carried out the most determined and persistent campaign was the mouthpiece of the coal owners, the *Daily Telegraph*. Dismissing Hall's allegations from the outset, the *Telegraph* conducted a campaign day after day because they are only too well aware of the real situation in the coalfields and the fact that the *Socialist Appeal* voices the true aspirations of the miners.

They based their campaign for our suppression on a sober estimation of our programme, printing sections of this programme in order to illustrate its dangers to their class. Their industrial correspondent underlined this in his remarks while interviewing us: "This paper is dynamite! Even the *Daily Worker* in its militant days didn't touch your programme!"

Nevertheless, at first sight it might seem astonishing that such a fearful assault should be waged on a small organisation and its press. The daily newspapers mentioned possess between them a circulation in a single day more than what the *Appeal* possesses in a year. Yet they are afraid! This arises out of the uneasiness of the ruling class at the present time. The masses of workers are dissatisfied with the existing state of affairs. The most reactionary sections of the ruling class are already thinking in terms of suppression and dictatorship as a means of keeping the workers in check. The workers are beginning to realise the shameless profiteering of the capitalists and the mockery of equality of sacrifice. That is why they want to silence those who consistently and untiringly fight for the interests of the workers. It is not our number today, but the fact that our programme will become the programme of the masses tomorrow, which has driven the most reactionary sections of the ruling class to take the offensive against us.

But the question can be asked: why should the miners' leaders appeal to the

Tories for aid? Apart from the irresponsible Mr. Hall, there is Mr. Will Lawther, the president of the Miners' Federation of Great Britain. It was they who raised the question first, and provided the right wing Tories and the coal owners with the opportunity of launching an offensive against the workers' press. The reason is that these "leaders" would resort to any vile means to defend their bureaucratic domination of the union and the privileges which flow from them.

The reasons for the monstrous slanders on the part of these union leaders arise out of the fact that they have lost the confidence of the miners in their leadership. Their shameless stand on the side of the coal owners in recent strikes has led to disgust and disillusionment among the rank and file. The miners are beginning to see that such rotten leadership can only lead to capitulation to the coal owners. The Trotskyists have been putting forward among the miners and other workers, the necessity of turning the unions into fighting organs really representative of the workers and to replace the present leadership by more militant ones. Now at the first signs of a threat developing to their positions, these leaders run whining to their masters for help, not scrupling to use such dirty weapons as the slander of "pro-Nazism".

The most encouraging feature of this attack, and one that bodes well for the future of socialism in Britain, is that while the coal owners, the capitalist press, the right wing Tories, the miners' leaders and the Stalinists united for a unanimous assault on the *Socialist Appeal*, we had the sympathy and support of the broad masses of the working class. The readers and supporters of the *Socialist Appeal* were angered and indignant at this vile attack. Not a single one faltered in support of their paper. Not only those who had read the *Appeal* in the past, but thousands of new sympathisers were gained. Dozens of letters were received from miners, soldiers, engineers and other workers, with whom we had never been in touch before, enquiring about our paper and organisation. Far from weakening, the attack strengthened us in the eyes of the working class.

The government has refused to suppress the *Socialist Appeal* at the present stage, on the grounds of our weakness. There is apparently no question of democracy and the freedom of the press involved! It is purely an estimate of strength and potentialities. When we gain the ear of tens of thousands of workers, then apparently all democracy will go by the board. So we see the ruling class is prepared to tolerate opposition, only so long as that opposition is not effective. The moment the working class evinces a desire for change, at that moment all rights of free speech and free press are cast aside and the rulers resort to methods of suppression, and ultimately to fascism. The only road to defeat fascism, both at home and abroad, lies in defending the rights and interests of the workers wherever they are menaced, and in marching ahead to the establishment of workers' power and socialism. That is the programme of the *Socialist Appeal*.

Workers! Trade unionists! Miners! Readers of the *Socialist Appeal*! It is your paper that is under attack! It is you and your rights they are attacking! And it is in your hands that the real defence of the *Socialist Appeal* lies.

This is but a dress rehearsal. Tomorrow the working class will be faced with even more powerful attacks, as the situation in Britain grows ever more tense. In the struggle, the workers need a fighting paper and a fighting leadership. Let your answer to the attacks on the *Socialist Appeal* be that you resolve to give it even greater support than in the past.

Join the ranks of the Workers' International League and help us to build a party that will make the programme of the *Socialist Appeal* a living reality.

New allies of Communist Party

By Ted Grant

[*Socialist Appeal*, Vol. 4 No. 12, September 1942]

The *Sunday Dispatch* is continuing its slander campaign against the *Socialist Appeal*. Under the title *Socialist Appeal still at it* the story is revealed of how "directives" from Germany are transmitted to the British Trotskyists through a "workers' challenge" station.

If this were true, surely the *Sunday Dispatch*'s diplomatic correspondent, the author of the article, would have supplied more details, such as the time and the date. Surely he would have notified the police, and formal charges would have been made against the Trotskyists.

But the pro-fascist *Sunday Dispatch* does not pursue the policy of truth. Taking a leaf out of the book of their mentor Hitler, they base themselves on the axiom—the bigger the lie, the more easily it will be believed.

The whole style, the whole method of presentation, the falsifications and the distortions, the amalgam dishonestly linking the policies of the ILP with that of the Trotskyists, all these savour of the familiar methods of Stalinism. Unable to attack the real ideas of Trotskyism, the Communist Party and its new-found ally, the *Sunday Dispatch* attempt to throw dust in the eyes of the workers by confusing the policies of two different working class parties, and link us both up with Hitler. It is clear that the article is written by an ardent supporter of the Communist Party.

Indeed it could have been written with the pen of W. Wainwright himself, the author of *Clear out Hitler's agents*.

Trotsky alone warned the workers

The entire article is based on falsification and slander. Our political position has been and is openly proclaimed in the pages of the *Socialist Appeal*.

The charge that we would seek a compromise peace with Hitler is reduced to a despicable lie upon one reading of any issue of the *Socialist Appeal*. We alone in the labour movement warned of the disastrous outcome of Hitler's coming to power. Trotsky alone advocated the policy which would have prevented Hitler's rise, the policy of the united front of all working class organisations which was attacked by Stalin in the following terms:

> "It is significant, that Trotsky has come out in defence of a united front between the communist and social democratic parties against fascism. No more disruptive and counter revolutionary class lead could possibly have been given at a time like the present." (*Daily Worker*, May 26 1932.)

The amalgam between the ILP and the Trotskyists

Both the *Sunday Dispatch* and the Communist Party attempt to depict the resolution of the Glasgow ILP which voted against the supply of arms for the USSR, as a Trotskyist resolution.

This is somewhat stupid when point 1 in our programme of demands is "The immediate despatch of arms and material to the Soviet Union under the control of the trade unions and factory committees." In any case, the defeating of this resolution arises, not from any lack of desire on the part of the ILP to assist the USSR, but from the sectarian attitude on their part, for which the Trotskyists have always criticised them. In the July issue of the *Socialist Appeal*, Marc Loris writes on this point:

> "At the ILP national conference an amendment was presented asking for the 'advocacy of the production and transport of war materials to the Soviet Union under workers' control.' The idea of tying the defence of the Soviet Union to the class struggle of the English workers is excellent. The slogan has an offensive character as much against the English bourgeoisie as against its agents, the Labourite and Stalinist leaders. But the leadership of the ILP hastened to oppose this proposition. The arguments of its spokesmen were, taken as a whole, that the proposals are impracticable. Thus the ILP leaders reveal once more their total incomprehension of the dynamics of revolutionary action. How render 'practicable' tomorrow that which is '[im]practicable' today?"

> "They have no idea. They find it very 'practicable' to praise the 'statesmanship' of Stalin, to insult Lenin by attending fraudulent ceremonies; but to call on the English workers to demand an accounting from the capitalists on aid to the Soviet Union, that is 'impracticable'!"

On the question of McGovern's attitude towards Munich, which the *Sunday Dispatch* triumphantly uses, and which the Communist Party never fails to use, the Trotskyists have always criticised the ILP on this question. It is one of the points which separates us. This position springs from the pacifist and centrist position of the ILP. *But at any rate, we stand whole-heartedly with the ILP against the foul allegation that this springs from the desire to help Hitler or Fascism.* The accusation is one that only the pen prostitutes of the pro-Fascist

Sunday Dispatch or the Communist Party falsifiers would dare to make.

The ignorant reference of the ILP defending the "Trotskyist" POUM in Spain is typical. The POUM was never Trotskyist as they claim, but precisely the Spanish version of the ILP. So it is natural that the ILP should defend its policies. We on the other hand consistently criticised the policies of the POUM for its participation in the popular front government which le*-d the Spanish workers to their defeat.

Dispatch praised fascism in all countries

In their frantic efforts to besmirch the revolutionaries, the Stalinists are willing to use any methods and any pro-fascist people or paper to suit their ends. And what is the record of these newfound friends and comrades-in-lies? These people, who now accuse the Trotskyists and the ILP of assisting fascism, are the very ones who have consistently supported fascism and reaction throughout the world. The question of Munichism is one on which they should keep silent. It was the *Sunday Dispatch* more than any other paper, which supported Chamberlain at that time. *And precisely because they wished to help Hitler.* They openly said so! The reference to Spain is even more injudicious. When the POUM was fighting on the barricades against Franco, they supported this butcher as the saviour of Christianity and civilisation! Their tender regard for the Soviet Union which they now manifest, is shown for the hypocrisy that it is by the fact that they incited the British government to allow a free hand to Germany in the East.

In one of the many articles which they published by Sir Oswald Mosley on their ideal of a fascist Europe of the future, he openly called for Germany to be allowed to attack the Soviet Union. Britain would gain the advantage from this by the mutual exhaustion of both Germany and the Soviet Union. This is, in fact, the secret policy of the *Sunday Dispatch* and its backers today.

While the revolutionaries were waging a struggle against fascism in all countries of the world, what was the attitude of the new knight-errant of the holy struggle against fascism?

While the brown murder bands were murdering the worker-militants (including the Trotskyists) and destroying the trade unions with terror and torture in the first moments of fascism in Germany, here are some samples of what the *Sunday Dispatch* was saying. In October of 1933, Geoffrey Harmsworth wrote:

> "The passionate sincerity of Hitler cried aloud. This was no cheap tub-thumping political firebrand but a fervent patriot and a realist. It is monstrously untrue to say that the Storm troops and Brown Shirts are a new German army in disguise. Germany does not want another war..."

In an article of October 22 1933, by Colonel T.C.R. Moore MP, we were told by the *Sunday Dispatch*:

"Germany welcomed her saviour, and largely owing to the obviously sincere and single-minded appeal of his policy he is today the adored leader of certainly 90 percent of the German population. Eight months ago Herr Hitler became Chancellor of the Reich. Today, and I now speak of experience barely a week old, the whole atmosphere of Germany has changed. Sobriety has replaced licence, patriotism has usurped communism, virtue has abolished vice."

"The servants of the law have crushed the masters of the gun. Women and children are safe; animals are mercifully treated; social services have received a new impetus..."

This is how the *Sunday Dispatch* smoothed over and justified the horrible atrocities of the Nazis. The article continues:

"These are some of the changes I have seen, but I realise that in making these changes there has been unjustified persecution, misery and suffering caused to many innocent German nationals of varied creed and faith. But experience has taught us to be tolerant of the ways of revolution. Eggs must be broken to make an omelette. Suffering is inevitable in the reconstruction of a state."

"But if I may judge from my personal knowledge of Herr Hitler, peace and justice are the keywords of his policy, and given time, the support of his people, and the goodwill of his colleagues, he will carry that policy to success."

On December 31 1933, the *Dispatch* published a special feature article by Mussolini, *The whole world going fascist?* To come closer home it was the *Dispatch* and the *Daily Mail* which were among the principal backers of Mosley and his black-shirt thugs in their attempt to organise fascism in Britain. Their pages were opened to Mosley and they gave him every possible publicity. On January 21 1934, on a special page was a picture of Mosley and a signed article by him entitled *Why we wear the black shirt*:

"The blackshirts have faced and overcome the socialist bullies of the razor, the knife, and the broken bottle, by standing together and fighting in the ordered ranks which the blackshirt makes possible. England already has to thank them for breaking the red terror of the streets, although greater ordeals may yet await them."

"Thus we wear the blackshirt for that combination of ideal and practical reasons which is so characteristic of the faith of fascism."

An ecstatic editorial of the same date was entitled *The blackshirts are coming.*

Thus they supported the paid thugs and hooligans in the ranks of Mosley's bands in their efforts to create an organisation to destroy the workers' movement and rights in Britain. On January 28 1934, they wrote this description of Mosley:

"To the world Sir Oswald Mosley; to blackshirts, the Leader."

"He quests for a better, healthier, happier England like a King Arthur knight for the Holy Grail."

On May 21 1934, this rag proudly announced that:

"The editor has purchased a limited number of seats to be presented to *Sunday Dispatch* readers for Mosley's Olympia meeting."

On the brutal thuggery at the fascist meeting in Olympia, which provoked an outcry in nearly the whole of the British press, the *Dispatch* headlined an article by G. Ward Price, friend of Hitler: *No communist badly injured. But blackshirts still in hospital. Elaborate 'red' plot miscarries. Armed interrupters wreck meeting.*

Their leader of June 17 1934, was headed *Mussolini-Hitler talks—hopes for peace* in which they say of these fascist gangsters:

"However that may be they have this in common. That each is the beloved leader of a great nation that regards him as its saviour and to which his lightest word is almost a divine command."

Their support of the Japanese militarists, of Hitler, of Mussolini was continued right up to the outbreak of the war. Now these gentlemen, aided, abetted and supported by the Communist Party, have the audacity to slander the international socialists. Tomorrow they would favour a deal with Hitler, Mussolini and Franco, if it suited the interests of their masters, the capitalist class. If the capitalists were threatened by the working class they would be the first to appeal to Hitler for help, just as their equivalents did in France. From this yellow rag the workers expect nothing different. But that the so-called Communist Party should assist and aid reaction by the peddling of slanders against the revolutionaries is a danger and a warning to the workers. They have linked themselves up with the most reactionary and pro-fascist section of the ruling class in this country, and the most foul anti-working class section of the capitalist press.

In the eyes of all honest workers the role of the Communist Party is becoming clear. It is becoming clear too that the reason the Communist Party and the *Sunday Dispatch* attack us is not at all that they think we are "pro-fascist"; *it is our programme they fear*. Despite the smallness of our numbers at present, they know that ours is the only programme which represents the interests of the working class; the programme of working class struggle against fascism at home and abroad; the programme which will lead to socialism.

In the teeth of the barrage of lies and slanders we are unafraid. We base ourselves on truth and honesty. We base ourselves on the interests of the working class. No matter the obstacles placed in our path, our programme will find the road to the workers, and the workers will find the road to our programme.

£10 Reward

To any member of the Communist Party who can prove that the so-called quotations from Trotskyist publications in their pamphlet "Clear out Hitler's agents" are not forgeries.

—Or—

To any member of the CP who can show one page of this pamphlet which does not contain a minimum of five lies.

Socialist Appeal

The ILP—A ship without a compass Labour leaders hold workers back

By Ted Grant

[Written: May 1942]
[*Socialist Appeal*, Vol. 5 No. 1, October 1942]

The "Socialist Britain Now" campaign, which was launched with such a ballyhoo by the leadership of the ILP, has fizzled out. No more than passing references to it appear, on rare occasions, in the pages of the *New Leader*. In place of this has come out attempts at horse deals and manoeuvres with the "left wing" of the Labour Party and an attempt to gain support on the basis of the so-called *Manifesto against race hatred*, which has been published in the pages of the *New Leader*.

It is necessary for the serious members of the ILP to draw a balance sheet of the results of the campaign and the policies of the ILP on the principle issues during the last few months. The leadership of the ILP has refused and is indeed incapable of doing so. But we will endeavour to.

Ridley attempts feebly to reply to the criticism of Loris by pointing out triumphantly that the LP has not decayed into an "open agent of imperialism". But when Lenin put forward the slogan of "*Labour to power*" in 1920 the Labour leaders were just as open agents of imperialism as they are today. Why then did Lenin, in a situation which could have easily become revolutionary—and we are in a "pre-revolutionary" situation today—put forward the slogan "Labour to power"? Because although the advanced guard may understand the role of the Labour leaders, that is certainly not true of the rank and file in the trade unions and Labour Party. Otherwise, quite obviously, they would have ceased to support the Labour Party and come over to the side of the revolution. But this is precisely the task of the revolution in Britain: *to win over the masses that support the Labour Party*. How to do it? Mere denunciation of the Labour Party leaders cannot achieve this. It can only be done by demonstrating to the masses, by *their own experience*, that their leaders are incapable of representing their interests. A proposal to the leaders addressed to the rank and file, demanding a break with capitalism and taking power on a programme such as that set out in the *Socialist Appeal*, cannot but awaken a response among the Labour workers.

The masses are dissatisfied with the present government, as the bye-elections have clearly shown. But they must be given *a practical, concrete alternative*. To suggest the ILP or ourselves, at the present stage, is obviously out of the question. Apart from anything else, the masses have not yet realised the necessity for the socialist revolution. But they are looking for an alternative "socialist" government to the present coalition with the bourgeoisie. The first steps of the awakening of the masses to activity would be in the direction of forcing a break with the present coalition with the Tories by the Labour and trade union leadership. These are carefully watching the masses and already their "left" wing are preparing, as the workers surge forward, to step out into open "opposition" in Parliament to the present government.

ILP forced to modify its attitude on Labour leaders

But alas, while contemptuously dismissing the Labour Party, at the critical moment the ILP say exactly the opposite of what they have been advocating.

The *New Leader* of July 11, reporting John McGovern's speech, stated:

> "The government is living in a fool's paradise...The government would not last a week but for the fact that Labour and trade union members are in it. They are the people who are protecting the government from being overthrown. They are the same people who, when British Forces suffered the comparatively small reverse in Norway, overthrew the Chamberlain administration. I am amazed to find the complacent attitude they have adopted and the way in which they are maintaining secrecy in what is regarded the nation's great peril."

This is of course true. Lenin pointed out that the British bourgeoisie could not continue to rule for 24 hours without the support of the Labour and trade union bureaucracy. This position has been further accentuated by the development of the war. But there is nothing "amazing" in this. As Trotsky pointed out on a similar statement of Brockway's, the superiority of the Marxist consists in his foresight and not being "amazed" at obvious things. But for McGovern and the ILP leadership the matter rests there. Tomorrow they could quite easily come to some sort of electoral arrangement with the Labour leaders. Only yesterday they were accusing the Trotskyists of attempting "to revive the fast putrefying corpse", because we demanded that the Labour leaders take power. Not many months ago, we read in the *New Leader*:

> "In fact everything indicates that this will mark the end of the Labour Party just as the last one did that of its Liberal predecessor, despite the valiant efforts of the Trotskyists to revive the fast putrefying corpse. The spirit in it died long ago. After all, even Christ gave up the dead as hope-

less after three days."

And here today we find that without the aid of the "corpse" the British government would not rule for a week! Thus the ILP is compelled to repudiate its position.

At the first outburst of indignation at repressions of the British government in India, the national council of the ILP issued a *Manifesto*. Now, the conduct of the first two Labour governments should have been a sufficient indication of the policy which the Labour ministers would pursue, yet this is what the *Manifesto* says:

> "We call on all liberty loving people in Britain and on all sections of the Labour movement to protest immediately and with the greatest strength. It will be the eternal shame of Labour ministers that they should share the responsibility for this crime, and the ILP hopes that members of the Labour Party will call for the repudiation of what has been done and the withdrawal of the Labour ministers from the government." (*New Leader*, August 15 1942)

Thus we see that at a moment of crisis, the ILP leadership is compelled to repudiate the fundamentally incorrect and sectarian policy they themselves have put forward. As to accentuate this we find Walter Padley, a member of the NAC and a delegate to the TUC, writing in the *New Leader* of September 5, as the final conclusion of his article *Will TUC face the real issue*, the following paragraph:

> "At this congress it is imperative that the demand be raised in the sharpest way for the ending of the coalition, for the establishment of a workers' government. For only along that road can the British workers solve their own problems, help Soviet Russia, and hasten the end of the war by a workers' peace."

At first one rubs one's eye in disbelief. There it is in black and white, an annihilating condemnation of the ILP's policy in the pages of the *New Leader* penned by the leaders of the ILP themselves. We hope that Ridley will hasten to the rescue in condemnation of this stealthy flirting with "Trotskyist" ideas. The ILP leadership is hoping that the Labour rank and file will demand the withdrawal of the Labour ministers from the government. Padley goes one step further and is urging the delegates to the TUC to end the coalition and move towards the setting of a "workers' government".

What is meant by this? An ILP government? Obviously not, or Padley would have said so. In any case it is patently ludicrous, if this is the meaning of the proposal, to demand of the delegates of the mighty mass organisations to place the (by comparison) insignificant ILP in power. What then does it mean? That the trade union leaders should take power as representatives of the dictatorship of the proletariat? If so, the idea is fantastic. Not even Padley would suggest, at the present stage, that the workers are ripe for this—or that these leaders were capable of carrying it out. It is as usual that the ILP leaders throw around slogans quite airily without bothering to think out the meaning of these slogans and ideas. It is clear that if the demand to end the coalition is seriously to be addressed to the Labour and the trade union leaders and gain support among the masses, it can only do so if coupled with the slogan *"Labour to power"*. Otherwise the demand is either ultra-left or opportunist. If the slogan of ending the coalition and setting up a workers' government is not meaningless, it can only be meant as a Labour government. But Padley does not mean this or that would have been the formula used. To be exact, Padley hasn't the faintest idea of what in the devil he does mean.

His article is perfectly in tune with policy of the ILP leaders. They combine opportunism with ultra-leftism and anything but precise, clear and unambiguous policies and ideas.

Where is the "Socialist Britain Now" campaign in all this? The disdainful and hopeless attitude to the Labour Party is apparently abandoned. The support of a small section of the "Socialist Britain Now" campaign has led to nothing. And the ILP leaders are compelled in a distorted way to reflect the blind alley in which they find themselves, and to attempt convulsively to find a solution. *But as always in a centrist manner.* If, instead of the isolated "Socialist Britain Now" campaign, the ILP leadership had adopted the correct policy and systematically appealed to the rank and file of the Labour Party and the trade unions, demanding the breaking of the coalition with the Tories and a fight for power on a socialist programme, even one so vague and ambiguous as the programme put forward by the ILP, then their position would have been considerably strengthened.

Brockway looks to Labour left and Common Wealth

As comrade Trotsky reiterated again and again, sectarianism always ends in opportunism. When his sectarian schemes are dashed to pieces by the class struggle, Fenner Brockway, (who is the theoretical leader of the ILP) makes haste to throw his principles overboard. Says Brockway in the *New Leader* of August 15:

> "The *objective* conditions for socialist revolution are developing. We must prepare for *subjective* conditions. How?

> 'The first step is to secure a Socialist Alliance. Not one party, but an alliance leaving liberty to its sections outside the terms of the alliance.

> 'The alliance should not be exclusively anti-war. Before the end of the war, pro-war and anti-war views in the past will not be the dividing line, but pro-socialist action and anti-socialist action. The alliance should be

based on four points:

"1. Anti-Vansittartism[1].

"2. Challenging the political truce with the object of securing the socialist government.

"3. A socialist and anti-imperialist example by the government.

"4. An offer of a socialist peace and aid to the socialist revolution in Europe.

"Where are the allies for this programme to be found? There is little to hope from the present government, but there is a small group of socialists and a few pacifists accepting the class struggle, who are reliable. There is also a nucleus of Labour MPs of sound working class instincts who will increasingly come out."

"There is the 'Common Wealth group'. They are middle class, reject the class struggle, and eschew the word socialism, but, nevertheless, they are significant and from them there will come the necessary elements in the middle class."

So, the differences between anti-war and pro-war are revealed apparently as a mere difference of opinion! The remarks on the Common Wealth group are even more revealing. Elsewhere, the *New Leader* in warmly welcoming the work of this group had occasion to remark in a leading article:

"It wants to see the war prosecuted more efficiently and, temporarily at least, accepts the national leadership of Mr. Churchill...It is sympathetic to the Labour Party, wants it to remain in the government, but at the same time is against the political truce."

And with this hotchpotch of confusion, Fenner Brockway attempts to palm off an alliance with these avowed supporters of Churchill as an alliance with the middle class! To that "nucleus of Labour MPs" why not immediately demand a

---

[1] Doctrine known as "Vansittartism", from Robert Gilbert Vansittart (1881 – 1957). As a senior British diplomat, during the war, Vansittart became a prominent advocate of an extremely hard line with Germany. Germany was regarded as intrinsically militaristic and aggressive. Nazism was just the latest manifestation. The German people enthusiastically supported Hitler's wars of aggression, so they must be thoroughly re-educated under strict Allied supervision for at least a generation. In 1943 he wrote: "In the opinion of the author, it is an illusion to differentiate between the German right, centre, or left, or the German Catholics or Protestants, or the German workers or capitalists. They are all alike, and the only hope for a peaceful Europe is a crushing and violent military defeat followed by a couple of generations of re-education controlled by the United Nations."

campaign for Labour to power even on the four-point programme outlined?

On August 8, the editorial in the *New Leader* laments:

"The disturbing feature of the British political situation is that so far there is no real alternative to the Churchill government".

So here is an admission that the ILP is incapable of giving any alternative lead. It is this incapacity which makes the ILP leaders clutch eagerly at the tail of all "left" movement in the parliamentary wing of the LP. It responds uncritically and is incapable of giving the movement an impetus from below, preferring secret negotiations with the opportunist elements at the head of the movement in the top. On July 18, the *New Leader* hopefully comments on developments within the LP:

"We hope that before long a united front may be achieved of all those who make this their first loyalty." (*Socialist Britain*)

On August 8, a front-page article headlined: *Labour revolt stuns leader*, continues:

"Last week's revolt of 49 Labour MPs stunned the leadership. The Labour ministers are demanding loyalty to the national government and the leaders of the parliamentary wing are insisting on discipline. A number of Labour members have made it clear, however, that their first loyalty is to the workers [!?] and that they will not hesitate to vote against the government on social issues when the workers are betrayed [!]...Strong speeches against the government were delivered by Labour MPs..."

ILP flirtations—A *Manifesto* without principles

On August 22, as a climax to this process, comes a new attempt at a fake "unity" with the *Manifesto against race hatred*. In the editorial of this date we read:

"Thus it comes about that members of the Labour Party, trade unionists, co-operators, shop stewards, intellectuals and artists, members of the ILP and of the Common Wealth, second-fronters and pacifists, are all associated in a common declaration."

"The broad scope of those supporting the *Manifesto* has led to criticism. We certainly differ. We differ on the war. But, even so, it is desirable immediately that all who reject Vansittartism and stand by socialism, should say so together, whilst in the long run we believe that the unity now indicated may prove more important than past or present differences on the war. The issue between capitalism, imperialism, and socialism may yet prove to be more crucial than the military issue."

"If, as we believe will be the case, the support is wide, the *Manifesto* may become the beginning of a unifying movement which will be of great significance for the future."

So the bankruptcy of the "Socialist Britain Now" campaign has not led the ILP leadership to a Marxian policy, but to a caricature of the parades which the Stalinists conducted at the time of their ultra-left line, i.e. the so-called "Amsterdam congress against war". The fate of this new set-up cannot be any different from that of these fake organisations.

The signature to this *Manifesto* commits the signatories to nothing. So vague is it that people who support the war, together with people who oppose it, can all join in signing it. Where then are the principles of the ILP? Their opposition towards the war is seen as a mere radical gesture, and not as principles.

"The issue between capitalism, imperialism and socialism may yet prove to be more crucial than the military issue." So apparently the ILP merely regard it as a question of a friendly political difference. As if the military could be separated from the political issues! As if war had ceased to be the "continuation of politics by forcible means"! Here we see how the ILP passes swiftly from sectarianism to opportunism and vice versa.

This *Manifesto*, while condemning Vansittartism, has not a word to say on the role of the present British government. And do not the ILP leaders know that Vansittart is merely an open spokesman for the policy of Churchill and the ruling class? Why then do they not demand that those who are opposed to an imperialist peace should prove this in deeds and not in empty words? No! To support the military adventure of the ruling class is to support and to prop up Vansittartism.

It is true that the *Manifesto* speaks of the necessity to make Britain socialist. But this remains a pious phrase and a gesture to lull that section of the workers who are becoming more critical of the position of the ruling class today. They can prate of the vested interests...and then continue blithely to support the government of big business par excellence. And Brockway and the ILP leadership can cover up this repulsive hypocrisy and go into ecstasies over a document which "deplores" Vansittartism and talks of the necessities of a "socialist peace" without indicating how this most desirable result will be achieved. Perhaps by appealing to the better nature of Churchill and the government, or to the cannibals of big business who are busily showing what their idea of the new world should be in India? Remember, the signatories, while all for a socialist peace, are supporting an imperialist war with Churchill, who stands for a super Versailles, at its head.

But Brockway and the ILP leaders only ask for the signature of a platonic declaration, which commits these lefts to nothing. The Labour leaders would have no objection to this. Morris has occasionally given an anti-Vansittart speech.

This does not mean to say that a united front could not be made on certain issues with elements in the Labour Party which support the war, or even with such an organisation as the Common Wealth group. But such a united front could only be on specific, limited issues, such as defence of the workers' press or democratic rights which these organisations claim to uphold. But to adopt a common programme with elements such as these indicates the complete lack of a Marxian principled position even on the question of the war by the leaders of the ILP.

To palm off the agreement with parsons, artists, even the four Labour MPs and the Common Wealth group, as a step towards winning the masses, is futile and stupid. These signatories represent nobody and nothing but themselves. The only serious movement which could be represented as a step in the direction of a "socialist peace" and against Vansittartism, could come as a movement to overthrow the present government. All else is a base deception and a sowing of illusions among the advanced strata of the working class. Any party which claims to represent the workers must demand deeds and not pretty words from its collaborators. If these elements are sincere in their desire to fight against the imperialist plans of British capitalism, their first step must obviously be to break with the British capitalists and their government. This is the acid test of their sincerity.

Here is where we get the difference between the policy and tactics of the ILP leaders and of a genuine Leninist party. To take advantage of the disagreements between the left wing and the official Labour leaders, which is now opening out under the pressure of the masses, is a correct thing to do. But a Bolshevik organisation would use this to achieve two things. The first to get the discontented masses mobilised and on the move against capitalism. The second, as a means of demonstrating to the masses the fact that the Labour leaders are not interested in the struggle for socialism but have betrayed the workers by going over to the side of the bourgeoisie. The test of the sincerity of these signatories would be to demand that they immediately begin, with the ILP, a campaign for the ending of the coalition, and for Labour to take power. The present campaign cannot have any more fortunate consequences than that of the "Socialist Britain Now". If it did gain any large following, the consequences would be even more pernicious. The combination of contradictory slogans and idea of pacifists, second-fronters, exploiters of the middle class discontent such as the Priestley-Acland group, would all move in different directions under the impact of events.

The way to win the middle class is [not that of the] leadership of the Common Wealth which "reject the class struggle and eschew the word socialism" and will inevitably end in the camp of reaction, even very possibly fascism.

The way to win the middle class is precisely by waging the class struggle, putting forward a programme which will include the interests of the middle class and showing them that their interests can be served only by linking their fate with that of the worker.

Shameful statements of parliamentary wing

The failure of the ILP to do this, their failure even to maintain a principled stand against those supporting Churchill and the imperialist war, such as the Common Wealth group, does not arise accidentally. Its sharpest expressions are seen in the antics of the parliamentary wing of the ILP, which dominates its leadership. The last few months have provided dozens and dozens of examples of the hollowness of their claim that they represent the forces of the socialist revolution in Britain. Their position on India and the colonial peoples, which will be dealt with in subsequent issues of the *Socialist Appeal*, provides another acid test. On July 4, Maxton had this to say on the position of the colonial peoples:

> "I associate myself with Mr. Creech Jones in the view that this House can either do the right thing, or be compelled later to surrender to an uprising of force, which will create a situation which intelligent people do not wish to see…I hope the government will not assume that when peace comes there will be a whole lot of rearrangements in the world and that every nation's possessions will not come under review…"

> "I would like to see a united states of Africa, for instance, run and controlled by Africans, the natives of the soil; but if the white races are to have a say as to how the wealth of that great continent is to be developed, I would like to see the United States of America have a part in it. I believe that America could teach up [!?] some things about the handling of colonial people, and I am more certain still that the Soviet Union and China could teach both of us things…"

What degrading and servile statements for one claiming to be a revolutionary. As if the American imperialist gangsters are one whit better than their British "allies". The masses in Cuba, Philippines, etc., can testify to the "civilising" mission of Yankee imperialism. America can teach even Hitler something about racial discrimination against subject peoples. The treatment of Negroes in the Southern states of America can testify to this. Already we see in Britain an importation by the American army of the Jim Crow policy against American Negro troops. It does not matter to the colonial slaves whether their masters fly the Union Jack or the Stars and Stripes as a symbol of their enslavement. And to piously hope that the slave masters, who are drenching all the continent in blood, *precisely for the right to exploit the colonial slaves and to defend their colonial loot*, will consent to a re-arrangement at home, is the measure of the "revolutionism" of Maxton and company.

Instead of boldly appealing to the workers and standing on the side of the colonial peoples in their just struggle against imperialism, Maxton attempts to frighten the imperialists, and himself, with the consequences of their failure to see reason *"which will create a situation which intelligent people do not wish to see!"* Perhaps the present bloody chaos which imperialism has created in the colonial areas and in Europe is a position acceptable to "intelligent people!" Yet his shameless appeal to the imperialists at home and his painting up of the American imperialists abroad, his appeals of "we" (and by this he associates himself with the imperialist gangsters) have a lot to learn from American capitalism—appear in the central organ of the ILP! To Maxton it is a question of "teaching" the imperialists the "evil" of their abominations or even learning from them, and not at all one of overthrowing them.

McGovern has capped this with a speech for which any party deeming itself Leninist would have demanded instant repudiation on pain of expulsion from its ranks. Yet it too naturally finds it way into the pages of the *New Leader* of July 11 1942. He was attempting to justify the shameful role the parliamentary clique had played at [the] Munich crisis[2] when they had supported Chamberlain:

> "We [!] are suffering from a considerable number of reverses and we do not want to see more reverses in which our men are decimated. To me the dangers seem tremendous."

> *"I believe, and said it at the time, that Members went too lightly into the war, believing it would be an easy task.* I have been accused time and time again, especially by my communist friends, of backing the then Prime Minister at the time of Munich. Apart from the fact that I have opposed war at every stage, I say it was a godsend to this country that the Prime Minister did not put us into war then. Bad as things are today, then there would have been sudden and swift disaster for the country. *We had a year's breathing space in which to prepare if we wished to do so."*

Here we see his so-called opposition towards war, as that of a "loyal oppositionist", concerned about the preparations of the bourgeoisie. Not on a class basis but on a basis of the military needs of the bourgeoisie. This is further reflected in the attitude adopted towards the second front:

> "The demand of the second front may compel the government; it may be blackmailed and driven into a second front before adequate preparations have been made...in Libya...I have been prepared to see military defeats because a large number of commandos and men were not trained

---

2 Adolf Hitler, Neville Chamberlain, Benito Mussolini and Édouard Daladier signed the Munich Agreement during the night between September 29 and 30. The deal conceded Germany the right to occupy the Czech Sudetenland by October 10.

in the art of this special type of warfare…"

And so on, he argues his case not from the political point of view, but from the military aspect, as any social-patriot would do. McGovern goes on:

"At the time the late Prime Minister [Chamberlain] was unseated, my blood boiled at the foul things that were hurled at him". As if it is the job of revolutionaries to sympathise with one side or another, when the capitalist snakes falls out with the capitalist crocodiles. Rather it would have been his duty to take advantage of the situation to show the masses the real aims of both.

Within the ILP, opposition to the parliamentary clique and their policy is usually smoothed over by arguments that after all they do not constitute the whole of the ILP. As though they were naughty children and not in one of the most important and authoritative positions as spokesmen for the party, quite apart from the fact that they are in the leadership of the ILP.

Lenin, in demanding a meticulous and uncompromising adherence to the principles of Marxism, once remarked that a spoonful of tar would spoil a barrel of honey. With the ILP it is not a case of a spoonful of opportunism but of a party leadership organically infected with the disease of centrism.

Those members of the ILP in the left wing seriously desirous of transforming the ILP into a genuine revolutionary party can only do so by a struggle against the sectarian and opportunist course of the leadership, especially of the parliamentary wing. In fighting for a correct policy, they will find that this is provided only by the method and policy of the Fourth International.

Jock Haston, national organiser of WIL

Wainwright and Doriot: birds of a feather

By Ted Grant

[*Socialist Appeal*, Vol. 5 No. 3, December 1942]

William Wainwright, modestly signing himself W.W., has written an article in *World News and Views* of November 21 1942, the pretended purpose of which is to expose Jacques Doriot, leader of the fascist Popular Party in France.

In reality, following the time worn methods of the "Communist" Party, the real aim is to slander and vilify the Trotskyists.

First Wainwright pretends to believe that Doriot is a Trotskyist. He is as much a Trotskyist as Wainwright himself could be described a Trotskyist. Both have the same credentials, i.e. Doriot at the service of Stalin slandered and lied about Trotsky's policies; now Wainwright jumps into the vacant space left by Doriot to fulfil the same purpose.

In order to understand this, it is only necessary to examine the biography of Doriot. He was one of the leaders of the French Communist Party from its earliest days. When the split came in Russia between Stalin and Trotsky, judging that Stalin would win, he supported him in the struggle and came out as a violent opponent against Trotskyism. Faithfully and cynically carrying out the policy of Stalin, he helped carry through Stalin's policy in 1925-1927, which led to the defeat of the Chinese revolution. It was here that he learned to practise the habit of lies and deception in the interests of the Stalinist "line". When on a delegation representing the communist workers, instead of warning the Chinese workers and peasants against the role of Chiang Kai-Shek and the Chinese capitalists, who would betray the revolution and slaughter the masses, Doriot kept silent. He kept silent to cover the policy of his then master Stalin. Just as Wainwright today covers up the crimes of Churchill, de Gaulle and Co. for the same purpose.

Doriot was sent by the Communist International as a member of an international delegation on a mission to China...This mission,

"passed through town after town where the unions had already been driven underground, and in Kanchow they received detailed reports on the murder of Chen Tsang-Shen, a local trade union leader killed by Chiang's orders only a few weeks previously." (*Tragedy of the Chinese revolution*, by H. Isaacs)

Doriot, *after* the betrayal of the Chinese revolution, wrote:

"The Kanchow incidents taught us a precious lesson. We knew from that moment on—well before the split—that the conflict between the bourgeoisie and the Chinese working class would take on the bloody forms it has since assumed..."

But, in obedience to Stalin's policy, he kept silent on this and attacked Trotsky and the Trotskyists, who were warning the workers precisely of the inevitability of what happened.

From 1927 to 1933 he faithfully followed the policy of the Communist International, which made the victory of Hitler inevitable: the policy of denouncing the socialists as social fascists and refusing a united front with them against fascism. Doriot in France denounced Trotsky as a social fascist and counter revolutionary, as obediently as the rest of the hacks in the Comintern, for demanding a united front of socialists and communists to prevent Hitler from coming to power.

Doriot was expelled in 1934, after the "Communist" Party had demonstrated, together with the fascists, for the overthrow of the liberal government on February 6. He was expelled from the CP for proposing a united front against the fascist bands! But Doriot never joined the Trotskyists. Just the contrary. He continued his attacks against Trotsky and the Trotskyists. He had been corrupted too well by the cynical school of Stalinism. It was but a short step for him to go over to fascism and offer his services to the capitalist class. It is significant that on the road to fascism he tarried for a while in the Popular Front in France. For the whole of his political life Doriot fought against Trotsky and Trotskyism.

But to return to Wainwright. Having failed with his forgeries and lies in the pamphlet *Clear out Hitler's agents* to convince the workers and even the advanced workers in the CP itself of the truth of the slander that Trotskyists are fascists, Wainwright attempts, by a new series of quotations, to prove that the policy of the Trotskyists is the same as that of Doriot. This time he selects passages from the *Socialist Appeal*. Let us have a look at these "quotations":

"The treaty between the Soviet Union and British imperialism...is primarily a conspiracy." (*Socialist Appeal*, July 1942)

Now read the *Socialist Appeal* of July 1942, from which this is taken:

"The ruling class is not interested in the defeat of 'Hitlerism' as such.

They are concerned only once and for all, with destroying the power of their German rival and obtaining domination of Europe and as much of the world as they can hold."

"The defeat of Hitler opens out the prospect of revolution in Germany and in the whole of Europe—a revolution which could not fail to spread to the British Isles. The ruling class has collaborated with the Soviet Union only because of the way in which Russia has fought the war as a 'national' war and not as part of the international struggle of the working class."

"It was because of this that the imperialists of Britain and America could even afford themselves the luxury of giving the Soviet Union a certain amount of aid. But they now desire further guarantees that after the war their position of domination will be firmly entrenched throughout the world—i.e. that the revolutions, which are inevitable in Europe, should be crushed. This is the meaning of the treaty between the Soviet Union and British imperialism. It is primarily a conspiracy against the German and European working class."

This quotation speaks for itself. Let us examine the second quotation, selected by Wainwright:

"We have resolutely opposed the policy of 'pressing' Churchill for a second front." (*Socialist Appeal*, November 1942)

Now read the *Socialist Appeal* from where this is taken:

"As against the short sighted policy of support for Churchill and Roosevelt, we have urged the independence of the labour movement from the capitalist class: we have fought for workers' control of the sending of arms to Russia; and we have resolutely opposed the policy of 'pressing' Churchill for a second front, knowing that such a military move would be undertaken by the imperialists at the moment of their own choosing for their own aims of dismembering the Soviet Union and stifling the European revolution by wresting control from their hands."

It will be observed that Wainwright has to pretend that these quotations are the beginning and end of sentences and for this purpose he obligingly adds full stops and capital letters where none exist! Just an old fashioned Stalinist custom! Wainwright uses his quotations to "prove" that the Trotskyists are in favour of fascism and opposed to the Soviet Union. One glance at the *Socialist Appeal* reveals that the articles were directed to demonstrate the real policy of Churchill and the British ruling class and the dangers to which the false policy of Stalin and the Comintern were leading the Soviet Union and the world working class.

Leaving aside the question of whether the opinions and ideas were correct or not, that was the point of view which we revolutionary socialists hold, and we firmly believe events will prove us correct. We claim this is the Leninist point of view. Why then did this Stalinist hack have to resort to lies and deliberate misrepresentation? If our point of view is incorrect, surely it should not be too difficult to prove this? Here we get the difference between Leninism and Stalinism. Marx and Lenin prided themselves on the fact that never once in the thousands of articles and books they wrote did they distort or lie on the position adopted by an opponent. And indeed it would be impossible to ever find a lie or perversion in the writings of Marx or Lenin. And for a very simple reason. They were so convinced of the correctness of their policies, that they knew any worker comparing their ideas with those of their opponents could not fail to arrive at the conclusion that they were right. Lenin even advised his supporters among the workers to read his opponents! Furthermore, he taught that lies and slander were the weapons of capitalist reaction. The weapon of truth is the most powerful weapon of all.

It is this tradition which Trotsky handed on to the Fourth International. Stalinism resorts to the methods of lies and slander. Wainwright, as a Stalinist, is without honour, without truth and without conscience. Methods such as these can only train and create...Doriots!

As for us, we shall continue on the path of Marxism. No amount of lies, slander or persecution will prevent us from answering the capitalists and Stalinists with the weapon of truth. And in spite of all, the truth will prevail. Our policy and ideas will become the policy of the working class, including the majority of the rank and file members of the Communist Party.

Open letter to Yorkshire miners

By WIL

[*Socialist Appeal* Cortonwood supplement,
c. January 1943]

Comrades,

On Wednesday, December 23, the Council of the YMA carried a resolution which stated:

> "That this council meeting authorises the officials to take legal advice as to what action, if any, can be taken in regard to the articles which are continually appearing in *Socialist Appeal*."

This resolution is aimed to silence our criticism of Hall and the present leadership at Barnsley and its policy. It carries the campaign to suppress the *Socialist Appeal* initiated by Hall last July a step further. It is a police substitute for an open discussion before the miners of Wombwell and Yorkshire.

The *Socialist Appeal* has had some hard things to say about Joe Hall. So also do we say hard things about any working class "leader" whose policy is against the interests of the workers. These are mild, let it be said, in comparison with statements made to the *Socialist Appeal* by *hundreds* of miners about their "leaders".

Although Hall has had every opportunity to reply to a public challenge which was issued on July 18 1942, he has not availed himself of the opportunity and attempted to refute our charges.

His latest move is an act of desperation.

Meanwhile the so-called Communist Party members and sympathisers in the Yorkshire area are peddling the story that the Trotskyists and their paper, the *Socialist Appeal*, are responsible for the present strike at Cortonwood. Every miner who is familiar with the events leading up to the strike will immediately recognise this as a lie, and will brand it as such.

In peddling these lies the "communists" echo the slanders of Joe Hall whose allegations were completely exposed as the lies that they are in Parliament, when the coal owners and Tory representatives attempted to use his allegations to get the *Socialist Appeal* suppressed.

"Why does a political organisation interfere in an industrial dispute?" is the trick question which the fakers ask. Any miner who deludes himself that it is possible to separate industrial from political questions is making a grievous blunder.

When the coal owners say that the present strike "holds up production and helps the Nazis," *that is a political action*; the coal owners who were responsible for firing the first shot in the industrial field attempt to throw the *political* responsibility for the outcome of the dispute on to the shoulders of the workers. The action of the government in allowing the courts to be used to intimidate the colliers, *is a political action.* The action of Hall and his colleagues, of tying the hands of the miners behind their backs, giving up the right to strike, and collaborating with the coal owners and their capitalist government, *is a political action.* So also is the action of the renegade "communists" who have deserted the workers and appealed to the miners to accept the cut in the interests of the "war effort."

It is no accident that the coal owners who are Tories in politics embrace Joe Hall who claims to be Labour. Nor is it an accident that Joe Hall who was the most bitter opponent of the Stalinists 18 months ago, now embraces them and endorses the political activities of the Communist Party and Young Communist League, while the Stalinists quote Joe Hall with great favour. For all these people have the same political aim: support for the present capitalist coalition and its repressive legislation against the working class. No matter what they may say in private or in the bedroom about "socialism after the war," their public activities and present day actions is detrimental to the interests of the working class.

The Socialist Appeal *is the organ of Workers' International League, a Trotskyist political organisation which continues the policy of revolutionary socialism.* The policy which made the Russian revolution. We oppose the present capitalist coalition, its repressive legislation against the workers, and all its other actions detrimental to the working class. We do not believe that this capitalist coalition is interested in conducting a war for democracy nor that it is capable of doing so, since it uses repression against the people in the colonies as well as at home. We believe that the only people who are really interested in or capable of conducting a war against fascism and reaction are the working class, and for that reason we say that political power must be in the hands of the workers.

In our view, the only way in which coal production can be thoroughly organised is by the nationalisation of the pits without compensating the present owners, who have sucked the blood of the miners for long enough, and by the operation of the pits under the democratic control of miners and technicians, who are the only people really capable of solving the question of production.

In the present dispute we believe that any honest working class organisation must come out openly in defence of the Cortonwood miners and assist them to the maximum in their present struggle.

These actions are *political acts* for which we take full responsibility before the workers.

Workers' International League (Fourth International)

THE I.L.P. AND THE FOURTH INTERNATIONAL

In The Middle of the Road
1934

by LEON TROTSKY

TWOPENCE

Published by
WORKERS' INTERNATIONAL LEAGUE
FOURTH INTERNATIONAL

Wainwright blunders again on the Chinese revolution

By Ted Grant

[*Socialist Appeal*, Vol. 5 No. 5, February 1943]

William Wainwright, who has been selected by the Stalinists for the job of hack-in-chief, is still at the old game of lying and slander. It must be admitted that the Stalinists have chosen well. Wainwright seems to take a delight in wallowing in his filth, and returns to his distortions and lies like a dog return to his vomit. It is positively embarrassing to have to reply to the "arguments" which he adduces.

For sheer unadulterated hypocrisy and deceit it would be hard even for Goebbels to beat Wainwright when on the job of "exposing" the Trotskyists. Nevertheless, in the latest batch of falsehoods, Wainwright, as usual with the tribe of Ananias[1], has given hostages to fortune. Any member of the Communist Party or any honest worker deceived by Wainwright need just glance at the *Socialist Appeal* to see the unscrupulous mendacity of the leadership.

In his zeal to discredit the Trotskyists, Wainwright invents the story that Wang Ching-Wei, the Japanese Quisling, is...a Trotskyist! It is an old Stalinist trick to confuse the workers by denouncing every renegade and police agent as a Trotskyist, and thus engender a hatred and distrust of the revolutionary socialists. Says Wainwright in his latest outcrop of lies:

> "Wang Ching-Wei, whose puppet government at Nanking has declared war on Britain and USA, is a kind of Chinese Doriot."

> "In 1938, Wang visited Europe. On his return he went over to the Japs. Instead of his 'leftism', he and his paper now shout about 'Asia for

---

[1] Christian believers in the early Church did not consider their possessions to be their own, but they had all things in common. According to the *Acts of the Apostles*, Ananias and Sapphira sold their land and donated the profit to the apostles, but withheld a portion of the sales for themselves. When Ananias presented his donation to Peter he replied, "Why is it that Satan has so filled your heart that you have lied to the Holy Spirit?" Ananias died on the spot. Three hours later his wife told the same lie and suffered the same fate.

the Asiatics'. One more example of Trotskyism being a cover for fascism."

Poor Stalinist slanderer! It would have been better for him to have invented a more plausible tale, instead of one which will prove a boomerang to his party. This fool has wandered into a subject which the Stalinists would prefer to be forgotten—the Chinese revolution.

Needless to say, Wang Ching-Wei is a capitalist politician and was never in the working class movement. The closest he ever got was when, with Chiang Kai-Shek and the other leaders, the Kuomintang was accepted as a "sympathising section" of the Communist International against the vote and protest of Trotsky and the Left Opposition[2].

During the Chinese revolution of 1925-27, Stalin and the Comintern defended this quisling creature against the advice and warning of Trotsky, and thus doomed the Chinese workers to be butchered and slaughtered by him. Just as today Wainwright defends Churchill, de Gaulle, Sikorski, and other imperialist rulers from Leninist criticism and thus prepares, insofar as it depends upon him, a like fate for the British workers.

Here we reproduce a quotation given by H. Isaacs in *Tragedy of the Chinese Revolution*, which shows the real position in China at that time:

"...addressing the fifteenth congress of the Communist Party of the Soviet Union, Chitarov, relating the events at Wuhan, said: '...One thing was left out of sight in connection with this—that while the bourgeoisie was retreating from the revolution [!] the Wuhan government [Wang Ching-Wei was head of this government—EG] did not even think of leaving the bourgeoisie. Unfortunately, among the majority of our comrades, this was not understood; they had illusions with regard to the Wuhan government. They considered the Wuhan government almost an image, a prototype of the democratic dictatorship of the proletariat and peasantry.' "

But it was on May 18 at the eighth Plenum that Trotsky had warned:

"...The leaders of the Left Kuomintang of the type of Wang Ching-Wei and company will inevitably betray you if you follow the Wuhan heads instead of forming your own independent soviets. The agrarian revolution is a serious thing. Politicians of the Wang Ching-Wei type, under dif-

---

2 The Kuomintang was admitted to the Comintern early in 1926 as a sympathising party (with Trotsky alone voting against). Kuomintang representatives attended both the VI and VII plenums of the Executive Committee of the Communist International. This, just a few months before Chiang Kai-Shek turned against the Chinese CP with the March 20 1927, coup and massacred many of its leaders, smashing the rising of the workers of Shanghai in April 1927.

ficult conditions, will unite ten times with Chiang Kai-Shek against the workers and peasants."[3]

Stalin, on the other hand, told the workers to trust Wang Ching-Wei. In Stalin's own words:

> "...without a policy of close collaboration of the lefts and the communists inside the Kuomintang...the victory of the revolution is impossible."

It was not at all surprising therefore, that Wang Ching-Wei could appear in person as guest of honour at the opening of the fifth congress of the Chinese Communist Party in Hankow on April 27, and announce that he and his colleagues "gladly accepted the perspectives of the Communist International..."

Trotsky continued to warn the workers against the faith placed by Stalin in capitalist politicians of the stamp of Wang Ching-Wei. In the same speech he sounded the alarm:

> "We say directly to the Chinese peasants. The leaders of the Left Kuomintang of the type of Wang Ching-Wei and company will inevitably betray you if you follow the Wuhan heads instead of forming your own independent soviets...Politicians of the Wang Ching-Wei type, under difficult conditions, will unite ten times with Chiang Kai-Shek against the workers and peasants. Under such conditions two communists in a bourgeois government become impotent hostages, if not a direct mask for the preparation of a new blow against the working masses."

On May 28, Trotsky had written in a letter to the Plenum:

> "The agrarian revolution cannot be accomplished with the consent of Wang Ching-Wei, but in spite of Wang Ching-Wei and in struggle against him...But for this we need a really independent Communist Party, which does not implore the leaders but resolutely leads the masses. There is no other road and there can be none."[4]

But again his pleas and warnings were brushed aside, the eighth Plenum of the Communist International condemned him for advocating soviets, and adopted a resolution in support of the Wuhan government, of which the following is an extract:

> "The executive committee of the Communist International deems erroneous the point of view of those who underestimate the Hankow government and deny its reality, its great revolutionary role..."

---

3 Trotsky, *Second speech on the Chinese question*, May 1927. This quotation is repeated twice in the article.

4 Trotsky, *Hankow and Moscow*, May 28 1927.

"In the present conditions in China, the Communist Party is for the war waged by Hankow. It is responsible for the policy of the Wuhan government, into which it enters directly. It is for facilitating the tasks of this government by every means..."

If it is "responsible for the policy of the Wuhan government", then it acknowledges responsibility for the murder of hundreds of thousands of Chinese workers and peasants by this government in China, after the defeat of the revolution caused by this policy. All this, mark, in the interests of what they called "national unity against imperialism." In China too, the CP acted as strike breakers and tried to prevent the peasants from taking the land in the interests of an agreement with the Chinese capitalists and their spokesmen. The results were—horrible defeat and slaughter of the masses.

Throughout the world, and in Britain today the CP, having learned nothing from these events, carries out the same policy. Acting on Stalin's same instructions, they curry favour with the capitalists in the interest of what they call "national unity."

The results of such a policy cannot be different from the results in China. To those who teach the workers to place no reliance on the capitalists and their agents, they reply with slander and vilification. That is Wainwright's job. But in doing it he had better keep off history. On some future occasion we will reply to his lies on Doriot with facts and documents. But the mere fact that the CP have to resort to such methods, more befitting to fascist reaction, is an indication of their fear that our position is becoming known and sympathetically viewed by members of the Communist Party. Despite the lying Stalinist leadership we will win to our banner the best elements in the Communist Party.

5 – WIL's pre-conference documents and updates [August and December 1942]

Introduction

The tumultuous growth of the WIL is reflected in the works of its first national conference of August 1942 (which was curiously denominated "pre-conference"). The group that before the war organised around 30 members had developed as a national organisation with more than 300 members. The WIL, unlike most of the groups that gathered around the Left Opposition and the Fourth International, was mainly proletarian in composition, organising a large majority of young workers. The scope and quality of the publications reflected this numerical and qualitative growth.

The conference political document *Preparing for power*, drafted by Ted Grant, reflect the confidence of the whole organisation in the revolutionary future.

The strengthening of the WIL also posed in different terms the future of the forces of Trotskyism in Britain, as the organisation became a powerful pole of attraction for all the best elements in the many groups that split in the permanent crisis of the official section of the Fourth International, the Revolutionary Socialist League.

After being rejected as the official section of the Fourth International in 1938, thanks to the manoeuvres of Cannon, the WIL grew steadily while the RSL splintered. In August 1942 already the WIL had emerged as the principal force of British Trotskyism. The conference voted a resolution that we reproduce in this section to appeal to the IS to step back on the previous decision and accept the WIL as an official section.

The last document is a draft update on perspectives written by Ted Grant after the conference. This is an important document showing the development of the position of the WIL with the approach of the second half of the war.

WORKERS' INTERNATIONAL NEWS

Vol. 5, No. 6   SEPTEMBER, 1942.   THREEPENCE

PREPARING FOR POWER

Revolutionary Perspectives and the Tasks of the Fourth Internationalists in Britain.

Published by
WORKERS' INTERNATIONAL LEAGUE
FOURTH INTERNATIONAL

WIN, Preparing for power, cover, 1942 (Ted Grant Archive)

Preparing for power
Revolutionary perspectives and the tasks of the Fourth Internationalists in Britain

By Ted Grant

[*Workers' International News*, Vol. 5 No. 6, September 1942]

The text of the thesis adopted at the national pre-conference of Workers' International League, August 22 and 23 1942, as revised for publication.

Tasks and perspectives

The whole world is now involved in the agonies of the imperialist conflagration. The few remaining "neutrals" are neutral in name only. They have been compelled to restrict consumption of the very essentials of life just in the same way as the actual belligerents—and sometimes to an even greater extent. Besides this, most of them are turning out armaments to the peak of their capacity for one or another of the great powers—with all that this implies. Few of them will avoid the actual shedding of blood. Ireland, Spain, Portugal, Turkey, and even Vichy France[1] will all be involved in the war in one way or another.

The Fourth International predicted long in advance that wherever the war started, it would inevitably and very rapidly, envelop the whole world. Everything had pointed to this: the contradictions of capitalism which the growth of the productive forces had intensified and aggravated; the sharpening imperialist antagonisms throughout the world; the incapacity of the leadership of the Second and Third Internationals to solve these contradictions. Between the first and second world imperialist wars, terrible national and social antagonisms were engendered and aggravated. With the failure of the workers' leadership to take power out of the hands of the bourgeoisie, these led inevitably to world war.

But the developments which have given the war its universality have at the

---

[1] In June 1940 the French Prime Minister, Pétain, signed an armistice with Hitler which allowed one third of France to remain unoccupied, with a government based at Vichy. The Vichy regime collaborated with the Nazis.

same time, far from strengthening imperialism, weakened it in the extreme. The very contradictions which led the imperialists to seek a way out in war will lead directly to revolutions. It is no longer a question of attempting to estimate where the weak link in the chain of capitalism might be. There are no strong links. There is not a single country, not even mighty America, which has the possibility of escaping terrific social convulsions and even civil war. Just as no one could state for certain where the war would begin, so it is with the social revolution. It may be Japan, China, Germany, the continent of Europe, Britain, or perhaps a colonial revolt in Africa. But just as the war had to spread inevitably throughout the world, so will the social revolution spread from country to country and continent to continent—and at an even greater speed.

Britain's decline as a world power

The decline of Britain as the invincible mistress of almost half the world is best seen in the loss of her position on the seven seas. Britannia has ceased to rule the waves. America, even before she had fired a shot in either hemisphere, announced a programme of naval expansion which would alone assure her unchallengeable superiority in a sphere which Britain has for centuries considered her own exclusive preserve; and a sphere too, in which the loss of first position exposes Britain to particular vulnerability in any conflict with the new master. Britain is thus at the mercy of her transatlantic "saviour".

Not only metropolitan Britain, but the empire too is in this position. Australia has already passed under the direct domination of America. The Australian premier has openly proclaimed that they must look to America for succour. The pooling of the industry of the United States and Canada is but a pale reflection of the penetration of American finance capital into what is now but a province of the USA. New Zealand and South Africa, although not so far on the road, are already travelling in the same direction.

South America, which in the past provided one of the biggest fields for British investments, has now become an American preserve. In the Far East, the situation is just as gloomy for the British bourgeoisie. Not only have Malaya and Burma fallen to the Japanese, but China now looks to America for arms and subsidies in her war against Japan. And in India, American influence makes itself felt more and more.

The British bourgeoisie and their man of the hour, Churchill, are compelled to accept this overlordship of American imperialism. There is nothing else they can do. Defeat in the present war at the hands of Germany means the end of imperialist Britain as a power of the first rank. Victory will mean a less spectacular decline to a second rate position under the patronage of America. This is the best that the British ruling class can hope for. In reality the process of decline has been going on for many years before the war. The altering relationship of forces between the powers was bearing less and less relationship to Britain's nominal position. The shattering blows of German and Japanese imperialism have served to reveal the true position and exposed the senility and decay of British imperialism.

The revelation of this weakness, particularly through the Japanese advance, to the hundreds of millions of colonial slaves in the British empire will lead to action on their part on the morrow. The colonial masses are being stirred by mighty events out of their apathy and indifference. It will be impossible for the paralytic hand of Whitehall to keep them in continued enslavement.

In addition, the working class in Britain is becoming more conscious and critical of the old school tie blimps in the colonial service and the armed forces, whose stupidity and incompetence is but a reflection of the fact that the British bourgeois system has completely outlived itself. A realisation of the enfeeblement and decline of the ruling class is beginning to crystallise itself in the consciousness of the masses. A mood of criticism on the basis of the past defeats has penetrated all strata of the population.

Britain's internal situation

Even before the crisis of world capitalism had resolved itself into the agony of a protracted death struggle between the imperialist rivals for world domination, the ruling class had perceived the necessity for a violent settlement with the British workers. The whole policy of the guiding layer of the bourgeoisie in the years before the war was conditioned by a preoccupation with the problems and tasks of *civil war*.

While the leadership of the mighty mass organisations—trade unions, Labour Party, Communist Party, not to speak of the Independent Labour Party (ILP)—was lulling the masses with the soothing routine of parliamentarism, the leadership of finance capital, soberly assessing the situation, was overhauling its plans for an armed struggle with the masses.

In the two years preceding the present war, army manoeuvres were, for the first time, based on the assumption that civil war was raging in Britain.

All these plans of the ruling class (utopian in any event except in the case of the complete paralysis of the leadership of the workers' vanguard) have been shattered by the course of events. The war has resulted in the fusion of the army with the working class far more than in any other period in history. (It may be remarked in passing, that it is in an effort to minimise or overcome this that the bourgeoisie has spent so much effort in attempting to incite the soldiers against the workers by demagogically contrasting "high" wages of the workers with low rates of pay in the army.)

The almost complete destruction of the European labour movement in the past eight or nine years has been accompanied by an apparently inexplicable strengthening of the British labour and trade union bureaucracy. Alone on the European continent (with the unimportant exceptions of Switzerland and Sweden, which exist by gracious consent of Hitler) the British labour organisations remained intact. This is explained by the fact that while her rivals were preoccupied with internal social conflict or intensive preparations for the coming war, Britain managed, for the last time perhaps, to increase her trade to nearly all markets. By these means she was enabled to grant slight illusory concessions to the working masses. As a result the few years preceding the war were among the most peaceful in the history of British capitalism. The class struggle suffered a lull with far fewer and less bitter strikes on the industrial field. The labour and trade union bureaucracy became more than ever associated with the interests of the employers as obedient and interested servants.

Because of the super-exploitation of the colonial masses the British imperialists were enabled to grant concessions to a privileged stratum of the British working class, and even to a certain extent, to raise the level of the whole of the British workers above that of the European workers. Basing herself on this, Britain's industries became archaic and outdated, instead of advancing as in Germany and America, on the basis of modern technique. Hopelessly outmoded from a technical standpoint, she has been fighting on the shoulders of the colonies. But the war is having its full effect on the British economy.

In the first nine months of 1941 Britain spent £3,495,761,703, while her ordinary income during that period was only £1,221,567,147. Less than a decade ago in 1931, the financial oligarchy engineered a crisis in order to throw out the Labour government ostensibly because of its refusal to cut unemployment benefit by £2,000,000 per year. Today the deficit amounts to more than this sum in a fortnight, and all the burdens of this are laid on the shoulders of the workers.

In every sphere the ruling class has revealed its complete senility and incapacity to even conduct its *own* war. The corruption and incompetence industrially and militarily, raises sharply in the minds of the workers *the question of the regime*. In the factories, chaos, waste and mismanagement, the incapacity to organise production because of the fetters of the profit system, assume a particularly baleful character when counterposed to the ever-increasing exhortations for the workers to "go to it". This is especially so when military defeats are justified by the "lack of equipment". Meanwhile the combines and big monopolies are assuming a stranglehold on the economic life of the nation. An unbridled clique of monopoly capitalists who control the banks, armaments manufacture and food combines are drawing greater dividends today more than ever before. It is not merely the despoliation of the working class, but the middle class is being completely ruined. The small shopkeepers and business people, professionals and clerks have been hard hit by the war.

The decay of the ruling class is so great that big sections are beginning to lose confidence in themselves. For the moment they have no substitute for Churchill. The complaints of Conservative members of Parliament of the inefficiency in industry and the army are but a glimpse of the fissures and internecine strife which are opening out within the ranks of the ruling class. And this at a time when the masses are not yet moving into action! All these symptoms are a reflection of the profound processes taking place within British society. Deep disillusionment and discontent at the moment find no outlet, but are simmering deep within the masses. All the conditions for social explosions are rapidly maturing.

The possibilities of fascism in Britain

The reluctant taking up of arms by British imperialism to defend her interests, compelled her to base herself on the hatred of the population for fascism—and even demagogically and confusedly, to intensify this hatred. Automatically this compelled the ruling class to dispense with its reserve weapon—the organisation of Mosley[2] fascists. Robbed of his basis, like the fascists in occupied Europe, Mosley logically became an agent for German imperialism—a British Quisling. Under these circumstances he could not hope to retain what small support he had gained prior to the war. Fascism finds its mass basis essentially among the petty bourgeoisie and the most backward strata of the population. British fascism had not penetrated the decisive sections of the petty bourgeoisie, not to speak of the backward strata of the working class. Mosley's position was untenable and the capitalists were compelled to put him in a safe place (comfortably, to be sure) behind bars as a protection against the working class and a sop to public opinion. Not to have done so would have led to his being torn to pieces by an infuriated British working class. His organisation vanished from the scene. It can be seen therefore, that there can be no question of fascism in Britain in the period opening up. Mosley could only come to power on the basis of German bayonets.

The bourgeoisie has no reserve weapons at the present time. The ruined middle class; the dissatisfied workers; the lack of confidence of the rulers themselves: all lay the basis, not for a turn in the direction of fascism, but for the most revolutionary period in British history. The fragile basis for the rule of the bourgeoisie rests in the failure of the leadership of the workers to offer an alternative to capitalist rule, which they justify by the threat from "foreign fascism".

Nevertheless the distrust and hostility towards the ruling class is increasing

---

2 Oswald Mosley entered British politics as a Tory, switched to Labour, then split to form the New Party, which he transformed into the British Union of Fascists in 1932. Thereafter he organised various fascist groups. The term Quisling came from Vidkun Quisling, a Norwegian army officer and Nazi collaborator, who became "minister president" in Nazi occupied Norway from 1940.

within all strata of the population. The eyes of the workers cannot remain closed to the incapacity and corruption of bourgeois rule. It confronts them in every sphere of their daily lives. This awakening is preparing for a revolutionary wave of such titanic proportions that even the great struggles of Spain and France will appear Lilliputian.

Fascism could only arise in the event of the defeat of this movement resulting from the betrayal of the Labour and Stalinist parties, and if we do not succeed in gaining the support of the decisive section of the British workers. On the basis of such a defeat the bourgeoisie would gradually regain confidence and prepare for its revenge. Basing itself on the despairing middle class and even backward sections of the workers disappointed in the failure of the revolutionary wave, the bourgeoisie could, in a short space of time organise a fascist movement—a "British Empire Protection Society," or some such organisation—and attempt to establish a precarious rule by a bloody and horrible repression of the working class. Lacking a social base, faced with the fact that the working class is the decisive section of the population—75 percent—a fascist regime in this country would of necessity be even more ruthless than Franco's.

The role of the Labour Party in British society

Immediately after the declaration of the war, the cloven hoof of the bourgeoisie was revealed. Draconic legislation, which if carried out would turn Britain into a totalitarian state on the approved model, was placed on the statute book with the tacit support of the Labour leaders. Nevertheless, in contradistinction to the "democratic" ally, France, no immediate attempt was made to put these laws into effect. The French bourgeoisie was compelled by the severity of the social crisis and the bitter mood of the workers to carry its repressive legislation into immediate effect, and, in the last analysis, at the decisive moment—as a safeguard against their own masses—to surrender to Hitler.

The same military crisis which resulted in the obliteration of Blum, Jouhaux[3] and company in France, placed the Labour leaders in Britain more firmly in ministerial positions. Much more than in the last war the capitalists lean for support upon their Labour agents. The course of the struggle on the continent; the chains which German imperialism has riveted upon the conquered and subject peoples, enabled the Labour bureaucracy to move confidently and surely to the path of open surrender to the bourgeoisie. The working class, not without some murmuring, faced with no alternative that they could see other than Nazi totalitarianism or support for their "own" government, supported the entry of the Labour ministers into the government. Thus the wors-

---

3 Leon Blum Socialist Party Prime Minister in the 1936-37 Popular Front government, Leon Jouhaux general secretary of the trade union federation, the CGT (1909-40).

ened international position and the difficulties of British imperialism strengthened the role of the Labour bureaucracy in the internal calculations of the bourgeoisie. Morrison and Bevin have been placed in those posts where the bourgeoisie expected there would be the most pressure from the masses—Home
Security and Labour. Under the signpost "against Hitlerism" the Labour leaders
have called for the utmost exertion on the part of the workers as exemplified by
the "inspiring" "go to it" slogan of Morrison.

In the last war the ministerial coalition of Labour with the bourgeoisie which
commenced in 1915, was ended in 1917 through the pressure of the disillusioned
workers exasperated by the privations at home and the predatory imperialist
policy abroad. A tremendous effect was created by the Russian revolution which
had immediate repercussions in Britain. The widespread swing to the left was
reflected in the attitude of the Labour leaders, who, scenting danger, were compelled to put forward pseudo-revolutionary speeches to maintain their hold on
the rank and file.

The revolutionary left, which later crystallised into the Communist Party of
Great Britain, destroyed its chance of winning a mass basis, precisely because it
failed to understand the necessity of keeping in close touch with the unclear feelings and aspirations of the masses, which in their beginnings could not but be in
the direction of the Labour Party. As Lenin had occasion to lecture the ultra-
lefts: it is very useful to chronicle the crimes of the Labour bureaucracy but that
is not sufficient to win the masses. This was the key to the weakness of the revolutionary forces in the first years. It is the key to all the subsequent developments, coupled of course, with the betrayal of Stalinism.

The experience of the first Labour government once again demonstrated the
strong roots which reformism has within the working class. The Communist
Party, at that time not yet completely degenerated, failed to gain a mass support,
despite the fact that Labour had shown itself utterly incapable of introducing
even one major reform in the interests of the masses. The embittered toilers
turned from the political to the industrial struggle. A revolutionary radicalisation of the masses began. It reached its culmination and greatest expression in
the general strike of 1926. The trade union wing of the Labour bureaucracy were
compelled by the upward swing to place themselves at the head of the movement which they hated and dreaded, if that movement was not to get completely out of their control. In order to cloak their activities they utilised the Russian
trade unions through the Anglo-Russian Committee[4]. This they were enabled to
do because of the policies of Stalin.

The defeat of the general strike, instead of "finally" exposing the role of the

---

4 Formed in 1925 as a bloc of the trade union leaderships, it helped to give left
wing credentials to the British TUC leaders who were to betray the general
strike in 1926. The committee folded when they walked out from it in 1927.

Labour and trade union leaders to the organised workers, led to the reinforcement of the Labour bureaucracy. The striving of the masses found its outlet in the formation of the second Labour government. The debacle of 1931 soon followed; the leadership revealed its true colours and went openly over to the camp of the class enemy. Yet, despite this, the masses of workers, with ranks almost intact, remained under the banner of Labour. Not of course without inner convulsions; the pressure from within forced a split of the left wing—the ILP broke away from the Labour Party.

The swing to the left of the labour bureaucracy

Since the crisis of 1931, even before the outbreak of the war, the top stratum of the Labour and trade union bureaucracy has completely degenerated and become more closely integrated with the bourgeois state machine. Simultaneously, they have taken to the outlook and ideology of the bourgeoisie. While the capitalists lean more heavily upon these strata, the dialectic of the process reveals that under the pressure of events a section of the bureaucracy is becoming completely separated from any mass basis. The deeper this process evolves, the more will the bourgeoisie find itself leaning on a vacuum. It is only the temporary inertia and inaction of the workers which enables these leaders to play their present role. But the reawakening of the masses will destroy their basis completely. The Labour bureaucracy has always operated the Labour Party as an electoral machine. It was purely for this purpose that a certain amount of activity was tolerated. But with the outbreak of the war and the fusion of the bureaucracy with the bourgeois state, there is no activity for the Labour Party branches as such. Moreover, the bureaucracy finds any sign of life within the party irksome, as it can only bring the tops into collision with the rank and file. On the other hand the trade unions, which have always been the backbone of the Labour Party, are continuing their existence and becoming more lively. This is reflected in the move of millions of workers to become organised.

But the unions too are becoming alienated from the stratum of the bureaucracy which has entered the government and upon whom the bourgeoisie lean most heavily, thus forcing them to come into sharp collision with the workers. This is leading directly and inevitably to a split within the trade union and

---

5 Ramsay MacDonald was Prime Minister in the 1929-31 Labour government. When he was unable to gain support for cuts in unemployment benefit in 1931, he split from Labour to form a national government with the Tories and Liberals.

6 Walter Citrine was TUC general secretary 1925-47, Ernest Bevin general secretary of the TGWU 1921-40 and Minister of Labour in Churchill's wartime coalition. Aneurin Bevan was regarded as the leader of the left in the Labour Party (hence the term Bevanites used for lefts in the party in the 1940s and 1950s); editor of Tribune 1940-45. Harold Laski was chairman of the party 1945-50. Emanuel Shinwell was a cabinet minister 1945-51.

Labour bureaucracy. The MacDonald experience[5] will at a later stage, be enacted once again, but now with different social implications. This tendency is already visible in the preliminary skirmishes between Citrine and Bevin[6] on the one hand, and more glaringly in the development of a left wing within the Labour Party. Even in the distorted reflection of Parliament, the pressure of the rank and file is evidenced. Aneurin Bevan, Shinwell, Laski, etc., represent this tendency. The "revolt" on the issue of conscription of the masses but not of wealth is a first indication of what is to come. Although the "lefts" made haste to come to peace on the welcome pretext given by Japan's entry into the war, tomorrow the differences within the working class will assume wider and more bitter proportions.

A split in the Labour Party is inevitable. The thoroughly rotten and decayed elements of the extreme right wing will step over into the camp of the ruling class as did MacDonald. The left will be driven to break the coalition and form an open opposition in Parliament, and what is more, they will almost certainly gain a majority. In 1931, in spite of the demoralisation among the masses, only the most degraded and corrupt of the Labour bureaucracy went openly over to the camp of the class enemy.

Already at the first signs of a critical spirit awakening, the Labour "lefts" have been forced into opposition. On the basis of the rising wave of discontent with potential revolutionary implications, it is inevitable that the decisive section of the trade union and Labour bureaucrats, including the majority of the parliamentary representatives, will be forced into an open clash with the capitalist class and a breaking of the coalition. In words at least, they will assume an extremely radical attitude. This process will depend to a large extent on a number of factors; especially the events which take place on the military fronts. These will have a greater or lesser effect on the subjective consciousness of the British masses, heightening or lowering the growth of the mass movement. For example, continued defeats in the Far East on a background of Russian successes will incense the workers and hasten their differentiation and regroupment towards the left. On the other hand, a defeat of the Soviet Union would temporarily have profound repercussions on the British as well as the international working class. Under these circumstances the workers would see no alternative but to cling to the coat tails of the bourgeoisie. The activity of the Stalinists will delay the more extreme manifestations among the workers; nevertheless the processes taking place have an inexorable logic in their development and direction.

Whatever delays may be imposed, these cannot be of any great duration—even in the event of the greatest catastrophe the working class movement of the world has ever suffered—the defeat of the Soviet Union. Despite all the efforts of the Labour leaders to canalise and give a parliamentary expression to the movement of the workers, it will be impossible for them to succeed. In this period the

Tribune group of left social patriots will in all probability step forward as the main organising centre of the leftward swing.

The Communist Party

Despite the handicaps of Stalinist policy, the revolutionary traditions of the October revolution and the militant activity conducted by the party over a period of years, resulted in the key militants in a number of areas turning to the Communist Party. Nevertheless, the Stalinists succeeded in penetrating only the advanced layer of the working class without gaining a widespread support among the masses.

During the "anti-war" period, despite their adventurous industrial policy they succeeded in extending their influence among the advanced sections of the industrial workers. It is a fact that the untiring work of the best CP militants (without any real lead from above) redounded to the credit and prestige of the Communist Party. In South Wales and in some parts of Scotland they succeeded in capturing leading positions among the miners. On the Clydeside, among the most class-conscious sections of the British workers, their roots extend deep into the shipbuilding and engineering industry. In other parts of the country they have succeeded in gaining influential points of support. The National Council of Engineers and Allied Shop Stewards came completely under the domination of the CP. With the extension of the aircraft industry they bade fair to completely dominate the leadership of the workers. Indeed in the event of a big upsurge among the workers, the Communist Party had the opportunity to capture a leading role, as did the French Communist Party at the beginning of the stay-in strikes in France.

However, with the new turn to class collaboration and strikebreaking, some sections of the party, already disillusioned with the rapid shifts in the policy of the tops, have become bewildered and disoriented. Hundreds of the best militants in the local areas have been driven from the party as "Trotskyists" and "agents of Hitler". Meanwhile wide sections in the factories and unions which followed in the wake of Stalinism because of past militancy in the industrial field, have become alienated. This strike-breaking policy has made it possible, by bold and militant leadership in the factories and unions, to win over those politically unclear militants who followed in the wake of Stalinism in the past.

The prospects of the Communist Party are dependent greatly on the fortunes of the Soviet Union. The peculiar situation is developing by the logic of the struggle, that where the party has its greatest grip—among the advanced workers—here it is fast losing ground. But from the backward strata now coming into political activity partly on the basis of their chauvinism and partly by their association with Russia, the CP is recruiting a new membership up and down the country. This shift was particularly noticeable in the composition of the delegates to their 1942 conference where more than half the delegates had been in the party not more than three years. The new element replaces in greater numbers those who have dropped out in disillusionment or attempted opposition to the "new" policy. But of course these are not so active as those they are replacing. However, despite the turn, large numbers, with secret misgivings perhaps, even the big majority of former members remained within the party.

Big successes for the Soviet Union or the failure of Hitler's offensive cannot but lead to more support for "communism" which will find distorted expression in the Communist Party. Stalemate on the Eastern front will have a similar result. A complete destruction of the Soviet Union on the other hand would lead to the obliteration of the Stalinist tendency, the most corrupt section of the apparatus, as with Doriot[7] in France, going over directly to the bourgeoisie; another section fusing with the Labour and trade union bureaucracy; while the remainder will drop out of politics altogether.

Given the continued resistance of the Soviet Union, the revolutionary wave will lead inevitably to a temporary strengthening of the CP. But this influence could not be of long duration. The strike breaking policy which is already repelling a section of the advanced strata of the workers will force the workers away from the Stalinists.

Despite the expulsions and attempts to stifle criticism by the use of a police regime within the party, the discontent of the workers is reflected in the ranks of the party. A reflection of this is in the statement of the political bureau issued in mid-1942 which admits to the fact that more energy is expended by the party membership in discussing the electoral policy of support for the Tories than in carrying out the party's agitation for the "second front." This criticism, which extends to all aspects of party policy, has forced the leadership to allege that the Trotskyists have become members of the Young Communist League and Communist Party and are doing serious harm to the party. This opposition, which is essentially revolutionary, must be reached and gained as adherents to the Fourth International. From here some of the best forces of the Fourth International will be recruited.

The Independent Labour Party

After years of complete isolation from the masses, the ILP is beginning to revive. Numbers of workers, especially from the youth, disgusted with the policy of the Labour Party and hostile to Stalinism, particularly in its present shameless phase of support for Churchill, are moving towards the ILP. The "left" policy, veiling centrist confusion, has resulted in a definite increase in membership. Whereas in the last few years it had completely lost touch with the workers in

---

7 Jacques Doriot, a leading member of the French CP, was expelled in 1934. He moved sharply to the right and founded the pro-fascist French People's Party.

the trade unions and industrial movement, it is now beginning to penetrate the fringes of the movement. As the only opposition force at by-elections of national importance, it has gained a certain standing among the workers who are becoming disillusioned with the present government.

In addition, the long-standing tradition of the ILP within the working class as the left wing of the workers' movement makes it inevitable, that without any other organisation in sight, leftward moving workers should gravitate almost automatically towards the ILP.

A steady growth within the coming months and years will be inevitable. Revolutionary repercussions will push the more "left" section of the workers towards the ILP. Under these conditions the ILP will be one of the most important recruiting grounds for the revolutionary party. It is not excluded in the event of a mass upsurge, that a fusion of the extreme left of the Labour Party with the ILP will take place to form a new centrist organisation. But even if it became a mass party, the ILP could not exist as such for long. The conflicting currents within it would break out in fractional struggles; splits and disintegration would take place and speedily shatter it to pieces. Even the relative stability which was achieved by the POUM in the Spanish revolution could not be attained by the ILP. The present cohesion in the ILP is based on its divorce from the necessity of any real activity. Its entry into the arena of mass politics would doom it to complete destruction.

On the other hand, a change in the weathercocks of the Labour Party, always sensitive to the mood of the masses, might lead the ILP leadership to drag at the tail of the Labour Party. But on whatever course events drive the ILP, it is necessary that the organisation prepare now to influence the worker revolutionaries in that party. A great part of our activity must be devoted towards the ILP. Even now in large numbers of branches there are workers who are thoroughly dissatisfied with the rotten compromising policy of the parliamentary clique and the whole centrist leadership. They are looking for a way out, honestly and sincerely seeking the revolutionary policy of Bolshevism.

The older layer of confirmed and crusted centrists has been supplemented by a younger and fresher layer entering politics in large numbers of cases for the first time. Numbers have entered since the war and are not anchored to the ILP like the older and more conservative elements. Especially necessary is the supplementing of the pressure of the revolutionaries within by pressure on the ILP from the outside. Proposals for joint activity against the bourgeoisie as well as against the Stalinist slander campaigns, etc, can break down the hostility which the leadership attempts to foster towards the Trotskyists.

The Labour Party tactic

The tactic of our organisation up to and including the first eighteen months of the war was to place the main emphasis on the Labour Party and especially the Labour League of Youth. That this was correct up to the outbreak of the war was indicated by the orientation of the ILP. Finding themselves isolated from the mainstream of the workers' movement and falling into complete decay, the ILP was compelled by the force of events, to turn towards the mass organisation of the working class. The leadership entered into discussions and conducted negotiations for re-entry into the Labour Party.

That advice of Trotsky which they so carelessly rejected in 1934, to turn to the Labour Party, they tardily adopted before the outbreak of war, giving it an opportunist tinge, and found no other course except capitulation to the Labour leaders. At that stage it seemed the most likely course of events that the political awakening of the masses would move completely on the traditional course and pass through the Labour Party.

But the outbreak of the war cut across the development of events and produced a different pattern. In line with the development of the war, our group has radically altered its organisational perspectives.

Far from growing in activity and political membership, the Labour Party machine in most areas has fallen to pieces. Branches and wards, executives of divisions and towns do not meet for months on end.

Under these circumstances total submersion into the Labour Party could serve only to separate the revolutionaries from the real struggles of the workers. Such a perspective is farcical and can serve only as a cloak for complete inactivity. The whole idea motivating the entrist tactic is to enter a reformist or centrist organisation which is in a state of flux, where political life is at a high pitch, and where the membership is steadily moving towards the left. It is essentially a *short-term* perspective of work in a milieu where favourable prospects exist for obtaining results in a relatively short space of time. It is dictated principally by the isolation of the revolutionary forces and the relative difficulty of reaching the ear of the masses.

None of the conditions for such a tactic are in existence at the present time. Any organisation operating it is doomed to stagnation without possibility of growth. Under these conditions a radical reorientation of the vanguard becomes necessary. In those areas where the Labour Party still shows signs of life, consistent work can achieve results. But in distinction to the previous position such work must be subordinated to the general strategy of building the Fourth International Party.

At the present time, political life within the working class exists in the unions and in the factories. Most of the members of the Labour League of Youth have been called up to the armed forces or work long hours in industry. Already enfeebled by the heavy hand of Transport House[8], the League of Youth has disappeared as a political force. Only in isolated cases does the League still function. So that this most favourable ground for revolutionary activity has dried up. With the youth cut off and the masses conspicuously absent, what can be achieved from penetrating the Labour Party at the present time? The answer is nothing. Far more fruitful than concentrating on attempting to create the left wing in the Labour Party will be the concentration on the trade unions, factory and shop committees where the militant workers are to be found *in a mood receptive to revolutionary ideas.*

The situation dictates that our tasks lie in the preparation of cadres among the widest strata of the advanced workers; of pushing and making known our banner among the widest strata of the working class; and struggling for leadership amongst the reactionary and reformist organisations.

The present period is characterised by a radicalisation and ferment within the working class without a mass *political* vent for this dissatisfaction. Insofar as the workers are moving at all at present, they are expressing themselves on the industrial field.

At a later stage they will turn to the Labour Party. But to come to workers who are advanced enough to look for a road out—with the disguise of the "left wing of the Labour Party" is idiotic. These workers will turn to the ILP or the CP but not to the so-called "socialist left of the Labour Party".

The proponents of entry into the Labour Party have their eyes glued to the future visage of the Labour Party and not to its present posterior. Using the example of the last war, they argue, correctly enough, that the first big revolutionary wave will immediately revive the Labour Party. It is true that already symptoms of a turn to meet this wave are to be seen on the part of the Labour leaders, especially the most shifty section. The speeches, particularly of the miners' MPs are reflecting the growing exasperation of the masses. *But history never repeats itself in exactly the same way.* The masses of the workers, above all, the *advanced stratum*, have a certain scepticism and cynicism towards the Labour leaders. The experience of the last two decades and the collaboration with the Tories in the government, have not failed to leave traces behind them in the consciousness of the workers.

It is useless to base the tactics of today on the *possibilities* of tomorrow; or more precisely, without preparing the ground on the basis of the existing situation it will be impossible to influence the events of tomorrow. The immersion into the Labour Party now will not influence those masses who might enter tomorrow in the slightest degree. Meanwhile all the favourable opportunities to

---

8 Transport House, the headquarters of the TGWU and the Labour Party for many years.

raise the banner of the Fourth International which will be present in the coming period, will be missed. More and more the workers will tend to break the bonds with which the Labour leaders have tied them to the fortunes of capital and advance on the road to *independent* action.

Careful attention must be paid to the processes taking place within the working class, but the necessity remains for the main activity round the general agitational and transitional demands, including the demand that Labour break with the capitalists and take power on a socialist programme. In the present period such activity can only find full expression through the medium of an independent organisation.

If as the result of the mass upsurge, hundreds of thousands and millions participate actively in the organisation of the Labour Party, *then will come the time to enter*. The present task is to prepare the way by winning and training the advance guard of the working class. In any event it is absurd to be tied down to a fetishism of organisations by an undialectical and rigid approach which is exactly the opposite of a flexible, elastic tactic of entrism, as it was first developed and put forward.

Trade unions and factory committees

In Britain, more perhaps than in any other country in the world, a correct policy towards the trade unions and factory committees is necessary for a young revolutionary party. Without a correct attitude on this question, our organisation would doom itself to vegetate in sectarian isolation. This is especially the case today when the workers are beginning to stir and awaken from the period of relative "peace" in industry which followed the debacle of the Labour Party in 1931, and when the whole of the working class is undergoing a transformation in its outlook.

This awakening of the working class is shown by the number of strikes that are taking place in formerly backward areas which were only partially organised before the war. Commencing with the unrest among the miners—always a barometer of the temper of the British workers—which has been followed by strikes on one coalfield after another. Small strikes have taken place among the dockers, railwaymen, engineers and shipbuilding workers. All these have for the present been limited to a local scale. But they are the first rumblings that give warning of the coming eruption.

The bourgeoisie and the Labour bureaucracy are looking with alarm on these signs of discontent among the workers, and have been compelled to retreat and compromise. They are afraid that by too stubborn opposition, they might release forces beyond their power to control. This process, however, is developing in a contradictory fashion. It can be seen, for example, that despite the terrific discontent among the highly class conscious workers in South Wales and

Clydeside, no big movement is taking place in these traditional storm centres. The reason for this has not been unwillingness on the part of the workers to fight. It is the stranglehold exercised by the Stalinists over the shop stewards and leading militants in these districts. Undoubtedly, but for this feature, there would already have been a general strike on the Clydeside, at least among the shipbuilding workers. Had the Stalinists been pursuing their pseudo-left line of the "people's government" period, they would today be at the head of a mass movement throughout the country. It is no exaggeration to say that they would probably have captured the rank and file militants in every union in industry. But the changing of the party line after Hitler's attack on Russia, revealed the true face of Stalinism: the Communist Party has come forward as the principal strike-breaking force at the service of the ruling class.

This offers a tremendous opportunity to the Fourth International, and one which must be utilised to the fullest possible extent. Once again it must be emphasised—face to the factories, the unions, the factory committees!

It is impossible for the Stalinists to dam up the tide of militancy of the British workers for any length of time. Their attempts to divert it into joint production committees will merely serve to discredit them at a later stage. The workers will learn from experience that this road leads not so much to increased production as to increased slavery. Revolutionaries must take into account the attitude of the workers to the question of production. In a false and distorted fashion the Stalinists have themselves raised the question of "control" of production through these committees. Their failure to achieve results will lead the workers to draw the conclusions of workers' control on the morrow.

It is noteworthy that already throughout the country militants in the factories and trade unions are becoming aware of the role of joint production committees and the strike breaking role of the Stalinists. This is especially so where we have members who can crystallise this opposition mood.

In the past, the best workers who sought a militant industrial policy were almost automatically dragged in the wake of Stalinism—even where they did not support the whole policy of the Communist Party. Now, many of them are instinctively refusing to accept the Communist Party's class collaboration policy. Such workers can be won to the programme of the revolution. They must be won to that programme and to the banner of the Fourth International!

Today our transitional programme takes on flesh and blood before our eyes. The response to our industrial slogans and propaganda has underlined the vital importance of partial, transitional demands. Our tiny voice and our inadequate forces have received a wonderful response from that part of the working class we have been able to reach. With an energetic application of our transitional programme this influence can be increased a hundred-fold in the period which lies immediately ahead.

The Stalinists have added their shrieks to the hallelujah of the Labour leaders' chorus of "go back to work" just at the time when the workers are becoming increasingly opposed to the treachery of Transport House. The Stalinist demagogues are, of course, much more skilful in putting over their blackleg policy, but, armed with a correct programme and attitude, these gentlemen can be dealt with by our comrades on the spot.

The struggle must be waged against the trade union bureaucracy no less than against Stalinism. The propaganda to remove strike breakers from the leadership of the trade unions, now comes to the fore. Within the unions there is developing a critical attitude towards the leadership. Some of the local officials of the unions are becoming radicalised and are pushing forward as militant leaders. Others of the local officials have remained with the bureaucracy through inertia. Either they will learn, or they will have to be thrust aside. What is outstanding at the present time is that the rank and file are to the left of even the militant elements among the leadership. But only a tiny section of workers have drawn the logical conclusions from the sabotage of the leadership. The majority are in opposition to the strike breaking officialdom, but are not fully conscious of the next step in the struggle. It is our task to provide that consciousness. We must fight to renew even the topmost strata of the trade union leadership; we must fight to convert the unions into organs of the revolution.

Even more vital than work in the unions, is work among the shop stewards in the factories. These are directly under the pressure of the workers on the job, and this is assuring that old reformist elements (and now the Stalinists) are being replaced by a fresh layer of militants. Workers who previously took no active interest in union affairs are today being pushed to offer themselves as alternative "unofficial" stewards.

As the struggle develops it will extend through the efforts of the local leaders, to other factories; from single localities to a regional and finally to a national scale. Spontaneously the workers will create fighting committees on a local and national scale which will embrace not only one industry but all the industries in the areas affected. This movement will give expression to the long dormant energies and power of the British proletariat and will assume tremendous scope. The Stalinists and Labour leaders will use "left" phrases in attempts to divert these energies into the channels of the bourgeoisie. They will only succeed in this if we fail to play our part in the struggle.

The leadership of this movement can be won if our key militants in the decisive areas can give a lead to the workers. Our small forces must be trained and prepared to give leadership to the workers on all problems that face them in industry. Our opportunities in the factories are unlimited. With a correct policy and a true orientation we can grow at a tremendous pace, a pace that will enable us to face the gigantic tasks which confront us, with confidence. *Face to the unions, factories and factory committees.*

Britain entering a pre-revolutionary period

Among the backward elements in the ranks of both civilians and soldiers there is to be observed an undercurrent of reactionary and anti-Semitic moods. The bourgeoisie has attempted to canalise these tendencies to suit its own interests, particularly by giving its campaign against the black market, a veiled anti-Semitic slant. But these moods are not based on, and do not represent, the dominant current, which is to the left.

Under the influence of the war and of Britain's changed position in the world, profound processes are taking place in the consciousness of broad sections of the working class. The age-old "conservatism" of the British masses had its real basis in the privileged position of Britain in the markets of the world, and the super-exploitation of the colonial masses. Now with that foundation crumbling, so also is the outlook, upon which it had been built. The main burdens of the war are now being shifted on to the shoulders of the British workers. Millions of them have been violently torn out of their customary routine and inertia by the war. The basis of "family life" has been shattered.

Women, the most oppressed and backward strata of the working class, as well as the youth, have been forced into industry and the armed forces. The old conception of a "tranquil" and "ordered" existence is being shattered by events. And as the conditions of the masses have changed, so has their consciousness. They have become responsive to new ideas and perspectives. The old faith in the ruling class and the acceptance of the continued coexistence of classes has virtually vanished. The unemployed have become re-proletarianised and the demoralised elements placed under the discipline and organisation of the army and industry. Large sections of the middle class have been reduced to the level of proletarians and forced into the factories.

The mood of discontent simmering among the workers and middle class has had no outlet yet. In fact, a great deal of it has been directed, for the present, even into patriotic channels.

Aroused principally by the incompetence of the ruling class in "fighting fascism" and backed up by the lessons of France where the capitalist class acted as direct capitulators to Hitler, this discontent has found no channel which leads to a genuine fight against fascism. The Labour and Communist parties accept the continued rule of the capitalists, and utter shrill warnings that any break in "national unity" will mean victory for Hitler! The ILP offers only pacifism.

In spite of this, the molecular changes within the ranks of the workers have proceeded apace. The "Churchill myth" has passed its apogee and is now on the downward grade. The mood of the masses has become increasingly critical and its waves are beating ceaselessly against the walls of class collaboration. Despite the efforts of the Bevins and the Pollitts[9] to stop the first little gaps in the dyke with their fists, the mighty mass pressure cannot for long be resisted. In a short space of time the wall must crumble.

If the ruling class, under the threat of revolution, were to attempt to capitulate to Hitler as the French bourgeoisie did, they would immediately provoke an uprising among the masses. Such an attempt at capitulation would compel the Labour leaders to place themselves at the head of the masses in order to continue the war. Because of the feeling that would be aroused among the masses, and because their own heads would be at stake, they would be compelled to wage a struggle to take control into their own hands. At least the left wing would do so. This would immediately precipitate the socialist revolution. But such a development is improbable in the extreme.

If, on the other hand, complete victory over Germany and Japan were to be gained by Britain (in reality the USA) this too could not prevent revolutionary repercussions among the masses. The programme of finance capital is utopian and insane. The idea that the British masses would tolerate the forcible holding down of the continent of Europe and Asia, not to mention Africa, is absurd. Once the masses compare the glittering promises about "after the war", of which they are sceptical even today, their indignation will rise to unprecedented heights when confronted with reality.

Freed from the nightmare of victory for the Nazis, neither the workers nor the soldiers would tolerate for long the outcome of the conflict which the capitalist class is preparing. Revolutionary explosions would be inevitable.

The prospect of stalemate and a compromise peace is even more remote. The antagonisms which brought about the war and have been sharpened by it, have now reached an unbearable tensity. Compromise could only come after the contestants were completely exhausted and the whole world was drained dry. This could only lead to further explosions. Long before the war had reached such a stage, and it would require several years, the endurance of the masses would have reached breaking point and the stability of the imperialist regimes would be put to the test. Revolution would begin in Europe or Asia and alter the whole balance of forces.

All three possibilities in regard to the war, therefore, lead to the same conclusion. The struggle between the classes in Britain must inevitably lead to the socialist revolution.

In the event of the failure of the working class to show a way out of the cri-

---

9 Harry Pollitt was general secretary of the British Communist Party 1929-56, except during the period of the Stalin-Hitler pact, when he favoured a Soviet agreement with British instead of German imperialism.

sis in which the bourgeoisie has placed society, a terrible social and political reaction would rage in Britain. The worsened position of British imperialism in the world market would dictate the need for the bourgeoisie to destroy all working class resistance to its imposition of lower standards of living, etc. A failure of the coming revolutionary wave would provoke outbursts of despair and hopelessness among the petty bourgeoisie and the backward strata of the working class. Basing itself on this mood, the bourgeoisie would, within the shortest space of time, create a fascist party and attempt to obliterate the organisations of the working class. *But this reaction would only arise after a defeat of the inevitable revolution.*

Taking the situation as a whole, it can be seen that more favourable opportunities exist for the British Trotskyists and for the success of the socialist revolution in Britain than for almost any other country.

The British working class has not suffered a severe defeat since the general strike of 1926 and the debacle of Labour in the general election of 1931. No big class struggles were waged in the last years before the outbreak of the war. The British workers are fresh and unjaded. They possess an overwhelming weight in British society. Concentrated as it is in big industrial cities, London, Glasgow, Birmingham, Liverpool, Leeds, Manchester, Swansea, etc, the working class finds its preponderating social weight still further increased.

That two and a half years after the outbreak of the most sanguinary battle for survival among the imperialist powers, most of the democratic rights of the working class, although formally abolished, are still intact, is a testimonial not of the strength of British imperialism, but indicates its Achilles' heel.

The ruling class is compelled to seek salvation in deceit and demagogy rather than in force. The continued, if precarious, existence of democratic rights gives us possibilities of growth in the most favourable of conditions. It arises out of the necessity on the part of the ruling class to disguise their imperialist war as one between democracy and dictatorship. It also arises, of course from the present dependence of the bourgeoisie on the shell of the organisations of the working class. All this gives us a unique opportunity of conducting our work legally, unhampered by the trammels which fascism and occupation have attached to our comrades on the continent.

The future is ours

The possibility exists for an unprecedented growth in influence and numbers in the shortest possible time. Today the problem consists mainly in preparing the basis for a rapid increase in growth and influence. *The Workers' International League will grow with the growth of the left wing.* It is necessary to break sharply and consciously, as the group is already doing, with the psychology and perspectives of the past. The most difficult period is in the past—isolated membership and the hostility or indifference of the masses. Big movements and big events *which we can influence* are on the order of the day. The group must not be caught unawares by the development of events.

It is necessary that the membership systematically face the workers and penetrate among the masses. Above all, it is necessary to bring the Fourth International before the masses of the workers as an independent tendency.

It is necessary that the organisation face up critically to the most vital of all factors: *the leadership and the organisation are lagging behind the development of events*. Objectively, conditions are developing and have already developed, which make for the speediest and most favourable growth and entrenchment of our organisation. But the basic weakness lies in the lack of trained cadres. The membership is for the most part young and untrained and lacks theoretical education. The organisation, despite the leap in influence, still maintains for the most part the habits and attitude of mind of the past—that is, of propaganda circles rather than of branches for agitation among the masses. The difficulties and tasks of the past period of the group's life are still reflected in its ideas and work. *On the basis of the new perspective a sharp break must be made with the past*.

It can be stated without exaggeration that the decisive question of whether the organisation will be able to face up to events will be determined by whether the leadership and membership can base themselves thoroughly in the shortest space of time, on these perspectives and face up to implementing them in the day to day work of the organisation. To develop deep and firm roots and to become known as a tendency and organisation throughout the country, and above all, among the advanced workers in the factories is the basic task of the organisation.

The disproportion in the situation in Britain lies in the lack of relationship between the ripeness of the objective situation and the immaturity and weakness of our organisation. Prospects of a swift impulsion of the masses leading to a spectacular growth of the organisation on the lines of the POUM in the Spanish revolution are rooted in the situation. But only if we realise the scope of the tasks and possibilities which history has placed before us. We will rise to the situation only *if in the interim, skeleton cadres are built throughout the country*. These cadres would serve as the bones on which the body of a powerful organisation could be built up from the new and fresh recruits who will come towards us as the crisis develops.

These tasks must be accomplished. Our untrained and untested organisation, will, within a few years at most, be hurled into the turmoil of the revolution. The problem of the organisation, the problem of building the party, goes hand in hand with the revolutionary mobilisation of the masses. Every member must raise himself or herself to the understanding that the key to world history lies in our hands. The conquest of power is on the order of the day in Britain—but only if we find the road to the masses.

Revolutionary audacity can achieve everything. The organisation must consciously pose itself and see itself as the decisive factor in the situation. There will be no lack of possibilities for transforming ourselves from a tiny sect into a mass organisation on the wave of the revolution.

Resolution on military policy[1]

By Ted Grant

[*Original document*, WIL pre-conference, August 1942]

Capitalism in decline is accompanied and characterised by wars and revolutions. The defeat of the post-war revolutionary movements in Europe and the East has made it possible for the capitalist class to plunge the world once again into the nightmare of modern war and militarism. This is evidence of the complete impotence of capitalism; it underlines the inability of the capitalist class to organise society on a peaceful basis and harness the economic laws and productive processes in the interest of humanity as a whole. For the second time within twenty-five years capitalism has plunged humanity into the bloody maelstrom of universal war. Out of the last war the only victory that was gained by the proletariat was the Russian revolution. In all other countries the revolutionary movements were defeated principally because of the failure of the leadership. Because of this failure capitalism has been able to plunge the world into the Second World War.

The decay of capitalism during the past twenty-five years has manifested itself above all in the rise of fascism. The tearing up of the Versailles Treaty by Hitler in 1935 inaugurated a new era of super militarism which was to lead to the period in which the entire peoples and resources of the world would be directly or indirectly engaged in war.

All the major problems of capitalism, all social problems will now be solved by force and clash of arms. To protect its right to exploit the peoples; to protect its right to retain control of the means of production, the capitalist class has been compelled by the inexorable logic of its system to extend its militarism over the entire circumference of the earth. Gone is the period of small, select professional armies, separated by artificial barriers from the mass of the people. The entire populations, male and female in the metropolitan states, are drawn into the vortex of capitalist militarism and war. The present impasse in which mankind finds itself can only be ended by the victory of the proletarian revolu-

---

[1] This resolution, drafted by Ted Grant, was presented to the WIL pre-conference but deferred to the internal bullettin for further discussion. We have checked this version with a previous draft. All changes have been identified in the footnotes.

tion. This is an elementary task if humanity is to survive with its cultural achievements of the past centuries and not be plunged into a period of the most degenerate form of barbarism.

The new war comes in circumstances which are by no means a mere repetition of those of the first holocaust. This applies above all to the question o   f power. If conditions were ripe in Russia in 1917 for the proletarian Revolution in 1917, they have become incalculably more so in other countries in the intervening quarter of a century. The question of power is placed on the order of the day for Britain no less than for the rest of Europe and the world. As the *Transitional Programme* of the Fourth International puts it.

> "The economic prerequisites for the proletarian revolution has already in general achieved the highest point of fruition that can be reached under capitalism. The question of power is raised today against a background of universal militarism and in conditions which are not merely a repetition of those of the First World War, but are a profound extension and development. The revolutionary party must perforce take this into account; its policies must likewise be not a mere repetition, but an extension and development."

The question of "democracy versus fascism" has nothing to do with the present battle. The existence of competing groups of capitalists who strive for world markets is the basic cause of the present conflict and not at all the so-called "ideology" of nations. In the interests of their class, capitalist democrats become fascists on the morrow. German and Italian fascism have many allies in the camp of the "democracies". Polish, and other European fascists have found full freedom and accord within the "democratic" ranks.

The defeat of the Popular Front regime in Spain at the hands of fascism had already unmasked the deception, that a successful war against fascism can be conducted under the leadership of capitalist democracy. The war in Europe and the crushing victories of Hitler, actively aided by the greed and cowardice of the whole class of bourgeois democrats, has consummated the exposure. The sellout of the French ruling class; the miserable capitulation of Laval and Pétain; the role of Churchill and the British ruling class—who were aware of the negotiations of the French capitulation, but kept silent—all this served to shatter any illusion that [capitalist democracy is really capable of waging a struggle against fascism][2]. The capitalist "democrats" are willing to sacrifice millions of lives of the duped workers and toiling people but they are resolute in their refusal to sacrifice one inch of their territory or one ounce of their property in the interests of the "nation" as a whole. In the final analysis, to save themselves from the wrath of their own masses, they are prepared to call in the fascists in one coun-

---

[2] We include this line that was deleted in the final resolution, we presume accidentally.

try after another; to retain the control of their property in their own hands, they pass over to the enemy.

No less complete and devastating has been the crushing of the reformist illusion of a peaceful and gradual progress within capitalism and its gradual transformation into a socialist society. All organisations which based themselves on this conception have been shattered in Europe by the onward rush of fascism ad reaction. At best these organisations of the working class—the traditional Labour and trade union organisations—were based on peace. The first test of imperialist war has shattered them as living functioning organs. Parties of a centrist or a pacifist nature, whose most extreme and "revolutionary" [statements] were protests against the horrors of war, but which do not base themselves on the revolutionary struggle to end the system which gave rise to war—these parties were shattered when the first test came. Mere protests against the war are futile and cannot take the workers a single step forward in the struggle against fascism, militarism and war. The working class requires a positive programme which bases itself on war as the characteristic feature of the present epoch, and takes this as a starting point for practical actions, which must lead to the taking of power and transforming the war into a genuine struggle for the liberation of the peoples of Europe and the world from Hitler or another form of oppression.

The British workers found themselves becoming not only militarised, but facing a fascism armed to the teeth which had succeeded in conquering the whole of Europe. The rise of fascism and its recent gigantic military victories have not left the British workers unmoved. They have no wish to become part of Hitler's "new order". The unending chaos and incompetence of the capitalist class both in the industrial and military spheres has caused a highly critical mood to spring up among the masses. This mood has not been at all for "peace" with Hitler. It has on the contrary been aimed towards a more vigorous and a different sort of prosecution of the war. It is this desire of the masses for a genuine struggle against fascism that the Labour and communist parties exploit to chain the workers to accept "national unity" with the capitalist class. It is, however, only [in] the absence of a non-pacifist alternative with a loud enough voice, that the second and third internationals have succeeded in keeping this mood within the narrow cracking banks of the chauvinist channel.

For a revolutionary party to come before the workers with a programme of "peace" would mean that such a party would condemn itself to complete isolation from the masses. On this basis it would not win the sympathy of the masses but their hostility. The workers do not want to see a victory for Hitler; this is testified by the results of peace programmes in by-elections where pacifist candidates invariably lose their deposits. If a programme of power is to be put forward in present day circumstances it cannot be pacifist—it must be military.

Even in Russia in 1917 a purely negative answer on the question of the defence of the country, against foreign conquerors could not, as Trotsky has pointed out, win the masses "who did not want a foreign conqueror". Once Lenin had recognised that power was not a perspective of the more or less distant future but was on the order of the day, his propaganda in relation to the war became more positive. No longer was there merely refusal to defend the bourgeois fatherland but measures were advanced which, said Lenin, "cannot be introduced without transforming the predatory war into a just war, without transforming the war waged by the capitalists in the interests of the capitalists into a war waged by the proletariat in the interests of all the toilers and exploited". How much more is it necessary today to advance such measures and such a policy of transforming the imperialist war into a just revolutionary war.

The apologists for American and British imperialism, the Stalinists and the social democrats, as well as the pacifists and centrists of various shades, lie prostrate or stand aghast before the onrush of Hitler's gigantic machine. These apologists for capitalism, agents of the class enemy within the ranks of the workers, sew the seeds of pessimism and defeat within the ranks of the working class. Undermining proletarian independence, sabotaging the class instincts on the part of the workers, thrusting them into the stifling and treacherous embrace of the ruling class, they call upon the workers to accept its militarisation and its military programme[3]. A successful defence of the rights which the working class still retains and the genuine struggle against fascism whether from within or without can only be waged by the struggle for the conquest of power by the working class. The Fourth International ceaselessly explains to the workers the necessity for class independence, the necessity to place no hope or confidence in the struggle "against fascism" in the ruling class, but ceaseless tries to win the majority to the idea of transforming the war into a struggle for their socialist emancipation[4].

World War II has posed the question in an even more categorical manner than the last: which is to prevail—the dictatorship of the capitalists or the dictatorship of the proletariat? The reformist programmes have been destroyed one after another, but the programme of Leninism and Trotskyism has stood the test; when the workers of conquered Europe rise again, the programme of the Fourth International will head their armies. In this programme too the masses of the East and the Americans will find their liberation. In contrast to the pessimists who preach defeatist adaptation to their imperialist masters, WIL is

---

3 In the first draft this sentence was followed with: "and in so doing they lay the basis for the victory of fascism whether of the Anglo-American or German variety."

4 In the first draft, this sentence was followed with: "It is not a question of a refusal to defend the bourgeois fatherland, but of conquest of power by the working class and the defence of the proletarian fatherland."

based upon the unassailable optimism in the future of the working class. It prepares the workers not only for the seizure of power and the establishment of the dictatorship of the proletariat, but for the defence of the victorious proletarian fatherland from external reaction and fascist aggression, as well as the liberation of the European masses from fascism and capitalist reaction.

War and militarism, which crushes all other organisations and disrupts all other programmes within the ranks of the working class, has provided a new test for the programme and cadres of the Bolshevik current. In line with the new period, WIL adapts its programme and tactics to the new conditions imposed upon the working peoples. The present period in Britain is characterised by the organisation of the wider sections of the working class into the military machine. Our programme must therefore take this into consideration as the point of departure. We present to the workers their own class programme, independent of and counterposed to that of the ruling class.

Pacifism, which characterised the attitude of the majority of the socialist internationalists in the last war, was responsible for isolating the revolutionaries from all the currents of the revolution in the decisive section of the armed forces. In the present period when the greatest masses in the history of Britain are organised in the army, navy, air force and Home Guard, a pacifist policy on the part of the revolutionary party would be sterile and lead to impotence in the face of great events. Essentially proletarian in the composition of our organisation, pacifism has nowhere reared its head as a tendency in our ranks or tinged the individual members of our cadres. Thus the unity and solidarity within our ranks has made it possible to adopt a clear and unambiguous attitude toward the problem of militarisation; has made it possible to fully assimilate the military policy of our international movement.

The imperialist war is not our war. The militarisation of capitalism is not our militarisation. In the same way as we oppose the exploitation of the workers in the factories and workshops, so we oppose the exploitation of the workers by the capitalist military machine. Just as we opposed the preparations of the imperialists for war before it broke out into open conflict, so we oppose the war today and the class which conducts it. But the war is here. We did not choose the arena: once confronted with this objective situation we base our programme on it.

Only with the mass of the workers will it be possible to conquer power and establish the socialist revolution. In this period the masses in the armed forces are to play a decisive role. Just as we seek to take over control of the industrial organisation of the country in the interests of the proletarian revolution, so we seek to take over control of the military machine. The capitalists seek at all costs to retain control of the armed forces—in the final analysis this is the main instrument of their rule. To maintain control they have centred all power in the hand of a caste of aristocratic and bourgeois professional officers. They have deliberately created a mysterious cult out of military theory and military strategy. Money is lavished on select schools to train their sons in the arts of military leadership. All this with the object of keeping the masses in ignorance of military theory and retaining control of the military machine. Bourgeois privilege, partly hidden in civil life, is unmasked in all its most reactionary features in the bourgeois military machine.

Meanwhile three years of military defeats for British imperialism has succeeded in raising the class character of the officer caste before the workers [and] has succeeded in exposing their incompetence as military strategists. All sections of the population are now discussing strategy and the "blimp" characteristics of the officer caste. Trained in working class and democratic organisations and conceptions, the working class queries the dictatorial methods and caste system of the Higher Command. In such a situation an independent military policy for the workers is essential. Such a policy must strive to organise the workers on their own class lines within the military machine. It must simultaneously seek to organise the workers into independent proletarian military organisations, controlled and officered by the working class and by workers' organisations[5].

Our proletarian military policy is a decisive question which separates our tendency from all other parties of the working class. It is an independent military policy designed to supplement our general political policy for the seizure of power.

In the first place our programme seeks to defend the interests of the workers in uniform from the exploitation of the bourgeois state and its officer caste. We demand the abolition of the dictatorial military regulations, which were framed in a period of semi-feudalism, and their substitution by laws based upon genuine democracy. Abolition of life and death powers of the officers over the worker soldiers; abolition of court martials and the rigorous punishments which they enforce. We demand that all the privileges of the officer caste be abolished. The treatment of officers as equals except in line of duty.

We demand an adequate wage based upon industrial conditions and accepted trade union standards. No financial victimisation of the soldier worker by the bourgeois state.

---

5 The following sentence was deleted in the final version of the resolution: "Just as in times of peace we stood for the active formation of workers' defence corps to defend the working class organisations and rights from fascist and reactionary violence, so in war times we stand for the defence of our rights from fascist attack from within or without, and this can only be undertaken under the control of the workers themselves."

We demand the setting up of state-financed schools, controlled by the trade unions and labour organisations, where workers can be schooled the arts and tasks of military technique and strategy. No appointed officers by the bourgeoisie, but election of officers from the ranks.

All the time we seek to break down the last barriers which separate the worker soldier from his industrial brother: full civil rights for the military to participate in politics and to be represented in all the democratic bodies of the nation. We demand that the Home Guard be dissolved into a workers' militia embracing the whole of the population, male and female. Only such a military force can guarantee the working class against invasion, only such a force can guarantee the population against Pétainism.

All the time we seek to propagate and legislate our military programme. We demand that Labour conduct a struggle for the implementation of these demands in Parliament and country.

The Fourth International is the only international workers' party equipped with a scientific Marxist programme. Our tendency alone retains an unshakeable confidence in the working class and its socialist future. We alone are ready to meet the capitalist class in the period of universal militarisation on its own ground. In Britain, it is our party alone, Workers' International League, which seeks to organise and lead the proletarian struggle for power on the conditions of today.

SUMMARY

of the

Final Report

of the
Commission of Inquiry
into the Charges made
against Leon Trotsky
in the

MOSCOW
TRIALS

Published by
WORKERS'
INTERNATIONAL
PRESS

WIL pre-conference appeal to the International Secretariat of the Fourth International[1]

By Political Bureau of WIL

[Resolution, WIL pre-conference, August 1942]

To the International Secretariat of the Fourth International

Dear comrades,

This, the first national conference of Workers' International League, held under the conditions of semi-legality imposed upon us by the present war politics of the British bourgeoisie, sends greetings to the International Secretariat, expressing our solidarity with it and through it to all sections of the Fourth International throughout the world.

It takes this opportunity to reaffirm its acceptance of the *Transitional programme of the Fourth International* and *The imperialist war and the world proletarian revolution* as its basic documents and as the guide to our programme in Britain.

In addressing ourselves to you, we once again express, by the unanimous vote of our membership, the desire to be acknowledged as an official section of the Fourth International.

The international conference of 1938 rejected the appeal of Workers' International League (then only a small minority group) to be accepted as an official section of the Fourth International, or to be recognised as a sympathetic section. This decision on the part of the conference was based on an entirely incorrect estimation of the British movement and its various components. The conference placed its trust in the "Unified Revolutionary Socialist League" in the hands of C.L.R. James, of Maitland and Tait, of Starkey Jackson. Today the "unified" organisation has splintered into no less than five fragments; C.L.R. James is now with the Burnham-Schachtman revisionists (his deviation had

---

[1] We have checked the resolution passed by the WIL pre-conference against a draft. All changes have been identified in the footnotes.

been noted by the WIL comrades in 1937); Maitland and Tait have adopted the stand of "conscientious objectors" opposing the war on "ethical grounds" and have decisively broken with Bolshevism; Jackson[2] has almost completely disappeared from the political horizon of the revolutionary workers. Meanwhile, despite the loss of R. Lee who returned to South Africa due to illness, and contrary to the prediction of the conference that the WIL would splinter into fragments and finish in the mire, the WIL has attracted to its ranks *all* the genuine militants of our tendency in Britain and stands today as the *only* representative of the Fourth International with a voice among the British working class.

In order to assist the IS in arriving at a correct decision, we present a short factual summary of the early development of the Fourth International in this country as well as a complete statement on the present situation on the forces of the British Trotskyists, especially since the "peace and unity" agreement signed in 1938 and adopted by the foundation conference of the Fourth International.

The initial cadres of the left opposition in the Communist Party of Great Britain were in the main petty bourgeois with a general low understanding of Bolshevik theory and a particularly low understanding of the practice of Bolshevik organisation. Its ideas were borrowed wholesale from the international left opposition, in particular from the American section. It made no attempt to concretise these ideas for Britain.

The spirit of a petty bourgeois discussion circle was fostered. No real attempt was made to acquaint the youth members and sympathisers of the theoretical differences between the Bolshevik Leninists and the Stalinist bureaucracy, nationally or internationally, or with the programme of the opposition. The leadership showed the greatest incapacity to train the younger elements or to conduct any decisive political action. Consequently the political level of the British opposition lagged behind that of almost every section of our movement internationally. These factors had an extremely demoralising effect on the worker elements within our ranks and among the contacts drawing close to our tendency.

It was possible for this loose collection of individuals to hold together while the general campaign for re-entry into the communist parties was the policy of the International Left Opposition, for in this country it enabled them to appear in public as "critics"[3] while binding them to no real programme of activity.

However, when the German betrayal revealed the full depths of Stalinist degeneracy, and impelled the International to consider the reform of the Comintern no longer possible and the perspective of the orientation towards the

---

2 In the draft it said: "and Harber".

3 We include the words "as 'critics' " from the draft, which we presume were mistakenly omitted in the final resolution.

new International was adopted, the semi anarchistic character of the British Bolshevik Leninists was revealed and their basic weaknesses exposed.

The directive given to the British section was a turn towards the centrist organisations as the main field of work. This perspective worked out by comrade Trotsky was fundamentally correct, but the tactic resulted in miserable failure due to the complete incapacity of the Trotskyists to carry this tactic out.

This turn towards the centrists marked the first of what was to be a series of disastrous splits. Incapable of acting as a unified body, the opposition burst asunder, one group entering the ILP, the other the Labour Party. This initial split took place without any thorough discussion or preparation, the factional lines running parallel to the personal alliances of the various individuals.

From 1934 until 1938 a continual series of splits took place. The "factions" were characterised by a core who, generally speaking, broke along lines of personal affiliation. The few who remained on the periphery of these "factions"— mainly fresh elements just turning to the Bolshevik-Leninist viewpoint—moved aimlessly from one faction to the other seeking a lead.

The Oehler split[4] in America came as a godsend to the various factions. A new variant arose in resplendent garb. "The principle of the independence of the Bolshevik Party" became the centre of the "new" and "higher" forms of political discussion. The axis of life changed and it now became possible to rationalise the lack of political decision. Since the "independents" borrowed their ideas for their use value, never once was a serious document produced for a genuine discussion.

During the whole of this period the International was completely misinformed as to the real situation in the British movement, either in its strength, what forms of work it carried out, its support among the workers or in any other aspect of its activities[5]. The survey of the archives of the IS will bear witness to this.

The Trotskyist groups which had evolved and disappeared were myriad. The Communist Left Opposition, the Marxist League, the Marxist Group, the Chelsea Action Group, the Revolutionary Socialist League[6], the Revolutionary Workers' League and the Workers' International League—all these in the London area alone, although others developed from time to time in the provinces. By September 1938 there were three distinct groups in existence in

---

[4] The draft text read: "The French party's turn to the Socialist Party and the Oehler split..."

[5] In the final resolution the following sentence was omitted: "The loose connection between the IS and the British movement facilitated this process."

[6] The draft added the "Unified Revolutionary Socialist League-Militant Labour League".

the London area—the Revolutionary Socialist League, the Militant Group and Workers' International League. In Edinburgh there was a grouping progressively evolving from the De Leonist standpoint to the programme of the Fourth International, the Revolutionary Socialist Party.

Added to these was an amorphous grouping containing some of the earliest leaders of the opposition, Groves, Sara, Wicks, Dewar, who while proclaiming themselves Trotskyists remained on the periphery of the Bolshevik movement and finally covered up Groves' capitulation to the Labour Party bureaucracy.

Each year without fail, a "unity" conference was called but without any serious preparation or intention. The soft elements who had proved incapable of any continuity of organised work appeared on the platform and played a preponderant role in the "discussions." Each year it became more and more obvious that a genuine unification among the old elements was precluded because of the determination of the "leaders" to retain their independence and because of the absence of a genuine ranks and file[7].

Such was the state in the British movement when the "peace and unity" conference was held in September 1938. In the bulletin circulated for pre-conference discussion, a copy of which is no doubt in the hands of the IS, the thesis of the WIL—*Tasks of the Bolshevik Leninists in Britain*[8]—was the only serious attempt to analyse the perspectives in the British labour movement and to outline the basic tactic which should govern our work.

The outcome of this conference is well known to the IS. Three groups, the RSL, MLL and RSP signed the unity agreement, the WIL remained outside. Arising from this conference two major decisions were made by the foundation conference of the Fourth International in relation to Britain, decisions voted on by none other than D. D. Harber, C. L. R. James and F. Maitland! These were:

1) It accepted the "unified" organisation set up in Britain—the RSL-MLL—as the official section of the Fourth and proclaimed that this unified grouping would have the full political, moral and material support of the International.

2) It rejected the application of WIL that it be recognised as an official or even a sympathetic section, attacking WIL for its "unprincipled clique politics" and proclaiming its inevitable degeneration and collapse.

Hardly had the ink dried on the "peace and unity" agreement and the American delegates departed for home when the cracks in the "unified" movement began to appear. These cracks rapidly widened into splits as the result of what we characterised in our document to the foundation conference as "a compromise with sectarianism."

---

7 In the final resolution the following sentence was omitted: "It was evident that unification would only take place on the basis of a programme of *work*."

8 Published in this volume.

The Edinburgh RSP broke away. The "lefts" followed suit, setting up the RSL which they proclaimed as the "official section of the 4th in Britain" since the official RSL-MLL, entrists in the Labour Party, had no open status as such. This was followed by a general disintegration of the majority of such provincial contacts or groups as the RSL-MLL retained.

Once again the old situation appertained but, as the result of the mistaken[9] intervention of the IS, it was more chaotic than at any time in the past.

During this period WIL continued its work. That we suffered to a certain extent from the denunciation by the International we will not deny[10]. But the general harmony within our ranks and the absence of any marked personal struggle coupled with a clear cut political perspective gave us a marked superiority in the orientation and organisation of our cadres.

A new phase began in the development of our movement. Whereas the years 1934 to 1939 witnessed a series of interminable splits, superficial reunifications, and splits again, the last year 1939 to 1940 has marked a period of genuine unification within the framework of WIL.

Provincial sections of the various groupings have one by one approached WIL for membership. The RWL had evolved from the official RSL-MLL disbanded[11], the large majority of its membership unconditionally entering the ranks of the WIL, the "leadership" retiring into the political wilderness. Resulting from the adoption of a resolution on the part of the majority member-

---

9 The draft read "unfortunate".

10 The draft read "is undoubted".

11 The following paragraph was cut: "The RWL which had evolved from the official RSL-MLL disbanded on the adoption of a resolution, 'that this organisation dissolves itself and that its members enter the WIL organisation...' The mover of the motion stated: 'I am moving this in view of the unification of the Trotskyist forces which is taking place within Workers' International League (the MLL is disintegrating, some of its best forces having already joined the WIL and others are likely to do so in the immediate future). Nobody suggests that the WIL is perfect nor does this entry mean that individual comrades retract any of the criticisms made in the past of the WIL. All this proposed entry means is that since there is a general and basic agreement on the *Transitional programme of the Fourth International* by the comrades of the WIL, the WIL today provides the nucleus for what we all hope will be the *real* British section of the Fourth, the revolutionary party. I am moving this resolution in the spirit that if it is accepted by the comrades, the entry into the WIL will not be made with the aim of building factions, cliques or "capturing the WIL", but with the honest intention of working together in the loyal spirit of comradeship.' "

ship of the RSP to enter the ranks of WIL[12] and become its Edinburgh local, the "leadership" of three expelled the entire membership resulting in their entry into our ranks and the isolation of Maitland and Tait from the militant revolutionaries in Edinburgh.

At the same time the membership of WIL rejected the proposals of the Molinier and his agents who were sent here to place before it the policy of this anti-Trotskyist sect.

The present situation finds the British Trotskyist movement in a more favourable situation than at any time in its history but one which is none the less unsatisfactory. The official recognised section of our movement, the RSL-MLL, has at all intents and purposes, collapsed. The comrades of the IS are aware that we are not given to overstatement in the interests of factional struggle. The MLL, a paper organisation within the Labour Party without a vestige of support in the rank and file of the Labour Party, was ignominiously thrown out by the Labour bureaucracy without a ripple. Not a single branch protested to the LP conference at its expulsion in May 1940. The last issue of the *Militant* appeared in June. It produces no publication, it holds no meetings, it conducts no discussion circles. In name it retains status of the British section of the Fourth International, in fact it has completely collapsed.

In contrast to this the WIL has moved slowly but steadily ahead. We have produced *every* important document of our international movement and sold them in thousands. The *semblance* of a genuine national organisation has been formed. Militants from our ranks play a leading role in workers' struggles in many parts of the country—in the trade union and the shop stewards' movement, particularly in heavy industry our comrades' voices are heard at conventions of the working class, a new feature in British Trotskyism. Our publications have appeared regularly and under the most adverse conditions and today they are the accepted Trotskyist publications in Britain.

Simultaneously with this advance in Britain we planted the flag of the Fourth International on Irish soil, having organised and developed the Irish section of the Fourth International which has made significant advances on the basis of the correct application of our tactic of entry into the Irish Labour Party. We hold leading positions on the Dublin constituency council of the Irish Labour Party.

---

[12] The following paragraph was cut: "In Edinburgh, a resolution was adopted in the Revolutionary Socialist Party that 'the RSP adopts the perspective of WIL and its tactic in building the revolutionary party of the Fourth International in Britain. It therefore terminates its independent existence as the Edinburgh RSP and becomes the Edinburgh local of WIL, accepting the discipline of WIL and operating under its central leadership. Because of the special conditions in the locality, the open propaganda platform now run by the RSP be continued under the control of the local section of WIL.' "

The leadership of the Dublin unemployed workers' movement is in the hands of the Irish section of the Fourth International. Our comrades have been imprisoned on several occasions as the result of their militant leadership of the Irish workers' struggles. The Catholic Action has been forced to conduct an extensive campaign through the Jesuit controlled paper—the *Catholic Standard*—against "the communists who are in the Labour Party under the direct instructions of Trotsky."

The consistent record of work conducted by WIL, the general collapse of the RSL-MLL at present recognised as the official section of the Fourth International in Britain, the fact that the voice of the Fourth International finds expression only through organs of WIL in this country, these underscore our request to official recognition as the British section of our tendency.

For the victory of the Fourth International in Britain.

For the victory of the Fourth International throughout the world.

INFORMATION

YOU MAY WANT TO KEEP

WHAT are Trotskyists? They are so called because of their professed adherence to Leon Trotsky who was banished from Russia for attempting to organise the downfall of the Soviet State. Later, Trotsky was convicted of contacting representatives of the German General Staff in an attempt to organise a Fifth Column in Russia.

This Fifth Column was unearthed by the Russians between 1937 and 1938. Some of them held important positions in Governmental and Army departments. They were tried, found guilty of assassination, wrecking, organising a network of spies for Germany, and planning to take advantage of war between Germany and Russia to overthrow the Soviet State. They confessed to have made contact with Hess. These Quislings were convicted. Many were shot. Some were imprisoned. **That is why there is no Fifth Column and no Quisling in Russia today.**

In France, the Trotskyists were active in disrupting the People's Front and sabotaging the French Alliance with Russia. Their leader, Doriot, was proved to have received Nazi money for his work. Today, he runs a newspaper for the Nazis in the country he helped to defeat.

In Spain, the Trotskyists were active in disrupting the unity of the people behind the Republican Government. They spread Nazi lies about Negrin. They staged an armed uprising to assist General Franco, Hitler and Mussolini.

In Britain they fought against the proposed Anglo-Soviet Alliance before the war, helping Hitler. They openly called for the violent overthrow of the Soviet State.

There are not many of them. But they are a virus that must be cleaned out of all contact with working-class organisations.

TREAT THE TROTSKYIST

AS YOU WOULD A NAZI

Issued by the Communist Party of Great Britain, 16 King St., London, W.C.2, and printed by the Marston Printing Co. (T.U. all depts.), at Beechwood Works, Beechwood Rise, Watford, Herts.

Stalinist propaganda put out against the WIL

Constitution of WIL (1942)

[*Workers' International News*, Vol. 5 No. 6,
September 1942]

Article 1. Name:

Workers' International League (Fourth International).

Article 2. Aim:

Workers' International League aims to organise the working class for the establishment of a workers' government (the dictatorship of the proletariat) which will end the present system of capitalist ownership of the land and the means of producing wealth and substitute in its stead the common ownership and workers' control of these means of production.

Article 3. Membership:

(a) Any person who accepts the principles and Constitution of WIL and who participates in its activities under the direction of the local, district and national bodies, is eligible for membership of the organisation.

(b) Application for membership shall be made in writing on the prescribed application form, or in such manner as may be directed by the CC and must be endorsed by two full members of the organisation.

(c) On acceptance in the local by a majority of members, application will be forwarded to the district committee for ratification or rejection and from there forwarded to the Central Committee for entry into the party register.

(d) Where no local of WIL exists, application for membership may be made direct to the district committee or Central Committee.

(e) Applicants accepted by the district committee shall be probationary members for three months, at the end of which period the application is reviewed by the district committee who will decide to admit the applicant to full membership, extend the period of probation, or exclude the probationary member.

(f) A probationary member may be expelled or admitted into full membership before the termination of the full three months probation.

(g) Members on probation are entitled to a voice on any question, but may not vote and are not eligible to serve as officials of the organisation or members of the district committee.

Article 4. Locals:

(a) The unit of WIL is the "local", which is based on an industrial or area group of not less than five. Where the local exceeds thirty members the district committee have the right to divide it into separate locals.

(b) Each local shall meet at least once weekly, elect officials once a quarter and conduct its business in accordance with the standing orders guide.

(c) Each local has the power within the limits of the Constitution to conduct its own business and procedure in accordance with the desires of its members.

(d) Locals shall elect, where necessary, a committee of not less than three, to facilitate the business of the organisation.

(e) Locals shall acquire premises and technical apparatus to conduct the business of the organisation in accordance with membership and financial position.

Article 5. District committee:

(a) District committees shall be set up in the following districts: London, Midlands, Yorkshire, Lancashire and North West England, North and North East England, Scotland, Wales; or in such districts as the national conference or Central Committee shall decide, and shall be constituted from delegates from locals within the established district. Large isolated locals may apply to the Central Committee for the same rights as district committees.

(b) District committees shall consist of delegates from not less than three locals, appoint all district officers and shall meet every month.

(c) District committees are responsible for the direction of all local activities in the district and have the power, within the limits of the Constitution, to decide their own procedure and business in accordance with the desires of district committee.

Article 6. National conference:

(a) A national conference of the membership represented by delegates from each organisational unit: local, district committees and Central Committee, shall be convened each year by the Central Committee and shall constitute the highest body of WIL.

(b) Locals are entitled to send delegates to national conference on the basis of one delegate for every 20 members or part of twenty, and shall contribute towards the fares in accordance with the number of delegates.

(c) District committees consisting of five or more locals are entitled to send delegates to the national conference and shall contribute towards the pool fare.

(d) Delegates to national conference shall be elected by ballot.

(e) Members are eligible for election as delegates to conference after completing six months full membership of WIL.

(f) Where locals exist which have no members who have the necessary qualifications as delegates, or where locals desire to send a delegate who is without the necessary membership qualification, they may be represented at conference by special application to the Central Committee which may grant voting and/or vocal rights.

(g) Locals and district committees are entitled to submit resolutions to conference agenda: CC resolutions to be submitted to the membership at least two months prior to national conference; final resolutions, together with the report of the CC shall be submitted to the membership at least three weeks prior to the national conference.

(h) Conference shall be ruled by a standing orders committee elected by conference.

Conference voting:

No binding mandate to its delegate by any body shall be recognised by conference. All delegates to conference shall participate with a free vote.

Decisions at conference:

Decisions at national conference shall be reached by simple majority.

Article 7. Central Committee:

(a) Between national conference full authority shall be vested in the hands of a Central Committee elected at conference by ballot and consisting of fifteen members.

(b) The Central Committee shall elect a political and organisational bureau for the conduct of its activities and shall meet at least every two months.

(c) The political bureau shall be in permanent session and shall be set up from full time and London members of the Central Committee and shall function from central headquarters, having full powers of national conference in between sittings of the Central Committee.

Article 8. National council:

(a) A national council shall be set up consisting of the Central Committee plus a delegate from each district committee and shall meet at least once every four months.

(b) The national council shall be an advisory body except as specified in article 9 and shall be responsible for maintaining close contact between the national members and the Central Committee.

Article 9. Special conferences:

Special conferences with the same power as annual conference may be called by the Central Committee or by more than one third of the national council.

Article 10. Amendments to Constitution:

Amendments to Constitution may be adopted by a simple majority at the national conference.

Article 11. Special powers:

In the event of an emergency, the constitution is suspended and all powers shall be delegated to the Central Committee or such committees as it may set up.

Article 12. Membership contribution:

Dues:

(a) Dues of WIL shall be a minimum of 1s per week to be divided into three parts: 6d shall be forwarded by the local treasurer to the Central Committee on the first of each month; 4d shall be retained by the local for its own funds; and 2d shall be forwarded to the district committee on the first of each month.

(b) Members two calendar months in arrears of dues are considered lapsed after due notice of arrears has been given, unless special application for reconsideration is made to the district committee.

(c) The district committee and Central Committee have the right to modify the dues of any member in the event of special application.

(d) Locals two months in arrears of dues shall be considered suspended by the Central Committee after due notice has been given.

(e) Members who are not fully paid up shall not be eligible for election as delegates to any conference or committee.

(f) Levies: locals, district committees and Central Committee have the right to impose levies on the members within the limits of the Constitution.

(g) Locals and district committees shall issue quarterly balance sheets of all finances in accordance with local standing orders guide.

(h) The Central Committee shall issue a balance sheet of all finances to each national conference.

Article 13. Democratic rights and discipline:

(a) The majority decisions of any body are binding on all the members within its jurisdiction.

(b) While co-operating in carrying out the decisions of the majority, all minorities have the right to express dissenting opinions within the organisation, to circularise the membership with any material stating these opinions, and to appeal to higher bodies against any decision with which they disagree. The Central Committee shall maintain a theoretical or internal discussion bulletin as a medium for expressing such dissenting opinions and shall publish material submitted for discussion within twenty-one days of receipt.

(c) The national conference shall define the limits of any discussion.

(d) Disciplinary action, including censure, reduction to probationary membership, suspension of membership, and expulsion may be taken by the body having jurisdiction against any member committing a breach of discipline or acting in a manner detrimental to the interests of WIL and of the working class.

(e) Charges against any member must be made in writing and the accused furnished with a copy; such charges are considered by the local at a meeting to which the accused member is invited and the recommendation of the local is acted upon by the district committee.

(f) Any member subjected to disciplinary action is entitled to appeal to the next higher body or to the annual conference, the disciplinary action in the meanwhile is upheld.

Article 14:

All who accept the principles and constitution of WIL hereby dedicate themselves to the task of fulfilling its aims and are required to enter the mass organisations of the working class for the purpose of fulfilling these aims.

Report of pre-conference, August 1942

By Political Bureau of WIL

[WIL, *Internal circular*]

The first national meeting of our organisation, our pre-conference, has now been concluded. Discussions were held on all the main political questions, India, industry, the new Constitution and the perspectives. A resolution on military policy was referred to the *Internal Bulletin* due to the lack of time and to insufficient discussion before adoption. The resolution of our American comrades and their general political ideas on this question was formally adopted by conference to express our complete solidarity with the military policy of the Fourth International.

Now that our position on the main strategical and tactical questions has been formally adopted and the new Constitution comes into force, it is necessary for the branches to tighten up on their work and put into force the new orientation of the organisation.

The pre-conference marks an epoch in the development of the British working class. It marks the "coming of age" of British Trotskyism. In the past the Trotskyist groupings in Britain were more or less compelled to exist as discussion circles without any real contact with the workers. Composed in great part of intellectuals and petit bourgeois elements, their discussions never passed beyond the academic stage. Ours is the first national conference in Britain of Trotskyists in which the delegates and membership were almost exclusively proletarian in composition.

This in itself is a tremendous step forward for our movement and a reflection of the process of development in British society today. The objective situation reveals itself as one tremendously favourable for the development of the revolutionary party. The delegates revealed the determination of our group to face up to the problems posed by history. The problem of transforming as swiftly as possible, the old outlook, habits and ideas, and prepare to transform our group into a party capable of leading the working class to the conquest of power.

The adoption of the new perspectives and the new Constitution formally marks the break with the old past of the group. The change from the group based primarily around study circles, to a propaganda group striving to integrate itself with, and face to, the masses. The delegates and the conference discussion revealed the hope and confidence that our young, weak and untried organisation would grow up to the tasks posed by history.

18 branches were represented by delegates; 4 were unable to attend. Many districts in which there are prospects of forming branches in the immediate future were represented by individual comrades who did not possess delegates' votes. Most of the industrial areas and cities were represented, but some important gaps are revealed where it becomes necessary immediately to find a basis, notably Manchester and Wales.

The age of the delegates revealed that we are composed in the main of young workers, although a few old seasoned fighters were present as well. The eagerness and anxiety of the delegates to get down to the job was the theme that ran right through the conference.

The whole tendency and outlook of the delegates, which expressed the feeling among the groups, was *outward*.

All delegates were members of trade unions. Miners, engineers, railwaymen, clothing workers, transport, sheet metal workers, aircraft, woodworkers, carpenters, building trade workers, etc., were represented at the conference. It was revealed that between 90 and 95 percent of the members of the organisation are members of trade unions. *The organisation is overwhelmingly proletarian in membership and outlook.*

The basic ideas of the conference which have thoroughly rooted themselves among the membership in the past year were accepted by the membership unanimously. The Constitution in which the new orientation of the group is embodied and the perspectives, apart from one or two minor points, were agreed on as the basis of our work in the coming period. The membership endorsed the turn away from the LP tactic and on to the road of building the revolutionary party as an independent force, without any hangovers from the old orientation being revealed. The old garment as cast aside and the new one donned without any attempt to cling to an outmoded tactic.

Conference understood the basic problem as the necessity to prepare and train the cadres for the coming revolution in Britain. Now that this basic idea will form the axis around which the whole of the activity of the group will revolve, it is necessary to strenuously and seriously implement the pre-conference decisions.

1. The education of our cadres, to assimilate theory, understand history, to speak and face up to the problems involved in transforming the group into an organisation which will be capable of conducting agitation among the masses.

2. Work within the factories, trade unions and factory committees on the lines of the discussion and documents to be systematically conducted.

3. A decisive turn towards the workers disillusioned with Stalinism.

4. The fraction in the ILP and the group itself to observe very carefully the developments within the ILP.

The leadership and the membership revealed the utmost confidence that with systematic work on the orientation indicated, it should be possible to double, and more, the membership by the time of the conference in a few months time.

Shortcomings in the organisation were: the production of the *Socialist Appeal* late in the month, which retarded the work of the organisation in the provinces; the inexperience and youth of a large proportion of the membership; the fact that as yet the theoretical level as revealed by the discussions is not as high among the membership as it should be; the weakness of some sections of the membership in numbers and connection with the workers.

Conference was a test of how far our organisation had developed. It revealed a certain lack of internal preparation on the part of the leadership in relation to documents and theses for discussion. Most of the energy had been expended on the external side of our work and not sufficient time spent on conference preparation. In this sense it revealed that we are not only in the process of forging an organisation but of forging a leadership itself.

The need was revealed for the leadership to systematically educate and raise the level of the membership. In this connection it is absolutely necessary to transform *Workers' International News* into a theoretical journal for the education of the members and close contacts, while the internal bulletin could be used for the purpose of educating the members, as well as for the purpose of discussing controversial questions.

The discussion on relations with the IS and the RSL revealed the determination of the membership to end the present ridiculous situation and to achieve a firm, principled, basis for fusion. The discussions with the RSL should serve as the basis for the education and inoculation of the membership against the sectarianism and ultra-leftism of all sects.

In itself, the conference is a water-mark of achievement for the Fourth International in Britain. It revealed the tremendous vistas of growth and work which stretch out in front of us. But the mood of the conference was not one of intoxication at the achievements already made.

The perspective before us is one which, for the first time, the Trotskyists can look forward hopefully to the *possibility* of playing a role in the great events to come. As far as the broad movement is concerned we have not even yet scratched the surface. *But the conference marked the beginning of a new stage.* It marked the beginning of the beginning. For the first time Trotskyists saw the historic possibility opening out in front of them, of influencing events not as spectators but as active participants. The delegates realised the immensity of the tasks and the immaturity of their forces to carry out these tasks. But they also saw the transformation of quantity into quality. We face these prospects and the coming events on an entirely different plane to that of two or three years back.

And that was the main achievement of the conference. The delegates left London determined to face up to the scope and limitless opportunities (only limited by the stature and numbers of our own forces) of the work which opens out before us. They went imbued with the faith and confidence that our organisation can form the nucleus that will build the party in the period opening ahead. At the same time, they went back with no false ideas of the relative weak forces at our disposal when compared to the objective tasks. They went back with the determination to do everything to remedy the weaknesses of the group and to make it a fit instrument of the British proletariat.

On balance, the organisation can be well satisfied with the success of the conference, despite the many weaknesses which it revealed. It can be well confident that by "common effort" all shortcomings will be rectified. But despite all weaknesses, the delegates know, our comrades know, that their party, their group, is the party and the factor in Britain which will transform the situation to the favour of the working class.

For the immediate attention of all locals

To implement conference decisions immediately it is necessary to prepare the group for the next step forward.

1. Locals should immediately elect delegates to form the DCs in the following districts: Scotland, Yorkshire, Lancs., Midlands, London. DCs in the provincial centres should be convened for the second week-end in each month, should elect officials and immediate notification and contact should be made with the centre.

2. Thorough discussions on perspectives should be undertaken, a review of local activity undertaken, and the local work brought into line with the decisions of the conference.

3. To facilitate the work of the Political Bureau and the Central Committee in training the membership locally, the first and third weeks of each month should be given entirely to local business and group activity. On the other weeks, a political discussion should be undertaken by the locals on the main political problems facing the workers, on the leading articles in our press, or on the letters of the Political Bureau when and as these are circulated for discussion.

4. The *Socialist Appeal* must be used even more vigorously than in the past as a national organiser.

Note: Minutes of the CC and the PB will not be circulated except to members of these bodies. To maintain the maximum contact between the locals a fortnightly report will be sent out from the centre to replace the old practice of circulating CC minutes.

Perspectives and tasks

By Ted Grant

[*Original draft document*, winter 1942]

The meeting of the national conference this year is a suitable time to check up on the ideas and perspectives adopted at the last conference and to modify or alter them in the light of the experience of the last twelve months, if that is necessary. The developments of the last period if anything have reinforced and given added weight to the conclusions embodied in our document *Preparing for power*. Our general perspectives remain fundamentally unaltered. There is no necessity then to repeat the basic ideas developed and adopted as the policy of the party.

Since last year the military position of British imperialism has completely changed. In the Pacific the onrush of Japanese imperialism has been checked and stemmed. In Europe the resistance of the Soviet Union has weakened and undermined the power of German imperialism. For two years the Nazi war machine has been battering itself to pieces in the vain endeavour to destroy the Soviet Union. The elite of the German troops lie buried on the plains of Russia. And meanwhile the flower of Soviet youth and a great part of the industrial wealth of the Soviet Union has been destroyed. The mutual destruction of these two powers suits the interests of British imperialism perfectly. For two years the British imperialists have had the opportunity of preparing their rearming on a tremendous scale, while their losses in equipment and manpower have been relatively small. As a result, far from facing the peril of imminent destruction the imperialists now face the prospect of victory over the Axis.

But what is important to note is that the changed position of British imperialism is not due mainly to her own efforts but to those of her "Allies". The changed prospects are due to the efforts of the Soviet Union and to the staggering armaments programme of American imperialism.

Thus the rosy prospects of British imperialism are somewhat illusory. It is thanks to her position as a base from which the United States can come to grips in a death-grapple with her most formidable competitor and rival that on the surface British capitalism's position as a world power has been strengthened and preserved. In fact this has been a means of concealing the stark reality of the decline and decay of British imperialism as a world power.

American imperialism has ruthlessly stripped the British capitalists of their foreign investments and grabbed strategic economic and political positions within the British dominions and colonies. Even in Europe the American bourgeoisie are manoeuvring for position so that Britain will not have the lion's share even there. The decline of British imperialism is concealed somewhat by the huge shipments of food and munitions under the lend-lease agreement to Britain by the American capitalists. But once this huge subsidy is withdrawn the position of the British bourgeoisie will become really serious. It is on this international background that political life has developed in Britain. The main line of development has proceeded on the lines sketched out in the perspectives. There has been a further growth of the radicalisation and discontent of the masses. This has proceeded apace despite the military victories which have been obtained in this period by the ruling class. The radicalisation has affected nearly all the strata of the population. The victories of the Common Wealth at the bye-elections have been a symptom of this process. Further illustration of this process has been the production by the ruling class of the Beveridge report as a means of harnessing and side-tracking the discontent of the workers with promises of "social "security" after the war. Even this measure has been regarded as too "revolutionary" by the decisive sections of the British capitalists who realise only too well that they will have a difficult job of surviving American competition after the war and are preparing the greatest attack on the standard of living which the masses have experienced for the past century.

Even more striking as a means of gauging the changes of consciousness among the masses has been the widespread scepticism and disbelief in the efficacy of the scheme as a means of ameliorating their lot with which the plan has been greeted, especially within the ranks of the working class. This has indicated the maturity and development of working class consciousness in the last quarter century and provides a favourable background to the development of the revolutionary party of the working class. Even a complete and decisive military victory for British imperialism in the next period cannot prevent tremendous revolutionary convulsions among the masses.

The situation which is rapidly developing in Ireland where the masses are moving left in a terrific wave is but a pale reflection of the process that will develop in Britain at a later stage. In Ireland, with a predominantly agricultural population, the Labour Party, the most left party in the political arena, has developed from a tiny force into a major factor of the situation. In Dublin they have won the majority of the population to their banner. Even in backward and reactionary Ulster the Orange workers are gravitating towards socialism. In the case of Ireland this development has taken place because of the steep fall in the standard of living of the population, due mainly to the deliberate economic measures adopted by Britain to exert pressure on Eire. A similar economic pressure will be exerted by American imperialism on Britain, once they have defeated the Axis. Thus the pressure of America will be one of the main levers of the revolutionisation of Britain. Except that if we wish to have a parallel with Eire it is to the developments in Dublin we would have to look rather than Eire as a whole. Britain with its rich proletarian tradition and its proletarian majority of the population far more swiftly and far more intensely will move towards the left under the impact of development of events both abroad and home.

Meanwhile developments during the course of the war within Britain are an indication of the events which are yet to come. Under the pressure of the masses the first dress rehearsal of how the Labour Party is going to react has taken place. Definite hints of the splitting away of the right wing have been given as was forecasted. The revolt of the majority of the Labour MPs on certain issues such as the Beveridge plan, in which they voted against the coalition, is another. Inevitably the LP will be driven into opposition at the first serious crisis, when an active mass movement has developed. The coalition will be smashed under the pressure of the Labour workers. Meanwhile the decisions of the last Labour conference do not in the least invalidate these conclusions. The shameful Vansittart resolution and the defeat of the resolution asking for the ending of the electoral truce did not in the least reflect the feelings of the rank and file Labour workers. They merely indicate how far the trade union bureaucracy and the Labour bureaucracy have degenerated and separated themselves from the masses. Possibly even in the coming year the LP might be compelled to end the coalition. Whether the coalition will be maintained or not does not depend in the least on the vote recorded at Westminster but on the movements of the class struggle in the next period. The inactivity and lifelessness of the LP organisations has continued over the country as a whole. But in some areas a definite revival of the LP is to be observed. The continuation of the truce will further stifle and kill the activity of the local Labour organisations. Only at a later stage will the LP revive, and form a fruitful ground for activity. At the present time the hopelessness of basing all activity within the LP has been completely confirmed. Nevertheless the most striking feature of the situation is the critical attitude of big sections of the Labour workers towards the leadership. This scepticism among the workers organised in the trade unions and the LP is an important capital for revolutionary socialism, and has had further reinforcement by the antics of the Labour leaders in the past 12 months. Of course the moment the masses swing forward the Labour leaders will be compelled to thrust forward their left face and will even use revolutionary phrases in order to keep control of the movement. It is virtually certain that then the broad masses will swing behind them. But the critical attitude and the suspicion of the policy of the Labour leaders will remain firmly fixed at the back of their minds. At the first signs of a failure to turn words into deeds they will look elsewhere for leadership. Hidden for the moment are some very nasty shocks and surprises for the Labour bureaucracy in the movement and ideas of the workers.

Communist Party

The first big wave of enthusiasm for communism which embraced millions of the workers after the entry of the Soviet Union into the war has now subsided. The CP in Britain had temporarily received a rich harvest in sympathy and support as a direct consequence of this mood among the masses. But the wholesale and vicious anti-working class activity of the Stalinists has had its effect. The strike-breaking and cynical betrayals of the interests of the workers wherever conflicts have broken out between the workers and the employers have aroused antagonism and hatred towards the Stalinists by most of the workers involved in such disputes. This flies so much in the face of tradition of class solidarity of the British workers that it has produced a violent reaction against Stalinism wherever workers have come in contact with it. The CP has definitely lost the support of tens of thousands of worker-militants, the natural leaders and fighters of the working class. Not only that, dozens and hundreds of the best elements of the CP refusing to stomach their vile policy have been expelled, driven out or simply dropped out of the CP. Even in their strongholds, South Wales and the Clydeside, especially the latter, the CP is losing ground. For a time the Red Clydeside tolerated the sell-out, out of their tradition of loyalty and their class instinct of wishing to support the Soviet Union. But now among the best sections of the workers the CP is falling to pieces. According to a document issued by the CP the sales of literature and dues collected have fallen tremendously in comparison with other areas. The dissolution of the Comintern has been the last straw and CP speakers attempting to explain it away outside factory gates on the Clyde have been received with jeers and insults from the workers.

So strong has been the reaction against the Stalinist blacklegs that the *Daily Worker* and the CP have had to tone down their attack on the workers. The *Daily Worker* in dealing with strikes no longer hysterically denounces the worker but writes against the strikes almost as "objectively" as the *Daily Mail*. This to prevent a complete loss of support among the workers. The CP has grown from the ranks of the more backward sections of the workers, among a section of the petit-bourgeoisie and even from formerly entirely non-political areas. The best elements are alienated by the support for the Tory candidates at the bye-elections and other phenomena.

Nevertheless the process does not develop in a simple fashion. The CP has lost heavily in influence in the last year. But it still remains as a strong force and on the basis of mass upsurge may once again increase its influence especially on the less conscious elements of the workers, and in those areas where the workers have not seen the Stalinist policy in action, in direct conflict with the workers at elections and during strikes. But the opening of a mass movement will pose tremendous difficulties for the leadership even if the present policy is "modified" under the influence of events. If the alliance with the Soviet Union is continued the CP will have to carry on the present policy despite the results. This opens up the prospects of serious clashes between the membership and the leadership. From the ex-members of the CP and the best elements who remain we can expect to make big gains.

It is not yet clear whether the subsidies from the Kremlin will continue to be sent or the funds will be cut off, through the agreement between Stalin and Anglo-American imperialism. If the funds are cut off it will cripple the CP. But even if not, the CP will undergo big tests in the coming period which will splinter it to pieces.

Independent Labour Party

The last twelve months have seen a steady growth in membership and support for the ILP. Big increases in membership can be observed. But already the centrist or rather left-reformist leadership is preparing to sell out to the reformists. This will immediately open up contradictions with the left workers in its own ranks. The perspective of growth of the revolutionary left will be further enhanced and reinforced by the influx of left workers from the Labour Party and outside attracted to the ILP as a left force. Our fraction within the ILP while it has achieved good results is still very weak. Not sufficient broad agitation around concrete issues has been systematically developed. The issues of internationalism and the attitude towards the Labour masses must be utilised as the basis of our activity among the ILPers. Strides have been made but a tightening up of the work will be necessary.

Industry and the unions

The key work of our party lies within industry and the unions at the present time. Events of the past 12 months have indicated the process taking place among the working class. After years of quiet the basic section of the workers are beginning to stir. Strikes among the miners, transport, railwaymen, engineers, shipping, etc., have taken place. The unions have received an enormous influx of members bringing the number of organised workers to the highest recorded in British history except for the peak year 1920. There is not a basic sector of industry where the mood of the workers is not turning towards the left. The ferment within the ranks of the advanced militants in industry, and the desire to co-ordinate the activities of the fighting elements against the attack of the bosses, taken in conjunction with the necessity to combat Stalinist treachery and the sabotage and indifference of the trade union bureaucracy, has led to the formation of the new organisation of shop stewards and militants. Similar in many respects to the Clyde workers' committee, which was set up for like reasons in the last war, the present organisation—while possessing many weaknesses and facing obstacles that the Clyde committee never had—nevertheless this council is on an entirely higher plane. The level of consciousness of the guiding layer is far above that of the workers who set up the Clyde workers' committee. The last

25 years of experience have lifted the movement to an entirely higher level. The movement though weak in its initial stages is looking towards a national orientation rather than limiting it to only one industry and one part of the country. We are already playing a leading role in this movement and by developing correct perspectives and [with] correct work should succeed in winning over to our banner the best industrial militants, who will be attracted to the militant programme of this organisation throughout the country in the coming period. These are the natural fighters and leaders of the working class who are selected on the basis of the actual struggle in the workshops and wield enormous influence among the workers. With a correct policy on our part they can through their actual experience draw the logical political conclusions and find their way into the ranks of the revolutionary party. These workers are of the finest revolutionary material and from them should come perhaps the biggest influx of members, certainly the most valuable portion in the coming period.

The general strategical orientation of the organisation has been borne out by the experience of the past 12 months. Modest but important gains have been recorded for the organisation and we have made steady if slow progress. We have been established as a definite tendency within the ranks of the labour movement. The period that opens up is one of sharp turns and sharp breaks in the situation. In the industrial as well as the political sphere a period of storms and crises looms ahead. The sharp breaks and crises in the situation must not take us unawares. Despite the strides which we have undoubtedly made the organisation is still very weak and shaky. Our trained cadres are still few and inexperienced. The process of building the cadres and building the party must be accomplished simultaneously. Twelve months' work and twelve months' experience indicates the necessity to continue on the path which has been mapped out at the last national conference.

BRITAIN'S War !
Production is in Chaos ●

*Britain's Millionaires pile up profits whilst
British Soldiers go to the front ill-equipped.*

MEETING

**TRADE UNIONISTS, SHOP STEWARDS,
FACTORY WORKERS,**

HEAR the case for

Workers Control of Production

At HOLBORN HALL,
Grays Inn Rd., W.C.1.

SUNDAY, FEBRUARY 22nd.

At 6.30 p.m.   Doors Open 6 p.m.

Speakers : **BILL ELLIOT, A.E.U.**
HAROLD ATKINSON, A.S.W.
SID BIDWELL, N.U.R.
TED GRANT, Editor "Socialist Appeal"
G. HEALY in the chair.

Auspices : Workers' International League

Published by E. Grant for W.I.L. 61, Northdown St., Kings Cross, N.1

Report on ILP work to the International Secretariat[1]

[*Original document*, presumably April 1935]

International Secretariat – International Communist League

Dear comrades,

We desire to bring to your notice the state of affairs now prevailing in the Bolshevik-Leninist[2] fraction in the ILP, known as the "Marxist Group".

Present position in the ILP

Since the 1934 annual conference the decline in the membership and influence of the ILP has continued steadily. The ILP has lost what little influence it had amongst the workers and ILP branches have become little groups averaging 4 to 12 active members whose main contact with the outside world consists in selling the *New Leader*, the party organ. Financially, the position of the party is even more desperate than before and it is only saved from bankruptcy by donations and loans from bourgeois and petty bourgeois sympathisers and members.

How has this development of the ILP reacted on the political consciousness of its members?

A year ago the then secret Bolshevik-Leninist fraction in the ILP had a little under thirty members, almost all active. All these were in London, where some ten branches supported our line at the 1934 winter divisional conference (which, by the way, was held in January, before most of the comrades of the Minority of the old Communist League had entered the party and before the fraction had

---

[1] This internal report to the International Secretariat of the International Communist League of April 1935—signed amongst others by Ted Grant—described the sorry state of the early groupings of the British left opposition, such as the Marxist Group in the ILP, and advocated the reorientation of Trotskyists towards entry in the Labour Party.

[2] For clarity, we have expanded the different abbreviations used in the original letter to signify Bolshevik-Leninist.

been organised). At the 1934 annual conference held at Easter of last year, 20 branches voted for the Fourth International.

Today the Marxist Group has a number of sympathetic groups in the provinces, and a paper membership of about 70 in London, of whom between 30 and 40 are active. The support obtained for our principles at the 1935 winter divisional conference was not substantially greater than was gained last year. At the 1935 annual conference, which has just taken place, the vote for the Fourth International was so insignificant that no count was taken; comrades who were present reckon it at not less than 6 and not more than 10. On the question of the relation to the Labour Party, the vote was also counted, but our support is estimated as being between 20 and 30 votes. The number of delegates at his conference was 110[3].

Since the entry of the Minority of the old Communist League into the ILP not one old member of the party has been won over to our position in the London division, all our support having come either from new members (whom, in most cases, we had converted to Bolshevik-Leninism before they joined the ILP), or from old ILPers who had, to a greater or lesser extent, adopted our position before we had entered—in most cases owing to the propaganda carried on by the old Communist League.

With regard to the internal position of the group of Bolshevik-Leninists, the position is far worse today that it was a year ago. A dangerous spread of centrist tendencies is to be observed within the group itself. This is of course due to the influence of the centrist environment, and has been accentuated by the fact that many of the old ILP comrades who have linked up with the Minority of the old Communist League since the latter entered the ILP have never been more than *left centrists,* who set a sentimental loyalty to the ILP *"their party"* above the principle of Bolshevik-Leninism. These comrades have come to us because they look upon our movement as the only way of saving the ILP. This tendency is manifested in a number of ways:

1) Making a fetish of doing ILP work and of "loyalty" to the ILP leadership and constitution. Naturally all Bolshevik-Leninists working in the ILP must expect to do a certain amount of ILP work (which mainly consists in selling the *New Leader*), also the constitution of the party must not be broken in such a way as to render expulsion possible—but some of the leading comrades of the Marxist Group carry this to the point where they are in danger of placing loyalty to the ILP higher than Bolshevik-Leninist principles. As an example of this, recently two South African comrades said in private discussion with comrade Johns, a member of the committee of the Marxist Group, that they thought that under certain circumstances the Labour League of Youth (Youth organisation of the Labour Party) might be found to be a better field for our work than the ILP.

---

3 Corrected in handwriting on the original to read 153.

At the next meeting of the Holborn Branch of the ILP (of which both comrade Johns and the South African comrades are members), comrade Johns, in the absence of the South African comrades, accused them of disloyalty to the ILP, inasmuch as they thought the Labour League of Youth a better organisation than the ILP, and on these grounds moved their expulsion from the branch and the party. Certain of our comrades managed to get this matter postponed for a time so that the comrades in question should have an opportunity for defending themselves.

2) Lack of concrete perspectives. No discussion of our perspectives for our work in the ILP has been held since the formation on the Marxist Group; it appears to be taken for granted by the leadership of the group that so long as the ILP exists so long must Bolshevik-Leninists continue to work inside it, to the exclusion of all work in other parties (such work, however fruitful the results, would of course be disloyalty to the ILP). The membership form which must be signed by all comrades wishing to join the Marxist Group begins by saying: "In becoming a member of the Marxist Group in No. 6 division, I recognise the necessity for a British revolutionary party, such as is not existing today, *and I believe that the ILP can be converted from its present centrist position to a revolutionary line*". The confession of faith contained in the part of the quotation which we have underlined still remains the official policy of the Marxist Group, despite growing doubts on the part of certain of the rank and file. Attempts to start a discussion on this question have been passed over by the leadership of the group, usually on the plea of "lack of time, owing to the necessity of discussing more important questions".

3) Organisational degeneration of the Marxist Group itself. Internally, the position of the group of Bolshevik-Leninists in this country is far worse than it was a year ago; a year ago the fraction was organised on the basis of local groups, which met every week and received reports from the committee, which also met weekly. Communications from the International Secretariat were discussed at committee meetings, and discussed among all members, with the exception of one or two who were considered not yet thoroughly reliable.

On the organisation of the wider open fraction (the Marxist Group) it was decided that until all members of the wider group were won over to our full position the inner Bolshevik-Leninist fraction should still function. *This decision has never been carried into effect*, and the inner fraction has now been liquidated in the outer one (Marxist Group)—with the result that there now exists no machinery by which the average member of the fraction (however reliable he may be politically) can be informed of communications from the IS. An attempt has recently been made to form a secret inner fraction within the Marxist Group, for this purpose of controlling policy and discussing the IS correspondence. Unfortunately, however, this attempt has been made by a small clique of the leadership on a basis of personal preference and/or ILP work done. At the first meeting which was called with this end in view, there were invited a number of members of the Marxist Group who were by no means yet fully won over to our principled position. The meeting was largely abortive—as a number of comrades walked out: some as a protest against the manner in which the meeting had been called, and others (the unreliable elements just mentioned), because they were opposed on principle to relations with any body outside the ILP. A second meeting has since been held, and we believe that this resulted in the formation of a small clique of perhaps half a dozen, which designs to guide the policy of the Marxist Group and maintain relations with the IS. On this we have little further information: a number of the oldest members of the group, who were known to be politically reliable, were not informed of this meeting, and one of them, who came along by chance (as the meeting was held in the private house of comrade) was asked to leave before the meeting began, while its purpose was concealed from him.

Attendances at the ordinary Marxist Group meetings continue to decline.

Such, comrades, is, in briefest outline, the position in the ILP and the Bolshevik-Leninist group working there in with its left centrist fellow-travellers; the unhealthy developments described above flow from the whole situation, in which a small group of Bolshevik-Leninists finds itself isolated in a centrist party, poor in working class contacts, and on the membership of which they make no apparent impression. The psychological pressure exerted by this environment upon our cadres cannot be overestimated, and it is no accident that most of the comrades who were in the leadership when the Minority of the old Communist League entered the ILP have withdrawn either wholly or partly from work in that party. Two of these comrades, (comrades, Kirby and Harber—both of whom attended the last Plenum of the IS), are now working in the Labour Party and Socialist League, where they have formed a Bolshevik-Leninist group. They both left the ILP individually, since they felt that they could work there no longer, and are now working for Bolshevik-Leninist principles in a new environment. These comrades now consider that such individual resignation is a tactical error, and carried to its logical conclusion might lead to the dislocation of the Bolshevik-Leninist forces in this country.

We considered it our duty to bring the above facts to your notice, and to warn you against accepting at its face value information sent by cliques of comrades, and to ask for your guidance in the present difficult situation. Naturally, the signatories of the present letter realise the fundamental necessity of keeping intact the scanty Bolshevik-Leninist forces in this country, and have no intention of taking any action detrimental to the principled unity of these.

Please write to us at the following [enclosed] address:

With communist greetings,

A.B. Doncaster—Member of ILP and Marxist Group.

E. Grant—Member of ILP and Marxist Group.

R. Porteons—Member of ILP and Marxist Group. I endorse the statement of facts contained in this letter so far as they refer to recent events but make reservations with regard to the theoretical presentation of them.

Stuart Kirby—Member of Labour Party and Socialist League and of Bolshevik-Leninist fraction therein.

D.D. Harber—Member of Labour Party and Socialist League and of Bolshevik-Leninist fraction therein.

S. Frost—Except the last two paragraphs.

W.G. Bryce—ILP.

All the comrades signing this letter are not acquainted with all the facts given, as some of them have only joined the ILP within recent months; all, however, are in agreement as far as the facts bearing on the present situation are concerned.

[We would like to thank Ian Hunter for making this letter available.]

"SOCIALIST APPEAL'

POLICY FOR THE R.O.Fs

HEAR THE CASE FOR

Workers' Control of Production

Meeting :

"GREYHOUND"

ORDNANCE ROAD ENFIELD

TUESDAY, JUNE 16th. 1942

6.30 p.m.

Speakers :

TED GRANT, Editor "Socialist Appeal"

G. HEALY, E.C. W.I.L.

A. ROY, A.E.U.

Chair : JIM PIPER. A.E.U. Shop Steward

Auspices :

WORKERS' INTERNATIONAL LEAGUE
Fourth International.

Clear out Hitler's agents! An exposure of Trotskyist disruption being organised in Britain

By W. Wainwright

[Pamphlet, Communist Party of Great Britain, August 1942]

This text by William Wainwright is one of the best examples of the Stalinist School of falsification and slander directed against Trotskyism. The instruction that Trotskyists "should be treated as you would treat a Nazi" or "treat him as you would treat an open Nazi" was launched in the middle of the war, as an incitement to murder any Trotskyist or indeed any militant of the ILP.

Clear them out!

There is a group of people in Britain masquerading as socialists in order to cover up their fascist activities.

The members of this group are very active. And dangerous.

They go among the factories, shipyards and coalfields, in the Labour, trade union and co-operative organisations. They try to mislead the workers with cunning deception and lies. They hide their black aims with "red" talk. They sow doubt, suspicion and confusion, retard production and try to undermine the people's will to victory.

They are called Trotskyists.

You've heard of the fifth column. The Trotskyists are their allies and agents in the ranks of the working class.

They are a greater menace than enemy paratroops. Because they seem to talk the language of workers, wear similar clothes, and get themselves jobs in Britain's factories, shipyards and pits.

> **Crime sheet**
>
> The people of the world accuse the Trotskyists of these crimes against humanity:
>
> *Russia*:
>
> > 1918—Attempt to assassinate Lenin.
> >
> > 1935—Attempt to assassinate Stalin.
> >
> > 1921—Organised spying for Germany in Soviet Union.
> >
> > 1936—Contacts with Hess. Plot to take advantage of Soviet-German war, overthrow government, seize power and give Ukraine to Germany and Eastern territories to Japan in return for services rendered.
>
> *France*:
>
> > Fought against Popular Front government.
> >
> > Worked to destroy Franco-Soviet pact.
> >
> > Accepted Nazi funds. Trotskyist leader Doriot now openly helping Nazis in France.
>
> *Spain*:
>
> > Staged armed uprising against Republican government at critical point in Spanish war against fascism. Opened sections of the front to fascists.
>
> *Britain:*
>
> > Worked against Anglo-Soviet pact before the war. Supported Chamberlain's Munich policy. Call for violent overthrow of Stalin and Soviet State. Aim to sabotage war production in Britain and hold up second front.

The Home Guard has been taught a quick way to deal with enemy paratroops and spies.

You must train yourself to round up these other, more cunning enemies, on whom Hitler depends to do his work for him in Britain.

This book is a simple training manual. It will explain to you the tactics of the strange war that Hitler is waging in your factory, organisation and home. It is a war of politics and sabotage, the counter-part of the war of tanks, planes and guns.

These men are *enemies*

What is a Trotskyist? Trotsky was a Russian who gathered around him an unscrupulous gang of traitors to organise spying, sabotage, wrecking and assassination in the Soviet Union.

They came together after the workers took power in Russia and had cleared out the capitalists.

They wormed their way into important army positions, working class organisa-

---

This happened in Moscow 1937

Scene. The Supreme Court of the USSR. Radek, the Trotskyist, is in the dock. Vyshinsky, the Public Prosecutor, is cross-examining him.

————————

Vyshinsky: What questions were raised in Trotsky's letter to you?

Radek: The victory of fascism in Germany. The growth of Japanese aggression. The inevitability of these countries waging war against the USSR. The inevitable defeat of the USSR. The necessity of the bloc [the Trotskyist group—Ed.] if it came into power, to make concessions.

Vyshinsky: Excuse me, please. Inevitable defeat: how did Trotsky and you picture that? And what was your and Trotsky's attitude towards defeat?

Radek: The attitude towards defeat was entirely positive because it was stated that this would create the conditions for the accession to power of the bloc, and it even stated more, that it was in our interest to hasten war.

Vyshinsky: Hence you were interested in hastening war and it was to your interest that the USSR should be defeated in this war? How was this put in Trotsky's letter?

Radek: Defeat is inevitable, and it will create the conditions for our accession to power, therefore, we were interested in hastening the war.

(Verbatim official report of the trial of Radek)

This man was a Trotskyist. Men like him are working in this country today.

tions, even government posts. They plotted with the Nazis to hand over large tracts of their country once they had weakened it sufficiently to make its defeat quite certain.

In the event of war, they undertook to open the gates to the enemy.

Like Quisling in Norway, Laval and Doriot in France, they were promised positions in a Nazi puppet government in return for services rendered.

They did a great deal of damage in Russia before they were caught. But their plot was unearthed. They were brought to trial. The guilty were executed or put in prison.

The whole world listened incredulously to the story that was unfolded at the Moscow trials.

It does not seem quite so strange today.

Do you remember Madrid and Barcelona, where the Trotskyists gave assistance to General Franco? Do you remember what happened when Belgium and Holland were invaded, when fifth columnists, who had hidden their real characters before, opened fire from the windows of their houses on their neighbours in the streets below? Remember France, where Doriot, chief Trotskyist, welcomed the Nazis with open arms, and is one of their most important men today?

It is time that Britain learned the lesson.

The Trotskyists want you to think they are advocates of a type of revolutionary political thought.

They are nothing of the kind. They have nothing in common with any organisation of the working class.

Trotsky's men are Hitler's men.

They must be cleared out of every working class organisation in the country.

The Trotskyist plan

Trotskyists oppose and hate the leaders of Russia. They want to see Russia defeated and Hitler victorious. They want to weaken Britain, Russia's ally.

But they do not say what they are after. They thrive only if they successfully deceive.

They know that British people are tolerant, easy-going and ready to give everyone except an obvious fascist a hearing.

They therefore use every opportunity to put forward cunning arguments and propaganda, to try to lead the people down the road of defeat.

If you examine what they say and write, you will find that it all boils down to these six aims:

1. Hold up supplies of arms to Russia.

2. Delay and sabotage the second front.

3. Hold up British production.

4. Undermine the Anglo-Soviet alliance.

5. Destroy the confidence of the people and Forces in Britain's ability to win.

6. Create conditions that will lead to a pro-Nazi government in order to do a deal with Hitler.

If this plan were entirely successful, Hitler would win the war.

Covers of CPGB pamphlets attacking Trotskyism and specifically targeting the WIL as Hitler's agents. W. Wainwright's *Clear out Hitler's agents!* was followed in February 1943 by the slanderous *Hitler's agents exposed!* by John Mahon. (Ted Grant Archive)

Even if only a tiny part of it were achieved, it would cost the lives of thousands of British workers in and out of uniform.

That is why you must equip yourself with the knowledge that will help you to pierce the Trotskyist deceptions, and expose them in their true colours.

Let us test some of their arguments, and see where they would lead the people.

"The Red Army has lost its morale and is therefore unable to resist the Nazi armies..."

"Stalin has sapped the strength of the Red Army by removing and executing over 90 percent of the highest and most qualified commanders..." (From Trotskyist papers)

These extracts come from the Trotskyist papers, and were spread by their speakers during the first months of the Nazi attack against Russia.

What was the purpose of these Nazi lies?

The Trotskyists hoped that people would think: "What's the use of sending arms to Russia? It will be all over before they get there. If they do arrive, the arms will fall into enemy hands."

Who else was trying to play this game?

Hitler, for one. Do you remember his boasts that Moscow would fall "before winter sets in"? Do you remember how the Nazis tried to get the world to believe that "Timoshenko's army groups are in headlong flight," and that "Russia as a military power is finished"? Do you remember how Hitler's friends in Britain gave the Red Army ten days, then six weeks, then six months to live?

They all had the same idea: to dishearten the British people and to delay the arrival of reinforcements on the Eastern front.

These arguments were made to look very stupid by the Red Army's heroic and magnificent fight.

But lies work well until they are found out—and then it may be too late.

"ILP opposes arms for Russia"

"Speaking at an ILP conference in Glasgow, Mr. John McGovern: 'The conference voted against a resolution moved by the Parkhead branch pledging it to assure the supply of all arms and equipment needed by the USSR.' " (Daily Herald, February 2 1942)

Mr. John McGovern, a leader of the Independent Labour Party, presided at the conference reported in this cutting. This organisation is riddled with Trotskyists, whose activities dominate it from top to bottom.

Why did they take this decision?

They cannot say: "Because we want to see Russia defeated." They have to cover up their intentions.

They say: "We agree to send arms to Russia—but only under workers' control."

Russia is a working class state. If Hitler were to win, the workers in control in Russia would be overthrown, and fascism installed instead.

The decision of this ILP conference means that those who were present pledged themselves to try to stop tanks, guns, planes and every other kind of war material going from Britain to its ally bearing the brunt of the struggle.

Hidden behind their slogan: "workers' control for Britain" is the Trotskyist aim to smash workers' control in Russia.

Which is what Hitler would pay them a fortune for—if they were successful.

The second front

"We don't want a boss class army on the continent."

"It will liberate Europe from its present tyranny but will only establish a new tyranny." (From Trotskyist papers and speeches)

Every week the second front is delayed is worth more than a fortune to Hitler: it is worth tens of divisions of men, hundreds of tanks and planes, thousands of guns.

That is why the Trotskyists and all Hitler's other friends in Britain are so busy peddling their poison against the second front.

While Hitler is hurrying in Russia and Egypt, they are organising a delaying action for him in Britain.

If the Trotskyists went about saying "We want Hitler to win," they wouldn't get very far with their propaganda.

So they wave a red flag and put their case in another way.

They would like you to believe that there is no difference between Churchill and Hitler. That British troops will carry out the same brutal atrocities in Europe as the Nazis. And that Stalin, Timoshenko and the other Soviet leaders, who have called for the second front, are partners in a plot to install a new kind of oppression in Europe.

For all these reasons, the Trotskyists say, you must prevent a British invasion of the continent.

Which means: let Hitler go on fighting his enemies one by one.

Do you remember Colonel Moore-Brabazon and Captain Margesson?

They were thrown out of the government by public pressure because they fought against the plan for a second front.

When Margesson went, Mr. James Maxton, a leader of the Independent Labour

Party protested and defended him: "I have never seen anything wrong with the conduct of Captain Margesson in doing his job," he said. (Parliament, February 24 1942)

Maxton and his partners do not want a second front. They don't want to fight fascism at all. "Man's struggle should be a struggle of the intellect," he told an audience in Glasgow (December 18 1941). "The struggle that is wanted in our day is not the struggle that takes us on to the battlefield," he said.

They won't fight fascism—but they'd jump at the chance of sending men to fight against Russia.

In 1938, an international organisation* of which Mr. Fenner Brockway was general secretary, called on Trotskyists all over the world to assist the "forces in Soviet Russia which are struggling against the Stalinist bureaucracy."

Today, Doriot, French Trotskyist, has organised a detachment of troops to fight Russia.

Mr. Fenner Brockway's organisation tries to do the next best thing: to delay, the opening of a second front in Europe.

British Production

"Why increase the bosses' profits?"

"Strike for higher wages." (From Trotskyist papers and speeches.)

The more arms we get, the stronger we will be to smash the Nazis.

The less arms we have, the better Hitler likes it.

So the Trotskyists try their hardest to hold up the production of arms.

Again they use the trick of waving a red flag. They talk about the boss's profits. They try to take the heart out of the workers. "Why slave when you are only piling up money for the boss?" they say.

They want you to go slow, not to give your best work, to be misled by their talk of strikes and the boss's profits into sabotaging our troops and the Red Army.

They want you to do in Britain, what the French, Dutch, Polish and Norwegian workers are doing on the continent.

But whereas Europe's workers are holding up supplies for the Nazis, the Trotskyists want you to hold up the weapons that will smash the Nazis.

Strikes are organised against Hitler in France. The Trotskyists want to cancel out these efforts against Hitler by organising strikes in Britain.

---

* Note in original: The so-called International Bureau for Revolutionary Socialist Unity.

Europe's workers are fighting and dying to help Britain to get ahead in the race to produce more arms. The Trotskyists want to offset all their courageous activity.

Arms, not arguments, is what our soldiers and the Red Army men need. Soviet workers don't worry if profits have been made on a tank sent from capitalist Britain.

To them and to our lads in Egypt and to the men who will invade the continent, a tank is a tank, and the more they get, the better they like it.

Who else wants to hold up British production, besides Hitler and his pro-Nazi friends?

Some coal owners would like to hold back good seams of coal until after the war. Some shipbuilding magnates are against expanding their industry because the cost of upkeep after the war would cut down their profits. Some steel manufacturers want to keep output down because scarcity raises prices. They also are worried about their post-war profits.

The Trotskyists, by their cunning talk, are helping these profiteers.

Anglo-Soviet alliance

> "Even if you did conclude a pact with Russia, it would, in my estimation, give no real aid." (*Hansard*, August 24 1939)

This cutting comes from the official report of a debate in Parliament. The speaker was Mr. John McGovern of the Independent Labour Party.

Nor is the Trotskyist opposition to an alliance with Russia new.

Mr. McGovern and his associates were foremost in this country in their opposition to the peace front with the Soviet Union which could have prevented war ever from starting. Instead, they backed Chamberlain's policy of appeasement and building up Hitler.

> "Do the government believe that in the event of a pact being successful the Russian government are willing to place their forces behind this country in any struggle which may take place?" asked Mr. McGovern. (Parliament, June 26 1939)

> "The Labour Party"—he protested—"are trying to foist Russia on to this country." (July 5 1939).

Today, Britain has at last formed an alliance with the Soviet Union. An alliance which will mean the salvation of humanity.

But the Trotskyists go on with their undermining work.

They cast suspicion on the leaders of the Soviet Union. They utter the same kind of slanders that pour out of the Nazi lie factories in Berlin against Stalin, Churchill and Roosevelt. They spread foul rumours of a possible British or Soviet separate peace with Hitler. They play on the people's impatience for the second front by sneers that we intend to fight to the last Russian, while at the same time they do everything they can to stop the second front from being opened.

Who else, in addition to Hitler, intensely dislikes our associations with Russia?

There's Major Cazalet, former member of the Friends of National Spain, an organisation which collected cash for fascist General Franco.

There's Lord Phillimore, formerly chairman of the same organisation and collector of funds for fascist General Mannerheim in Finland.

These are the people, and there are others like them, whose activities receive the support of the Trotskyists and the ILP.

Public confidence

The Trotskyists aim to undermine the confidence of the people and the Forces in Britain's ability to win.

They go around whispering: "What are we fighting for?"

Mr. Maxton, too, told an audience in Glasgow:

> "You will bleed yourselves white in this war, and at the end, you will be so sick, you won't care whether you have won or lost."

Every Nazi victory is used by them as an opportunity to run down Britain, to attack the government, to dishearten the people, and to paint a picture of the impossibility of facing up to the fascists.

They want you to believe that the fight is hopeless, that the whole government is rotten, that Germany has a monopoly of military experts.

In the debate on Libya, the ILP members lined up with those who were trying to bring about the government's downfall.

The British people are fighting for dear life against the most cunning, brutal and treacherous enemy of mankind. The Nazis, wherever they have conquered, have destroyed the trade unions, the cooperatives, the labour and communist parties, all organisations of the people and have instituted a rule of terror against the population.

We are fighting, not only to liberate the peoples of Europe and to enable them to restore all their working class organisations, but to defend our own trade unions, our own organisations that have been built up by years of sacrifice and struggle.

Victory means the possibility of going forward to create those conditions that will lead to socialism.

Defeat means the end of working class organisations, and goodbye to all ideas of socialism for generations.

That is why the Trotskyites do everything they can to dampen down the peoples' enthusiasm, resolution and will to win, by their lies about the aims for which this war is being fought.

A deal with Hitler

British workers want to get the best possible output of war materials. They want to see this country fighting the total war of a free people in arms. They are quite naturally impatient at the slow way Britain is getting into her stride, angry at the waste they see, bitter at the mistakes that take place.

They look at Russia, and see that socialism is a more efficient way of running a country than is capitalism.

This is when the Trotskyist enemy of Russia comes round with his poison.

"You want to get efficiency in industry?" he asks. "You will never do it under capitalism," he says. "First you must abolish capitalism, and get workers' control, socialism."

Why do they say this?

Not because they want socialism. All they want to do is to stop everyone pulling together in the fight against fascism. They want to disrupt the unity of the British people. They want the workers to fight Churchill instead of Hitler.

Would this bring socialism? Of course not. It would give fascism its chance.

Hitler would be able to carry on his attack on Russia without fear of a second front in the West; and after weakening Russia, he would then be able to turn on Britain.

Instead of socialism, British workers would get Nazism.

That's the plan of the Trotskyists.

They know that to defeat Hitler, every section of the people, Conservative, Liberal, Labour and Communist workers, middle-class and capitalist class must fight as allies in a united struggle against their common enemy.

"We want socialism now." (Trotskyist papers)

They know that Hitler won his victories in the past because of the divisions inside the countries he attacked.

They aim to sow those divisions in Britain, to prevent the national unity of the people from presenting a solid front against fascism.

A clue

What kind of a government would they like instead of the present one? Mr. John McGovern, of the ILP, gave us a clue:

> "If I had to choose between Hitler and the Prime Minister, I should not know exactly on which the choice had to fall." (Official report of Parliamentary debates, July 1 1942)

This is the man who waves a red flag and calls himself a "socialist." He had no difficulty in making up his mind to support Chamberlain when he was backing Hitler.

He is against Churchill: Churchill signed the Anglo-Soviet alliance. He backed Chamberlain: Chamberlain opposed this alliance and built up Hitler.

What a Record!

When Chamberlain signed the pact with Hitler at Munich, Mr. McGovern said: "Well done thou good and faithful servant." (*Hansard*, October 6 1938). Mr. Chamberlain's policy of "appeasement," he described as "the road of peace." (September 3 1939).

His partner, Mr. Maxton, was equally emphatic with his praise for the Munich pact:

> "I congratulate the Prime Minister (Mr. Chamberlain) on the work he did in these three weeks." (October 4 1938)

> "On an occasion like this I do not wish to say a controversial word, but simply to agree with the step which has now been taken." (September 28 1938)

Mr. Maxton defended Hitler's aggression with:

> "What objections can you have to Herr Hitler wanting to defend the people of his own race and of his own nationality wherever they may be?" (October 4 1938)

Their whole record is one of support for the most reactionary pro-fascist forces in Britain and for the Nazis abroad.

> "We were ridiculed when we stood for peace when Abyssinia was conquered...When Czechoslovakia was over-run we wanted peace, and we were called Chamberlain's allies and Hitler's allies," said Mr. McGovern. (*Hansard*, October 3 1939)

> "I was in favour, as Hon. Members know, of non-intervention on the Abyssinian issue," said Mr. Maxton. (*Hansard*, April 14 1937)

When Spain was invaded by Mussolini and Hitler, the Trotskyists and the ILP were attacking the Spanish peoples' government and backing the organisation of fascist spies and Trotskyists working for General Franco behind the republican lines, which covered up its real aim by calling itself the "Party of Marxist Unity" (POUM).

Mr. McGovern summed-up his policy:

> "If we say to Mussolini, 'You must withdraw these troops, and if you do not we will use our power to see that supplies are cut off; and we are prepared to use every pressure against you,' then Mussolini will be driven into an enlarged war. Am I going to advocate that the people of Britain must go into Spain and fight on behalf of the Spanish government? Am I to say that they are to go into China and fight for the Chinese? Am I to say they are to go into Abyssinia and fight on behalf of the Abyssinians? The test is: 'Am I prepared to go myself?' and I say 'No.' " (October 21 1937)

At the time when it was still possible to stop fascism's march across Europe by presenting the firm united front of all peoples, the ILP, like the "appeasers", raised the bogey of war to try to frighten Britain into passivity and inaction.

Today we are paying the price.

Guernica has been followed by Coventry, Lidice and the other towns and villages of the countries that have been plunged into war by the pro-Nazis who covered up their aims by shouting the slogan of "peace."

Puddings and shirts

There's an old saying: "Never judge a pudding by the shirt you boil it in." Also: "The proof of the pudding is in the eating."

Apply these sayings to the Trotskyists.

The pudding is their so-called policy. The shirt is a red one, to cover up what's inside the pudding.

Those Spanish workers who ate the Trotskyist pudding have found out that it was poisoned alright. So also have the workers of France.

It is an old, old trick that the Trotskyists use.

Hitler and Goebbels use it. They call their party the National Socialist Workers' Party. That's what "Nazi" stands for. It is neither national nor socialist. German workers are finding out the lie today.

Spanish Trotskyists called their organisation the Party of Marxist Unity. It worked for the fascists.

French Trotskyists called theirs the People's Party. It sold the people to Hitler.

British Trotskyists call themselves "militant socialists" and other titles of a similar character. They are neither militant nor socialist, but the very reverse. The Independent Labour Party has ceased to be independent or labour, but carries out a policy which Hitler couldn't better.

So don't be taken in by the red flag, the red tie, the socialist sounding speeches and articles.

Ask yourself: "Where will this lead me? Whom will it help?" and you'll be able to see through the Trotskyist trickery and deception.

Don't say to yourself: " It's a good thing there aren't many of them in this country. We don't have to worry."

It is true that the Trotskyists are few in number. But they started in a small way in other countries too. They were not rooted out in time, and were able to deceive many people, who discovered their treachery when it was too late.

France

In France, the Trotskyists are led by Jacques Doriot, who was thrown out of the Communist Party which discovered in time what manner of man he was.

He opposed the People's Front in France. His argument was: "I don't want workers to associate with capitalists." He slandered the Soviet Union, and was in the front ranks of the attack against the Communist Party. When the People's Front government suppressed the fascist party, Doriot formed a new party which the fascists joined so that they could continue their work.

Now he is completely unmasked. He is Hitler's best assistant. He runs a paper for the Nazis and leads the fight against the brave people who are resisting the fascist enemy, handing them over to the fascist executioners.

The Trotskyists disrupted French unity against fascism: now they support unity with fascism against the people.

Spain

In Spain, "The main enemy of the people in the rearguard are the Trotskyists: they are the bitterest enemies of our cause, the direct agents of Franco in our ranks," said Jose Diaz, Secretary of the Spanish Communist Party (Report to Central Committee, 1937)

The Trotskyist organisation was called the POUM. Of them, the *Valencia Socialist* paper wrote:

> "Spies and traitors! When will we have done away with them or when will
> they have done away with us? Are they spies in the service of a party, or
> is it a party in the service of spies?" (October 24 1937)

And again:

> "The POUM is the refuge of spies...the most dangerous acts of sabotage
> have been entrusted to two spies who are members of the POUM. The
> most dangerous of those who have been arrested belong to this party."

Mr. Maxton, however, supported this organisation.

> "The POUM...is a political party of the same viewpoint as my own party
> in this country." (House of Commons, January 19 1937)

And Mr. Fenner Brockway handed Gorkin, leader of the POUM, the sum of £100 at a meeting in Brussels in 1936, "to be placed at the service of the POUM in their struggle." (Official report, published in London at the ILP headquarters).

Under the slogans of "workers' control", the POUM succeeded in hampering production for the Spanish fight against fascism. Under the slogan of "collectivise the peasantry", they sent armed bands to shoot peasants who did not agree with communal farming, with the object—in which they largely succeeded—of preventing the harvesting of crops and the cultivation of food. At a critical moment for the republican government, they staged an armed uprising in Barcelona.

The Trotskyists and the ILP in Britain still boast of their support for the POUM, and are defending the fifth columnist activities of its leader, Gorkin, who has now made his way to Mexico.

The cover

The Trotskyists pretend they support Russia but disagree with Stalin's leadership. This is only another cover to hide their aims.

Right from the first days of the Russian revolution the Trotskyists have tried to bring about its downfall. Before the Russian workers took power, the Trotskyists tried to lead them to defeat.

The Independent Labour Party has conducted a consistent campaign of lies and attacks against the Soviet Union. Philip Snowden, one of its former leaders and partner of Ramsay MacDonald, wrote some venomous attacks against the young Soviet Union in the *Labour Leader* (the forerunner of the *New Leader*). When the editor protested, she soon found herself out of the editorial chair. They protested when the people of Menshevik Georgia, which they called an "ILP state", and which plotted with the interventionists to restore capitalism in Russia, drove out the traitors and joined the Soviet Union. They protested when the Trotskyists and other fascists were brought to trial in Moscow.

Now the British Trotskyists are trying to carry on the work the Russian Trotskyists left undone, and are actively engaged in a campaign designed to bamboozle the British people.

Don't under-estimate the danger because of their small numbers.

Be on the alert for the Trotskyist disruptors.

These people have not the slightest right to be regarded as workers with an honest point of view.

They should be treated as you would treat a Nazi.

Clear them out of every working class organisation and position.

What to do with the Trotskyists

First—remember that the Trotskyists are no longer part of the working class movement.

Second—expose every Trotskyist you come into contact with. Show other people where his ideas are leading. Treat him as you would treat an open Nazi.

Third—fight against every Trotskyist who has got himself into a position of authority, either in your trade union branch, local Labour Party or co-op. Expose him and see that he is turned out.

Warning

Many workers, trade unionists and Labour Party members, unthinkingly express views which sound Trotskyist. Don't confuse these honest but muddled opinions with Trotskyism.

The real Trotskyist is a bitter enemy of Stalin and the other trusted leaders of the Soviet Union. That's his fingerprint, whatever else he may say. And that's how you can spot him. As for the people who are genuinely confused, your job is to explain. Explain. Explain. Get them to read this booklet. If they haven't time, explain what is in it to them.

Factory workers:
be on your guard
Clear out the bosses' agents!!

By WIL

[Leaflet, 1942]

Under the guise of a struggle against "Trotskyism" the leadership of the so-called "Communist" Party have instructed their members in the factories to launch a campaign of lies and slander against leading shop stewards and prominent trade unionists.

The object of this campaign is twofold:

1. It seeks to undermine the strong rank and file trade union movement which has been built up in the factories during the last few years.

2. It is the "all clear" signal to reactionary employers to victimise and frame-up active trade unionists.

You must know the truth

"Communist" Party policy today fully supports the handful of profiteers who run this war in their own interests. Those who carry out *that* policy in the factories are doing the bosses' dirty work. They are *bosses' men* who must be exposed and cleared out.

When our brothers in the mining industry were on strike for better conditions against the tight-fisted tyranny of the coal owners it was the "Communist" Party which urged its members to blackleg and scab.

The "Communist" Party alleges that supporters of the Socialist Appeal are agents of Hitler. *This is a lie.* We defy any member of the Communist Party to defend this lying statement in open debate. The Socialist Appeal stands for the complete destruction of fascism whether it be of the Nazi, Mosley or any other variety. It advocates as the first step towards a genuine struggle against Hitlerism the expropriation of the millionaire armament kings and the nationalisation of the war industries under *workers' control*.

Here are the real facts

Fact No. 1—Communist Party policy helped Hitler conquer Europe.

When Hitler rode roughshod over the continent, the "Communist" Party accused Britain and France of starting the war.

"The war did not develop out of the British and French desire to liberate humanity from fascism, but to protect their Empires against German claims, and further was *started by Great Britain and France and not by Germany.* Therefore the Soviet Union considers itself justified in the first place in making an agreement with Germany to prevent itself being involved in an imperialist war." (Moscow paper *Trud*, January 21 1941)

"Above all the conclusion must be drawn that Germany's actions in the present instance were forced on it...Britain and France wanted to undermine Germany's military positions and fundamentally to improve their own positions. Germany was not desirous of falling into a worse position and was *compelled* to adopt counter measures." (*Daily Worker*, April 12 1940)

Fact No. 2—The Communist Party wanted peace with Hitler.

On October 4th 1939 Hitler was offering peace.

"We are against the continuance of this war. We demand that negotiations be immediately opened for the establishment of peace in Europe." (Communist Party special statement, *Daily Worker*, October 4 1939)

Fact No. 3—The Communist Party policy helped Hitler invade the Soviet Union by confusing British workers.

When Hitler massed his Panzer divisions on the Eastern front, this is what the "Communist" Party told the British worker *the day before he marched*:

"Even before the arrival of Sir Stafford Cripps, the British ambassador in USSR and particularly after his arrival, British and in general the foreign press, began an intense dissemination of rumours on the 'proximity of war between USSR and Germany'...Despite the obvious nonsensical character of these rumours, responsible Moscow quarters have still found it necessary, in view of these rumours, to authorise Tass to state that these rumours constitute clumsily concocted propaganda by forces hostile to USSR and to Germany and interested in the further extension and unleashing of war." (*World News and Views*, June 21 1941)

Fact No. 4—Before June 22 1941 the Communist Party carried out Hitler's dirty work in Britain—today they do Churchill's dirty work.

They tell you that Churchill is a great statesman but this is what they said on October 11 1940:

> "Churchill is chiefly known to the workers as the breaker of the general strike, the Home Secretary who sent troops against striking miners and railwaymen, and the fomentation of intervention against the struggling Soviet republic.

> "Let the Labour leaders fawn on him as they will. The rank and file of the labour movement do not trust this man. No new world or reconstruction will come from him. His words long ago lost their charm. There are perhaps many Tories who already realise that they have not only chosen a leader, but also a liability." (*Daily Worker*, Editorial, October 11 1940)

Lies and confusion

That is all the "Communist" Party has to offer the British workers.

When Stalin has a pact with Hitler they *support Hitler* and oppose Churchill.

When Stalin has a pact with Churchill they *support Churchill* and oppose Hitler.

Their policy is completely dependent upon the pacts that Stalin signs and not upon the needs of the British or international working class.

The *Socialist Appeal* continues *Lenin's* policy and *opposes both Churchill and Hitler*. It fights for working class power as the only real answer to fascism.

Fellow workers—do not be deceived by the lies and slanders of the Communist Party. Urge a debate in your trade union branch between a representative of the Socialist Appeal and the *Daily Worker*—between Workers' International League and the Communist Party. This is the best way to expose the false political position of these people. Like Hitler their policy is the bigger the lie the more people will believe it, but once brought face to face with the truth they have no answer.

Factory Workers

BE ON YOUR GUARD

Clear Out the Bosses' Agents!!

UNDER the guise of a struggle against "Trotskyism" the leadership of the so-called "Communist" Party have instructed their members in the factories to launch a campaign of lies and slander against leading shop stewards and prominent trade unionists.

THE object of this campaign is twofold:

1. It seeks to undermine the strong rank and file trade union movement which has been built up in the factories during the last few years.

2. It is the "all clear" signal to reactionary employers to victimise and frame-up active trade unionists.

You must know the Truth

"COMMUNIST" Party Policy today fully supports the handful of profiteers who run this war in their own interests. Those who carry out THAT policy in the factories are doing the bosses' dirty work. They are BOSSES' MEN who must be exposed and cleared out.

WHEN our brothers in the mining industry were on strike for better conditions against the tight-fisted tyranny of the coal-owners it was the "Communist" Party which urged its members to blackleg and scab.

Thesis of Indian Fourth Internationalists[1] 1941

The following document is a section of a thesis adopted in the latter part of 1941 by the formation committee of the Bolshevik-Leninist Party of India as the programme on which all Marxist revolutionists could form a single revolutionary party. Together with certain other groups, the original committee has now constituted the Bolshevik-Leninist Party of India as an adherent of the Fourth International. The party is now centring its agitation on the central slogan of the constituent assembly.

Together with the Ceylon Socialist Party (the Lanka Sama Samaja Party) and a recently-formed organisation in Burma, our Indian comrades have established the Federation of Bolshevik-Leninist Parties of Burma, Ceylon and India, for the revolutionary destiny of these three peoples is closely linked together.

The native princes

The revolt of 1857 represented the last attempt of the old feudal ruling class of India to throw off the British yoke. This revolt, which despite its reactionary leadership laid bare the depth of mass discontent and unrest, alarmed the British rulers, and led to a radical change in policy in India. Seeking for bases of social and political support, the British abandoned the policy of annexing the Indian states within British India, instead guaranteeing the remnants of the feudal rulers their privileged and parasitic positions in innumerable petty principalities, buttressing their power and protecting them against the masses, and

---

[1] This is the founding document of the Indian Trotskyist movement, which took place in the winter of 1941. We publish it in this appendix with its original introduction as it was published in *Workers' International News* (Vol. 5 Nos. 3&4, 1942) in conjunction with the article by Ted Grant and Andrew Scott *The road to India's freedom.*

receiving in return the unqualified support of these elements for the British rule. The princes of the Indian states, maintained at the cost of a chaotic multiplication of administrative units, are today only the corrupt and dependent tools of British imperialism, and the feudatory states, checker-boarding all India as they do, are no more than a vast network of fortresses erected by the British in their own defence. The variety of the states and jurisdiction of the feudal princes defies a generalised description but they bolster alike the reactionary policies of imperialism in India. The despotism and misgovernment practiced by the great majority of these rulers in their territories have created and perpetuated conditions of backwardness extreme even in India, including the most primitive forms of feudalism and slavery itself. Their collective interests are represented by the Chamber of Princes, instituted in 1921, which is the most reactionary political body in India.

The landlords

The most solid supporters of British rule in India, after the princes, are the landlords. In fact the majority of the princes are no more themselves than glorified landlords, playing the same parasitic role as the landlords of British India. The landlords of India have a record of medieval oppression, of rack-renting and usury, and of unbridled gangsterism over a disarmed peasantry, which has made them the most hated exploiters in India. The rapid extension of landlordism in modern times through the development of intermediary and new parasitic classes on the peasantry, has not only increased the numbers of those who receive land rents, but firmly linked their interests with those of the Indian capitalist class, by ties of investment and mortgage. The political role of the landlords has always been one of complete subservience to British imperialism, as well as the greatest obstacle in the way of agricultural development which demands a thorough-going democratic revolution in the agrarian field and the liquidation of landlordism in all its forms.

The second half of the nineteenth century saw the rise of an Indian capitalist class in Bombay and other industrial centres. The Indian bourgeoisie of the early period, conscious of its own weakness and dependent position in economy, offered no challenge whatever to British rule. But the deep economic conflict between their own interests and those of the twentieth century, [forced them] to utilize the national political movement to strengthen their bargaining power against British imperialism.

The Indian bourgeoisie

The bourgeoisie, in the absence of any competing class and especially of an independent proletarian movement, assumed complete leadership of the national political movement through its party, the Indian National Congress. The bourgeois leadership of the movement was clearly demonstrated in 1905, by the choice of the economic boycott of foreign goods as the method of struggle against the partition of Bengal. The aims of the bourgeoisie were defined during this period as the attainment of "colonial self-government within the Empire" as junior partners of the imperialists. They abandoned the struggle and adopted a policy of co-operation with the British after the grant of the Morley-Minto reforms[2], their own aims being satisfied for the moment.

The last years following the First World War, and the years which immediately followed it, were marked by the development, for the first time since 1857, of a mass struggle on a national scale against imperialism based on the discontent and unrest of the peasantry and the working class. This discontent was especially marked in Bombay, where the wave of working class strikes was on a scale hitherto unknown in India, and reached its highest point in 1920 for which year the number of strikes reached the gigantic total of 1.5 million. The Montague-Chemsford reforms[3] were designed to meet this rising threat by buying off the bourgeois leadership, and they succeeded to an extent that the section of the bourgeoisie who wanted whole-hearted co-operation with the government seceded from the Congress to form the Liberal Federation (1918). But the growth of the mass movement compelled the Congress bourgeoisie either to enter the struggle or be isolated from the masses. Launching under its own banner the passive resistance movement, and later the mass civil disobedience movement of 1921-22, the Congress entered the struggle but only to betray it from the inside.

The mass movement which, despite its timid and unwilling leadership, had attained the undeniable character of a mass revolt against the British Raj, was abruptly called off when at its height by the bourgeois leader Gandhi, and a period of demoralisation followed for the masses. The reactionary and treacherous character of the bourgeois leadership was shown clearly in the Bardoli resolution of 1922, which condemned the no-tax campaign of the peasantry and insisted on the continuation of rent payment to the landlords, assuring the *zamindars* (landlords) that the Congress "had no intention of attacking their legal rights." The bourgeoisie thus demonstrated its reactionary attitude toward the land question in which lies the main driving force to revolution in India.

With the worsening conditions of the late 1920s, the mass struggle developed again at a rising tempo, and was again led to defeat by the Congress (1930-34). The aims of the new struggle were limited by Gandhi beforehand to the celebrated 11 points which represented exclusively the most urgent demands of the Indian bourgeoisie. Nevertheless the movement developed in 1930 far beyond

---

[2] The Indian Councils Act of 1909 allowed the election of Indians to the various legislative councils in India for the first time.

[3] The Government of India Act of 1919 introduced self-governing institutions gradually to India, subject to British rule.

the limits laid down for it by the Congress, with rising strikes, powerful mass demonstrations, the Chittagong Armoury raid, and the risings at Peshawar and Sholapur. Gandhi declared openly to the Viceroy that he was fighting as much against the rising forms of revolt as against the British imperialists. The aim of the bourgeoisie was henceforward to secure concessions from imperialism at the price of betraying the mass struggle in which they saw a real and growing threat to themselves. The Gandhi-Irwin settlement[4] was a settlement against the mass movement, and paved the way for a terrific repression which fell on the movement during its ebb in 1932-34.

Since 1934 Gandhi and the leaders of the Congress have had as their chief aim that of preventing the renewal of a mass struggle against imperialism, while using their leadership of the national movement as a lever to secure the concessions they hope to obtain from imperialism. They see in the rising forces of revolt, and especially in the emergence of the working class as a political force, a threat to their own bases of exploitation, and are consequently following an increasingly reactionary policy. Reorganising the party administration so as to secure to the big bourgeoisie the unassailable position of leadership (1934), they transferred the centre of activities to the parliamentary field and to working the new Constitution in such a way as to secure the maximum benefits to the bourgeoisie, until the intransigence of the British parliament and the Indian government in the war situation and the withdrawal of many of the political concessions of provincial autonomy again forced the Congress into opposition (1939). The Congress bourgeoisie then engaged in a restricted campaign of individual "non-violent" civil disobedience with narrowly defined bourgeois aims and under the dictatorial control of Gandhi himself. By this move they hoped to prevent the development of a serious mass struggle against imperialism, the leadership of which will be bound to pass into other hands.

The main instrument whereby the Indian bourgeoisie seeks to maintain control over the national movement is the Indian National Congress, the classic party of the Indian capitalist class, seeking as it does the support of the petty bourgeoisie and if possible of the workers, for its own aims. Despite the fact that under these conditions revolutionary and semi-revolutionary elements still remain within the fold of the Congress, despite its mass membership (five millions in 1939), and despite the demagogic programmatic pronouncements (constituent assembly, agrarian reform) which the Congress has repeatedly made, the direction of its policy remains exclusively in the hands of the bourgeoisie as also the control of the party organisation, as was dramatically proved at Tripuri and after. The Indian National Congress in its social composition, its organisation, and above all in its political leadership can be compared to the Kuomintang, which led the Chinese revolution of 1925-27 to its betrayal and

---

4 The agreement between Gandhi and Irwin, signed on March 5 1931, put an end to the Civil Disobedience movement.

defeat.

The characterisation of the Indian National Congress as a multi-class party, as the "national united front," or as "a platform rather than a party," is a flagrant deception and calculated only to hand over to the bourgeoisie in advance the leadership of the coming struggle, and so make its betrayal and defeat a foregone conclusion.

The more open reactionary interests of the Indian bourgeoisie find expression in many organisations which exist side by side with the Congress. Thus the Liberal Federation (1918) represents those bourgeois elements who co-operate openly with the imperialists. The sectional interests of the propertied classes are represented by various communal organisations, notably the Moslem League (1905) and the Hindu Maha Sabaha (1925) which are dominated by large landlords and bourgeois interests and pursue a reactionary policy in all social and economic issues, deriving a measure of mass support by an appeal to the religious and communal sentiments of the backward masses.

The petty-bourgeois intelligentsia

Because of their position of dependence on the capitalist class and in the absence of a real challenge to their leadership from the proletariat, the various elements of the urban petty bourgeoisie and of the petty-bourgeois intelligentsia have always played a satellite role to the bourgeoisie. The radicalisation of the petty bourgeoisie under imperialism found its first and strongest expression in the prolonged terrorist movement in Bengal and elsewhere, the failure of which, despite the heroism of its protagonists, demonstrated finally the utter inability of the petty-bourgeois intelligentsia to find an independent solution of its own problems.

Today the urban petty bourgeoisie find its political reflection mainly in the various organisations within the fold of, or under the influence of the Indian National Congress, such as the Forward Bloc, the Congress Socialist Party, the Radical Democratic Party of M. N. Roy, etc.

Within the Congress, the petty-bourgeois leaders have repeatedly lent themselves to be used by the bourgeoisie as a defensive colouration before the masses, bridging with their radical phrases and irresponsible demagogy the gap between the reactionary Congress leadership and the hopes and aspirations of the masses. Thus the demagogy of Bose and Nehru, as well as the "socialist" phrases of M. N. Roy and the Congress Socialist Party, to say nothing of the "Marxism" of the national united fronters of the Communist Party of India, have in turn served the Ghandian leaders as a smoke screen for their own reactionary manoeuvres.

The humiliating capitulation of the Congress Socialist Party to the Congress leadership, the conversion of M. N. Roy and his Radical Democrats to imperialist war-mongering, and the departure of Subhas Chandra Bose from the Indian scene, are symptoms of the diminishing political role of the petty-bourgeois intelligentsia, which however theatrically it may posture before the masses in normal times, exposes in times of growing crisis its political bankruptcy, and exists only to be utilised by the bourgeoisie in its deception of the masses.

The peasantry

The peasantry comprises the vast majority of the Indian population (70 percent). The stagnation and deterioration of agriculture, the increasing land hunger, the exactions of the government, the extension of parasitic landlordism, the increasing load of rural debt and the consequent expropriation of the cultivators are together inevitably driving the peasantry on to the revolutionary road. Peasant unrest, leading frequently to actual risings—Santal rebellion of 1855, Deccan riots of 1875[5]—have been a recurring motif in Indian history. In the last two decades, and especially since the world economic crisis (1929) the peasant movement has been on the rise and has taken on a more and more radical character.

It is precisely the depth and scope of the agrarian crisis that places the revolution against imperialism on the order of the day, contributing to it the driving force and the sweep which are necessary to accomplish the overthrow of the ruling power. Nevertheless the agrarian revolution requires the leadership of another class to raise the struggle to the level of a national revolution. The isolation and the scattered character of the peasant economy, the historical and political backwardness of the rural masses, the lack of inner cohesion within the peasantry and the aims of its various strata, all combine to make it impossible for the peasantry to play an independent role in the coming revolution.

The invasion of moneyed interests has sharply accelerated the disintegrating tendencies within the peasantry. The creation of a vast army of landless peasants, sharecroppers and wage-labourers on the land has immensely complicated the agrarian problem and rendered necessary revolutionary measures of the most far-reaching character. The basic antagonism between landlord and peasant has not been reduced by the entry of finance capital into agriculture, since

---

5 The *Santal rebellion* was a native rebellion of the Santal people in Eastern India (now Jharkhand) against both the British colonial authority and the corrupt upper caste *zamindari* system. It lasted from July 1855 to May 1856. The British revenge was ruthless: every village of the Santals was attacked, plundered, their women raped and whipped and their teenagers castrated. In May and June 1875, peasants of Maharastra in some parts of Pune, Satara and Nagar districts revolted against increasing agrarian distress. The *Deccan Riots* of 1875 targeted conditions of debt peonage (*kamiuti*) to moneylenders. Peasants rioted to get hold of and destroy the bonds, decrees, and other documents in the possession of the moneylenders.

this did not bring with it any change for the better in farming methods or in the system of land tenure. On the contrary, the landlord-peasant antagonism has been given a sharper emphasis by the extension of parasitic claims on the land and the overthrow of landlordism by the transference of the land to the cultivator remains the primary task of the agrarian revolution. Nevertheless, this basic antagonism has been supplemented by a new one, which is reflected in the growth of an agricultural proletariat in the strict sense of the word. Beside this, the invasion of finance capital has made the problems of mortgage and of rural debt more pressing in some parts of India than in others, and these facts taken together will probably give to the agrarian revolution, at least in some areas, an anti-capitalist character at a very early stage.

Leadership of the peasantry

The leadership of the revolution, which the peasantry cannot provide for itself, can come only from an urban class. But the Indian bourgeoisie cannot possibly provide this leadership, since in the first place it is itself reactionary through and through on the land question, sharing as it does so largely in the parasitic exploitation of the peasantry. Above all, the bourgeoisie, on account of its inherent weakness and its dependence on imperialism, is destined to play a counter-revolutionary role in the coming struggle for power.

The leadership of the peasantry in the petty-bourgeois democratic agrarian revolution that is immediately posed can therefore come only from the industrial proletariat, and an alliance between the proletariat and the peasantry is a fundamental prerequisite of the Indian revolution. This alliance cannot be conceived in the form of a "workers' and peasants' party" or of a "democratic dictatorship" in the revolution. The revolutionary alliance between the proletariat and peasantry can mean only proletarian leadership of the peasant struggle and, in case of revolutionary victory, the establishment of the proletarian dictatorship with the support of the peasantry.

The peasant movement

The growth of the peasant movement in recent times has led to the formation of various mass organisations among the peasantry, among which the most important are the Kisan Sanghs (peasant committees) which are loosely linked up in a district, provincial, and finally on an all-India scale in the All-India Kisan Sabha, whose membership in 1939 was 800,000. These associations, whose precise character varies from district to district, are in general today under the control and influence of petty-bourgeois intelligentsia elements who, as pointed out before, cannot follow a class policy independent of the bourgeois, although the growing mass pressure upon them is reflected in the more sharply radical demands they are forced to put forward. There is no means of deciding in advance the exact role of the Kisan Sanghs in the coming revolution. This will be determined by the correlation of forces within them, which in turn will depend largely on the consciousness and militancy of the lower layers of the peasantry and the measure of control they exercise in the Kisan Sanghs. But it can be stated beforehand, on the basis of the experience of the Russian and Chinese revolutions, that the existence of Kisan Sanghs on however wide a scale does not offer a substitute for the separate organisations of poor peasants and agricultural labourers in rural soviets, under the leadership of the urban working class. Only the soviets can assure that the agrarian revolution will be carried out in a thorough-going manner.

The working class

The industrial proletariat is the product of modern capitalism in India. Its rapid growth in the period since 1914 can be illustrated by a comparison of the Factory Acts statistics for 1914 and 1936:

	No. of factories	No. of workers employed
1914	2,936	950,973
1936	9,329	1,652,147

The numerical strength of the industrial proletariat can be estimated at five millions, distributed mainly as follows (1935 figures):

(a) Workers in power driven factories (including those of the "Native states"): 1,855,000

(b) Miners: 371,000

(c) Railwaymen: 636,000

(d) Transport workers: 361,000

(e) Plantation workers: 1,000,000

The Indian working class is chiefly employed in light industry (cotton, jute, etc) but also to some extent in the iron, steel, cement, and coal mining industries. The degree of concentration in industrial establishments is relatively high, owing to the recency of industrial development and the typically modern character of many of the new enterprises. The proletariat holds a position in Indian society which cannot be gauged by its actual size; the true gauge is the vital place it occupies in the economy of the country. The wage rates of the Indian proletariat are among the lowest, the living conditions the most miserable, the hours of work the longest, the factory conditions the worst, the death rate the highest in the civilised world. The fight to remedy these intolerable conditions and to protect themselves against the steadily worsening conditions of exploitation bring the workers directly to the revolutionary struggle against imperialism and the capitalist system, the destruction of which is necessary for their emancipation.

Working class struggles

The record of proletarian struggle in India dates back to the last century, but the movement took on an organised character only in the post-war period. The first great wave of strikes (1918-21) signalled the emergence of the Indian working class as a separate force, and gave to the national political movement during this period a truly revolutionary significance for the first time in its history. In 1920, on the crest of this strike wave, the Indian Trade Union Congress was formed. The second great strike wave of the late twenties, especially in Bombay, showed an immense advance in the working-class movement, marked by its growing awakening to communist ideas. The increasing millions of the workers and the growing influence of the communists caused the trade union movement to be split in two by those leaders who sought the path of collaboration with the bourgeoisie. Thus the reactionary Trade Union Federation was formed in 1929. The policy of the reactionary labour leaders was facilitated by the disastrous "red trade union" policy followed by the Communist Party of India on orders from the Comintern bureaucracy. With the arrest of the communist leaders on a trumped-up charge (the Meerut conspiracy case) and the further splitting of the Trade Union Congress in 1931, the wave of working-class struggle subsided once more. It was [during] this period (1930-31) that the Communist Party of India, which commanded the confidence of the awakening workers, made the grievous political mistake of standing aside from the mass movement which was again assuming revolutionary proportions.

The tendency towards economic recovery commencing in 1936, combined with the mass activities in connection with the election campaign of the Congress, led to a revival in the mass movement which entered once again on a period of rise. The Congress ministries saw a resurgence of the working-class strike movement with the Bengal jute strike (1937) and the Cawnpore textile strike (1938), a resurgence which was arrested only by measures of increased repression introduced by the government since the outbreak of war, but not before the Indian working class had clearly demonstrated its attitude towards the imperialist war, particularly by the mass political anti-war strike in Bombay of 80,000 workers.

Left groups

The Communist Party of India, which alone in the last two decades could have afforded the Marxist leadership that above all things is needed, made instead a series of irresponsible mistakes, which find their expression in the bureaucratically-conceived policies of the Comintern. In conformity with its false central programmatic aim, the "democratic dictatorship" of the proletariat and the peasantry, the CPI fostered the growth of workers' and peasants' parties from 1926 to 1928, at the expense of an independent working-class party. This policy was shelved in 1929 to make way for an ultra-left sectarian policy (in the celebrated third period days of the Comintern) the signal expression of which came in the splitting of the trade union movement by the formation of "red trade unions". This sectarian policy of the CPI led to its isolation from the mass struggle of 1930-31 and made the bourgeois betrayal of the struggle so much the easier. In the period of ebb which followed (1934) the CPI was illegalised and has remained so since. From 1935 onwards the CPI (again at the behest of the Comintern now openly and flagrantly the tool of the Soviet bureaucracy) reversed its policy once more and held out the hand of collaboration to the bourgeoisie through the policy of the national united front which credited the bourgeoisie with a revolutionary role. The CPI was transformed into a loyal opposition within the Congress, having no policy independent of that organisation, a state of things which continues today.

Mechanically echoing every new slogan advanced by the Comintern to suit the changing policies of the Soviet bureaucrats, the CPI has shown its reactionary character by its attitude towards the imperialist war. With its false theory of national united front, the CPI is making ready to repeat its betrayal of the Chinese revolution by handing over the leadership of the revolutionary struggle to the treacherous bourgeoisie. The Communist Party of India, because of the prestige it seeks to obtain from the Russian revolution and the Soviet Union, is today the most dangerous influence within the working class of India.

Openly preaching collaboration with the bourgeoisie, and today with the British imperialists at war, is the party of M. N. Roy. With a narrowing base within the working class, Roy has turned for a following to the labour bureaucrats supporting the war and to the bourgeoisie itself.

The Congress Socialist Party (1934) has from the beginning followed a policy of utter subservience to the Congress bourgeoisie, and remains today completely without a base within the working class. Surrendering its claim to an independent existence, the CSP has been split wide open by the communists who worked inside it, and is today an empty shell devoid of political substance.

To the left of the Communist Party, disgusted with its bureaucratic leaders and its reactionary policies, there exists a number of small parties and groups, occupying more or less centrist positions. Such are the Bengal Labour Party

(Bolshevik Party of India), the Red Flag Communist (Communist Party) led by S. N. Tagore, etc. Without a clear-cut revolutionary policy and without making a decisive break organisationally and politically with the Comintern, these parties and groups are unable to offer the working class the independent leadership it requires. Nevertheless these groups and parties contain many tried fighters and able Marxist theoreticians, who would be invaluable in a revolutionary working-class party.

This party can be only the Bolshevik-Leninist Party of India, the party of the Fourth International in India, which alone with its revolutionary strategy based on the accumulated experience of history and the theory of permanent revolution in particular, can lead the working class of India to revolutionary victory. This party has still to be built on an all-India scale, though many groups exist already whose fusion in the formation committee of the Bolshevik-Leninist Party of India has provided the nucleus for its formation.

Despite its subjective weakness in organisation and consciousness, inevitable in a backward country and in the conditions of repression which surround it, the working class is entirely capable of leading the Indian revolution. It is the only class objectively fitted for this role, not only in relation to the Indian situation but in view of the decline of capitalism on a world scale which opens the road to the international proletarian revolution.

The permanent revolution

India faces a historically belated bourgeois-democratic revolution, the main tasks of which are the overthrow of British imperialism, the liquidation of a semi-feudal land system, and the clearing away of feudal remnants in the form of the Indian Native states. But although bourgeois-democratic revolutions occurring in the advanced capitalist countries in previous centuries found leadership in the then rising bourgeoisie, the Indian bourgeoisie appeared on the scene only after the progressive role of the bourgeoisie in the world as a whole has been exhausted and is incapable of providing leadership to the revolution that is unfolding in India.

Connected with and dependent on British capital from the beginning, the Indian bourgeoisie today displays the characteristics of a predominantly compradore bourgeoisie, enjoying at the best the position of a very junior partner in the firm British Imperialism and company. Hence, while they have been prepared to place themselves through the Indian National Congress at the head of the anti-imperialist mass movement for the purpose of utilising it as a bargaining weapon to secure concessions from the imperialists, the bourgeois leaders have restricted the scope of the movement and prevented its development into a revolutionary assault on imperialism. Incapable from the very nature of their position of embarking on a revolutionary struggle to secure their independence, and fearful of such a struggle, the bourgeois leaders have maintained their control over the mass movement only to betray it at every critical juncture.

Secondly, unlike the once revolutionary bourgeoisie of former times which arose in opposition to the feudal landowning class and in constant struggle against it, the Indian bourgeoisie has developed largely from the landowning class itself, and is in addition closely connected with the landlords through mortgages. They are therefore incapable of leading the peasants in the agrarian revolution against landlordism. On the contrary, as is clearly demonstrated by the declared policy and actions of the Congress both during the civil disobedience movements and in the period of the Congress ministries, they are staunch supporters of *zamindari* interests.

Finally, unlike the bourgeois-democratic revolutions of former times, the revolution in India is unfolding at a time when large concentrations of workers already exist in the country. The industrial proletariat numbering five millions occupies a position of strategic importance in the economy of the country which cannot be measured by its mere numerical strength. It is important to remember, moreover, that a hitherto uncalculated but indubitably very high proportion of these workers is employed in large concerns employing several hundreds of thousands of workers. The high degree of concentration of the Indian proletariat immeasurably advances its class consciousness and organisational strength. It was only in the post-war years that the Indian working class emerged as an organised force on a national scale. But the militant and widespread strike waves of 1918-21 and of 1928-29, which were the precursors of the mass civil disobedience movements of 1920-21 and of 1930-33, testify to the rapidity of the awakening. These workers are in daily conflict not only with the British owners of capital, but also with the native bourgeoisie. Faced by the threat of the working class, the Indian bourgeoisie has grown more conservative and suspicious. With every advance in organisation and consciousness of the workers, the bourgeoisie has drawn nearer to the imperialists and further away from the masses. It is clear that not a single one of the tasks of the bourgeois-democratic revolution can be solved under the leadership of the Indian bourgeoisie. Far from leading the bourgeois-democratic revolution, the Indian bourgeoisie will go over to the camp of the imperialists and landlords on the outbreak of the revolution.

The urban petty bourgeoisie, daily becoming declassed and pauperised under imperialism and declining in economic significance, cannot even conceive of playing an independent role in the coming revolution. Since, however, there is no prospect whatever of improving their conditions under imperialism, but on the contrary they are faced with actual pauperisation and ruin, they are forced into the revolutionary road. The peasantry, the largest numerically and the most atomised, backward and oppressed class, is capable of local uprisings and partisan warfare, but requires the leadership of a more advanced and centralised class for this struggle to be elevated to an all-national level. Without such leadership the peasantry alone cannot make a revolution.

The task of such leadership falls in the nature of things on the Indian proletariat, which is the only class capable of leading the toiling masses in the onslaught against imperialism, landlordism and the native princes. The concentration and discipline induced by its very place in capitalist economy, its numerical strength, the sharpness of the class antagonism which daily brings it into conflict with the imperialists who are the main owners of capital in India, its organisation and experience of struggle, and the vital position it occupies in the economy of the country, as also its steadily worsening condition under imperialism, all combine to fit the Indian proletariat for this task.

But the leadership of the working class in the bourgeois-democratic revolution poses before the working class the prospect of seizing the power and, in addition to accomplishing the long overdue bourgeois-democratic tasks, proceeding with its own socialist tasks. And thus the bourgeois-democratic revolution develops uninterruptedly into the proletarian revolution and the establishment of the dictatorship of the proletariat as the only state form capable of supplanting the dictatorship of the Indian bourgeoisie in India. The realisation of the combined character of the Indian revolution is essential for the planning of the revolutionary strategy of the working class. Should the working class fail in its historic task of seizing the power and establishing the dictatorship of the proletariat, the revolution will inevitably recede, the bourgeois tasks themselves remain unperformed, and the power will swing back in the end to the imperialists without whom the Indian bourgeoisie cannot maintain itself against the hostile masses. A backward country like India can accomplish its bourgeois-democratic revolution only through the establishment of the dictatorship of the proletariat. The correctness of this axiom of the theory of permanent revolution is demonstrated by the victorious Russian revolution of October 1917, and it is confirmed on the negative side by the tragic fate of the Chinese revolution of 1925-27.

In India, moreover, where the imperialists are the main owners of capital, the revolutionary assault of the workers against imperialism will bring them into direct and open conflict with the property forms of the imperialists from the moment the struggle enters the openly revolutionary stage. The exigencies of the struggle itself will in the course of the openly revolutionary assault against imperialism demonstrate to the workers the necessity of destroying not only imperialism but the foundations of capitalism itself. Thus, though the Indian revolution will be bourgeois in its immediate aims, the tasks of the proletarian revolution will be posed from the outset.

But the revolution cannot be stabilised even at this stage. The ultimate fate of the revolution in India, as in Russia, will be determined in the arena of the international revolution. Nor will India by its own forces be able to accomplish the task of making the transition to socialism. Not only the backwardness of the country, but also the international division of labour and the interdependence—

produced by capitalism itself—of the different parts of world economy, demand that this task of the establishment of socialism can be accomplished only on a world scale. The victorious revolution in India, however, dealing a mortal blow to the oldest and most widespread imperialism in the world will on the one hand produce the most profound crisis in the entire capitalist world and shake world capitalism to its foundations. On the other hand it will inspire and galvanise into action millions of proletarians and colonial slaves the world over and inaugurate a new era of world revolution.

9 781900 007351